IMPORTANT:

HERE IS YOUR REGISTRATION CODE TO ACCESS
YOUR PREMIUM McGRAW-HILL ONLINE RESOURCES.

For key premium online resources you need THIS CODE to gain access. Once the code is entered, you will be able to use the Web resources for the length of your course.

If your course is using **WebCT** or **Blackboard**, you'll be able to use this code to access the McGraw-Hill content within your instructor's online course.

Access is provided if you have purchased a new book. If the registration code is missing from this book, the registration screen on our Website, and within your WebCT or Blackboard course, will tell you how to obtain your new code.

Registering for McGraw-Hill Online Resources

To gain access to your McGraw-Hill web resources simply follow the steps below:

USE YOUR WEB BROWSER TO GO TO: **www.mhhe.com/lumpkin6e**

CLICK ON **FIRST TIME USER**.

ENTER THE REGISTRATION CODE* PRINTED ON THE TEAR-OFF BOOKMARK ON THE RIGHT.

AFTER YOU HAVE ENTERED YOUR REGISTRATION CODE, CLICK **REGISTER**.

FOLLOW THE INSTRUCTIONS TO SET-UP YOUR PERSONAL UserID AND PASSWORD.

WRITE YOUR UserID AND PASSWORD DOWN FOR FUTURE REFERENCE.
KEEP IT IN A SAFE PLACE.

TO GAIN ACCESS to the McGraw-Hill content in your instructor's **WebCT** or **Blackboard** course simply log in to the course with the UserID and Password provided by your instructor. Enter the registration code exactly as it appears in the box to the right when prompted by the system. You will only need to use the code the first time you click on McGraw-Hill content.

Thank you, and welcome to your McGraw-Hill online Resources!

REGISTRATION CODE

V16D-5BEX-FOCI-0BBS-DGUC

0-07-297392-7 T/A LUMPKIN: INTRODUCTION TO PHYSICAL EDUCATION,
EXERCISE SCIENCE, & SPORT STUDIES, 6/E

INTRODUCTION TO PHYSICAL EDUCATION, EXERCISE SCIENCE, AND SPORT STUDIES

SIXTH EDITION

Angela Lumpkin, B.S.E., M.A., M.B.A., Ph.D.
Dean, School of Education
University of Kansas

Boston   Burr Ridge, IL   Dubuque, IA   Madison, WI   New York
San Francisco   St. Louis   Bangkok   Bogotá   Caracas   Kuala Lumpur
Lisbon   London   Madrid   Mexico City   Milan   Montreal   New Delhi
Santiago   Seoul   Singapore   Sydney   Taipei   Toronto

The *McGraw·Hill* Companies

 **Higher Education**

INTRODUCTION TO PHYSICAL EDUCATION, EXERCISE SCIENCE, AND
SPORT STUDIES, SIXTH EDITION
Published by McGraw-Hill, a business unit of The McGraw-Hill Companies, Inc., 1221 Avenue
of the Americas, New York, NY, 10020. Copyright © 2005, 2002, 1998, 1994, 1990, 1986 by The
McGraw-Hill Companies, Inc. All rights reserved. No part of this publication may be reproduced
or distributed in any form or by any means, or stored in a database or retrieval system, without
the prior written consent of The McGraw-Hill Companies, Inc., including, but not limited to, in
any network or other electronic storage or transmission, or broadcast for distance learning.
Some ancillaries, including electronic and print components, may not be available to customers
outside the United States.

This book is printed on acid-free paper.

1 2 3 4 5 6 7 8 9 0 FGR/FGR 0 9 8 7 6 5 4

ISBN   0-07-285166-X

Vice president & editor-in-chief: *Emily Barrosse*
Publisher: *Bill Glass*
Executive editor: *Nick Barrett*
Director of development: *Kate Engelberg*
Senior developmental editor: *Michelle Turenne*
Executive marketing manager: *Pam Cooper*
Media producer: *Lance Gerhart*
Project manager: *Catherine R. Iammartino*
Senior production supervisor: *Carol A. Bielski*
Senior designer: *Gino Cieslik*
Media project manager: *Kathleen Boylan*
Manager, photo research: *Brian J. Pecko*
Cover design: *Gino Cieslik*
Typeface: *10/12 Garamond*
Compositor: *Interactive Composition Corporation*
Printer: *Quebecor World Fairfield Inc.*

Library of Congress Cataloging-in-Publication Data

Lumpkin, Angela.
   Introduction to physical education, exercise science, and sport studies / Angela
Lumpkin.-- 6th ed.
    p. cm.
   Includes index.
   ISBN 0-07-285166-X (softcover: alk. paper)
   1. Physical education and training. 2. Sports. 3. Physical education and
training--Vocational guidance--United States. I. Title.
GV341.L85 2005
613.7'1'023--dc22

                   2004044888

www.mhhe.com

Contents

UNIT TWO

HISTORY AND DEVELOPMENT OF PHYSICAL EDUCATION, EXERCISE SCIENCE, AND SPORT

UNIT THREE

**THE CHANGING NATURE OF PHYSICAL EDUCATION,
EXERCISE SCIENCE, AND SPORT**

Preface

Introduction to Physical Education, Exercise Science, and Sport Studies provides students with an exciting opportunity to discover the diversity of physical education, exercise science, and sport and the wealth of careers available in these fields. Students are introduced to the heritage, current programs, and future potential of the field they are considering. This book introduces students to these multifaceted fields and involves them in assessing potential careers in physical education, exercise science, and sport.

The intent of this book is to broaden students' understanding of how the philosophies and programs of physical education, exercise science, and sport evolved, as well as to present the current status of these fields. Inherent within the changing nature of physical education, exercise science, and sport is a need to examine how Title IX of the 1972 Education Amendments, the inclusion into classrooms of physically and mentally challenged individuals, the increased emphasis on physical activity and fitness for all ages, past programs in this country and in Europe, and various philosophies and ethical perspectives have affected and will continue to influence what professionals in these fields will do in the twenty-first century.

No longer are physical education, exercise science, and sport just for schools or colleges, although teaching in these settings is certainly an important endeavor. By learning about careers in leisure services, athletic training, corporate fitness, sport management, fitness club instruction and management, recreation for all ages and abilities, coaching, cardiac rehabilitation, and a variety of other activity-related pursuits, students will gain a clearer perspective of the future role physical education, exercise science, and sport should play in American society. Individuals who accept the challenges of these careers will help women, minorities, senior citizens, individuals in lower socioeconomic classes, individuals with disabilities, students, and many others benefit from active, fit lifestyles. Practical suggestions are provided to help students choose and prepare for careers. To enhance this process, the importance of physical education, exercise science, and sport as expanding and diverse fields of service, enjoyment, and employment is emphasized throughout the book.

NEW TO THIS EDITION

The sixth edition of this book provides insights into the increasing emphasis on exercise science and careers associated with preparation in allied fields. Throughout the book, more information has been provided on exercise science, physical activity, and fitness and the importance of these to the future of each person. Each chapter has been updated with revisions and expansions of key topics and includes some of the latest research to stimulate students' critical thinking and continued study. New photos throughout the book help reinforce students' learning of key concepts in the text. The review questions, student activities, suggested readings, and websites have been revised and updated, as needed. Finally, important terms are defined where they first appear within each chapter to reinforce the content.

Chapter 1   Physical Education, Exercise Science, and Sport Studies—Dynamic Fields

- Expansion of the importance of physical activity
- Additional information from the surgeon general's *Report on Physical Activity and Health*
- New Career Perspective for a personal trainer

Chapter 2   Exercise and Sport Sciences

- Added Research View on the scientific method
- Expanded information about technology associated with the exercise and sport sciences

Chapter 3   The Profession of Physical Education, Exercise Science, and Sport Studies

- Added information about exercise science and fitness
- Revised information about obtaining certification in athletic training
- Added standards for new teachers

Chapter 4   Philosophy of Physical Education, Exercise Science, and Sport

- Added information about several codes of ethics or conduct
- Added sample of a philosophy of a personal trainer
- New Career Perspective for a sport philosopher

Chapter 5   Selecting a Career

- Added information about job opportunities, educational and other experiences needed, and salary ranges

Chapter 6   Preparation for a Career

- Added information about the importance of internships and certifications
- Updated information about certifications
- Added examples of courses in graduate programs in some of the exercise and sport sciences
- Added contents of a portfolio to use for prospective employers

Chapter 7   Sport in the Ancient World and Our European Heritage

- Added information about the beginning of strength training
- New Career Perspective for a physical therapist

Chapter 8   Early American Physical Education and Sport

- Added information about the "father of physical culture"
- New Career Perspective for a teacher/coach

Chapter 9   Twentieth-Century Physical Education, Exercise Science, and Sport

- Added information about the history of exercise science
- Added information about how exercise science helps to dispel myths about physical activity
- Expanded information about inclusion in physical education
- New Career Perspective for an elementary physical education teacher

Chapter 10   Opportunities and Challenges in Physical Education and Exercise Science

- Expanded focus on the value of physical activity
- Added information about competencies of sport managers
- Expanded emphasis on exercise science
- New Career Perspective for a director of campus recreation

Chapter 11   Issues in Sports

- Added information about nutritional supplements and sport performance
- Expanded information about Title IX
- Expanded information about minorities in sport
- Added information about drug testing

Chapter 12   Living Actively in the Twenty-First Century

- Expanded information about exercise science
- Revised Career Perspective for a former sport manager working in a new leadership role

Appendix A   Revised and updated listing of professional journals along with contact addresses, including websites

Appendix B   Revised and updated list of certifying organizations

Glossary   Revised several definitions and added over a dozen new definitions

CONTENT DESIGN

Written in a conversational and personal style, *Introduction to Physical Education, Exercise Science, and Sport Studies* is designed for students enrolled in their first course related to exercise science, sport management, physical education, athletic training, or other related majors.

An overview of the field is stressed rather than an in-depth examination of the disciplinary areas. The relevant topics discussed include practical suggestions for selecting and obtaining a job in the chosen career; current issues affecting job selection; girls and women in sport; minorities in physical education and sport; the standards and assessment movement; teacher, coach, athletic trainer, and exercise specialist certifications; educational values of sports; and the importance of physical activity for all.

The book's three units are self-contained and may be read in any order, although each is important to a full understanding of the field. Unit One provides foundational information in the first four chapters before focusing on careers. As defined in Chapter 1, physical education is a *process through which an individual obtains optimal physical, mental, and social skills and fitness through physical activity*. Exercise science is broadly defined as the *scientific analysis of the human body in motion* and encompasses exercise physiology, biomechanics, kinesiology, anatomy, physiology, motor behavior, and some aspects of sports medicine. Sport is operationally defined as *physical activities governed by formal or informal rules that involve competition against an opponent or oneself and are engaged in for fun, recreation, or reward*. The cognitive, affective, and psychomotor development objectives of physical education and sport indicate how physical education and sport can contribute to improvements in quality of life for all. Chapter 2 provides an in-depth look at the exercise and sport sciences, such as exercise physiology, athletic training, and sport management. An explanation of organizations in the field precedes a discussion about preparation programs for school and nonschool careers in Chapter 3. The five traditional philosophies and discussion of ethics presented in Chapter 4 provide reference points for the development of a personal philosophy.

A career emphasis is integrated throughout and given special attention in Chapters 5 and 6. Chapter 5 describes more than 50 careers in education, recreation, fitness, sports, business, and athletics. Students learn about job responsibilities, prerequisite education and preparation, and potential availability of positions. Chapter 6 provides practical ideas for preparing for careers, with an emphasis on the importance of internships, volunteer experiences, and obtaining certifications. Recommendations for writing a résumé, developing a portfolio, and seeking a job are provided.

Unit Two covers the history and development of physical education, exercise science, and sport from early cultures through today. Athletics in Athens and Sparta, European gymnastics programs, and sports and games in Great Britain are emphasized in Chapter 7 in terms of their influence on programs in the United States. In Chapter 8, early American physical education, exercise science, and sport are traced from early sporting diversions through the formalized gymnastics programs of the late 1800s. Chapter 9 completes the chronology of evolving programs that are diverse in philosophy, clientele, and activity.

Unit Three describes issues and trends in physical education, exercise science, and sport. Chapter 10 examines the value of physical activity for everyone; exercise science program developments; unique features of elementary, middle, and secondary school physical education; standards and accountability; legal liability; career burnout; and instructional challenges facing physical educators. The beneficial outcomes and associated issues of sports for girls and women, minorities, senior citizens, individuals with disabilities, youth, school and college students, and Olympic athletes are addressed in Chapter 11. The final chapter looks at the image and role of physical education, exercise science, and sport in all settings in the twenty-first century.

SUCCESSFUL FEATURES

Key Concepts

Each chapter begins with statements that highlight the major topics to be discussed. These provide students with both a focus and direction for framing the key ideas to learn.

Introductions

The first paragraphs in the chapters briefly set the stage for and preview the text. They help students gain further perspective on the relevance of the content.

Illustrations

More than 140 photographs help students see the diversity of physical education, exercise science, and sport and potential careers in these fields. The photographs also reemphasize the popularity of sports and activities for all and help reinforce important concepts.

Boxed Material

Throughout the text, specially highlighted information is designed to enhance students' understanding and provide additional insights into the profession.

Definition Boxes

Selected definitions of key terms are boxed throughout the chapters at their first mention to reinforce meanings and for ease of studying.

Summaries

A summary paragraph at the conclusion of each chapter emphasizes the primary areas of importance, thus complementing the initial key concepts. These summaries help students focus on the major items discussed.

Career Perspective

A unique feature of this book is the integration of biographical sketches of sport, exercise science, and physical education professionals in several diverse careers. The featured individuals list their job responsibilities, hours, course work, and degrees, discuss experience needed for their careers, describe satisfying aspects of their careers and job potential, and offer suggestions for students.

Review Questions

To enhance retention of each chapter's content, students are encouraged to answer the review questions. Rather than seeking rote memorization of facts, these questions stress understanding key concepts.

Student Activities

Like the review questions, student activities encourage students to think about and use the chapter content in greater depth and to extract practical ideas for career application. These activities also encourage active participation in the learning process.

Suggested Readings

Suggested readings furnish students with additional information and potential resources for further study. The annotations are especially beneficial for expanding students' knowledge.

Web Connections

Each chapter provides students with annotations about content that can enhance learning at the URLs provided.

Glossary

A comprehensive glossary of important terms reinforces students' understanding of the terminology used in the book and in physical education, exercise science, and sport.

Appendixes

An appendix of professional journals, mailing addresses, websites, and foci provides easy references for purchasing these periodicals or learning more about their availability. A second appendix gives addresses for several organizations that certify coaches, athletic trainers, and fitness leaders.

INSTRUCTOR'S RESOURCE MATERIALS

Instructor's Resource CD

An Instructor's Manual and Test Bank accompany the text. The Instructor's Manual is available online to those who adopt the text. The manual includes practical teaching suggestions, chapter overviews, instructional objectives, and additional annotated readings. The Test Bank contains more than 450 multiple choice, true/false, matching, and essay test items with separate answer keys, and suggested audiovisual materials.

Computerized Test Bank

McGraw-Hill's Computerized Testing is the most flexible and easy-to-use electronic testing program available in higher education. The program allows instructors to create tests from book-specific test banks. It accomodates a wide range of question types, and instructors may add their own questions. Multiple versions of the test can be created. The program is available for Windows, Macintosh, and Linux environments. It is located on the Instructor's Resource CD.

PowerPoint Presentation

A comprehensive and extensively illustrated PowerPoint presentation accompanies the text for use in classroom discussion. The PowerPoint presentation may also be converted to outlines and given to students as a handout. You can easily download the PowerPoint presentation from the McGraw-Hill website at www.mhhe.com/lumpkin6e. Adopters of the text can obtain the login and password to access this presentation by contacting their local McGraw-Hill sales representative.

INTERNET RESOURCES

Online Learning Center

www.mhhe.com/lumpkin6e   This website offers resources to students and instructors. It includes downloadable ancillaries, web links, student quizzes, additional information on topics of interest, and more.

Resources for the instructor include:

- Instructor's Manual
- Downloadable PowerPoint presentations
- Links to professional resources
- Lecture outlines
- Additional web links

Resources for the student include:

- Flashcards
- Internet activities
- Interactive quizzes
- Learning objectives
- Career opportunities

Health and Human Performance Website

www.mhhe.com/hhp   McGraw-Hill's Health and Human Performance Discipline Page provides diversity, text ancillaries, a "how to" guide to technology, study tips, and athletic training exam preparation materials. It includes professional organization, convention, and career information, and information on how to become a McGraw-Hill author. Additional features of the website include:

- This Just In—This feature provides information on the latest hot topics, the best web resources, and more—all updated monthly.
- Faculty Support—Access online course supplements, such as lecture outlines and PowerPoint™ presentations, and create your own website with PageOut.
- Student Success Center—Find online study guides and other resources to improve your academic performance. Explore scholarship opportunities and learn how to launch your career.
- Author Arena—Interested in writing a textbook or supplement for the college market? Read the McGraw-Hill proposal guidelines and links to the Editorial Marketing teams, and meet and converse with our current author.

PageOut: The Course Website Development Center

www.pageout.net   PageOut enables you to develop a website for your course. The site includes:

- A course home page
- An instructor home page
- A syllabus (interactive, customizable, and includes quizzing, instructor notes, and links to the Online Learning Center)
- Web links
- Discussions (multiple discussion areas per class)
- An online grade book
- Student web pages
- Design templates

This program is now available to registered adopters of McGraw-Hill textbooks.

ACKNOWLEDGMENTS

Without the help of numerous individuals, this book would not exist. First and foremost, my parents, Janice and Carol Lumpkin, instilled in me a love for learning, provided me with many educational opportunities through personal sacrifice, and continually encourage all of my endeavors. I dedicate this book to them with my love. My sister, Vernell Berry, and my brother, Phillip Lumpkin, who are also dear friends, and their families provide me with love and encouragement, too.

I also appreciate the invaluable help given to me by the reviewers, who have provided valuable suggestions for this revision:

Leigh Ann Danzey-Bussell
Marian College (IN)

Sharon Stoll
University of Idaho

Pauline Entin
Northern Arizona University

Scott Frazier
University of Wisconsin–Stevens Point

James Racchini
Frostburg State University

Last, but significantly, I want to thank the outstanding professionals at McGraw-Hill Higher Education, and especially Michelle Turenne. It has been a pleasure to be associated with each of them. Their commitment to the publishing of quality books is unmatched. It is my hope that this book will awaken and kindle the interest of those who read it to select careers in physical education, exercise science, and sport.

Angela Lumpkin

PRINCIPLES AND SCOPE OF PHYSICAL EDUCATION, EXERCISE SCIENCE, AND SPORT STUDIES

© Corbis/Vol. 103

CHAPTER

1

PHYSICAL EDUCATION, EXERCISE SCIENCE, AND SPORT STUDIES— DYNAMIC FIELDS

KEY CONCEPTS

- Today's physical education, exercise science, and sport studies programs have the potential to improve the quality of life for everyone.
- The purpose of physical education, exercise science, and sport studies is to enhance lives through participation in physical activity. The growing interest in health and fitness contributes to the achievement of this purpose.
- Cognitive development, affective development, and psychomotor development objectives are achieved through today's programs in these dynamic fields.
- The allied fields of health, recreation, and dance share some curricula and purposes.
- The continual challenge facing physical educators, exercise scientists, and leaders in sports programs remains to instill in Americans of all ages the importance of participating in regular physical activity.

Children love to move because it is fun. Adults choose to engage in physical activity because they find it enjoyable. With increased leisure time, people of all ages are seeking out instructional, recreational, and competitive physical activity and sport programs. This interest promises a dynamic future for professionals who want to contribute to the well-being and quality of life of others. The millions who enroll in aerobic dance classes, join fitness clubs, bowl in leagues, hike, camp, swim, jog, climb, sail, walk, skate, and engage in many other physical pursuits already have determined that these activities are fun. Many also value the mental, social, and physical development resulting from their regular participation.

Although many people highly value maintaining a physically active and fit lifestyle, others are not yet convinced. Motivating this latter group is the challenge awaiting you when you begin your career. Historically, the term *physical educator* has been used to encompass professionals in various careers who teach fitness

Aerobic activities develop cardiovascular endurance, an important aspect of physical fitness. (Photo courtesy Bob Hilliard.)

and sport skills. This descriptor identifies individuals who are committed to using physical activities to develop the whole person.

To help you meet the challenge to contribute to the wellness of others, this text introduces you both to the current concepts and objectives in the dynamic fields of physical education, exercise science, and sport studies and to their rich heritage. Past physical education programs provide the foundation for today's broader programs in the United States, shaping the way we structure and describe these fields. Understanding the definition and objectives of physical education today and in the past will help you conceptualize the breadth and depth of these fields. Understanding current affective, cognitive, and psychomotor domains of learning will ensure that you know what physical education, exercise science, and sport studies programs seek to accomplish.

WHAT IS PHYSICAL EDUCATION? WHAT IS EXERCISE SCIENCE? WHAT IS SPORT?

Physical education, exercise science, and sport are allied fields that share a common heritage and have grown more distinctive with the knowledge explosion and through disciplinary specificity. They relate to, but are not synonymous with, exercise, play, games, leisure, recreation, and athletics. Defining each of these terms can help clarify the distinctions and similarities. **Exercise** involves physical movement that increases the rate of energy use of the body. **Play** refers to amusements engaged in freely, for fun, and devoid of constraints. **Games,** usually implying winners and losers, can range from simple diversions to cooperative activities to competitions with significant outcomes governed by rules. Freedom from work or responsibilities describes **leisure,** which may or may not include physical activity. Similarly, **recreation** refreshes or renews one's strength and spirit after work, with or without physical activity. **Athletics** are organized, highly structured, competitive activities in which skilled individuals participate.

Definitions

Sports may be played both for exercise and as a game. Sports participants may use their leisure time to play games recreationally. Some describe bridge and chess games as sports, while others claim that rock climbing, fly fishing, and skydiving are sports. When the rules governing the skill levels required of participants and the significance placed on the outcome are rigidly structured, sport becomes athletics. Usually *sport* refers to a contest in which the outcome is viewed as important by the players, who will emerge as either winners or losers. Broadly defined, **sports** are physical activities governed by formal or informal rules that involve competition against an opponent or oneself and are engaged in for fun, recreation, or reward.

exercise:
physical movement that increases the rate of energy use of the body

play:
amusements engaged in freely, for fun, and devoid of constraints

games:
activities ranging from simple diversions to cooperative activities to competitions with significant outcomes governed by rules

leisure:
freedom from work or responsibilities so that time may or may not be used for physical activity

recreation:
refreshing or renewing one's strength and spirit after work; a diversion that occurs during leisure hours

athletics:
organized, highly structured, competitive activities in which skilled individuals participate

sports:
physical activities governed by formal and informal rules that involve competition against an opponent or oneself and are engaged in for fun, recreation, or reward

Traditionally, the definition of physical education has been restricted to formal instruction in a school or college. However, instruction in physical activities also can occur in an aerobics center, a sports club, a corporate fitness program, or a recreational league. In these settings, people learn skills, develop fitness, and commit to enhancing their physical well-being. The National Association for Sport and Physical Education published its *National Standards for Physical Education* in 1995. These build on the definition of a physically educated person.

According to its guidelines, a physically educated person:

- HAS learned skills necessary to perform a variety of physical activities
- IS physically fit
- DOES participate regularly in physical activity
- KNOWS the implications of and the benefits from involvement in physical activities
- VALUES physical activity and its contribution to a healthful lifestyle in order to pursue a lifetime of healthful physical activity.

Revised in 2004, there are now six national standards for physical education:

- Standard 1: Demonstrates competency in motor skills and movement patterns needed to perform a variety of physical activities
- Standard 2: Demonstrates understanding of movement concepts, principles, and tactics as they apply to the learning and performance of physical activities
- Standard 3: Participates regularly in physical activity
- Standard 4: Achieves and maintains a health-enhancing level of physical fitness
- Standard 5: Exhibits responsible personal and social behavior that respects self and others in physical activity settings
- Standard 6: Values physical activity for health, enjoyment, challenge, self-expression, and/or social interaction

To encompass the various outcomes experienced by all people in diverse programs, **physical education** is defined as a process through which an individual obtains optimal physical, mental, and social skills and fitness through physical activity. In recent years, many colleges have chosen to rename their departments, using terms such as *kinesiology, exercise science, human movement,* and *sport studies.* **Exercise science** describes the scientific analysis of the human body in motion. This broad term encompasses exercise physiology, biomechanics, kinesiology, anatomy, physiology, motor behavior, and some aspects of sports medicine. Researchers are exploring how to maximize the potential of human movement through physiological, biomechanical, and psychological studies. Practitioners are applying these findings to improve the quality of life for all who incorporate physical activity into their lives. Thus, the term *exercise science* rather than *physical education* may more broadly define what people know and do relative to human movement.

physical education:
a process through which an individual obtains optimal physical, mental, and social skills and fitness through physical activity

exercise science:
the scientific analysis of the human body in motion; broadly encompasses exercise physiology, biomechanics, kinesiology, anatomy, physiology, motor behavior, and some aspects of sports medicine

QUALITY OF LIFE

What does "quality of life" mean? Is it happiness, wellness, health, fitness, or fun? Maybe it refers to leisure time, relief from stress, safety from harm, or the absence of disease. In today's world *quality of life,* although defined individually, increasingly means a long and healthy life. Inherent therein is the concept that a feeling of well-being or some level of fitness enhances life. Maybe it is an outgrowth of Americans' search for the fountain of youth, but fitness, or at least the appearance of fitness, appears to be valued.

This commitment to fitness is not a fad; it has become an integral part of life for many. Executives may choose where to take a job based on the availability of exercise programs, or employers may hire only healthy and fit employees. Families often plan vacations and leisure time around various recreational and sports activities. Thousands of people sign up for marathons, 10-kilometer road races, and fun runs. Walking has become popular for people of all ages. Sporting goods and sports clothing sales continue to gross millions of dollars. Sports facilities, such as health clubs, aerobics centers, tennis courts, swimming pools, and golf courses, are increasingly attracting people who take both their health and sports seriously.

A number of factors in contemporary life have reemphasized the importance of physical activity (see the Research View box "Physical Activity"):

- The threat of cardiovascular disease has contributed to a realization of the need to exercise the heart muscle.

- Poor nutritional habits have adversely affected the health of thousands.

- Longer life expectancies have raised the consciousness levels of many people who not only want to live longer but also want to enjoy their later years.

- Technological advances have reduced the amount of exercise inherent in our daily lives while providing greater amounts of leisure time and discretionary income.

- Stress proliferates as a frequent by-product of technology and a highly competitive business world.

In each case, exercise, along with a knowledge of how the body functions in response to activity, can enhance fitness and the overall quality of life. R. Tait McKenzie's *The Joy of Effort,* depicted on page 8, certainly captures the ecstasy of participating in sport for the pleasure it offers.

Millions of people in the United States, however, do not participate in any physical activity because they lack motivation, time, money, skills, or knowledge. To encourage participation is the role of physical educators, exercise scientists, and leaders of sports programs. Are you willing to accept responsibility for changing attitudes and developing programs to get inactive people involved? Teachers, can you sell your students on the value of physical activity? Sports leaders, can you persuade participants to adhere to, rather than drop out of, their sports programs? Exercise scientists, can you activate lethargic participants? The

⌕ RESEARCH VIEW

Physical Activity (information and data from the Centers for Disease Control)

The Importance of Physical Activity
(www.cdc.gov/nccdphp/dnpa/physical/importance/index.htm)
Regular physical activity substantially reduces the risk of dying of coronary heart disease, the nation's leading cause of death, and decreases the risk for stroke, colon cancer, diabetes, and high blood pressure. It also helps to control weight; contributes to healthy bones, muscles, and joints; reduces falls among older adults; helps to relieve the pain of arthritis; reduces symptoms of anxiety and depression; and is associated with fewer hospitalizations, physician visits, and medications. Moreover, physical activity need not be strenuous to be beneficial; people of all ages benefit from participating in regular, moderate-intensity physical activity, such as 30 minutes of brisk walking five or more times a week.

Recommendations for Physical Activity
(www.cdc.gov/nccdphp/dnpa/physical/recommendations/index.htm)
- Adults should engage in moderate-intensity physical activities for at least 30 minutes on five or more days per week; **or**
- Adults should engage in vigorous-intensity physical activity three or more days per week for 20 or more minutes per occasion.

Physical Activity Data
(www.cdc.gov/nccdphp/dnpa/physical/stats/stats.htm)
- 26.2 percent meet one of the above recommendations for physical activity.
- 46.2 percent get insufficient physical activity.
- 27.6 percent are inactive.

Obesity
(www.cdc.gov/nccdphp/dnpa/obesity/trend/index.htm)
- In 2000, the prevalence of obesity, defined as having a body mass index score of 30 or more, was 38.8 million, or 19.8 percent of adults in this country, which reflects a 61 percent increase since 1991.
- An estimated 15 percent of children and adolescents ages 6 to 19 years are overweight.

R. Tait McKenzie's *The Joy of Effort* won the King's Medal at the 1912 Stockholm
Olympic Games. (Courtesy the University of Tennessee Press.)

opportunity to make a difference is boundless since less than 50 percent of our
population exercises regularly.

The contribution of physical education, exercise science, and sport to the
quality of life can be enhanced by encouraging participation in team sports and
individual sports. Schools, recreation departments, and large corporations offer
league competitions in baseball, volleyball, basketball, football, soccer, and softball. Within these settings, team members learn and demonstrate teamwork, cooperation, communication skills, and the ability both to lead and to follow. Team
camaraderie may lead to lifelong friendships and the willingness to place the
team's benefit above individual goals. Although some of these sports can become
ageless pursuits, many individuals discontinue participation because their teams
lack sufficient players or because of the physical demands of the sport.

Individual sports are often called "lifetime sports" because of the greater likelihood of continued participation throughout life. Most of these sports can be engaged in by an individual either alone or with only one other person. Aerobics,
bowling, fishing, golf, hiking, jogging, racquetball, swimming, tennis, walking,
and weight lifting are the most popular of these sports and activities. They can be

Aerobic activities are important for all ages and both genders.

engaged in recreationally or competitively through leagues, tournaments, and organized events. Individual sports, like team sports, can teach fair play, self-confidence, and how to win and lose graciously, as well as specific sports skills.

Typically, school athletic teams and city or business recreational leagues attract skilled participants or those at least moderately comfortable with their skills. Those lacking skills, however, are often relegated to spectator roles or to their easy chairs in front of their televisions, video games, or computers. More instructional programs and beginning-level leagues and teams are needed for individuals of all ages. Unfortunately, there is frequently an overlap between the lower skilled and the economically disadvantaged. Because of their cost, tennis, golf, and swimming, for example, have often been categorized as upper-class sports. Therefore, tax-supported recreation departments need to provide opportunities for these and other activities for all individuals.

Senior citizens, a growing percentage of the U.S. population, also have recreational needs. For example, exercise has been found to reduce osteoporosis (a breakdown of calcium in the bones), especially for women in their post-menopausal years. Senior citizens need activities matched with their capabilities.

On the other end of the spectrum, children have many needs for physical activity that remain unfulfilled. Daily physical education from kindergarten through the twelfth grade would greatly enhance children's movement skills and fitness capacities. Nonschool sport programs can also provide opportunities for physical activity and play. For each of these groups, increased fun-filled opportunities for physical activities will contribute to the development of a healthy lifestyle. You, as a coach, recreation leader, personal trainer, or teacher, hold the key to unlocking this door of opportunity for others.

IMPORTANCE OF PHYSICAL ACTIVITY

In 1997, 77 percent of adults age 18 years and older were not vigorously active on a regular basis. Forty percent of American adults in 1997 engaged in no leisure-time, physical activity. More than 25 percent of adult Americans are overweight.

Healthy People 2010, published by the federal government in 2000, continued to report disturbing statistics (as did Healthy People 2000, published in 1990) about the poor status of Americans' overall health. Millions of citizens were overweight and inactive, and suffering the consequences of unhealthy lifestyles.

The Healthy People 2010 goals listed in Box 1-1 are important guidelines for the work of physical educators, exercise scientists, and sports leaders.

In 1996, the first-ever Surgeon General's report on *Physical Activity and Health* emphasized that Americans could substantially improve their health and the quality of their lives by participating in regular physical activity. Despite the Healthy People 2000 goals, the patterns and trends in physical activity reported

Walking is a moderate activity that can be enjoyed throughout life.

Development and maintenance of fitness is a lifelong pursuit.

Daily physical education leads to skill development so that individuals can play at high skill levels as adults. (Photo courtesy Lisa Sense.)

BOX 1-1   HEALTHY PEOPLE 2010

Healthy People 2010 is a national health promotion and disease prevention initiative that seeks to unite agencies at all levels in their efforts to improve the health of all Americans, eliminate disparities in health, extend lives, and improve the quality of life. Healthy People 2010 builds on initiatives pursued over the past two decades to achieve national health objectives. Healthy People 2010 seeks to attain two overarching goals and specifically addresses physical activity and fitness in Objective 22.

Goal 1: Increase Quality and Years of Healthy Life

Healthy People 2010 seeks to help individuals of all ages increase life expectancy and improve their quality of life.

Goal 2: Eliminate Health Disparities

Healthy People 2010 seeks to eliminate health disparities among different segments of the population. These include differences that occur by gender, race or ethnicity, education or income, disability, living in rural localities, or sexual orientation.

Objective 22: Deals with Physical Activity and Fitness—to Improve Health, Fitness, and Quality of Life through Daily Physical Activity

Physical Activity in Adults

22-1. Reduce the proportion of adults who engage in no leisure-time physical activity.
>**Target:** 20 percent.
>**Baseline:** 40 percent of adults age 18 years and older engaged in no leisure-time physical activity in 1997.

22-2. Increase the proportion of adults who engage regularly, preferably daily, in moderate physical activity for at least 30 minutes per day.
>**Target:** 30 percent.
>**Baseline:** 15 percent of adults age 18 years and older were active for at least 30 minutes five or more days per week in 1997.

22-3. Increase the proportion of adults who engage in vigorous physical activity that promotes the development and maintenance of cardiorespiratory fitness three or more days per week for 20 or more minutes per occasion.
>**Target:** 30 percent.
>**Baseline:** 23 percent of adults age 18 years and older engaged in vigorous physical activity three or more days per week for 20 or more minutes per occasion in 1997.

Muscular Strength/Endurance and Flexibility

22-4. Increase the proportion of adults who perform physical activities that enhance and maintain muscular strength and endurance.
>**Target:** 30 percent.
>**Baseline:** 19 percent of adults age 18 years and older performed physical activities that enhance and maintain strength and endurance two or more days per week in 1997.

22-5. Increase the proportion of adults who perform physical activities that enhance and maintain flexibility.
>**Target:** 40 percent.
>**Baseline:** 30 percent of adults age 18 years and older did stretching exercises in the past two weeks in 1995.

BOX 1-1   HEALTHY PEOPLE 2010 (CONTINUED)

Physical Activity in Children and Adolescents

22-6. Increase the proportion of adolescents who engage in moderate physical activity for at least 30 minutes on five or more of the previous seven days.
   Target: 30 percent.
   Baseline: 20 percent of students in grades 9 through 12 engaged in moderate physical activity for at least 30 minutes on five or more of the previous seven days in 1997.

22-7. Increase the proportion of adolescents who engage in vigorous physical activity that promotes cardiorespiratory fitness three or more days per week for 20 or more minutes per occasion.
   Target: 85 percent.
   Baseline: 64 percent of students in grades 9 through 12 engaged in vigorous physical activity three or more days per week for 20 or more minutes per occasion in 1997.

22-8. Increase the proportion of the nation's public and private schools that require daily physical education for all students.
   Target: 25 percent of students in middle and junior high school and 5 percent in senior high school.
   Baseline: 17 percent of students in middle and junior high school and 2 percent of students in senior high school were required to take daily physical education in 1994.

22-9. Increase the proportion of adolescents who participate in daily school physical education.
   Target: 50 percent.
   Baseline: 27 percent of students in grades 9 through 12 participated in daily school physical education in 1997.

22-10. Increase the proportion of adolescents who spend at least 50 percent of school physical education class time being physically active.
   Target: 50 percent.
   Baseline: 32 percent of students in grades 9 through 12 were physically active in physical education class more than 20 minutes three to five days per week in 1997.

See the Healthy People 2010 website for more information: www.health.gov/healthypeople/default.htm.

in the Surgeon General's report indicated little progress and even some decreases in activity. A few of these low participation levels included the following:

- Approximately 15 percent of adults and about 50 percent of individuals 12 to 21 years old in this country engage in vigorous physical activity at least three times a week for at least 20 minutes.

- Approximately 22 percent of adults in this country engage in sustained physical activity at least five times a week for at least 30 minutes.

- About 25 percent of adults and 25 percent of individuals 12 to 21 years old in this country engage in no physical activity.

- Daily attendance in high school physical education classes between 1991 and 1995 declined from approximately 42 percent to 25 percent.

These data verified the significant challenge facing this nation and confirmed a national concern for the physical welfare of most citizens.

As the Surgeon General's report on *Physical Activity and Health* concluded, people of all ages and both genders can benefit from regular physical activity. Significant health benefits can be obtained by including a moderate amount of physical activity in our weekly routines (e.g., 30 minutes of brisk walking, 15 minutes of running, or 45 minutes of playing volleyball on most, if not all, days of the week). Regular physical activity improves health by reducing the risk of premature death, dying from heart disease, developing diabetes, developing high blood pressure, or developing colon cancer. Daily, moderate physical activity helps reduce blood pressure in people who already have high blood pressure, reduces feelings of depression and anxiety, helps control weight, helps older adults become stronger and better able to move about without falling, and promotes psychological well-being. Other conclusions and recommendations of this landmark report are provided in Box 1-2.

BOX 1-2   SELECTED CONCLUSIONS AND RECOMMENDATIONS FROM THE SURGEON GENERAL'S *REPORT ON PHYSICAL ACTIVITY AND HEALTH*

1. Public health recommendations have evolved from emphasizing vigorous activity for cardiorespiratory fitness to including the option of moderate levels of activity for numerous health benefits.

2. Recommendations from experts agree that for better health, physical activity should be performed regularly. It is also acknowledged that for most people, greater health benefits can be obtained by engaging in physical activity of more vigorous intensity or of longer duration.

3. Experts advise previously sedentary people embarking on a physical activity program to start with short durations of moderate-intensity activity and gradually increase the duration or intensity until the goal is reached.

4. Experts advise consulting with a physician before beginning a new physical activity program for people with chronic diseases, such as cardiovascular disease and diabetes mellitus, or for those who are at high risk for these diseases. Experts also advise men over age 40 and women over age 50 to consult a physician before they begin a vigorous activity program.

5. Recent recommendations from experts also suggest that cardiorespiratory endurance activity should be supplemented with strength-developing exercises at least twice per week for adults in order to improve musculoskeletal health, maintain independence in performing the activities of daily life, and reduce the risk of falling.

6. Physical activity has numerous beneficial physiologic effects. Most widely appreciated are its effects on the cardiovascular and musculoskeletal systems, but benefits on the functioning of metabolic, endocrine, and immune systems are also considerable.

7. Many of the beneficial effects of exercise training—from both endurance and resistance activities—diminish within 2 weeks if physical activity is substantially reduced, and effects disappear within 2 to 8 months if physical activity is not resumed.

BOX 1-2   SELECTED CONCLUSIONS AND RECOMMENDATIONS FROM THE SURGEON GENERAL'S *REPORT ON PHYSICAL ACTIVITY AND HEALTH* (CONTINUED)

8. Higher levels of regular physical activity are associated with lower mortality rates for both older and younger adults.

9. Even those who are moderately active on a regular basis have lower mortality rates than those who are least active.

10. Regular physical activity for cardiorespiratory fitness decreases the risk of cardiovascular disease mortality in general and of coronary heart disease mortality in particular.

11. The level of decreased risk of coronary heart disease attributable to regular physical activity is similar to that of other lifestyle factors, such as keeping free from cigarette smoking.

12. Regular physical activity prevents or delays the development of high blood pressure, and exercise reduces blood pressure in people with hypertension.

13. Regular physical activity is associated with a decreased risk of colon cancer.

14. Regular physical activity lowers the risk of developing non-insulin-dependent diabetes mellitus.

15. Regular physical activity is necessary for maintaining normal muscle strength, joint structure, and joint function. In the range recommended for health, physical activity is not associated with joint damage or development of osteoarthritis and may be beneficial for many people with arthritis.

16. Weight-bearing physical activity is essential for normal skeletal development during childhood and adolescence and for achieving and maintaining peak bone mass in young adults.

17. Low levels of activity, resulting in fewer kilocalories used than consumed, contribute to the high prevalence of obesity in the United States.

18. Physical activity may favorably affect body fat distribution.

19. Physical activity appears to relieve symptoms of depression and anxiety and improve mood.

20. Physical activity appears to improve health-related quality of life by enhancing psychological well-being and by improving physical functioning in persons compromised by poor health.

21. Most musculoskeletal injuries related to physical activity are believed to be preventable by gradually working up to a desired level of activity and by avoiding excessive amounts of activity.

*Taken from www.cdc.gov/nccdphp/sgr/chapcon.htm.

Physical activity has numerous beneficial physiological effects on the cardiovascular and musculoskeletal systems, but it also benefits the metabolic, endocrine, and immune systems. Maintaining normal muscle strength, joint structure, and joint function occurs only when activity is sustained. Many of the beneficial effects of endurance and resistance activities diminish within two weeks if physical

Individuals of all ages are seeking to achieve the healthy benefits of physical activity. (Photo courtesy Lisa Sense.)

activity is substantially reduced, and effects disappear within two to eight months if physical activity is not resumed. Thus, the health benefits can be enjoyed only if physical activity becomes a regular part of a person's life.

PURPOSE

What exactly do physical education, exercise science, and sport programs seek to accomplish? A **purpose** is a stated intention, aim, or goal. Used interchangeably, these terms describe desirable long-range achievements that will occur only after many hours of effort and incremental progress. Working to make the dean's list this semester, earning an athletic grant-in-aid based on performance as a walk-on athlete, getting invited into an academic honor society, and saving money from a part-time job to purchase a car are all examples of goals. Whether you call it an aim, a goal, or a purpose, each is achieved by meeting several objectives, such as spending long hours studying or perfecting athletic skills. To help each person make these attitudinal and behavioral changes, the purpose of physical education, exercise science, and sport programs is to optimize the quality of life through a long-term commitment to enjoyable physical activity and sport experiences that will meet varied needs in a changing world.

> **purpose:**
> a stated intention, aim, or goal

A purpose provides the answer to the question *why*. Physical education, exercise science, and sport programs must add value to the lives of participants, or

WEB CONNECTIONS

1. www.health.gov/healthypeople/default.htm
   This site includes extensive information about the Healthy People 2010 initiative, including steps to ensure good health.

2. www.cdc.gov
   The Centers for Disease Control provide a plethora of information and data about health topics.

3. www.nih.gov
   The National Institutes for Health provide fact sheets, results from clinical trials, health information via hotlines, MEDLINEplus, and many other resources.

4. www.fitness.gov
   Visit this site of the President's Council on Physical Fitness and Sports to learn more about its activities to coordinate and promote opportunities in physical activity, fitness, and sports for all Americans.

5. www.cdc.gov/nccdphp/sgr/sgr.htm
   Read the text of the Surgeon General's report on *Physical Activity and Health* as well as gain access to other publications from this office.

6. www.healthfinder.gov
   This service of the U.S. Department of Health and Human Services provides a wealth of information about health and nutrition topics.

they cannot be justified. A "roll out the ball" physical education class that results in no development of physical fitness or motor skills should be changed. A school sports program that fails to teach fair play, cooperation, and self-control cannot be defended. A corporate or community fitness or sport program that is poorly organized, results in injuries and attrition because it is not based on sound physiological principles, and is not fun for the participants is doomed to failure. Conversely, the purpose of physical education, exercise science, and sport programs is to ensure that each person benefits physically, mentally, socially, and emotionally. Most people enjoy being active, which is why these opportunities exist. An improvement in the quality of their lives will be the desired and valued outcome that you can help them achieve.

Physical activity, physical fitness, health, and wellness are components essential to the achievement of the purpose of physical education, exercise science,

physical activity:
all movements that can contribute to improved health

physical fitness:
developed through endurance and resistive exercises of sufficient frequency, duration, and intensity to enhance heart and other bodily functions

health-related fitness:
attaining the level of well-being associated with heart function (cardiovascular endurance), muscular function (strength and endurance), and flexibility as a deterrent to debilitating conditions

skill-related fitness:
achieving levels of ability to perform physical movements specific to a sport, such as serving a tennis ball effectively, or a physical activity, such as executing safe and proper technique in an aerobics class

health:
wellness of body and mind; absence of disease or illness

wellness:
mental, emotional, spiritual, nutritional, and physical factors that lead to healthy behaviors

and sport. **Physical activity** includes all movements that can contribute to improved health. **Physical fitness** is developed through endurance and resistive exercises of sufficient frequency, duration, and intensity to enhance heart and other bodily functions. **Health-related fitness** refers to attaining the level of well-being associated with heart function (cardiovascular endurance), muscular function (strength and endurance), and flexibility as a deterrent to debilitating conditions. **Skill-related fitness** refers to achieving levels of ability to perform physical movements specific to a sport, such as serving a tennis ball effectively, or a physical activity, such as executing safe and proper technique in an aerobics class. **Health** refers to the wellness of body and mind. It also encompasses the absence of disease and illness, such as coronary heart disease, high blood pressure, and depression. **Wellness** includes the mental, emotional, spiritual, nutritional, and physical factors that lead to healthy behaviors. Each of these elements is vital to a person's quality of life.

OBJECTIVES OF PHYSICAL EDUCATION, EXERCISE SCIENCE, AND SPORT PROGRAMS

The objectives of physical education, exercise science, and sport programs are often stated more specifically than the purpose because they consist of particular learning outcomes. Professional colleagues and the general public often learn about a program's worth through an examination of its objectives and their fulfillment.

Through the years, physical education, exercise science, and sport objectives have increasingly focused on the whole person. Dudley Sargent, a recognized leader in physical education for college students in the late 1800s and early 1900s, suggested that physical education achieves hygienic, educative, recreative, and remedial objectives. Outcomes that he noted in his programs included improved

Tennis skills learned at a young age can lead to enjoyable sports participation throughout life. (Photo courtesy Lisa Sense.)

health, fun, reduction of illness and injury, and enhanced knowledge about how the body moves and learns. Clark Hetherington, one of the "new physical educators," helped lead the transition from exercising methodically to developing the entire person. In 1910, he recommended that physical education programs seek to achieve organic, psychomotor, character, and intellectual objectives.

In 1934, the American Physical Education Association's (today's American Alliance for Health, Physical Education, Recreation and Dance) Committee on Objectives listed the following as desired objectives:

- Physical fitness
- Mental health and efficiency
- Social and moral character
- Emotional expression and control
- Appreciation

In 1950, these objectives were restated as follows:

- To develop and to maintain maximum physical efficiency
- To develop useful skills
- To conduct oneself in socially useful ways
- To enjoy wholesome recreation

In 1965, the American Association for Health, Physical Education and Recreation stated five major objectives (*This is physical education,* 1965):

- To help children move in a skillful and effective manner in all the selected activities in which they engage, in the physical education program, and in those situations that they will experience during their lifetime.

- To develop an understanding and appreciation of movement in children and youth so that their lives will become more meaningful, purposive, and productive.
- To develop an understanding and appreciation of certain scientific principles concerned with movement that relate to such factors as time, space, force, and mass-energy relationships.
- To develop through the medium of games and sports better interpersonal relationships.
- To develop the various organic systems of the body so they will respond in a healthful way to the increased demands placed on them.

Before examining the objectives that guide physical education, exercise science, and sport programs, it is essential to understand how these objectives relate to those of education.

In 1918, the Educational Policies Commission stated seven objectives of education:

- Health
- Command of fundamental processes
- Worthy home membership
- Vocation
- Citizenship
- Worthy use of leisure time
- Ethical character

In 1938, these were consolidated into

- Self-realization
- Human relationship
- Economic efficiency
- Civic responsibility

Through all of these objectives, educational leaders sought to develop the whole child. Justification for any educational program was based on what contributions it could make. Since the 1930s, physical education has verified its value as a school subject by demonstrating its alignment with Benjamin Bloom's domains of learning: cognitive, affective, and psychomotor objectives. Educators, physicians, legislators, and parents have affirmed that school programs have helped achieve the educational objectives listed in Box 1-3. The domains of learning encompass mental, physical, social, and emotional components. School physical education and sport programs are unique because they contribute to the all-around person. The psychomotor objective focuses on the development of motor skills and physical fitness. Activities in these programs include an integration of cognitive abilities for optimal learning. Through participation in physical activities, individuals learn to value and appreciate themselves and others, as well as the experiences.

**BOX 1-3   EDUCATIONAL OBJECTIVES WHOSE ACHIEVEMENT
IS ENHANCED THROUGH PHYSICAL EDUCATION,
EXERCISE SCIENCE, AND SPORT PROGRAMS**

Physical

- Reduce risk of coronary heart disease, diabetes, obesity, high blood pressure, and colon cancer
- Improve muscular strength and endurance, flexibility, and cardiovascular endurance
- Regulate weight and improve body composition
- Promote overall health and fitness
- Strengthen bones
- Develop movement skills

Mental

- Improve academic performance
- Increase interest in learning
- Improve judgment
- Promote self-discipline
- Encourage goal setting and achieving these goals

Psychological and Social

- Improve self-confidence, self-esteem, and self-control
- Strengthen peer relationships
- Reduce the risk of depression
- Promote healthier lifestyles

Cognitive Development

Cognitive development focuses on the acquisition, comprehension, analysis, synthesis, application, and evaluation of knowledge. Preparation in physical education, exercise science, and sport studies includes studying the body's structure and function, history and philosophy, growth and development, sport marketing, sport finance, sport ethics, sport law, motor learning, biomechanics, sport psychology, sport sociology, and exercise physiology. Regardless of the setting, content learned in such courses is essential for teachers and leaders to understand and disseminate information and for program participants to comprehend and apply what they have learned.

cognitive development:
an educational outcome that emphasizes the acquisition, comprehension, analysis, synthesis, application, and evaluation of knowledge

Increased cognitive involvement usually leads to better execution of a skill and to a better understanding of the activity. In meeting cognitive objectives, teachers in all settings need to explain not only *how* but especially *why* the body's movements result in certain outcomes. For example, they can explain why hand position, release technique, and follow-through are critical to the success of throwing a ball. Teachers in all settings need to emphasize learning rules, strategies, skills, safety principles, and proper etiquette. An example of a measurable cognitive learning outcome would be: "A participant will demonstrate knowledge of the rules of tennis by answering at least 15 out of 20 questions correctly."

Performance in reading, math, language, and other subjects may be enhanced through participation in certain physical activities; plus, content in these areas can be incorporated into physical activities. In addition, mental fatigue from studying or working can be reduced through exercise so that a subsequent classroom session or job task becomes more productive.

Affective Development

Affective development emphasizes the formulation of attitudes, appreciations, and values; this domain contains both social and emotional dimensions. In the social realm, both individual and group needs are met while positive characteristics are developed. Learning self-confidence, courtesy, fair play, sportsmanship, and how to make value judgments through cooperative activities benefits all students. In team sports, decision-making abilities, communication skills, and affiliation needs are enhanced, as long as the outcome of the event is not overemphasized. Individuals' values and attitudes toward involvement in physical activity are solidified, as are appreciations for participation and performance when the achievement of realistic personal goals is paramount. On the emotional side, self-discipline, fun, learning how to win and lose, tension release, self-control, and self-expression are enhanced through the give-and-take of challenging oneself and competing with and against others. An example of an affective learning outcome would be: "Students take turns tossing balls to classmates in such a way that the classmate can catch at least 8 out of 10."

> **affective development:**
> an educational outcome that focuses on the formulation of attitudes, appreciations, and values, including both social and emotional dimensions
>
> **psychomotor development:**
> an educational outcome that emphasizes the learning of fundamental movements, motor skills, and sports skills

Psychomotor Development

Movement undergirds all physical education, exercise science, and sport programs that seek to achieve the objectives of **psychomotor development,** which is an educational outcome that emphasizes the learning of fundamental movements, motor skills, and sports skills. Although any person can learn fundamental movement skills, children learn more easily because they do not have to break habitual inefficient motor patterns. Also, if the basic locomotor, manipulative, and

Flexibility, muscular strength and endurance, and cardiovascular endurance are the essential components of physical fitness.

perceptual-motor skills are learned early, they provide the foundation for lifelong enjoyment of physical activity.

Movement concepts include body awareness; spatial awareness, including space, direction, level, and pathways; qualities of movement such as time, force, and flow; and relationships with objects and with people. Walking, running, jumping, leaping, and sliding are some of the basic locomotor movements; conversely, stretching, twisting, pushing, lifting, and swinging are nonlocomotor movements. Manipulative skills, involving propelling or absorbing force from an object, include throwing, catching, striking, and kicking.

Developing and improving fundamental movement skills and game or sport skills are important objectives, since sport, aquatic, and dance skills begin with learning basic and efficient movement patterns. Children need to explore their bodies' capabilities as they learn to walk, run, or jump independently, in conjunction with others, or by using a piece of equipment. Similar principles can apply as individuals experiment with solving other movement challenges. Manipulative skills are developed by exploring the potential of hoops, ropes, balls, rackets, bats, and other implements. Perceptual-motor skills, such as the eye/hand coordination needed to strike a ball with a racket or the reaction time needed to judge how quickly a partner's thrown ball will arrive, are also important skills. Once these abilities are mastered developmentally and independently, skills such as catching, throwing, and batting can be incorporated into lead-up games and sport situations. An example of a psychomotor development learning outcome would be: "The participant will use the proper technique in successfully executing at least 7 out of 10 dominant-hand basketball layups."

Physical Fitness

Health-related physical fitness includes cardiovascular endurance, muscular strength and endurance, flexibility, and body composition. The ability to sustain physical activity that requires oxygen for exertion indicates cardiovascular endurance, the most essential component of physical fitness. Similarly, the ability to exert and sustain maximal force against a resistance constitutes muscular strength and endurance. Flexibility gained by statically stretching the muscles improves the range of motion in the joints. *Body composition* refers to the percentage of fat in the body. Caloric expenditure through exercise helps regulate body composition. Agility, balance, neuromuscular coordination, speed, and power also contribute to physical fitness. Agility permits quick changes in direction during activity. A person's balance, or state of equilibrium, stabilizes the body in preparation for future movements or actions. Neuromuscular coordination, including reaction time, integrates the senses with motor function. Speed permits rapid execution of a movement, while power combines speed with muscular strength.

Figure 1-1 summarizes the objectives of physical education, exercise science, and sport. It is essential to recognize that these objectives interrelate rather than exist in isolation. For example, while learning to hit a tennis ball, people not only enhance their eye/hand coordination but also learn proper body position for a

Physical education helps children develop fitness and psychomotor skills as they learn to enjoy activity. (Photo courtesy Bob Hilliard.)

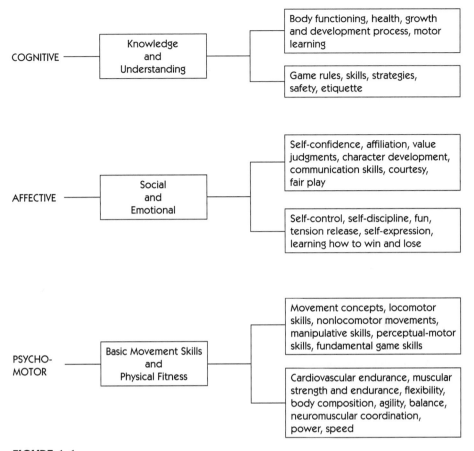

FIGURE 1-1

Objectives of physical education, exercise science, and sport studies.

level swing and cooperation with those with whom they take turns tossing the ball. Box 1-4 provides several examples of how the objectives of physical education and sport are achieved and interrelated. It should also be emphasized that the breadth of the outcomes sought in physical education, exercise science, and sport programs makes it challenging to maintain a focused field of study.

ALLIED FIELDS

Health, recreation, and dance have traditionally been allied in purpose with physical education, exercise science, and sport, although their programs differ somewhat in emphasis. Coaching, another allied field, is often a combined career with teaching physical education in the schools. Today personal trainers, athletic trainers, sport managers, sport psychologists, exercise physiologists, and others help achieve the purpose and objectives of physical education, exercise science, and sport programs.

BOX 1-4   EXAMPLES OF PHYSICAL EDUCATION, EXERCISE SCIENCE, AND SPORT OBJECTIVES

Cognitive Development

- The participant will explain the principles for playing zone defense in basketball.
- The participant will analyze the technique for executing a flat tennis serve.
- The participant, using the entire stroke (whole teaching method), will synthesize the principles of learning the crawl stroke in swimming.
- The participant will apply knowledge of cardiovascular functioning in establishing a personal fitness program.
- The participant will evaluate another person's weight-lifting technique and provide corrective feedback.

Affective Development

- The participant will express appreciation for the excellence of an opponent's high-level performance.
- The participant will enjoy playing hard and doing his or her best, regardless of the outcome of the contest.
- The participant will cooperate and take turns with others.
- The participant will demonstrate fair play in unsupervised activities.
- The participant will value the rights of others and the regulations governing the situation.

Psychomotor Development

- The participant will improve eye/hand coordination by weekly practicing racquetball forehand and backhand shots. (motor skill development)
- The participant will explore ways to manipulate a ball without using the hands. (motor skill development)
- The participant will design and perform a one-minute dance that includes the use of two locomotor movements and two objects. (motor skill development)
- The participant will demonstrate the proper technique for executing a volleyball spike. (motor skill development)
- The participant will execute four exercises designed to improve flexibility of the shoulders. (physical fitness)
- The participant will develop and implement a daily program of at least 30 minutes of aerobic activity. (physical fitness)
- The participant will engage in a weight-lifting program at least three times a week. (physical fitness)

Health

Many of the early school and college physical education programs in the 1800s emphasized health benefits as their primary justification. For example, at Amherst College, beginning in the 1860s, the president supported a physical education program to help students become and stay healthy. As was the case with many other institutions, the person charged with directing this program was a physician. In the twentieth century, the dual role of the health/physical educator separated as colleges prepared physical education teachers for jobs that focused on teaching physical activities, especially in alignment with educational objectives rather than health objectives. Because health and physical education programs share the goal of good health, and because school health classes are often assigned to physical educators (who at best have minimal academic preparation in this field), acceptance of health as a separate discipline in schools has been gradual.

Although the disciplines of health and physical education share some content and objectives, each also seeks to achieve unique outcomes. Physical activity and sports participation contribute to fitness and overall well-being. Health, in addition to being the traditional absence of disease, encompasses soundness of body, mind, and spirit. School health curricula include the study of nutrition; mental and emotional health; avoidance of abuse of tobacco, alcohol, and other drugs; and human sexuality. Community and corporate health programs focus on disease prevention, smoking cessation, safety and first aid, child care, weight loss and control, and stress management.

Hypokinetic disease refers to those diseases and health problems associated with physical inactivity and a sedentary lifestyle. Coronary heart disease, high blood pressure, stress, ulcers, obesity, and low back pain often afflict individuals who fail to engage in regular exercise. When school, work, and family place few physical demands on our bodies, these degenerative diseases may develop. Health education and physical activity can help alter or deter the disease process.

In 1992, the American Heart Association identified physical inactivity (along with high blood pressure and high cholesterol) as a primary risk factor for coronary heart disease. Millions need to realize that participating in regular physical activity and exercise is essential to good health (see the Research View box "National Physical Activity Status and Goals").

Soccer helps develop sports skills and physical fitness. (Photo courtesy Lisa Sense.)

RESEARCH VIEW

National Physical Activity Status and Goals

Date	Agency/ Initiative	Status/Goals
1987	U.S. Congress	Resolution 97 encouraged educational agencies and governments to provide quality, daily physical education programs for all K–12 children.
1990	Healthy People 2000 Goals	Increase to at least 50% the proportion of children and adolescents in first through twelfth grade who participate in daily physical education at school. Increase to at least 50% the proportion of physical education class time that students spend being physically active, preferably in lifetime physical activities.
1996	Surgeon General's *Report on Physical Activity and Health*	Nearly half of American youths 12 to 21 years of age are not vigorously active on a regular basis. Moreover, physical activity declines dramatically during adolescence. Daily enrollment in physical education classes declined among high school students from 42% in 1991 to 25% in 1995. Only 19% of all high school students report being physically active for 20 minutes or more in daily physical education classes.
2000	Healthy People 2010 Goals	Increase the proportion of adolescents who engage in moderate physical activity for at least 30 minutes on five or more of the previous seven days. Increase the proportion of the nation's public and private schools that require daily physical education for all students. Increase the proportion of adolescents who spend at least 50% of physical education class time being physically active.
2001	*Shape of the Nation* from the National Association for Sport and Physical Education	Forty-eight states (Colorado and South Dakota are the exception) have some type of mandate for physical education. Illinois is the only state that requires daily physical education for all students, but does permit waivers. All students in grades K–8 in Alabama are required to take physical education. A majority of high school students in grades 9–12 take physical education for only one year. Actual class times at all grade levels vary widely and are most frequently less than the recommended minutes per week. Certified physical educators are required to teach physical education in 4 states in elementary schools, 38 in middle grades, and 47 in high schools.

Recreation

Recreation, a diversion that occurs during leisure hours, renews and refreshes one's strength and spirits after work. Today most recreation programs are separate from physical education, exercise science, and sport studies programs, although they share many objectives. This change reflects the important role of recreational activities for people of all ages. Schools, businesses, communities, and families have increasingly offered activities for fitness and pleasure as each of these groups accepts some responsibility to educate for healthy use of leisure time. Businesses provide work site fitness centers, sponsor sports teams, and offer a variety of fitness activities for employees and their families.

Because many Americans are enjoying increased leisure time and larger discretionary incomes, the recreation services industry is growing rapidly. Also, as the American population ages, more and more retired persons are seeking appropriate recreational outlets. No longer can municipal recreation departments fulfill their missions simply by sponsoring youth leagues in the traditional team sports. Americans also want adult competitive leagues, instructional clinics, open facilities for family outings, organized trips and moderate exercise programs for seniors, and child care so that parents can recreate. Environmental concerns have led many people to expect resource management by state and national authorities to preserve the beauty of nature and access to it for outdoor recreators. Schools and colleges have expanded their curricula to include the lifetime activities of backpacking, canoeing, rock climbing, and downhill skiing. Thus, some shared outcomes with recreation programs are evident.

Dance

Bodily movements of a rhythmic and patterned succession usually executed to the accompaniment of music constitute **dance.** Both as physical activity and as performing art, dance varieties include aerobic, ballet, ballroom, folk, clogging, jazz, modern, square, and tap. Dance can provide participants opportunities for aesthetic expression whether in a beginner's class or on stage. People of all ages can dance for fitness and for fun. Some schools and most colleges have dance specialists, yet many dance classes, especially for females, are taught by physical educators who sometimes have had minimal preparation in this field.

> **dance:**
> bodily movements of a rhythmic and patterned succession usually executed to the accompaniment of music

Introduction to Nonteaching Fields

Many individuals are interested in careers in exercise science, sport, and physical activity programs that do not involve teaching. Opportunities certainly abound in these areas, as will become evident as you read this book and explore the plethora of learning experiences you will encounter during your college years. While historically a common heritage is shared, in recent decades the information explosion has created new venues for working in fields that contribute to human

Rafting has become a popular recreational activity. (Photo courtesy Terry Dash.)

welfare as broadly defined. For example, with the increase in life expectancy, providing leisure time programs for senior citizens who are healthy and can engage energetically in human movement activities is an expanding field of employment. With the emphasis on constantly improving motor skills, exercise scientists in exercise physiology, biomechanics, sport psychology, and motor learning are conducting research studies to identify approaches that will improve how athletes perform. To offset increasing obesity and inactivity associated with a technological world, individuals are seeking fitness programs to help them attain and maintain healthy lifestyles. With increased leisure time, people of all ages are participating in a diversity of sporting pastimes as well as being entertained by athletes of all ages. Sport managers and recreation specialists organize these programs.

Each of the nonteaching fields makes its unique contribution to the attainment of shared objectives of physical education, exercise science, and sport. As Table 1-1 indicates, the contributions made to others as well as personally enjoyed are extensive for each objective.

SUMMARY

Physical education, exercise science, and sport programs aim to improve the quality of life and the physical well-being of participants. People of all ages enjoy playing games, engaging in recreational activities, and exercising to maintain good health. Competitive, rule-bound sports provide opportunities to test one's skills against opponents. Through all of these programs, the all-around development of the individual is enhanced during activity. The purpose of these programs is to optimize quality of life through enjoyable physical activity and sport experiences. Educational objectives through cognitive, affective, and psychomotor (physical fitness and motor skill) development are sought and achieved. Several of these objectives are shared with the allied fields of health, recreation, and dance. A significant challenge facing physical education, exercise science, and sport professionals is to help all Americans participate in regular physical activity so they can enjoy the associated health benefits.

TABLE 1-1

NONTEACHING PHYSICAL ACTIVITY CAREER CONTRIBUTIONS

Job Title	Those Served	Cognitive	Affective	Psychomotor
Fitness director	Participants in a corporate fitness program	X	X	X
Coach	Athletes	X	X	X
Sport psychologist	Athletes	X	X	X
Exercise physiologist	Subjects in a research study on motor performance	X		X
Athletic trainer	Athletes	X	X	X
Sport marketer	Professional athletes and fans		X	X
Recreation director	Senior citizens recreational program	X	X	X
Sporting goods salesperson	Customers who purchase products		X	X
Personal trainer	Members of a health and fitness club	X	X	X

Lifetime recreational activities, such as rock climbing, are part of some school and college curricula. (Photo courtesy Aram Attarian.)

CAREER PERSPECTIVE

JIM WHITTAKER

Owner and President of Velotek Training & Alta-Sport, LC
Lawrence, Kansas

EDUCATION

B.S., Psychology, with emphasis in health and behavior
modification, University of Kansas
M.S., Physical Education, with emphasis in exercise
physiology, biomechanics, and health, University of Kansas

JOB RESPONSIBILITIES AND HOURS

Jim owns his own event promotion business (www.alta-sport.com) and coaches cycling
(www.Velotek.com). He provides custom training programs to amateur and professional
road and off-road cyclists in North America, serves as a personal trainer for athletes and
special populations, and promotes and manages bicycle races and triathlons. Jim's primary job responsibilities include coaching, designing and implementing training programs, and managing and promoting sporting events. In completing these, Jim uses his
background and experiences in accounting, sales, marketing, customer service, and technology. Since his hours are flexible, there is no normal work schedule. But, being self-
employed, he often works long hours and needs to be available at any time to meet the
needs of customers, such as when coaching athletes who call for assistance outside of
normal workday hours and especially in the spring and summer. Depending on the
scope of work and quality of services provided, the salary range for a small-business
owner in this field is $30,000 to $75,000.

SPECIALIZED COURSE WORK, DEGREES, AND WORK EXPERIENCES NEEDED FOR THIS CAREER

It is helpful for coaches to have experience playing in their chosen sports to augment
their scientifically based, technical knowledge. Strength and conditional specialists do
not necessarily need experience in any sport. To promote sporting events, marketing
skills and sales experiences are imperative. For both types of positions, a person must
have good interpersonal skills. The most important courses for Jim were sports psychology, general psychology, exercise physiology, and anatomy, but he adds that business
and marketing classes would have been helpful had he taken those. However, Jim notes
that courses completed should not be permitted to stifle creativity and initiative, which
are essential to small-business ownership. He believes that a master's degree helps to
distinguish among applicants in the marketplace. Other distinguishing marks are the
certifications Jim holds: ASCM Exercise Test Technologist; NSCA Certified Strength
and Conditioning Specialist; NSCA Certified Personal Trainer; and USA Cycling Elite
Level Cycling Coach.

SATISFYING ASPECTS

Jim really enjoys helping people believe in their abilities on and off the playing field. He
takes special pleasure in seeing clients progress as their belief in themselves and their

confidence grow. Because of the flexible work schedule that self-employment allows, Jim appreciates being able get up when he wants and go to bed when he chooses. He likes to treat others the way he wants to be treated. It is rewarding to run all aspects of his business and learn new skills. It is also challenging: The workload varies during the year, resulting in the stress of large events and projects; high levels of energy and commitment are demanded year round; and it is often difficult to balance private life with the job, especially when working at home.

JOB POTENTIAL

Jim views self-employment in this field of exercise as unlimited. He stresses that it is important not to grow the business too quickly and to focus on what is important, not just the bottom line.

SUGGESTIONS FOR STUDENTS

Jim states, "*Never, never* give up on your dreams!" He advises that even though others will discourage starting and managing your own business, be patient, work hard, and have some fun. He suggests studying business and marketing as well as completing core exercise classes. Jim says that although advanced education provides the tools to think, it is up to you to do something with what you have learned and to overcome the greatest challenge: to set out by yourself.

REVIEW QUESTIONS

1. How can physical education, exercise science, and sport contribute to an improved quality of life?

2. How do physical education, exercise science, and sport relate to athletics, leisure, and play?

3. What is the relationship among physical education, exercise science, and sport? What are the differences?

4. How do physical education, exercise science, and sport objectives relate to general educational objectives?

5. What types of knowledge are important within the cognitive domain of physical education, exercise science, and sport? Give examples of each.

6. How are the social and emotional outcomes of the affective objective achieved in physical education, exercise science, and sport programs?

7. What are the three major components of physical fitness?

8. What are the two overarching goals of Healthy People 2010?

9. How do health, recreation, and dance relate to physical education, exercise science, and sport?

10. What is the primary recommendation of the Surgeon General's report on *Physical Activity and Health*?

STUDENT ACTIVITIES

1. Interview three individuals of different ages (for example, below 18, mid-30s, and over 60) to determine what role physical activity plays in their lives.

2. Ask at least two friends who are not majors in your field what they think physical education, exercise science, and sport are.

3. Write a one- or two-page description of how you would incorporate three movement concepts or skills into a youth soccer program.

4. Write a one-page summary of how the three domains of physical education, exercise science, and sport objectives have influenced your life and career choice.

5. In groups of three to five students, develop several strategies that would effectively change the physical activity patterns of children, teenagers, and adults. Present two-minute reports to the class.

REFERENCES

This is physical education, Washington, DC, 1965, American Association for Health, Physical Education and Recreation.

Healthy people 2010, Washington, DC, 2000, U.S. Government.

National Standards for Physical Education, Reston, VA, 2003, National Association for Sport and Physical Education.

Physical activity and health, a report of the Surgeon General, Washington, DC, 1996, Department of Health and Human Services.

SUGGESTED READINGS

Corbin CB, Pangrazi RP: How much physical activity is enough? *JOPERD* 67(4):33, 1996. It is recommended that inactive people need some physical activity. Beginners need to start slowly and then progress; adults need at least 30 minutes of moderate-intensity physical activity most days; some vigorous activity is recommended. Implementing the FIT formula (frequency, intensity, and time) helps to achieve and maintain high levels of physical fitness and weight control, and some weekly activity designed to build muscular strength and endurance and flexibility is encouraged.

Dorman SM: Healthy People 2010 online, *J of Sch Health* 70(3):113, 2000. Health promotion and education resources that are available online from the federal Healthy People 2010 initiative are presented.

Foret CM, Clemens JM: The elderly's need for physical activity, *JOPERD* 67(4):57, 1996. Based on their entry-level health status, seniors need to participate in properly administered exercise programs that help them improve their functional capacity.

Gill DL (ed.): Quality of life: through movement, health, and fitness, *Quest* 48:245, 1996. This issue contains 14 papers presented at the 1995 meeting of the American Academy of Kinesiology and Physical Education. All of these papers focus on quality of life through movement, health, and fitness.

Hue O, Gallis DL, Prefaut C: Pulmonary function during cycling and running in triathletes, *J of Sp Med & Phy Fit* 43(1):44, 2003. This article reports on research on the lung functioning of triathletes during two phases of their competitive events.

Keating XD: The current often implemented fitness tests in physical education programs: problems and future directions, *Quest* 55(2):141, 2003. The author describes some of the issues associated with fitness tests and makes some suggestions for change.

Knehans AW: Childhood obesity: why is this happening to our children? *J of the Okla St Med Assn* 95(8):539, 2002. This comprehensive article examines the numerous factors that have contributed to the medical crisis of childhood obesity.

Morrow JR, Blair SN: Promoting the Surgeon General's *Report on Physical Activity and Health:* activities of the NCPPA, *Quest* 51(2):178, 1999. The authors advocate for collaborative activities and coalitions to help deliver the message of the Surgeon General's report on the essential relationship between physical activity and health and to work to achieve the goals of Healthy People 2010.

Pangrazi RP, Corbin CB, Welk GJ: Physical activity for children and youth, *JOPERD* 67(4):38, 1996. Children should be encouraged to participate in sporadic, high-volume, moderate-intensity physical activities. These should be individualized and enjoyable so that youth learn behavioral skills that lead to lifetime activity.

Stewart KJ, Turner KL, Bacher AC, Deregis JR, Sung J, Tayback M, Ouyang P: Are fitness, activity, and fatness associated with health-related quality of life and mood in older persons? *J of Cardiopulmonary Rehab* 23(2):115, 2003. These researchers report on how physical activity contributes to positive lifestyles for older individuals.

2

EXERCISE AND SPORT SCIENCES

KEY CONCEPTS

- An academic discipline includes a body of knowledge that is scholarly and theoretical and seeks to gain greater insights.
- Ten exercise and sport sciences continue to make significant contributions to the knowledge base of their disciplines.
- As a multidisciplinary field, the exercise and sport sciences share content knowledge with technology and the humanities.

A critical issue in the fields of physical education, exercise science, and sport studies is whether they can be considered academic disciplines. The major question debated in the 1960s (Henry, 1964) was whether physical education possesses a body of knowledge that is formally organized and merits scholarly study. Starting in the 1980s, an emphasis on the theoretical and scholarly content of physical education over its practical aspects resulted in attempts to rename this field using a more scholarly descriptor. This chapter gives an overview of the contributions of 10 exercise and sport sciences to determine whether physical education, exercise science, and sport studies warrant such a categorization.

WHAT IS AN ACADEMIC DISCIPLINE?

An **academic discipline** is a formal body of knowledge discovered, developed, and disseminated through scholarly research and inquiry. The components of an academic discipline include

academic discipline:
a formal body of knowledge discovered, developed, and disseminated through scholarly research and inquiry

- A body of knowledge
- A conceptual framework
- Scholarly procedures and methods of inquiry
- Both the process of discovery and the end result

If physical education, exercise science, and sport merit the distinction of being called academic disciplines, these criteria must be met.

A *body of knowledge* refers to an area of study that seeks answers to important questions. Participants in a field attempt to gain information and to contribute to the knowledge available to others. Physical educators have discovered and reported information that is of value to researchers and practitioners in other fields. Examples of their contributions include studies about the effects of drugs on physical performance, the importance of feedback to learning, and the role of sports in developing cultures. In these and many other studies, physical educators and exercise scientists examine the physiological, psychological, historical, or sociological impact of physical activity on people.

Similarly, research studies in an academic discipline must be guided by a conceptual framework. Proper hypotheses and experimental designs, strict controls, absence of bias, accurate reporting of findings, and interpretive analyses should characterize each attempt to gain new knowledge. This process requires stringent adherence to protocol to give credibility to the results.

Scholarly procedures and methods of inquiry are built on this conceptual framework. For example, the sport historian must not rely on secondary, and often inaccurate, sources in examining significant events. Motor development specialists must evaluate the role of genetics and the environment in assessing readiness to learn. The exercise physiologist must control extraneous variables when analyzing the effect of a treatment, such as consuming a different diet or taking a specific drug, on a training regimen.

In seeking knowledge, the process of discovery and the end result are equally important. How the researcher collects data influences the findings; therefore, accuracy in reporting and interpretation is vital. Also, replication studies should verify the results consistently.

Other characteristics of an academic discipline include a substantial history and tradition, a broad scope that is unique in comparison with other fields, and a specific language. Thus, for physical education, exercise science, and sport studies to qualify as academic disciplines, they must contribute to the body of knowledge by using a conceptual framework, scholarly procedures and methods of inquiry, theoretical processes of discovery, and analysis of the end results.

THE SCIENTIFIC FOUNDATION OF THE EXERCISE AND SPORT SCIENCES

Before describing the exercise and sport sciences, it is important to realize that our scientific foundation is multidisciplinary. As discussed in Chapter 3, **pedagogy** is the art and science of teaching, and teachers study learners and how to enhance their learning. Numerous academic fields of study provide many of the principles and methods of scientific inquiry used by researchers. One cornerstone is biology, the study of life

pedagogy:
the art and science of teaching

and life processes. On these biological facts and information are built anatomy, physiology, chemistry, and physics.

Anatomy and physiology are the studies of the structure and function, respectively, of the human body. Chemistry is the study of the composition, properties, and reactions of matter. The specialization of biochemistry focuses on biological substances and processes, such as how the body's cells use food to obtain energy through respiration. The study of physics examines interactions between matter and energy, including various types of motion and forces. These and other sciences rely on applied mathematical concepts and computations.

History, philosophy, including sport ethics, psychology, and sociology are often called social sciences because they seek knowledge in more experiential

TABLE 2-1		
RELATIONSHIPS AMONG DISCIPLINES		
Influencing Discipline	*Exercise and Sport Science*	*Shared Research Interests with*
Anatomy Biology Chemistry Physiology	Exercise physiology	Motor control and learning Sport biomechanics Athletic training Sport and exercise psychology
Anatomy Physical therapy Physiology Psychology	Athletic training	Exercise physiology Sport biomechanics Sport and exercise psychology
Physiology Psychology	Motor development	Motor learning
Anatomy Physiology Psychology	Motor control and learning	Exercise physiology Motor development Sport biomechanics
Mathematics	Sport biomechanics	Exercise physiology Motor control and learning Athletic training
History Philosophy Sociology	Sport history	Sport philosophy Sport sociology
Accounting Ethics Finance Law Management Marketing	Sport management	Sport ethics and philosophy Sport sociology
History Philosophy	Sport philosophy	Sport history Sport sociology
Physiology Psychology Sociology	Sport and exercise psychology	Exercise physiology Athletic training Sport sociology
History Philosophy Sociology	Sport sociology	Sport history Sport philosophy

ways than do the "hard" sciences just described. The historian seeks to record and analyze past events. In the pursuit of wisdom through intellectual and logical means, the philosopher investigates the causes and laws underlying reality. The sport philosopher also seeks to understand the nature, value, and artistic aspects of sport to learn how and why people perceive or believe as they do. The psychologist examines mental processes and behaviors. The sociologist studies human behavior in society. After we discuss the 10 exercise and sport sciences, refer to Table 2-1 to examine the relationships among these and the influencing discipline and to Figure 2-1 to see the interrelations among the 10 exercise and sport sciences.

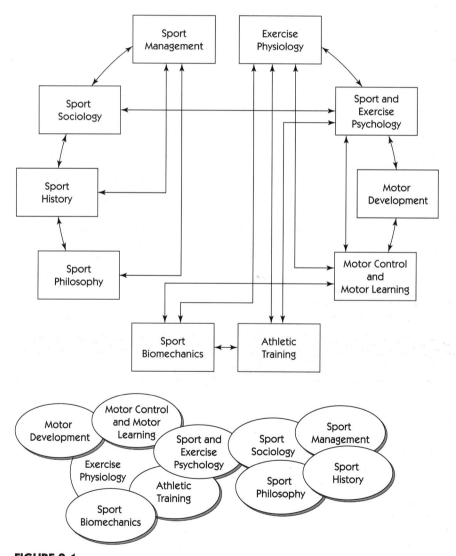

FIGURE 2-1

Exercise and sport sciences: two depictions of their interrelationships.

EXERCISE PHYSIOLOGY

The study of bodily functions under the stress of muscular activity is called **exercise physiology.** As described in Chapter 8, George Fitz helped establish the first exercise physiology laboratory at Harvard University over a century ago, through which he advocated using research to substantiate or refute physical activity claims. Exercise physiology, which became the cornerstone of early collegiate physical education programs, grew in stature after the establishment of the American College of Sports Medicine in 1954. This organization brought together (or rejoined—see Chapter 8) the medical and scientific communities in the shared quest to investigate all aspects of the impact of physical activity on the body.

> **exercise physiology:**
> the study of bodily functions under the stress of muscular activity

The study of exercise physiology is built on an understanding of the anatomical and physiological bases for human movement, including the 208 bones in the human skeleton; the joint structure, which includes cartilage, ligaments, and muscular attachments; the muscular system; the nervous system; and the circulatory and respiratory systems. More than 400 muscles, through a system of levers in conjunction with the skeletal system, provide the physiological key and guide

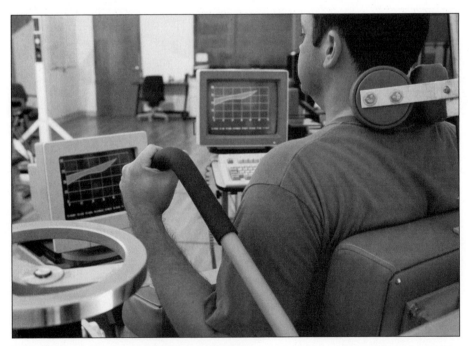

Technology has enhanced exercise physiology research.

to human movement. This potential for motion is released through the initiation of the nervous system and the biochemical reactions that supply muscles with energy.

Exercise physiologists measure the metabolic responses of the body to exercise and training through various endurance, flexibility, and strength programs. In these projects, they may examine changes in the cardiovascular system, stroke volume, pulse rate, blood composition, and other physiological parameters. Other researchers study how the body utilizes carbohydrates, fats, and proteins during exercise; the effects of diet, smoking, and temperature on performance; and differences between trained and untrained individuals based on a variable such as sleep, diet, or gender.

Because of their expertise in understanding bodily functions under the stress of muscular activity, exercise physiologists are often consulted about or given responsibility for prescribing and monitoring exercise programs for cardiac patients. Specialists in cardiac rehabilitation monitor exercise paradigms for individuals who have experienced cardiovascular trauma or prescribe preventive programs for people demonstrating coronary disease risk factors. Biomechanists and exercise physiologists often work together to design the most appropriate training programs for elite athletes, such as those at the United States Olympic Training Center in Colorado Springs.

Researchers in exercise physiology often prescribe workouts on treadmills to monitor oxygen uptake and expired carbon dioxide, take heart rate and function measurements, and analyze the chemical activities of the body. Exercise physiologists also conduct joint research projects with athletic trainers concerning the prevention and rehabilitation of injuries and with physicians in the areas of muscle biopsies and blood lactate analyses.

Exercise physiologists are interested in studying how the body utilizes food relative to energy output. They have found that numerous factors, such as sleep, drugs, work, and stress, influence how the body reacts to a specific diet or exercise paradigm. Biochemical and physiological tests isolate those nutritional factors that most dramatically affect performance. Studies include the effects of marathon training on nutritional needs, the risks or benefits of vitamin supplementation, and the effects of caffeine on various heart parameters. Nutritional information also is vital for the athlete in training who needs to maintain a specific weight, for the individual with a disabling condition who is minimally active, and for the senior citizen whose metabolic rate has slowed.

Exercise physiologists conduct research on how environmental and age factors affect exercise. They also study the interrelationships among disease, bodily functions, and health within the context of exercise. In recent years, exercise epidemiology has emerged to examine how physical activity affects mortality. Research on the effects of asthma on respiration has helped exercise physiologists develop training programs for athletes who has exercise-induced asthma. Exercise physiologists collaborate with athletic trainers to design rehabilitative programs as well as developmental programs to enhance sport performance (see the Research View box "Exercise Physiology").

RESEARCH VIEW

Exercise Physiology

In studying how the body functions during muscular activity, exercise physiologists may conduct research to answer these questions:

- What are the metabolic responses of nonfit adult bodies during endurance training?
- What is the most effective method for developing and maintaining muscular strength for female volleyball players?
- How do various diets or nutritional supplements affect the performances of elite athletes?
- What types of fitness programs are appropriate for senior citizens?
- How do individuals with high levels of cardiovascular fitness differ in their stroke volume, blood lactates, perceived exertion, and pain tolerance from those who engage in no cardiovascular fitness training?
- What kinds of fitness routines should an exercise physiologist prescribe for participants in a cardiac rehabilitation program?
- What should be the optimal frequency, intensity, and duration for an effective off-season baseball team's conditioning program?
- What effect does ethnicity have on athletic performances such as sprints in track or rebounding in basketball?
- What is the current physical fitness status of school-age children?

ATHLETIC TRAINING

Athletic training is the study and application of the prevention, treatment, and rehabilitation of sports injuries. The term *sports medicine* involves physicians, who may be general practitioners, orthopedic surgeons, or other specialists. Physicians often are responsible for clearing athletes for practice and competition as well as attending to the needs of athletes in events in which the risks of injury are high. Athletic trainers are involved with athletes almost daily. They help design appropriate sport conditioning during the preseason, postseason, and off-season; they tape, preventively as well as protectively, athletes before activity; they are responsible for assessing injuries at the

athletic training:
the study and application of the prevention, treatment, and rehabilitation of sports injuries

🔍 RESEARCH VIEW

Athletic Training

The athletic trainer studies the prevention, evaluation, management, and rehabilitation of injuries through seeking answers to questions like these:

- What type of flexibility training will help prevent injuries in football?
- Why do more female athletes suffer from anterior cruciate ligament damages than do male athletes?
- What should athletes who seldom play during competitions do to maintain their cardiovascular conditioning?
- What is the optimal type of weight training for youth below age 12?
- What is the optimal rehabilitation program for a soccer athlete recovering from a hamstring strain?
- What is the athletic trainer's role in evaluating an injury in the absence of a physician?
- How does an athletic trainer deal with a gymnast who suffers from anorexia?
- What is the best treatment for ankle sprains?
- What is the athletic trainer's role in the nutrition of athletes?

time they occur, providing immediate and appropriate first aid, and supervising the rehabilitation process on the recommendation of a physician.

Extensive knowledge of the anatomy and physiology of the body and skill in applying this knowledge to injury situations are essential for athletic trainers. Sometimes they need to be able to console injured athletes and keep them from trying to return to competition or practices too quickly. At other times, athletic trainers need to encourage athletes to work more diligently during their rehabilitation (see the Research View box "Athletic Training").

Athletic trainers are expected to use various treatments, such as ultrasound, whirlpool, ice massage, or heat. These professionals constantly help athletes play despite minor injuries by using the above treatments or various taping techniques.

The National Athletic Trainers' Association (NATA) seeks to enhance the quality of health care for athletes and those engaged in physical activity as well as advance the profession of athletic training through education and research in the prevention, evaluation, management, and rehabilitation of injuries. NATA was founded in 1950 and has grown to more than 22,000 members; over 100 universities and colleges offer NATA-approved curricula. NATA publishes the *Journal of Athletic Training*, a quarterly scientific journal.

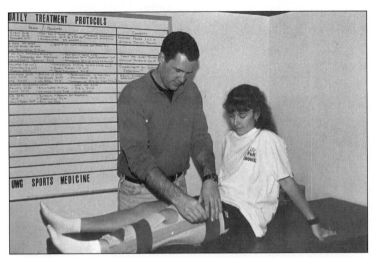

Athletic trainers apply splints to immobilize injured areas such as legs. (Photo courtesy Bob Hilliard.)

MOTOR CONTROL AND LEARNING

Motor behavior is a broad term that encompasses motor control, motor learning, and motor development. **Motor control** is an area of study that deals with the neurophysiological factors that affect human movement; **motor learning** is the study of the cognitive processes underlying motor acts associated with skill acquisition through practice and experience. Motor development is discussed in the next section. Research in solving industrial problems (such as safe and efficient movements in the workplace) and military needs (such as pilot selection and training) laid the foundation for the emergence of the fields of motor control and motor learning. Led by Franklin Henry, Alfred Hubbard, Arthur Slater-Hammel, and Dick Schmidt, motor control and motor learning specialists expanded their research and published scholarly manuscripts in journals such as the *Journal of Motor Behavior.* They completed studies dealing with

> **motor control:**
> an area of study that deals with the neurophysiological factors that affect human movement
>
> **motor learning:**
> the study of cognitive processes underlying motor acts associated with skill acquisition through practice and experience

- Closed-loop theory—investigated how feedback following slow and discrete movements can be used to improve subsequent motor performances.

Motor learning knowledge, such as use of various types of feedback, can enhance an archer's performance. (Photo courtesy Lisa Sense.)

- Open-loop theory—investigated how motor patterns, such as striking skills, can be generalized to a variety of sports or settings, with or without limited feedback.

- Dynamic systems theory—investigated how degrees of freedom in joints and muscles, along with neural control, can lead to enhanced motor performance.

- Types of practice—investigated the appropriateness and effectiveness of massed or distributed, blocked or random, mental or physical, and full or reduced speed practice sessions.

- Cognitive processes in learning motor skills—investigated how knowledge of results and knowledge of performance affect subsequent motor patterns.

- Transfer of learning—investigated how motor skills learned in one setting can be generalized to another sport.

- Types of feedback—investigated how intrinsic, extrinsic, terminal, concurrent, visual, verbal, constant, and interval feedback influence motor performance.

- Special needs—investigated how individuals with special needs, including the aging, can regain and maintain their balance, coordination, reaction time, fundamental movement skills, and fitness levels.

The fields of motor control and motor learning grew out of the area of psychology dealing with human performance and behavior. Whereas motor control focuses on the neurophysiological factors of how and why people move as they do, motor learning integrates the cognitive processing of information with motor skill acquisition. Specialists in motor control and motor learning examine the variables that lead to improved performance of motor skills by responding to questions such as these:

- How and why do people's muscles respond differently to similar stimuli?

- How do massed and distributed types of practice affect motor performance?
- How do neurological responses to cues affect motor performance?
- What type (and with what frequency) of feedback should be provided to enhance motor skill acquisition?
- What type of practice, mental or physical, is optimal for the learning of a skill such as putting a golf ball or shooting a basketball free throw, and why?
- What is the relationship among a student's learning style, information-processing system, and ability to learn a motor skill?
- How do varying cognitive abilities affect the learning of motor skills?
- What is the interrelationship between information processing and skill acquisition?
- How does a person's reaction time influence the learning of motor skills?
- How does the aging process affect motor control and motor learning?

The objective of these researchers independently, as well as collectively, is to understand and enhance human movement. In motor control, it is essential to investigate the neuromuscular pathways to improve the learning of motor skills. In motor learning, it is essential to build on this information and add knowledge of feedback and optimal practice methods. Motor control researchers may use imaging or manipulation to help children with special needs learn new motor patterns, whereas motor learning researchers may use verbal and kinesthetic cues to help young athletes learn complex motor skills such as heading a soccer ball.

MOTOR DEVELOPMENT

Motor development is the maturation and changes in motor behavior throughout life. Researchers in this field examine factors that influence the performance of motor skills, including developmental differences that occur over time. Movement competencies are influenced by contributions from genetics as well as the environment. Throughout life, individuals continually progress from unskilled movements to the demonstration of complex motor skills with accommodations made for age and any physical limitations. Motor development encompasses the process and results of motor behavior as well as the factors that affect it.

motor development:
the maturation and changes in motor behavior throughout life

Motor development historically has been closely aligned with developmental psychology, such as through studies that examined behavioral sequences and the maturational process. Anna Espenschade's article "Motor Performance in

Motor development researchers examine the process and sequence of learning movement skills. (Photo courtesy Judy Young.)

Adolescence, Including the Study of Relationships with Measures of Physical Growth and Maturity," published in 1940, described one of the early models for motor development research. This study and related research by Lawrence Rarick, Vern Seefeldt, and others supported the positive influence of physical growth and development on motor performance. Educational psychology studies in perceptual-motor development concluded that improved motor skills lead to an enhancement of academic performance and that cognitive development positively affects skill acquisition over time. These findings were especially important because data from studies in this area were used to justify school physical education programs for children. In recent years, researchers have found that dynamic systems, more than cognitive processes, account for enhanced motor performance.

Specialists in motor development investigate questions such as these:

- When are children developmentally ready for weight training and cardiovascular training programs?
- What are the hereditary and environmental factors that most significantly influence obesity in children?
- How and why do weight training and cardiovascular training programs combat decreases in strength and endurance associated with advancing age?
- What are the characteristics of children who are developmentally ready for competitive sports?
- What are the developmental stages for learning the fundamental movement skills?
- How does socioeconomic status, which affects nutritional health, affect the development of motor skills?
- How does a person's developmental level limit his or her ability to learn or enhance a motor skill?
- What factors determine the relationship between cognitive development and motor development in learning a complex motor skill?
- How does gender affect developmental readiness in motor development?
- What are the developmental stages for learning fundamental sports skills?

Much of the research in motor development is associated with children as they learn fundamental motor skills. However, adults also can learn new perceptual-motor skills. Longitudinal studies are especially beneficial in determining the varied factors that determine what, how, and why motor performance emerges. Interdisciplinary research, such as with exercise physiologists or motor learning specialists, not only strengthens present understanding but also paves the way for improved motor behavior.

SPORT BIOMECHANICS

Sport biomechanics is the study of the effects of natural laws and forces on the body through the science and mechanics of movement. Biomechanists study the musculoskeletal system, the principles of mechanics, and activity analyses. They examine the force of muscular contractions; flexion, extension, pronation, and supination of the muscles during activity; the composition of muscle fibers; equilibrium, center of gravity, and base of support; transfer of momentum; and projection of the

sport biomechanics:
the study of the effects of natural laws and forces on the body through the science and mechanics of movement

Biomechanical analyses are used to enhance sports performances. (Photo courtesy John R. Stevenson.)

body or an object. Their findings have contributed to improved athletic performance and have been used to prevent injuries, which is of special interest to physical therapists and athletic trainers. For example, through biomechanical analysis, minor flaws in throwing technique for the discus or stride length for sprinting can be identified and corrected to enhance distance or reduce time. Scientific answers can be provided to questions such as: What kind of shoe support is needed for individuals participating regularly in aerobics? What type of weight training is appropriate for judo or volleyball players? What type of exercise program is best for increasing joint flexibility for senior citizens?

Biomechanists explain movement in relation to acceleration, energy, mass, power, torque, and velocity. They rely on mechanical principles such as force application and absorption, leverage, and stability. Use of cinematography (motion picture photography) has become common among coaches and teachers for the analysis of performance. Electromyography is the measurement of electrical discharges from a muscle to study the action potential and the sequence of muscular activity. An analysis of the position and movements of joints is possible with electrogoniometry. Biomechanists also measure muscular forces using a force platform, determine speeds or frequencies using a stroboscope, and record movements and electrical responses (such as heart rate) using a telemeter. Computer-assisted analyses have helped isolate components of physical skills that can then be corrected or changed to improve efficiency.

Interest in the science of applying mechanics to human movement can be traced to the early 1900s, when the focus was on understanding anatomy and physiology. Notable curricular and research emphases during the following decades included body dynamics, efficiency of work, cinematic studies of sports skills, mechanical analysis of human performance, electromyography, and neurophysiology. Several scholars, such as Ruth Glassow, Thomas Cureton, Gladys Scott, and John Cooper, conducted kinesiological studies grounded in the scientific foundation of physical education and sport that provided the basis for the development of this field. The founding of the International Society of Biomechanics and its publication of the *Journal of Biomechanics* were leading forces in the emergence of biomechanics as a specialty (see the Research View box "Sport Biomechanics").

🔍 RESEARCH VIEW

Sport Biomechanics

The sport biomechanist investigates questions such as these:

- What are the optimal design and composition of the pole used in pole vaulting?
- How can a sport biomechanist use computer-enhanced images to analyze and improve the performance of sport skills?
- What biomechanical factors contribute to muscular and joint injuries in baseball pitchers?
- How can fundamental movement skills such as running, jumping, and throwing be taught most effectively and efficiently?
- What mechanical principles are most important for reducing injuries and increasing the attainment of strength goals in weight-training programs?
- How does weight transfer affect force and aerodynamics in striking motions?
- Biomechanically, why did the crawl stroke and the Fosbury flop revolutionize swimming and the high jump, respectively?
- What are the most effective approaches for increasing an athlete's vertical jump?
- How and why does stride length differ for a sprinter versus a distance runner?
- What biomechanical factors contribute to an effective tennis serve?

SPORT HISTORY

Sport history is the descriptive and analytical examination of significant people, events, organizations, and trends that shaped the past. Sport historians investigate the past seeking to explain how, what, when, where, and why things occurred. Descriptive history explores events, individuals' contributions, and pivotal happenings using primary sources such as archeological artifacts, original writings, and eyewitness accounts. Such firsthand information is judged to be reliable and accurate, especially when confirmed by other primary sources. When no original information is available, secondary sources must sometimes be used to document history. History reported in secondary sources, however, must be verified meticulously to ensure accuracy. The narrative approach is often used in descriptive history to chronicle events, individual lives, and developments.

sport history:
the descriptive and analytical examination of significant people, events, organizations, and trends that shaped the past

⌕ RESEARCH VIEW

Sport History

The sport historian may examine questions such as these:

- What was the significance of Greek athletes competing in the nude?
- Why were African Americans excluded from Major League Baseball?
- Why were women initially excluded, and only begrudgingly included, in the modern Olympic Games?
- What role did the Industrial Revolution play in the growth and development of organized sport?
- What factors contributed to the establishment of the National Football League? How and why did its relationship with college football evolve as it did?
- How have sports played a role in the Americanization of various immigrant groups in this country?
- How and why was basketball spread internationally?
- How did upper-class sport affect the popularity of organized sport in this country?
- What role has gambling played in sports?
- Why do many consider the National Collegiate Athletic Association the most powerful amateur sports organization in this country?

Vital to an understanding of why events happened as they did is the more difficult interpretive or analytical work of historians. Such analyses attempt to explain the significance of historical events within their historical and social contexts. Sport historians record biographies, examine organizations and their activities, describe trends and movements, and analyze how and why societal events occurred as they did.

A clear understanding of modern sports depends on an examination of the significant events and practices of the past. Changes in this country that have influenced the emergence and predominance of sport include colonialism, the expanding frontier, rural life, the industrialized age, military involvement, the information age, and the explosion in technology. Seminal works that laid the foundation for the emergence of the field of sport history include Foster Dulles's *Americans Learn to Play* (1940), John Betts's *America's Sporting Heritage, 1850–1950* (1974), and Robert Boyle's *Sport—Mirror of American Life* (1963). Led by physical educators, the North American Society for Sport History was established to legitimize the rising academic interest in this field. Through its *Journal of Sport History,* this organization, which includes individuals from a diverse group of disciplines, serves as the central forum for the promotion of sport history (see the Research View box "Sport History").

SPORT MANAGEMENT

Sport management is the study of the management of personnel, programs, budgets, and facilities in various sports settings. It includes the management functions of planning, organizing, directing, and evaluating, as well as the business components of marketing, accounting, economics, finance, and law. This field encompasses the spectator sport and fitness industries, sporting goods sales, and recreational and educational sport programs.

> **sport management:**
> the study of the management of personnel, programs, budgets, and facilities in various sports settings

Academics and practitioners in sport management are interested in learning the answers to questions such as these:

- What amenities are important for increasing attendance at sporting events at the high school, college, and professional levels?
- How can private health and fitness clubs attract and retain members?
- What recreational and leisure-time activities are of most interest to individuals of all ages?

Today's sport managers depend on data and technology to achieve team and organizational goals.

- How can professional sports teams in smaller metropolitan areas financially compete with Major League Baseball given the disproportionate revenues in comparison to teams in larger metropolitan areas?

- What economic factors are involved in joining a major college athletic conference? How does such a change affect the college's revenue- and nonrevenue-producing sports?

- What are the legal liabilities for a professional franchise when fans are injured or cause injury to other fans?

- What leadership and management characteristics or traits are most important for the success of a sport manager?

- What are the costs and benefits of awarding naming rights to a stadium or an arena?

- How is market research important in sports?

- What responsibility do sport managers have for the ethical conduct of their athletes?

Professionals working in the management of sport and leisure programs in the 1980s recognized the need to study and develop an essential body of knowledge. The North American Society for Sport Management (NASSM) was established to promote, stimulate, and encourage research, scholarly writing, and professional development in the area of sport management. This cross-disciplinary field encompasses management, leadership, and organizational behavior in sport, sport ethics, sport marketing, sport finance, sport economics, sport business in the social context, legal aspects of sport, and sport governance. NASSM's *Journal of Sport Management* provides a venue for the publication of theoretical and applied aspects of management related to sport, exercise, and play in a variety of settings, such as professional sports, intercollegiate athletics, interscholastic sports, health and sport clubs, and recreational sports.

The sport industry, broadly defined, involves sport products and services, all of which need sport managers. Career options exist in professional sports, intercollegiate athletics, high school sports, recreation programs, the leisure and travel industry, private and public health and sports clubs, and sporting goods businesses.

Sport managers need to be competent in a number of areas to qualify for such careers. These include communication skills, facility and event management abilities, sport marketing skills, financial management skills, and personnel management abilities.

SPORT PHILOSOPHY

Sport philosophy analyzes sport from aesthetic, epistemological, metaphysical, and ethical perspectives. That is, sport philosophers examine the beautiful and ugly and the good and bad in sport as well as seek to understand how and why people play and engage in sport. Every person

sport philosophy:
analyzes sport from aesthetic, epistemological, metaphysical, and ethical perspectives

has a philosophy, although it may be unstated. One's philosophy is revealed in the particular thought patterns, behaviors, and aspirations one has. Sport philosophers analyze concepts, make normative statements that guide practical activity, and speculate or extrapolate beyond the limits of scientific knowledge. Within the schools, sport philosophers examine how physical education contributes to both educational objectives and social values by explaining the nature, importance, and reason for play. Meeting people's needs, relating physical activity to human performance of all kinds, and enhancing the quality of life for others are the roles of sport philosophy outside the schools.

The sport philosopher seeks truth and understanding by investigating questions such as these:

- What is the meaning of competition to the athlete?
- Why do sports fans become so avid in their support of an athletic team?
- How and why does sport lose its element of fun for many competitors?
- Why is sportsmanship considered integral to sport?
- Does participation in sport lead to the development of moral values? If so, how does this occur?
- Why is "taking out an opponent" considered ethical by some athletes?
- What is the significance of a feminist sport perspective?
- What is beautiful about sport?
- What is the role of play in life?
- Why is sport of such paramount interest to millions in this country?

The early roots of today's sport philosophy grew out of an eclectic philosophy of education and, subsequently, physical education. The various factors that have influenced sport philosophy include the progressive education movement (including developmentalism), traditional philosophical systems (such as idealism, realism, pragmatism, naturalism, and existentialism), and specialized research investigating the nature, relationships, and values of sport. The establishment of the Philosophical Society for the Study of Sport and the publication of the *Journal of the Philosophy of Sport* helped establish the identity of this new field.

Most individuals in physical education and sport use philosophy to analyze issues of today. For example, what are the moral values depicted in films like *Chariots of Fire* or *Hoosiers*? (See other suggested films and videos in Box 2-1.) Why do problems such as gambling, unscrupulous sports agents, and a lack of sportsmanship plague intercollegiate athletic programs today? Why do so many athletes, even at the high school level, use anabolic steroids? What lesson is learned by youth soccer players when the congratulatory hand-slap at the end of the game is eliminated because members of one team spit on their hands and then slapped their opponents' hands? Sport philosophy seeks to understand why such actions occur, and what values they reflect.

**BOX 2-1   FILMS AND VIDEOS RELATED TO SPORT HISTORY
AND SPORT PHILOSOPHY**

- *Bang the Drum Slowly: Friendship and Compassion*—An examination of motivations and actions of major league baseball players
- *The Black Athlete*—Through interviews, the status of African Americans in sport is portrayed
- *Brian's Song*—The true story of the deep and courageous friendship between Gale Sayers and Brian Piccolo of the Chicago Bears
- *Chariots of Fire*—Harold Abrahams and Eric Liddell lead the British track and field team to victories in the 1924 Olympic Games
- *Do You Believe in Miracles*—The winning of the gold medal in Olympic ice hockey
- *Eight Men Out*—The scandal of the Chicago White Sox throwing of the 1919 World Series
- *Going for the Gold. . . The Story of Black Women in Sports*—A profile of 17 African American women athletes
- *A Hard Road to Glory*—The compelling story of the early rise of African American athletes
- *Hoosiers*—A small-town (Hickory) team wins the Indiana high school basketball championship in 1952
- *A League of their Own*—The story of the beginning of the All-American Girls' Professional Baseball League
- *The Natural*—Roy Hobbs seeks superstardom, but leads his team to a play-off victory only one year
- *Rocky Bleier*—The true story of a Vietnam veteran who rehabilitates from a war injury to start for the world champion Steelers
- *"There Was Always Sun Shining Someplace": Life in the Negro Baseball Leagues*—Tells the story of the Negro Baseball Leagues, with interviews of some of the stars
- *A Winner Never Quits*—Describes a high school team and the roles of the players, cheerleaders, and coaches

SPORT AND EXERCISE PSYCHOLOGY

Sport and exercise psychology is the study of human behavior in sports, including an understanding of the mental processes that interact with motor skill performance. Theories and laws of learning, the importance of reinforcement, and the linking of perceptual abilities with motor performance contribute to this body of knowledge. Sport and exercise psychologists utilize this information when studying topics such as achievement motivation, arousal,

sport and exercise psychology:
the study of human behavior in sports, including an understanding of the mental processes that interact with motor skill performance

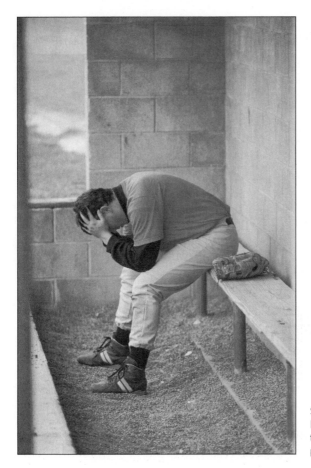

Sport psychologists help athletes learn to use visualization to enhance their performance after poor performances.

attribution, and personality development. Achievement motivation research examines how individuals perceive themselves and their accomplishments. Excitement and relaxation (as well as tension reduction) are among the parameters of arousal studies. The study of causal attribution weighs the importance placed on ability, effort, luck, and task difficulty relative to contest outcome. Aggression, competitiveness, anxiety, independence, extroversion, and self-confidence are among the personality traits researched. Sport and exercise psychologists also examine the influence of group dynamics, exercise addiction, and enhanced body image on people who are physically active.

The mental aspect of sports has intrigued researchers for years. Some have stated that at the elite level of sport, where all athletes are highly skilled, the outcome of the contest is overwhelmingly dependent on mental preparation and cognitive execution. Coleman Griffith is credited with conducting the initial sport psychology research, even though earlier researchers had stated that there were psychological benefits from participating in sport and physical activity. The prolific research coming from Griffith's Athletics Research Lab at the University of

⌕RESEARCH VIEW

Sport and Exercise Psychology

The sport and exercise psychologist studies how to enhance motor performance through an examination of and interventions in areas such as these:

- How does an athlete's self-efficacy (how one feels about one's self and abilities) affect performance?
- Why is stress reduction essential to success in sport?
- What role does mental imaging play in the execution of motor skills?
- How does participation in physical activity affect performance in cognitive tasks?
- What is the relationship between the body's psychological and physiological responses within sports?
- How does attribution influence the way an athlete deals with winning and losing?
- What is the difference in the arousal states of football linemen and elite golfers, and how can these be shaped?
- How does the traditional pep talk given by a coach prior to a competition affect individual athletes?
- What are the most effective techniques for relaxation training?
- Why are sport psychologists increasingly hired by individual athletes and teams?

Illinois, along with early writings like John Lawther's *The Psychology of Coaching* (1951), Bryant Cratty's *Psychology and Physical Activity* (1967), and Robert Singer's *Motor Learning and Human Performance* (1968), laid the foundation for the emergence of this field of study. The founding of the North American Society for the Psychology of Sport and Physical Activity in 1967 and the Association for the Advancement of Applied Sport Psychology in 1985, and their publications, the *Journal of Sport Psychology* (later the *Journal of Sport and Exercise Psychology*) and the *Journal of Applied Sport Psychology,* respectively, strengthened the development of this discipline.

Applied sport psychology focuses on understanding psychological theories and techniques to help athletes improve their performance. This area has grown in popularity as coaches and athletes seek a competitive edge. Specific strategies assist athletes in managing stress, concentrating more effectively, and maintaining confidence. Sport psychologists help athletes achieve their physical potential by improving their mental state (see the Research View box "Sport and Exercise Psychology").

The clinical interventions used by sport psychologists include relaxation training, biofeedback, breath control, desensitization, and mental imaging. These interventions help athletes cope with the pressures of competition.

SPORT SOCIOLOGY

Sport sociology is the study of social units and processes within the sporting context. This discipline examines the role of sports in human society by seeking to determine why people play and how participation in various physical activities influences them. The sport sociologist examines play, games, sports, recreational activities, and leisure-time pursuits in analyzing the expected outcomes of fun, relaxation, self-expression, wish fulfillment, and social interaction. The dynamics of socialization may reveal examples of racial and gender integration, exclusion, affiliation, competition, cooperation, conflict, rivalry, teamwork, and fair play.

> **sport sociology:**
> the study of social units and processes within the sporting context

Sport sociologists investigate sport as a game and as an institution. They examine the concepts of social mobility, class and gender stratification, status, racial and ethnic discrimination, team dynamics, social consciousness, and social values. Understanding the sociology of sport requires dealing with the relationship between sports and social institutions.

Sport is woven into the daily and seasonal fabric of American society. The social significance of sporting pastimes emerged from the British emphasis on sports in private boarding schools for boys in the mid-1800s. Schoolmasters and fathers came to believe that manly virtues learned through playing sports would prepare upper-class youth for their anticipated leadership roles in business, politics, and the military. This emphasis on character development through sports was adopted by organized sports in this country and has influenced attitudes toward sports at all levels. As an outgrowth of these perspectives about the role of sport in society, books such as Thorstein Veblen's *The Theory of the Leisure Class* (1899), Frederick Cozens and Florence Stumpf's *Sport in American Life* (1953), and Roger Caillois' *Man, Play and Games* (1961) blazed the trail for the subsequent development of the discipline of sport sociology. In the 1960s, publications and presentations by Gerald Kenyon, John Loy, and others led to the identification of sport sociology as a unique field of study. Publications such as the *International Review of Sport Sociology* and the *Sociology of Sport Journal,* as well as the establishment of the North American Society for the Sociology of Sport, marked its emergence and acceptance as a distinct discipline. Sport sociology moved from a positivist, empirical-analytical paradigm that focused on describing and analyzing the social order of sport to an interpretive research model. Scholars of this genre examined sport cultures from a variety of theoretical and methodological perspectives with an emphasis on interpretation. Today many sport sociologists take a critical inquiry approach that not only analyzes and interprets social dynamics but makes suggestions for transforming social structures.

The sport sociologist addresses questions such as these:

- What sociological factors may have contributed to a mother purchasing a death contract on a girl who beat out her daughter for a spot on the high school cheerleading squad?
- Why did a sophomore in high school commit suicide after leading his team to the state football championship?
- What are the sociological factors that have contributed to the inequitable funding of girls' and women's athletic teams?
- Why are so few African Americans hired to coach professional and college sports teams?
- How are males and females socialized differently in and through sport?
- Why do approximately half of all children drop out of organized sports by age 12?
- Why are athletes permitted to act in violent ways during sporting events that would be illegal if the same acts occurred outside of sport?
- Why has television been allowed to dictate rule changes and starting times for sporting events?
- How do socioeconomic factors affect individuals' participation in physical activity and sport?
- Does sport mirror society, or does society mirror sport?

As shown in Figure 2-1 and in the Research View, each of these exercise and sport sciences have important disciplinary components. Take the Exercise and Sport Sciences Quiz in Box 2-2 to review the key areas of emphasis for each science. All of the exercise and sport sciences contribute to the greater whole. Rather than being mutually exclusive, they interact with one another.

Humanities

Although the humanities are not a part of the exercise and sport sciences, they have made a significant contribution to sports. The humanities, which encompass the areas of art, literature, and music, are noteworthy from both historical and practical perspectives. Archaeological discoveries from early civilizations verify the significance attached to physical activity for survival, group affiliation, religious worship, and enjoyment. From Myron's *Disco-bolus* during the Greek

RESEARCH VIEW

Examples of Research Areas for Exercise and Sport Scientists

Through the **scientific method,** exercise and sport scientists make observations, develop hypotheses, conduct experiments, analyze data and information, report findings, and establish theories or draw conclusions. This process, used by researchers in each of the exercise and sport sciences, leads to the establishment of new truths and a broader understanding of the topic examined. Furthermore, the results may have a significant impact on sport performance or quality of life. Below are listed some topical areas that exercise and sport scientists may study to give you a better understanding of the breadth of these fields:

> **scientific method:**
> the process of making observations, developing hypotheses, conducting experiments, analyzing data and information, reporting findings, and establishing theories or drawing conclusions

- Structure and function of skeletal muscles that lead to the development of muscular strength and endurance
- Types of training programs, such as isometric, dynamic resistance exercise, aerobic, and interval, as they relate to cardiovascular endurance
- Nutrition and drugs as they affect performance, body composition, and disease
- Injury prevention, such as the use of proprioceptive neuromuscular facilitation to enhance flexibility; the implementation of treatment modalities, such as the immediate application of ice; and rehabilitation techniques, such as electrical stimulation
- Kinetics of human movement, including the laws of inertia, acceleration, and gravity; force; velocity; and gait analysis
- Psychological factors that affect performance, such as relaxation, arousal, and anxiety
- Neural control of movement, including muscular electrical activity, depth perception, peripheral vision, and anticipation
- Learning of motor skills though feedback, various types of practice, and transfer
- Developmental readiness for strength and endurance training, as well as the impact of aging on reaction time, balance, muscular fiber composition, and bone density

(continued)

- The historical examination of games and sports relative to the participants, types of events, frequency, venues, and the importance placed on these factors
- The role sport plays in the leisure-time pursuits of individuals and groups
- Individuals' attitudes, beliefs, and values as illustrated by how they view truth, perceive the world, and interact with others
- The commercial and experiential impact of sport, exercise, and fitness on individuals of all ages in a variety of settings

zenith to R. Tait McKenzie's *The Joy of Effort* (which received the King's Medal in the Fine Arts Competition at the 1912 Stockholm Olympic Games; see page 8) to a wall fresco of the first women's Olympic marathon champion Joan Benoit, art has vividly shown the beauty of human movement.

Homer's *Iliad* and *Odyssey* verify the importance of athletics in Greek times. According to several presenters at conferences of the North American Society for Sport History, some literature in the United States today, as well as that of earlier times, affirms the socialization role of sports.

BOX 2-2 EXERCISE AND SPORT SCIENCES QUIZ

1. Which of the exercise and sport sciences studies oxygen utilization during cardiovascular exercise and metabolic responses to exercise and training?
2. Which of the exercise and sport sciences describes and analyzes the past?
3. Which of the exercise and sport sciences studies how people learn skills, especially through practice and feedback?
4. Which of the exercise and sport sciences studies how sport influences social units, processes, and institutions?
5. Which of the exercise and sport sciences analyzes the impact of motion, force, and energy on sport performance?
6. Which of the exercise and sport sciences analyzes the developmental patterns associated with movement and skill performance?
7. Which of the exercise and sport sciences uses extensive knowledge of the body to help athletes stay injury free and return to competition safely?
8. Which of the exercise and sport sciences seeks to understand why people act as they do based on their values?
9. Which of the exercise and sport sciences involves providing sports products and managing sporting events?
10. Which of the exercise and sport sciences uses various mental coping strategies to aid sports performance?

WEB CONNECTIONS

1. www.nata.org
   This site for the National Athletic Trainers' Association lists all the requirements for obtaining certification and provides other helpful information for individuals interested in this field.

2. www.nassm.org
   Visit this site to learn more about the North American Society for Sport Management, its services, and membership.

3. www.naspspa.org
   Learn more about the multidisciplinary North American Society for the Psychology of Sport and Physical Activity and its work to improve the quality of teaching and research in sport psychology, motor development, and motor learning and control.

4. www.pesoftware.com/Technews/news.html
   Bonnie Mohnsen publishes this online newsletter for K–12 physical educators to help them in their use of technology in physical education.

5. www.nassh.org
   Learn more about the activities of the North American Society for Sport History at this site.

6. www.isbweb.org
   Check out this site for more information about the International Society of Biomechanics, which promotes the study of all areas of biomechanics at the international level, with special emphasis on the biomechanics of human movement.

7. www.uwm.edu/~aycock/nasss/nasss.html
   Examine this site of the North American Society for the Sociology of Sport, which promotes the sociological study of play, games, and sport.

Music provides the rhythm for movement experiences for all ages. The Greeks exercised to the music of the lyre, and music became a vital component of German school gymnastics in the 1800s. Children in elementary physical education today frequently experiment with and explore movement to the accompaniment of their favorite songs. In the 1980s, the addition of music to exercise routines helped popularize aerobics. Athletic team practice sessions, weight-training workouts, and daily jogs often include music. Art, literature, and music can enhance the focus on the development of a fit body, the socializing nature of sport, and the free experimentation of movement, thereby facilitating the application of the body of knowledge comprising the exercise and sport sciences.

Technology

Inseparably linked with the exercise and sport sciences is the use of technology. As mentioned in several previous sections, much of today's research relies on technology-based equipment that makes it possible to collect and analyze data. For example, biomechanists use motion analysis and technology to examine and improve the position and movement of joints to enhance the techniques and performances of elite athletes. Exercise physiologists analyze cardiac output measures, such as oxygen consumption, gas exchange, and chemical reactions, to obtain immediate and valid data for exercise prescription. Sport psychologists use biofeedback techniques to monitor arousal levels. Athletic trainers monitor conditioning programs and injury rehabilitation for thousands of athletes using technologies such as radiography and bone imaging. Sport managers utilize a plethora of software packages to monitor financial and statistical records.

Regardless of the computer platform, the operating system chosen, or the types of software used, the exercise and sport scientist is limited in contributing to the body of knowledge in the field without being technologically literate. In

Pat Monk's *American Dream Machine* in an unusual yet lifelike manner depicts one type of sport. (Photo courtesy Pat Monk.)

searching for information, exercise and sport scientists and their students can access a wealth of information through compact disc read-only memory, or CD-ROMs, which store about 300,000 typewritten pages of text that can be easily retrieved using word searches. *Medline* (*Index Medicus*) and *SPORT Discus* offer vast information in the exercise and sport sciences.

Internet (the network of computers that links individuals worldwide) access to the World Wide Web is an essential research and communications tool. Using the browser of a program such as Netscape or Explorer, anyone can gain access to an amazing range of resources. This includes the entire Encyclopedia Britannica (www.britannica.com), search engines such as Google (www.google.com), and the Library of Congress (http://lcweb.loc.gov). From instant messaging to data collected on personal digital assistants (PDAs), exercise and sport scientists rely on technologies to complete their work.

Technological innovations in sports equipment raise ethical as well as pragmatic questions. Are competitions occurring on a "level playing field" when an athlete from a more affluent nation has the latest and greatest vaulting pole, while an athlete from a Third World country does not? Do the new designs in golf clubs and balls take away from the skill level required for elite or even recreational players? Does some sports equipment, such as face masks in football, help increase the risk of injuries to opponents as well as protect athletes from injury? Do athletes choose to ignore research showing that some drugs enhance performance but have harmful side effects? Research is also needed to determine the effectiveness (or possible harmful impact) of new fitness equipment. For example, how effective for weight reduction and overall physical fitness are power chutes or power harnesses? Do abdominal slides or exercise balls help burn fat and tone muscles? Responding to these questions constitutes only a few examples of how technology helps exercise and sport scientists understand human movement and enhance sport performance.

SUMMARY

An academic discipline includes a body of knowledge, a conceptual framework, and scholarly procedures and methods of inquiry. Based on the heritage of physical education as a teaching profession, the exercise and sport sciences have drawn from and contributed to the knowledge base in multiple academic disciplines. Integral to the emergence and acceptance of the exercise and sport sciences as recognized academic disciplines are the extensive scholarly and scientific research studies that have informed the academic community as well as the general public about the importance of physical activity. The exercise and sport sciences have improved the human movement experiences of individuals of all ages and skill levels. Research findings have helped prevent health-related disabilities as well as assisted in the rehabilitation of individuals who have suffered from medical maladies. Despite critics who claim that our fields have no unique body of knowledge, scholars in the exercise and sport sciences have made significant contributions to a broader understanding of the historical, sociological, psychological, and physiological roles of exercise and sport in the lives of everyone.

CAREER PERSPECTIVE

RENÉ REVIS SHINGLES
Associate Professor
Central Michigan University
Mount Pleasant, Michigan

EDUCATION
B.A., Health and Physical Education, University of North Carolina at Chapel Hill
M.S., Physical Education: Athletic Training/Sports Medicine, Illinois State University
Ph.D., Psychosocial Aspects of Sport and Physical Activity, Michigan State University

JOB RESPONSIBILITIES AND HOURS
As a university associate professor and certified athletic trainer, René teaches in a sports medicine/athletic training curriculum accredited by the Commission on Accreditation of Allied Health Education Programs. Courses taught include Introduction to Athletic Training, Therapeutic Exercise and Modalities, Health Care Administration, and Pharmacology for Health Professionals. She also coordinates all curriculum activities in the Athletic Training Program. As a clinical supervisor in the Injury Care Center, René evaluates the student staff, keeps records, and writes reports. Her typical work hours are 8:00 A.M. to 6:00 P.M. Some evening and weekend hours are also required for class preparation, student evaluations, and center supervision.

SPECIALIZED COURSE WORK, DEGREES, AND WORK EXPERIENCES NEEDED FOR THIS CAREER
Certification by the NATA Board of Certification and experience as a volunteer, intern, or employed athletic trainer are essential prerequisites to teaching in this area. Licensure or registration as an athletic trainer is required in some states. René states that all athletic training courses, sport sciences classes such as exercise physiology, and courses in instructional methodology have been beneficial in her current position. A master's degree is the minimal academic credential for a college position, although a doctor's degree in athletic training/sports medicine or a related area is the standard for a tenure track position.

SATISFYING ASPECTS
René enjoys sharing her experiences and developing relationships with students who want to become athletic trainers. She finds it rewarding to work with and mentor future professionals.

JOB POTENTIAL
René holds a tenured position that carries the opportunity to advance from assistant to associate to full professor. Depending on experience and academic degrees held, assistant professors at her university get starting salaries of about $37,000. Research, scholarly publications, and teaching proficiency are required for promotion in rank and achievement of tenure. Salary increases and additional responsibilities are usually associated with advancement.

SUGGESTIONS FOR STUDENTS

Obtaining a terminal (doctorate) degree is essential for teachers to advance in higher education. René advises students to get involved in professional organizations (such as NATA and AAHPERD) and to appreciate and cultivate relationships with mentors.

REVIEW QUESTIONS

1. What are the characteristics of an academic discipline?
2. What is exercise physiology, and how has it become the leading disciplinary foundation of sports?
3. What is biomechanics?
4. What is the difference between motor development and motor learning?
5. Within which of the exercise and sport sciences would research studies on mental practice to improve performance be conducted?
6. Why is sport history relevant?
7. Describe the various content areas that comprise sport management.
8. Describe the scope of responsibilities for an athletic trainer.
9. What role would a sport psychologist play with a professional athlete?
10. How would a sport historian and sport sociologist collaborate in research of mutual interest to them?

STUDENT ACTIVITIES

1. Select 1 of the 10 exercise and sport sciences and describe its contributions to sport.
2. Volunteer to help a faculty member or a graduate student conduct a research project specific to 1 of the 10 exercise and sport sciences.
3. Read two research articles that contribute to the body of knowledge in exercise and sport sciences. Summarize the major points of each article, the scholarly procedures and methods of inquiry used, and the end result of each study.
4. Invite a specialist in each of the exercise and sport sciences to your class or majors club to present an overview of each field of study and how it interrelates with the others.
5. Divide the exercise and sport sciences into the following groups:

    • Motor learning, motor development, and sport psychology
    • Exercise physiology, biomechanics, and athletic training
    • Sport history, sport philosophy, sport sociology, and sport management

Conduct a class debate about the relative significance of the contributions of each of these groups.

6. Interview one of your professors who works in one of the exercise and sport sciences. Describe the type of research conducted by this person.

REFERENCE

Henry FM: Physical education: an academic discipline, *JOHPER* 35(7):32, 1964.

SUGGESTED READINGS

Bloom G, Stevens D, Wickwire T: Expert coaches' perceptions of team building, *J of Ap Sp Psy* 15(2):129, 2003. The authors examine what successful coaches believe are the most importance aspects of building a cohesive team.

Escamilla RF, Fleisig GS, Zheng N, Lander, JE, Barrentine SW, Andrews JR, Bergemann BW, Moorman CT: Effects of technique variations on knee biomechanics during the squat and leg press, *Med & Sci in Sp & Exer* 33(9):1552, 2001. These researchers describe their findings on how the knee functions using various techniques during two weight-lifting exercises.

Goldsmith PA: Race relations and racial patterns in school sports participation, *Soc of Sport J* 20(2):147, 2003. This article provides an in-depth exploration of the various racial issues involved in school sports.

Guttmann A: Sport, politics and the engaged historian, *J of Cont Hist* 38(3):363, 2003. This sport historian provides a detailed explanation with examples of the interrelationships between sport and politics.

Hynes-Dusel J: Motor development in elementary children, *Strategies* 15(3):30, 2002. This practical article describes key issues associated with how young children learn motor skills.

Kilduski NC, Rice MS: Motor learning—qualitative and quantitative knowledge of results: effects on motor learning, *The Amer J of Occup Ther* 57(3):329, 2003. The authors explain how important the knowledge of results is to the learning of motor skills. They suggest that individuals need both quantitative and qualitative information as they progress in learning.

Lehnus DL, Miller GA: The status of athletic marketing in division 1A universities, *Sp Mkt Q* 5(3):31, 1996. Data from questionnaires returned by university presidents, athletics directors, and marketing personnel revealed that the two most important problems facing college athletics in the next decade will be gender equity and inadequate finances. Marketing professionals can help with generating new revenues, but indicate a need for greater understanding by others about the function or concepts of sport marketing.

Parker J, Pitney W: Professional preparation—are content and competencies enough? strategies to encourage reflective practice among athletic-training students, *JOPERD* 74(2):46, 2003. The authors suggest how educators, through their supervisory practices, can teach athletic training students to become reflective practitioners.

Rejeski WJ, Foy CG, Brawley LR, Brubaker PH, Focht BC, Norris III JL, Smith ML: Older adults in cardiac rehabilitation: a new strategy for enhancing physical function, *Med & Sci in Sp & Exer* 34(11):1705, 2002. This article reports on a clinical trial for older adults comparing a standard cardiac rehabilitation program with a group-mediated cognitive–behavioral intervention in which the latter led to greater improvement in physical function.

Thomas JR: Children's control, learning, and performance of motor skills, *Res Q Exer & Sport* 71(1):1, 2000. In this text of the 1999 McCloy Lecture, the author discusses the characteristics of children that influence their motor skills, whether children's failure to use cognitive strategies accounts for deficits in motor performance, and how children develop motor expertise and control their movements.

3

THE PROFESSION OF PHYSICAL EDUCATION, EXERCISE SCIENCE, AND SPORT STUDIES

KEY CONCEPTS

- Careers in physical education, exercise science, and sport are characterized by the components of a profession.
- The American Alliance fulfills its objectives through the programs of its associations and through conventions, publications, and other activities that benefit its membership and the people they serve.
- Many professional organizations promote the study of and involvement in human movement, sports, leisure activities, fitness programs, and other related pursuits.
- Physical education, exercise science, and sport specializations in athletic training, coaching, fitness, sport management, exercise physiology, and therapeutic fields prepare students for diverse careers following the completion of specialized course work.
- Issues facing physical education, exercise science, and sport studies include program viability, teacher/coach conflict, fragmentation, and legal issues.

Physical education has long been recognized as a part of the teaching profession, evidenced by its affiliation with the National Education Association since 1937. Even earlier, in 1885, a group of teachers and other interested individuals formed the Association for the Advancement of Physical Education to encourage the exchange of program and instructional ideas. Today the American Alliance for Health, Physical Education, Recreation and Dance, along with multiple allied organizations, promotes a broad discipline that encompasses physical education, exercise science, health, sports, dance, and leisure. This chapter describes many of these associations, along with their purposes, publications, and services. To understand physical education, exercise science, and sport, it is important to know the educational background needed to enter many physical education, exercise science, and sport careers; therefore, the teaching option and some non-traditional specializations are described.

THE DISCIPLINE–PROFESSION DEBATE

Since the 1960s, a debate has raged within traditional physical education programs at the college level concerning whether it should be classified as a discipline or a profession. Academicians in recent decades claim that the only way their research can be accepted as meritorious, and thereby their status within academe enhanced, is to disassociate from their historical roots. Conversely, advocates of physical education as a profession stress that our only justifiable uniqueness is "educating the physical." Let us examine this debate more fully.

Physical educators have long viewed themselves primarily as practitioners who taught knowledge, skills, and values. Although many early physical educators in the colleges held medical degrees, most physical educators in the schools and colleges received degrees from teacher training institutions. They studied the scientific foundations but emphasized the application of this knowledge for the development of movement and sports skills. Starting in the 1930s, physical education aligned itself closely with educational goals while specifying that it made a unique contribution to the education of the whole child. Teachers in the schools, who were often the coaches, enthusiastically supported the belief that theirs was a practical field.

In contrast, the acquisition of knowledge for its own sake rather than for any applied purpose was the rallying cry of the academicians, especially those in the exercise and sport sciences. They focused on researching, conceptualizing, and theorizing. Those who emphasized that the broadening field of physical education must defend itself through scholarly writings and publications seemed worlds apart from the practitioners in the gymnasium. As this chasm widened in the 1970s, the academicians established numerous specialized organizations that provided outlets for their research in scholarly journals and through presentations at annual conferences.

The debate continued as those involved in disciplinary research sought knowledge for its own sake, while teachers desired ways to improve instruction. As society became increasingly specialized in all areas and the quality of the scholarship produced by academicians improved, this disciplinary approach began to influence students' selection of majors. Simultaneously, many school physical education programs experienced cuts that resulted in a reduced demand for teachers. Students selecting nontraditional career options in physical education, exercise science, and sport, such as in athletic training, corporate and community fitness, and sport management, quickly exceeded the number choosing teacher education. The physical education generalist who could teach, coach, and work in a recreation program or a camp gave way to the disciplinary specialist.

PHYSICAL EDUCATION AS A PROFESSION

Before looking specifically at physical education as a profession, we need to define what a profession is. A **profession** is a learned occupation that requires training in a specialized field of study. The characteristics of a profession include

profession:

a learned occupation that requires training in a specialized field of study

- A complex, systematic body of theoretical knowledge

- Individuals who have attained extensive knowledge and experience through a formal educational process

- Standards and competencies for entry into the profession, often through a certification process

- Mechanisms and opportunities for growth and development within the field to ensure adherence to established standards, competencies, and practices

- A socially valuable service that has received societal recognition and status

- Governance by a code of ethics to protect those served

Physical educators and exercise and sport scientists must have at least a bachelor's degree and frequently have advanced study and training in an extensive body of knowledge that takes considerable time and effort to learn. Individuals in these fields share research findings and new ideas while serving people throughout society.

While the above describes physical education as a profession, Chapter 2 presented the exercise and sport sciences as academic disciplines. Are these contradictory or complementary perspectives? Physical education, exercise science, and sport studies include the 10 specialized disciplines described in the previous chapter, any of which can be a career emphasis. As individuals continue to specialize, they most often take on the identity of exercise physiologists or sport managers, even though their areas of work are based on physical activity. Historically physical education has been one of the teaching professions. It has retained the characteristics of a profession even though it has expanded into teaching in numerous nonschool settings and into nonteaching, activity-related careers. Thus, physical education, exercise science, and sport studies have broadened to encompass aspects of both an academic discipline and a profession.

PEDAGOGY

As mentioned in Chapter 2, pedagogy is the art and science of teaching. The pedagogist (or teacher) must provide an effective learning environment that focuses on successful practice opportunities. Each student or participant should

RESEARCH VIEW

Pedagogy

Teachers, in their continuous process to enhance their pedagogical practices, seek answers to questions like these:

- What instructional strategies should be used to meet the various learning styles and multiple intelligences of a diverse class of students?
- How much class time should be devoted to providing instruction, allowing for practice, giving feedback, dealing with discipline problems, managing equipment distribution, and checking attendance?
- What adjustments, if any, should be made to provide the optimal learning environment?
- How do the genders of teachers and students affect the number and quality of interactions?
- How can students become engaged in developing personalized fitness programs?
- What role should students have in the selection and implementation of their physical education curriculum?
- What type of grouping, homogeneous or heterogeneous (or both), should be used to increase student learning?
- How can a middle school coach design and implement an athletic program focused on skill development and fun?
- Why and how should a personal trainer adapt strength training programs for adolescents, unfit adults, or senior citizens in a cardiac rehabilitation program?
- What is the most effective method of giving feedback to students learning new motor skills?
- Describe how to develop and implement an accurate and effective assessment process.

spend most practice time "on task" rather than being subjected to management or organizational distractions such as waiting to use equipment. Each individual needs to be sequentially challenged by the movement experience or sports skill to achieve success while being motivated to pursue additional learning (see the Research View box "Pedagogy").

The first objective for effective pedagogical practice is to use class or practice time optimally. Each teacher must plan extensively to ensure that equipment is readily accessible, handouts explaining the day's lesson are prepared for distribution, and instructional learning cues appropriate for students with heterogeneous abilities are ready for use. The good teacher is also prepared to handle management tasks (such as calling roll and passing out equipment) and discipline problems with minimal loss of instructional and practice time. Each day's lesson is sequentially structured to provide maximal opportunities to practice each new skill.

The second essential criterion of exemplary teaching focuses on helping students or participants achieve success and challenge themselves to higher levels of skill development. Specific, corrective feedback and positive reinforcing comments about proper execution of a skill or movement must be provided by the teacher. Only when each participant, with his or her individual limitations, enjoys learning will that person want to continue. A feeling of success is the key to this enjoyment.

The primary reason people choose a career in teaching is the pleasure and reinforcement they receive when their students learn, enjoy the learning process, and continue to participate and develop their skills. Teaching is personally more than financially rewarding. This feeling of success occurs when teachers plan and implement innovative curricula, commit to the improvement of student-to-student and teacher-to-student interactions, assess students' performance to ensure that learning is occurring, and continually evaluate their work and make enhancements.

Pedagogical researchers seek to improve the instructional process through observation, analysis, and evaluation. By examining the amount of academic learning, direct instruction, and management time, one can determine how teachers' and students' behaviors influence learning. Research studies also look at teachers' expectations for students, the classroom learning climate, and the type and amount of feedback—all critical to student learning.

An essential component of practice time is receiving specific, positive feedback from teachers. (Photo courtesy Bob Hilliard.)

ADAPTED PHYSICAL EDUCATION

Adapted physical education prepares teachers to provide specialized programs for individuals with diverse abilities and limitations. Based on federal protection of individuals' rights and changing societal attitudes, school children with disabilities are increasingly being placed in regular classes, including physical education. **Inclusion** is the placement of students with physical, mental, behavioral, or emotional disabilities or limitations into regular classes with their peers. The inclusion of students who have hearing limitations, are wheelchair-bound, have attention deficit disorders, suffer from cerebral palsy, or are autistic presents significant challenges to the physical educator, who must help these and all other students achieve cognitive, affective, motor skills, and physical fitness goals (see the Research View box "Adapted Physical Education").

adapted physical education:
a program for exceptional students who are so different in mental, physical, emotional, or behavioral characteristics that, in the interest of quality of educational opportunity for all students, special provisions must be made for their proper education

inclusion:
the placement of students with physical, mental, behavioral, or emotional disabilities or limitations into regular classes with their peers

Through adapted physical education, individuals with disabling conditions can develop physically by achieving their individual goals. (Photo courtesy Bob Hilliard.)

RESEARCH VIEW

Adapted Physical Education

Adapted physical educators seek to provide specialized programs for individuals with special needs based on the answers to research questions such as these:

- What are the most effective adaptations that can be made for the wheelchair-bound student during a softball unit of study?

- How can instructional strategies be used to accommodate students with attention deficit disorder?

- What curricular planning and implementation methods should the classroom teacher and the adapted physical educator utilize to meet the needs of children with emotional and behavioral disorders?

- Why are equipment adaptations essential for children with intellectual limitations? Which of these are most effective for the learning of fundamental movement skills?

- What types of evaluations and assessments should be used with children with learning disabilities who are placed in inclusive physical education classes?

- How can learning outcomes other than those associated with physical development be designed so that children with special needs can succeed?

- What are the most effective instructional strategies for the physical education curriculum portion of an Individualized Education Program for a child with cerebral palsy?

- Describe the conditions under which a child with special needs would be placed into a "pull out," adapted physical education class.

- What curricular adaptations should be made to help a gifted child who is obese become physically fit?

- What are the pros and cons of pairing a student with special needs with a student without special needs during physical education classes?

Individualized programs or modified activities are needed to help all students have successful learning experiences. To make this approach effective, differently sized and weighted pieces of equipment, choices in task dimensions and goals, and variety in evaluation measures should be used. Peer tutors, collaborative teaching, and cooperative learning activities have proven effective in inclusive classes.

Adapted physical educators can work with other physical educators to reap the benefits of inclusive classrooms. Students gain respect for those who appear different. They demonstrate greater social acceptance, display changed attitudes, and recognize their fellow students as having equal status. The collaboration

WEB CONNECTIONS

1. www.ashaweb.org
   Learn more about the American School Health Association and its programs and services for promoting the health of the nation's youth at this website.

2. www.aahperd.org
   The American Alliance for Health, Physical Education, Recreation and Dance offers an array of information and services via this comprehensive website.

3. www.pecentral.org/index.html
   This PE Central site contains a plethora of information to assist teachers in helping children become physically active and healthy for a lifetime.

4. www.pelinks4u.org
   This site provides a wealth of information for developing skillful and healthy movers.

5. www.activeparks.org
   Learn about all the programs and services offered by the National Recreation and Park Association.

6. www.ncpad.org/
   A plethora of information about adapted physical education awaits the visitor to this site of the National Center on Physical Activity and Disability.

among students, as well as among the teachers who design curricula, positively influences learning. Inclusion implies that special resources, personnel, and curricular adaptations make it possible to educate all children with special needs, mild to severe, in regular classrooms.

Physical educators are increasingly sharing their expertise with and borrowing from the various therapeutic fields. The value of exercise in retarding osteoporosis and other degenerative diseases carries broad implications for recreational activities for senior citizens. Physical therapists and athletic trainers are seeking the best programs for injury rehabilitation. Exercise physiologists are working with physicians in the prescription of exercises for individuals who have suffered heart attacks. Recreational therapists and adapted physical educators together may provide appropriate activities for disabled employees and school children. In each of these cases, the medium of exercise is involved and, through consultation, the best activities are prescribed.

NATIONAL ORGANIZATIONS AND SERVICES

The American Alliance for Health, Physical Education, Recreation and Dance (AAHPERD, or the Alliance) has grown from 49 to more than 30,000 members and served these members for over a century. One reason for the widespread influence of AAHPERD is that many professional groups have merged into its structure. In 1937, as a department of the National Education Association, the former American Physical Education Association became the American Association for Health and Physical Education. (It became an alliance in 1974.) Recreation was added to its title in 1938; dance was added in 1979.

The Alliance is an educational organization designed to facilitate and promote the purposes and activities of its members, associations, and affiliated groups. The Alliance's mission is to promote and support creative and healthy lifestyles through high-quality programs in health, physical education, recreation, dance, and sport, and to provide members with professional development opportunities that increase knowledge, improve skills, and encourage sound professional practices. AAHPERD's mission is achieved through the following purposes:

- To develop and disseminate professional guidelines, standards, and ethics
- To enhance professional practice by providing opportunities for professional growth and development
- To advance the body of knowledge in the fields of study and in the professional practice of the fields by initiating, facilitating, and disseminating research
- To facilitate and nurture communication and activities with other associations and other, related professional groups
- To serve as their own spokespersons
- To promote public understanding and improve government relations in their fields of study
- To engage in future planning
- To establish and fulfill other purposes that are consistent with the purposes of the Alliance

The Alliance is headquartered at 1900 Association Drive, Reston, VA 20191-1599. For more information about the Alliance, call 1-800-213-7193 or visit the Alliance website at www.aahperd.org. The services provided by the Alliance include holding an annual national convention; publishing brochures, research abstracts, conference proceedings, and other information pertinent to its fields of interest; positively influencing public opinion and legislation; and providing consultant services.

Periodicals published by the Alliance include the *Journal of Physical Education, Recreation and Dance,* which includes articles of a broad and practical nature, and the *Research Quarterly for Exercise and Sport,* which reports research findings. *Update,* published in newspaper format, keeps the membership apprised of current events and legislation. Issues of *Update* include notices of job vacancies and information about graduate assistantships.

The Alliance is divided into six national associations through which it accomplishes its goals. The *American Association for Active Lifestyles and Fitness (AAALF)* represents numerous special-interest groups that fill particular niches to achieve its purposes as well as those of the Alliance. These councils and societies conduct conferences, publish position papers, and collaborate in promotional initiatives in areas such as aging, aquatics, adapted physical activity, administration, facilities, international relations, measurement, physical fitness, and safety.

The *American Association for Health Education (AAHE)* promotes health education in schools, public and community health agencies, business and industry, and colleges. Among the health issues vigorously addressed by AAHE are drug use prevention, HIV prevention and AIDS education, and cultural awareness and sensitivity. AAHE offers continuing education credits for health education professionals through a credentialing process using its *American Journal of Health Education.*

The *American Association for Leisure and Recreation (AALR)* seeks to enhance the quality of American life through the awareness and promotion of leisure and recreational experiences. In addition to helping integrate the concepts of positive leisure attitudes and values into education, AALR professionals formulate and disseminate leisure knowledge, trends, and delivery methods. This organization's commitment to uplifting the human spirit has resulted in efforts to conserve cultural and natural resources so individuals can enjoy life-enriching experiences. The "Leisure Today" feature in the *Journal of Physical Education, Recreation and Dance* focuses on the provision of leisure and recreational programs for all populations, including older individuals and those with special needs. In collaboration with the National Recreation and Park Association, the AALR accredits programs and has developed standards for evaluating services delivered by community, park, and recreation agencies.

The *National Association for Girls and Women in Sport (NAGWS)* seeks to improve and expand sport opportunities for girls and women at all levels of

The National Association for Sport and Physical Education of the American Alliance for Health, Physical Education, Recreation and Dance serves over 20,000 members through various projects and programs. (Photo courtesy Mary Ellen Saville.)

BOX 3-1 NATIONAL ASSOCIATION FOR SPORT AND PHYSICAL EDUCATION

Physical Education Councils

- Council on Physical Education for Children
- Middle and Secondary School Physical Education Council
- Council for School Leadership in Physical Education
- Council on Professional Preparation in Physical Education
- College and University Physical Education Council

Academics

- Biomechanics
- Curriculum and Instruction
- Exercise Physiology
- Motor Development
- Sport History
- Sport Philosophy
- Sport Psychology
- Sport Sociology

Sport Councils

- Coaches Council
- National Council of Athletic Training
- National Council of Secondary School Athletic Directors
- National Intramural Sports Council
- Sport Management Council
- Youth Sports Coalition

competition. It advocates for the initiation and enhancement of opportunities for sports participation and leadership for females. NAGWS helps coordinate the annual celebration of National Girls and Women in Sports Day. Through collaborative work with other associations, NAGWS is an advocate for equity in sport.

The *National Association for Sport and Physical Education (NASPE)* supports quality physical activity programs for children and adults. NASPE crusades for quality, daily physical education for each school student through conferences, print ads, public service announcements, and observance of the National Physical Education and Sport Week (May 1–7). Specialized councils serve NASPE members through conferences and workshops, convention programs, and the establishment of guidelines and position statements, such as "Developmentally Appropriate Physical Education Practices for Children." NASPE publishes *Strategies,* which includes practical articles for physical educators and coaches. (See Box 3-1 for a list of specialty councils and academies.)

The *National Dance Association (NDA)* advocates for standards, assessments, and sound professional practices in dance education. It promotes dance pedagogy and the creative process, movement training, and performance practices. The NDA through its publications, conferences, and collaborations helps

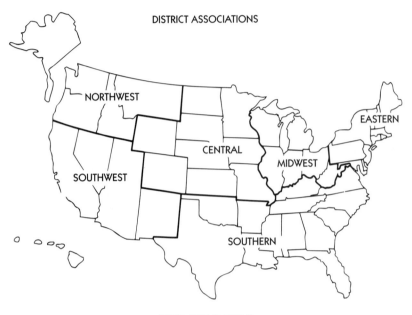

STATE ASSOCIATIONS

NORTHWEST DISTRICT
Alaska
Idaho
Montana
Oregon
Washington

CENTRAL DISTRICT
Colorado
Iowa
Kansas
Minnesota
Missouri
Nebraska
North Dakota
South Dakota
Wyoming

SOUTHWEST DISTRICT
Arizona
California
Guam
Hawaii
Nevada
New Mexico
Utah

SOUTHERN DISTRICT
Alabama
Arkansas
Florida
Georgia
Kentucky
Louisiana
Mississippi
North Carolina
South Carolina
Oklahoma
Tennessee
Texas
Virginia

MIDWEST DISTRICT
Illinois
Indiana
Michigan
Ohio
West Virginia
Wisconsin

EASTERN DISTRICT
Connecticut
Delaware
Washington, D.C.
Maine
Maryland
Massachusetts
New Hampshire
New Jersey
New York
Pennsylvania
Puerto Rico
Rhode Island
U.S. Virgin Islands
Vermont

FIGURE 3-1

District and state associations.

disseminate resources in dance curriculum, program development, and professional development.

Each of the national associations comprising the Alliance provides opportunities for student involvement. This begins by joining the Alliance, which can be done online at http://member.aahperd.org/aahperd/template.cfm?template=../ssl/membership-form.cfm. Students are invited to attend the Alliance's annual convention, participate on committees and councils through the national associations, and read the Alliance's journals and other publications. Since the future of physical education, exercise science, and sport studies depends on students who join the profession and take an active role, it is essential that these opportunities remain beneficial and interesting. Involvement often begins at the college level, where clubs for majors in physical education, exercise science, athletic training, sport management, and other fields exist. Through these collegiate experiences, students develop leadership abilities, learn more about their fields of study from professors and guest lecturers, and have fun with friends. Often these major clubs participate in service learning activities by providing after-school fitness programs for at-risk kids, conducting events for Special Olympics, or assisting with fundraising events for the American Heart Association or American Cancer Society. These service activities not only give back to the community but also strengthen and expand students' knowledge and skills.

The Alliance is divided into six district associations that share the goals and activities of the Alliance while providing leadership opportunities and services within each region (see Figure 3-1). Membership in the Alliance and in a district is combined, thus enabling professionals to attend their district conventions and the Alliance's annual conventions. During these conventions, the Alliance provides a job placement service where graduates can learn about vacancies and interview for jobs. Nonconvention workshops, clinics, and seminars provide Alliance members with the latest research findings, innovative activities, and teaching approaches, as well as opportunities for personal enrichment and growth.

Similarly, state associations give professionals the opportunity to learn different coaching techniques, acquire new skills, and interact and exchange information with other members at their annual conventions. Students, especially you, should take advantage of state conventions. Not only will you learn from these experiences, but you may also make contacts with individuals who later hire you or help you get a job.

Thus, physical education, exercise science, and sport studies provide enrichment opportunities to members as they prepare themselves to serve others. They are joined in their efforts by related groups that seek to share knowledge for the benefit of all.

ALLIED ORGANIZATIONS

Although AAHPERD is the largest organization of professionals supporting those involved with physical education, health promotion, fitness, leisure, dance, and related specialties, it shares its interests with numerous other groups. The discussion that follows briefly describes some of these organizations.

Athletic Training

The need to establish professional standards and disseminate information led to the establishment in 1950 of the National Athletic Trainers' Association (NATA), which publishes the *Journal of Athletic Training* for its members. The NATA works with the American Academy of Family Physicians, American Academy of Pediatrics, American Orthopaedic Society for Sports Medicine, and Commission on Accreditation of Allied Health Education Programs to establish, maintain, and promote appropriate standards of quality for educational programs in this field. Athletic trainers cooperate with medical personnel, athletic personnel, individuals involved in physical activity, and parents and guardians in the development and coordination of responsive athletic health care delivery systems. Among the services provided by athletic trainers are injury prevention, risk management, assessment and evaluation, therapeutic modalities, nutritional aspects of injury and illness, psychosocial intervention and referral, and acute care of injury and illness.

Exercise Science

Exercise scientists in clinical settings are committed to helping people of all ages learn more about the importance of physical activity to their health and well-being. While most individuals can and should begin and maintain a regular exercise program, often under the direction of an exercise scientist, some people may require a doctor's permission and possibly even an exercise prescription if a cardiac, pulmonary, or metabolic condition exists. Exercise scientists in laboratory settings are dedicated to the analysis of human movement to determine the effectiveness of various exercise programs and to the integration of scientific research into educational and practical applications of exercise.

The American Society of Exercise Physiologists, founded in 1997, enhances discussion and collaboration among exercise physiologists throughout the profession and helps set standards for the collegiate preparation of exercise physiologists. Members are scholars and practitioners in the fields of fitness, health promotion, rehabilitation, and sports training. Its *Journal of Exercise Physiology,* which focuses on research in this field, is published online at www.css.edu/users/tboone2/asep/fldr/fldr.htm.

The American College of Sports Medicine (ACSM) was founded in 1954 by individuals drawn from medicine, physiology, and physical education. Among its objectives are advancing scientific research dealing with the effects of physical activities on health and well-being; encouraging cooperation and professional exchange among physicians, scientists, and educators; initiating, promoting, and applying research in sports medicine and exercise science; and maintaining a sports medicine library. The ACSM encourages research publications on injury prevention and rehabilitation and on the environmental effects of exercise, nutrition, and other factors through its publications: *Medicine and Science in Sports and Exercise, Exercise and Sport Sciences Reviews,* and *ACSM's Health and Fitness Journal.*

Fitness

While a balanced, nutritious diet in combination with regular physical activity leads to healthier living, poor eating habits and inactivity contribute to related health problems, such as obesity, type 2 diabetes (high blood sugar), high blood pressure, heart disease, stroke, and some types of cancer. Nutritional workshops, such as those offered by professionals in health clubs and recreation departments, include recommendations about food selection (with an emphasis on fruits and vegetables), food preparation (broiled rather than fried foods; seasoning with spices rather than fats), smaller serving sizes, and healthy snacks (such as low-fat yogurt, baby carrots, or air-popped corn), as well as tips about losing weight. Personal trainers and exercise science specialists in private clubs and public agencies offer a wealth of advice about increasing one's physical activity. They might advise their clients to make simple lifestyle changes, such as using the stairs instead of the elevator, parking the car farther from destinations, and taking daily walks around the mall or neighborhood for enhanced health. Teachers of aerobic activities usually include dancing, walking, jogging, swimming, and cycling in their programs to help participants increase their cardiovascular endurance. In classes, individually, or with the assistance of a personal trainer, adults of all ages are encouraged to lift weights, use resistance bands, and do push-ups or sit-ups to increase muscular strength and endurance, reduce injury risk, and maintain strong bones.

The National Strength and Conditioning Association (NSCA), founded in 1978, is composed of teachers, personal trainers, collegiate strength and conditioning coaches, physical therapists, sports medicine physicians, and sport science researchers. It promotes the total conditioning of athletes for optimal performance. It publishes the *Journal of Strength and Conditioning Research* and *Strength and Conditioning Journal.*

The value and importance of joining and participating in a professional organization are multifaceted. First, membership entitles each person to receive journals, newsletters, directories, and other materials to help keep the practitioner up to date on the latest techniques, research, methodology, and applications. Second, many of these organizations sponsor conferences and workshops, which provide additional opportunities to stay current through timely updates and to interact with and learn from colleagues in similar careers. Third, organizational affiliation may lead to service on committees and leadership opportunities where you can contribute to the promotion of standards and share your expertise with others. Fourth, job announcements in newsletters and placement centers at conferences may lead to career advancement. Thus, professional involvement enlivens your career.

The basic objectives of all professional groups are to exchange information, to learn, and to serve. To enhance both your knowledge about and commitment to your chosen career, you should seek opportunities through these organizations to grow professionally. By exchanging program ideas and instructional and motivational techniques, members can improve their abilities to serve others and learn how to communicate their goals and activities to colleagues and to the general public. Sharing of experiences and research generates many ideas for further study. Therefore, as a young professional, you are encouraged to join your college, state, and national associations and one or more organizations in your interest area. You should also begin to read physical education and sport periodicals, such as those listed in Box 3-2, to help you more fully understand your profession.

Higher Education

In 1978, the National Association for Physical Education in Higher Education (NAPEHE) was formed by a merger of the National Association for Physical Education of College Women and the National College Physical Education Association for Men. Since the merger, NAPEHE has continued the publication of *Quest* and its conference proceedings.

Since 1926, the American Academy of Kinesiology and Physical Education has been the highest honorary group in health, physical education, and recreation. Its more than 125 active members have contributed scholarship and professional services, especially in colleges and universities. Some research studies are published annually in *The Academy Papers*.

Health

Since 1927, the American School Health Association has sought to improve health instruction, healthful living, and health services in the schools. Although originally only for physicians, membership is now open to anyone engaged in school health work. This association publishes the *Journal of School Health*.

Recreation

The National Recreation and Park Association (NRPA) is dedicated to improving the human condition through improved park, recreation, and leisure opportunities as well as developing and expanding its programs and services and addressing environmental concerns. NRPA facilitates the training of personnel who conduct community recreation programs. *SCHOLE: A Journal of Leisure Studies and Recreation Education, Journal of Leisure Research, Therapeutic Recreation,* and *Parks and Recreation* are NRPA publications.

The National Intramural-Recreational Sports Association (NIRSA) was begun in 1950 to provide an opportunity for college intramural directors to meet annually to exchange ideas and information. With the expansion of college programs into recreational services of all kinds, the association assumed its present name in 1975. Sharing innovative program ideas, reporting research, and discussing policy and procedures highlight its annual convention and the *NIRSA Journal*.

Other Exercise and Sport Sciences

In 1967, psychologists and physical educators founded the North American Society for the Psychology of Sport and Physical Activity to promote this increasingly

BOX 3-2   PHYSICAL EDUCATION, EXERCISE SCIENCE, AND SPORT JOURNALS

ACE Fitness Matters

ACSM Health and Fitness Journal

Adapted Physical Activity Quarterly

American Fitness Magazine

American Journal of Clinical Nutrition

American Journal of Health Education

American Journal of Sports Medicine

Clinics in Sports Medicine

Exercise and Sport Sciences Reviews

Fitness Management Magazine

Health and Fitness Journal

Journal of Aging and Physical Activity

Journal of Biomechanics

Journal of Applied Biomechanics

Journal of Applied Physiology

Journal of Applied Sport Psychology

Journal of Athletic Training

Journal of Cardiopulmonary Rehabilitation

Journal of Exercise Physiology

Journal of Leisure Research

Journal of Orthopaedic and Sports Physical Therapy

Journal of Motor Behavior

Journal of the Philosophy of Sport

Journal of Physical Education, Recreation and Dance

Journal of Sport and Exercise Psychology

Journal of Sport History

Journal of Sport Management

Journal of Sport Rehabilitation

Journal of Sport and Social Issues

Journal of Strength and Conditioning Research

Journal of Teaching in Physical Education

Measurement in Physical Education and Exercise Science

Medicine and Science in Sports and Exercise

Motor Control

Palaestra

Parks and Recreation

Pediatric Exercise Science

Performance Training

(continued)

BOX 3-2   PHYSICAL EDUCATION, EXERCISE SCIENCE, AND SPORT JOURNALS (CONTINUED)

Quest

Research Quarterly for Exercise and Sport

SCHOLE: A Journal of Leisure Studies and Recreation Education

Sociology of Sport Journal

Strategies: A Journal for Sport and Physical Education

Strength and Conditioning Journal

The Physical Educator

The Physician and Sportsmedicine

The Sport Psychologist

Maintaining muscular strength and endurance is important throughout life.

popular field of study. The Association for the Advancement of Applied Sport Psychology, founded in 1986, promotes research and intervention strategies in sport psychology. It publishes the *Journal of Applied Sport Psychology*. Since 1973, the North American Society for Sport History has encouraged scholarly research in all aspects of this discipline of sport, conducted an annual conference, and published the *Journal of Sport History*. The North American Society for Sport Management, established in 1985, focuses on the professional development of practitioners and researchers in this specialization. Articles in the *Journal of Sport*

Management encompass both the theory and application of management to sport settings. Appendix B lists several organizations, such as the NSCA and ACSM, should you seek to obtain certification to work in the fitness industry.

UNDERGRADUATE SPECIALIZATIONS

Assuming you are considering a career in physical education, exercise science, or sport, this section of the chapter introduces you to the various options or specializations that exist in many colleges and universities. This discussion will prepare you for Chapter 5, which describes many careers related to physical education and sport, and Chapter 6, which explains many specific programs and certifications.

Professional preparation programs in physical education traditionally have been oriented toward teacher education, although today most colleges offer a variety of specializations, such as exercise science, sport management, and athletic training. As the demand for teachers decreased dramatically in the late 1970s, colleges and universities revised their curricula to include the increasingly popular sport- and fitness-related specializations. This expansion in the fields of fitness, leisure, recreation, athletics, and sport resulted in diverse career opportunities for students specializing in these areas.

Athletic Training Option

Many students opt to specialize in athletic training, which deals with the prevention, treatment, and rehabilitation of sports injuries. Athletic trainers work with coaches to develop conditioning programs to optimally prepare athletes for competition. Trainers also provide supportive taping to help ensure safe participation. When injuries occur, athletic trainers are the primary caregivers, conducting on-site assessments of the severity of injuries. If injuries are minor, first aid measures and administration of ice, whirlpool, ultrasound, or other treatments fall within their purview. Under a physician's supervision, athletic trainers rehabilitate athletes suffering from more serious conditions, such as loss of mobility due to a broken bone or surgery. In addition, athletic trainers often counsel athletes to help them deal with injuries and rehabilitation.

Regulations governing athletic trainers in schools vary depending on the state. This situation, however, places the athletic trainers, athletes, and schools at risk when proper care is not given. Almost all colleges, professional teams, and sports medicine clinics stipulate that applicants must hold certifications from the NATA Board of Certification for employment (see Box 3-3).

In schools, athletic trainers can expect to teach at least a partial load of classes (if they hold a teaching certification) because these positions are seldom full time. However, it is difficult to meet certification requirements for athletic training and for teaching in less than five (and maybe more) years due to the strict course work and clinical hours each requires. Salaries are determined by the local school district's salary schedule and are based on years of experience and

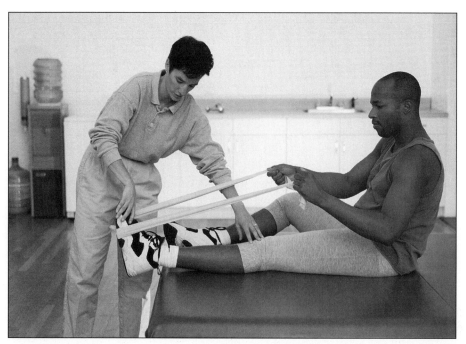

Careers in athletic training are available in schools, colleges, professional leagues, and clinical settings.

educational degrees. Additional stipends for extracurricular work are possible. Annual salaries range begin around $30,000 and advance depending on respon-sibilities, experience, and education.

Depending on the size of the institution and the number of trainers, col-lege athletic trainers may be full or part time. They may teach in an accredited athletic training program or in some other field. They may serve one team (such as football) or be responsible for all the intercollegiate sports teams. De-pending on the job description, salaries can vary widely, from $30,000 to $100,000 a year.

Another popular career choice for athletic trainers is in a clinical setting. These jobs may be affiliated with a hospital (with a rehabilitative focus) or in a private clinic that serves the public. Individuals helped by athletic trainers may have suffered sports-related injuries or need assistance in returning to activity after inactivity or some non-sports-related injury.

Coaching Option

Coaching specializations or minors are popular choices for undergraduates who want to continue their involvement with sports. Interscholastic and youth pro-grams need individuals who want to coach young athletes. The demand for coaches of school teams exceeds the supply because of increased numbers of girls' teams, the hiring of fewer new teachers, and the resignation of tenured physical educators from coaching but not from teaching. The millions of children

BOX 3-3 CERTIFICATION IN ATHLETIC TRAINING

An athletic trainer, who is educated and experienced in the management of health care problems associated with physical activity, works with physicians and other health care personnel as an integral member of the health care team in secondary schools, colleges and universities, professional sports programs, sports medicine clinics, and other health care settings.

The National Athletic Trainers' Association Board of Certification (NATABOC) upholds the standards for the profession by providing a certification program for entry-level athletic trainers and recertification standards for certified athletic trainers. A candidate must satisfy the basic requirements, successfully complete an entry-level athletic program accredited by Commission on Accreditation of Allied Health Education Programs in no less than two academic years, and pass a three-part national certification examination.

Basic Requirements

- Graduate at the baccalaureate level from an accredited college or university located in the United States
- Hold a current certification in cardiopulmonary resuscitation
- Receive endorsement of the certification application by a NATABOC-certified athletic trainer or accredited curriculum program director

Curriculum Requirements

Students must demonstrate competencies in these areas of instruction:

- Assessment of injury or illness
- Exercise physiology
- First aid and emergency care
- General medical conditions and disabilities
- Health care administration
- Human anatomy
- Human physiology
- Kinesiology/biomechanics
- Medical ethics and legal issues
- Nutrition
- Pathology of injury or illness
- Pharmacology
- Professional development and responsibilities
- Psychosocial intervention and referral
- Risk management and injury or illness prevention
- Strength training and reconditioning
- Statistics and research design
- Therapeutic exercise and rehabilitative techniques
- Therapeutic modalities
- Weight management and body composition

(continued)

BOX 3-3   CERTIFICATION IN ATHLETIC TRAINING (CONTINUED)

Associated with these courses, students must complete a minimum of two academic years of clinical experience in athletic training rooms, athletic practices, and competitive events at various levels under the direct supervision of a certified athletic trainer. These clinical experiences must include exposure to upper-extremity, lower-extremity, equipment-intensive, general medical experiences of both genders, and opportunities for observation of and involvement in the first aid and emergency care of a variety of acute athletic injuries and illnesses.

Certification Exam

Students must successfully complete written examination, written simulation, and practical section questions developed to assess knowledge on subject matter from the six domains of athletic training that comprise the educational competencies for the health care of the physically active:

- Risk management
- Assessment and evaluation
- Acute care, general medical conditions and disabilities, pathology of injury and illness, pharmacological aspects of injury and illness, and nutritional aspects of injury and illness
- Therapeutic exercise and therapeutic modalities
- Health care administration and professional development and responsibilities
- Psychosocial intervention and referral

See www.nataboc.org/candidates/Online/reqs/purpose/index.htm, http://www.cewl.com, and www.caahep.org/caahep/standards/at_01.htm for additional information.

---

competing on youth sport teams deserve coaches who know how to teach fundamental skills while making sports fun.

Almost all youth league coaches, however, are volunteers. Regardless of the type of employment of these volunteers, they need a basic knowledge in first aid, coaching concepts, human growth and development, and exercise and sport sciences. Although a few independent programs offer educational opportunities and certifications for these coaches, most volunteers demonstrate minimal competence.

Few individuals only coach in the schools; the dual role of teacher/coach characterizes most. Typically the teacher/coach is paid according to a state or district salary scale, along with a stipend for coaching. These amounts and salaries vary widely. Whereas states require subject matter certifications for teachers, only a few specify that coaches must show competencies or complete certain courses. Coaching curricula in colleges typically include courses in first aid, care and prevention of athletic injuries, anatomy, physiology, exercise physiology, coaching theory, coaching techniques in specific sports, human growth and development, sport management, and sport psychology.

Coaching and teaching are often combined into one career in schools and colleges.
(Photo courtesy Kitty Harrison.)

Fitness Option

A specialization in fitness prepares students to enter myriad careers in this growing field. One appealing feature is the opportunity to help others attain and maintain healthy lifestyles. Another is the pleasure of associating with people who value fitness. Although fitness specialists avoid most of the discipline problems and management minutiae in the schools, they typically work during other professionals' leisure hours.

Regardless of the setting, the fitness specialist must have a strong scientific background, such as in biomechanics and exercise physiology, especially if any activity programs are being designed and prescribed. A knowledge of business and management not only helps in entry-level positions but is essential for career advancement. Fitness specialists typically find jobs in corporate, industrial, and community fitness settings; health, fitness, and sports clubs; or recreation departments. However, there are also job opportunities on cruise ships, at resorts, or as personal trainers. Salaries in the fitness industry vary from hourly rates at the minimum wage to over $100,000 for some personal trainers.

Sport Management Option

The burgeoning sports industry attracts graduates who seek to apply business and management knowledge to sports settings. The best academic preparation encompasses the triad of management foundations, sports applications, and an internship or work experience within the field. It is imperative that students understand that careers in this area are "bottom line," or profit oriented. There-fore, courses in accounting, economics, finance, organizational behavior, and law are important. Built on these should be applications courses such as sport man-agement, sport law, facility management, sport ethics, and personnel manage-ment. The culminating experience that links this knowledge and application is the internship. Salaries in sport management careers vary widely, from entry-level salaries of less than $30,000 to hundreds of thousands in upper management positions with professional sports teams.

Exercise Science

The academic preparation of the exercise science student focuses on the sci-ences. Usually courses are completed in biology or zoology, anatomy, physiol-ogy, chemistry, exercise physiology, biomechanics, and possibly biochemistry. Also beneficial is the development of strong statistical and computer technology skills, along with a background in nutrition. This strong scientific foundation also helps prepare a student to pursue advanced degrees for a college professorship. On the practical side, exercise prescription skills are necessary to qualify for many positions, such as those in corporate fitness programs, clinical settings, or cardiac rehabilitation centers. Experiences gained through an internship or part-time work are decided advantages when entering this specialization. Salaries are determined by the degree held, work setting, and level of experience.

Physical Therapy, Adapted Physical Education, and Therapeutic Recreation

The therapeutic field encompasses physical therapy, adapted physical education, and therapeutic recreation. Whether in schools or in clinics, specialists in these fields help individuals with disabling conditions. Majors in physical therapy prepare students for the licensing exam through course work based on the sci-ences and extensive clinical experiences. The adapted physical educator may in-struct one on one, in a special school, or within inclusive classrooms. Activities outside of schools are used by the therapeutic recreation professional to enhance mobility, self-confidence, and independence. Internships or experiences working with people with different disabling conditions facilitate the application of thera-peutic knowledge and skills.

Teaching Option

Teacher certification following graduation from an accredited degree-granting institution is the goal of graduates choosing a teaching option. Teacher prepara-tion courses may be taken throughout the undergraduate years or concentrated in just two years following the completion of general education courses taken at a junior or community college or at a four-year institution. Certifications for physical education may include those for prekindergarten (P) through grade 6,

Physical therapists focus on helping individuals rehabilitate from injuries.

grades 5 through 8, grades 7 through 12, P through grade 12, health education, and dance.

The National Council for Accreditation of Teacher Education (NCATE) allows learned societies, such as the National Association for Sport and Physical Education, to recommend guidelines for the professional studies component of its standards. These guidelines, containing all the attitudes, knowledge, and skills required of a physical education teacher, have been subdivided into three elements: academic, professional, and pedagogical. Aquatics, dance, exercise, games, sports, and other leisure pursuits are components of the unique academic content of physical education. Motor development, sport management, motor control and learning, sport philosophy, sport biomechanics, exercise physiology, sport history, sport and exercise psychology, sport sociology, and athletic training as discussed in Chapter 2, provide the intellectual and theoretical bases for studies in physical education. The professional aspect of the undergraduate program develops an awareness of and commitment to the various educational, research, and service activities of physical education, exercise science, and sport

BOX 3-4   STANDARDS FOR NEW TEACHERS

Many teacher preparation programs are based on the 10 principles developed by the Interstate New Teacher Assessment and Support Consortium of the Council of Chief State School Officers:

Principle 1: The teacher understands the central concepts, tools of inquiry, and structures of the discipline(s) he or she teaches and can create opportunities that make these aspects of subject matter meaningful for all students.

Principle 2: The teacher understands how children learn and develop, and can provide learning opportunities that support their intellectual, social, and personal development.

Principle 3: The teacher understands how students differ in their approaches to learning and creates instructional opportunities that are adapted to diverse learners.

Principle 4: The teacher understands and uses a variety of instructional strategies to encourage students' development of critical-thinking, problem-solving, and performance skills.

Principle 5: The teacher uses an understanding of individual and group motivation and behavior to create a learning environment that encourages positive social interaction, active engagement in learning, and self-motivation.

Principle 6: The teacher uses knowledge of effective verbal, nonverbal, and media communication techniques to foster active inquiry, collaboration, and supportive interaction in the classroom.

Principle 7: The teacher plans instruction based on knowledge of subject matter, students, the community, and curriculum goals.

Principle 8: The teacher understands and uses formal and informal assessment strategies to evaluate and ensure the continuous intellectual, social, and physical development of the learner.

Principle 9: The teacher is a reflective practitioner who continually evaluates the effects of his or her choices and actions on others (students, parents, and other professionals in the learning community) and who actively seeks out opportunities to grow professionally.

Principle 10: The teacher fosters relationships with school colleagues, parents, and agencies in the larger community to support students' learning and well-being.

*Courtesy of Interstate New Teacher Assessment and Support Consortium, a program of the Council of Chief State School Officers.

studies. These include studies of curriculum models, organizational structures, diagnostic and evaluative procedures, and problem-solving techniques. Knowledge about teaching and learning physical skills constitutes the pedagogical element. Abilities to plan, implement, and evaluate learning are observed in a supervised student teaching experience. (See Box 3-4 for guiding principles regarding what new teachers should know and be able to do.)

These specializations, while not the only ones available, illustrate the variety of alternative career choices in physical education and sport. Chapter 5, "Selecting a Career," will assist in your career choice and career development process.

Teachers help individuals of all ages and in various settings learn new skills.

SELECTED ISSUES FACING PHYSICAL EDUCATION, EXERCISE SCIENCE, AND SPORT

The issues facing physical education, exercise science, and sport today include program viability, role conflicts between physical educators and coaches, an identity dilemma in name and image, fragmentation in the field, and legal issues. Each of these situations and some suggestions for actions that can be taken to ameliorate them are briefly described next.

Program Viability

The greatest challenge for most physical education programs is inadequate resources. No longer can schools and colleges expect to receive budgetary increases. In many states, educational budgets have been cut, some substantially. During tight economic times, the so-called nonessential subjects, such as physical education, art, and music, are reduced, if not eliminated. Corporate fitness programs, public recreation agencies, and even private clubs may reduce their leagues, operating hours, and staff to withstand financial shortfalls or zero-growth budgets. No longer can teachers expect an ever-increasing revenue stream. Rather, we must expect to meet our goals with the same or fewer resources. We may have to be more frugal with our meager equipment allocation through careful maintenance and repair. We may have to charge fees for participation, while always providing alternative payment methods for those who would otherwise be excluded. We may have to market our programs better to increase private support.

Role Conflicts between Physical Educators and Coaches

Many physical educators in schools and small colleges also coach. In fact, some obtain degrees in physical education to increase the likelihood of obtaining coaching positions. Because of the overlap in instructional knowledge and skill content, this joint career seems most appropriate. When these individuals commit equally to teaching students of heterogeneous ability levels and to coaching the highly skilled, all students benefit.

Conflicts occur, however, because of time and energy constraints, unequal rewards, self-imposed and external pressures, and personal preferences. Most physical educators are expected to teach a full class load and then coach after school. This schedule results in long days. For those coaching multiple sports, these long days continue season after season. Some coaches rapidly experience burnout, causing them to quit. Others gradually lose enthusiasm and begin slacking off in one of their roles—usually their classes.

Compensation for the teacher/coach varies widely. Teaching salaries are usually established by the school district based on years of experience and academic degree(s). Coaching stipends usually are salary supplements. In small colleges, there will likely be more equity in salary and workload for the teacher/coach. Fringe benefits, such as bonuses, use of a car, or club memberships, may help compensate a person for coaching duties.

Pressures to win, whether self-imposed or from external sources, accompany sports competitions. Although most people have no interest in the quality of classroom instruction provided by the teacher/coach, hundreds or even thousands may pass judgment on one's ability to develop a successful team. Accompanying these pressures, which in the worst case may cause one to be fired, are the public prestige and status of being a coach.

Another potential source of conflict is preference for one role. Often the teacher/coach finds coaching highly skilled athletes and building a strong team more rewarding than the daily routine of teaching, especially when many students, unlike most athletes, do not want to learn. A personal preference often leads to a disproportionate allocation of time and energy to the coaching role.

Resolution of this role conflict is difficult because the conflict usually develops gradually. The teacher/coach needs to continually assess the commitment given each responsibility to ensure that it is equitable. Regardless of the pressures, rewards, constraints, and preferences, the teacher/coach as a professional is ethically expected to serve competently in both roles. Suggested strategies to ameliorate some of the teacher/coach conflict might include

- Encouraging school administrators to define, evaluate, and reward teaching and coaching roles separately
- Allowing the athletic director to specify team responsibilities and lines of authority to preclude potential conflicts between teaching and coaching duties

- Urging school administrators and athletic directors to work together to relieve the excessive pressures placed on coaches by athletes, parents, and team supporters
- Helping coaches balance the time and energy spent in meeting the responsibilities of both teaching and coaching

Identity Dilemma in Name and Image

The field is no longer singularly unified by its traditional name—*physical education*. Although schools continue to use the term, many people disparagingly refer to the instruction occurring in its classes as "gym," "phys ed," "recess," or "play." Many fail to respect the profession because physical educators have sometimes failed to teach its skills, knowledge, and values.

Most colleges and universities, in attempting to align themselves with a multidisciplinary content that is recognized as academic, have chosen names such as kinesiology, human performance, and exercise science. This disassociation from physical education has also grown out of the dramatic shift in students' major fields of study from preparing to teach physical education in the schools to specializing in exercise science, athletic training, and sport management. Although many outside the schools educate others in performing physical activities, they prefer titles such as tennis pro, aerobics leader, personal trainer, exercise physiologist, athletic trainer, and coach.

Changing the public's perception of physical education rests squarely on the shoulders of those in the field. School physical educators must design and teach quality programs that they proudly demonstrate to parents, school administrators, school board members, and legislators. College physical education instructional programs must also provide quality instructional opportunities for their students in a variety of activities. However, these two groups may become the only ones that retain the name of physical education.

Fragmentation

Beginning in the 1960s, the field of physical education has divided into specializations that focus on the research-based exercise and sport sciences described in the previous chapter. Moving away from an instructional emphasis in school and college programs of physical education, these theoretical fields have sought to gain recognition and status as academic disciplines with unique contributions. While these academic disciplines investigate various aspects of human movement, they emphasize gaining deeper understandings rather than limiting their work primarily to teaching physical activity.

Primarily associated with universities, this fragmentation has divided the traditional field of physical education into narrowly defined areas of study and encouraged professors to specialize in one of these exercise and sport sciences. With this new commitment to the creation of new knowledge, a dissonance has occurred between practitioners in the schools and researchers in the universities. Often research studies in exercise science and sport studies fail to have practical application to helping children learn and achieve the objectives of physical education. Within the profession, fragmentation has resulted in the establishment and growth of specialized organizations and in a loss of membership and involvement in the

American Alliance for Health, Physical Education, Recreation and Dance. These discipline-specific organizations are attractive to specialists because colleagues nurture and encourage strong research and conduct conferences with singular foci.

Legal Issues

In what many consider a highly litigious society, professions that serve people face numerous situations in which injuries and other problems can occur. Chapter 10 includes more in-depth information about legal concerns, especially as they relate to negligence; here we present a few examples of professional responsibilities. Exercise scientists have to be aware of legal concerns, such as ensuring that subjects involved in research projects are fully informed about any potential risks and provided an "informed consent" form that explains all aspects of their participation in the study. Exercise scientists, athletic trainers, and physical therapists must comply fully with physicians' directions when prescribing exercise programs and movements or risk lawsuits for operating outside their levels of expertise. Sport managers must ensure that sporting venues are safe for all spectators by anticipating and providing emergency procedures for all potential hazards, including heart attacks, bomb threats, and earthquakes. Those who hire individuals in the physical education, exercise science, and sport fields must check references to verify academic credentials and the absence of criminal or harassing behaviors. All employees in these fields are expected to comply with all laws and administrative policies and procedures to ensure equitable and fair treatment of all participants, regardless of skill level, gender, ethnic background, or other minority status. Inequitable treatment may lead to lawsuits or even more severe reprisals.

SUMMARY

This chapter focuses on being a professional rather than on joining a profession. Physical education, exercise science, and sport studies are characterized by extensive training in a disciplinary body of knowledge and service; therefore, communication among colleagues is essential. The services provided by the Alliance will enhance development of each component of the profession. The Alliance's six national associations are composed of professionals in leisure and recreation, health, fitness, sport, physical education, dance, and related fields. Numerous other professional associations provide avenues for collaboration and individual career development. Journals and conferences are the two most noteworthy services provided by these organizations. Become involved while you are a student. Participate in conferences, attend workshops, and read publications of professional organizations to prepare for your chosen career.

Undergraduate specializations include athletic training, coaching, fitness, several exercise and sport sciences, and teaching. Various career options await graduates with specialized knowledge and skills in one of these fields.

As a young professional, you can make a significant contribution to the quality of life of those you serve as a teacher, researcher, or program leader. You have the opportunity to become a role model by planning and implementing effective programs that meet the activity needs of diverse groups. Rather than reacting, you can become proactive by promoting the values of physical education, exercise science, and sport and implementing exemplary programs.

CAREER PERSPECTIVE

RICHARD J. CAREY, ATC/L
Health Educator/Athletic Trainer
Lyons Township High School
Western Springs/LaGrange, Illinois

EDUCATION
A.A., Pre-Physical Therapy, Grays Harbor Junior College (WA)
B.A., Health Education, University of Washington
M.S., Health Education, Pennsylvania State University

JOB RESPONSIBILITIES AND HOURS
As the head athletic trainer, Rich is responsible for 26 girls' and boys' teams at two campuses. He covers all home and away football games and home events for all other sports. He prepares athletes for practices and competitions, plans and administers conditioning and rehabilitation programs, maintains athletes' treatment records, coordinates two training rooms, and supervises 24 student trainers. He also teaches three classes of health education to sophomores and two classes of sports medicine to juniors and seniors. Monday through Friday, Rich works from 7:30 A.M. to 7:00 P.M. and on Saturday from 7:30 A.M. to 5:00 P.M. These are typical hours for an athletic trainer who also teaches. In addition, he works longer hours when back-to-back sports competitions occur.

SPECIALIZED COURSE WORK, DEGREES, AND WORK EXPERIENCES NEEDED FOR THIS CAREER
Certification by the National Athletic Trainers' Association and a college degree in education with the appropriate teaching certification are required. Some states also require regulation (Illinois requires licensure) in athletic training. Rich recommends obtaining emergency medical technician training as well as instructor certification in cardiopulmonary resuscitation, first aid, and AED (automated external defibrillation). He emphasizes the importance of attending sports medicine workshops and symposia whenever possible. Many of these sessions build on one's undergraduate and graduate education and provide the opportunity to obtain required continuing education units.

SATISFYING ASPECTS
Rich enjoys helping others recover from an injury or illness. He likes serving as a counselor for teens during their injury recovery period with its emotional ups and downs. Keeping up to date to teach his health education class is a pleasant challenge for him. The two months off in the summer help compensate for the long hours worked during the school year.

JOB POTENTIAL
At Rich's school, one's salary increases with educational hours and years of continuous service in sports. The salary range is $44,000 to $93,000 for teaching, with a $6,000 to $30,000 stipend for athletic training. Professional time is available for speaking and publishing, with the school paying part of the associated expenses.

SUGGESTIONS FOR STUDENTS

Rich recommends accumulating the highest educational degrees possible. You must be willing to relocate from your home in securing a position. Certification in a teaching field other than health and physical education, when coupled with athletic training certification, may enhance your employment options. Personally, Rich stresses that one's physical and mental health must be high, with sufficient stamina to work long hours. As an athletic trainer, you must be able to deal with all kinds of people and demonstrate a great sense of humor. You must also show a genuine understanding and supportive attitude during an athlete's convalescence period. In the classroom, you need to use diversified strategies to teach health and decision-making skills. Rich suggests teaching *with,* not *at,* your students. He adds that if you work hard and remain dedicated, you can attain any goal you desire as a teacher/athletic trainer.

REVIEW QUESTIONS

1. What are the characteristics of a profession?
2. How can you justify physical education, exercise science, and sport studies as professions?
3. How has the American Alliance for Health, Physical Education, Recreation and Dance sought to achieve its mission?
4. What types of services are provided by the National Association for Sport and Physical Education?
5. What opportunities are available for students through majors clubs?
6. What are the purposes of the American College of Sports Medicine?
7. What is the purpose of the National Strength and Conditioning Association?
8. According to the National Council for Accreditation of Teacher Education, in what three elements of physical education must a prospective teacher gain knowledge?
9. What is required for certification as an athletic trainer?
10. What are several career possibilities for individuals specializing in the exercise and sport sciences?

STUDENT ACTIVITIES

1. Join the American Alliance for Health, Physical Education, Recreation and Dance.
2. Write to one physical education, exercise science, or sport organization that interests you (other than the AAHPERD) and request information about possible careers.
3. Read at least one article from any two of the periodicals listed in Box 3-2 on pages 85 and 86. Describe its key points.

4. Write a one-page statement defending the importance of being a professional.

5. Attend at least one professional workshop or clinic during this school year.

6. In small groups, prepare a five-minute defense for the importance and advantages of joining a professional organization.

7. Interview one person in each of the undergraduate specializations to gain more information about their careers. Write a one-page report about each, or share this information in a two-minute class presentation.

8. Select one of the professional organizations and give a two-minute presentation about its unique programs and services.

9. Read one position paper or publication of one of the six Alliance organizations and write a one-page report about it.

10. Discuss and debate this situation: The Board of Trustees of Midwest College has directed the president to cut programs on campus due to the current financial crisis. The president has decided that physical education, intramurals, and athletics are expendable because they contribute little to achieving the mission of the college. The president has formed three task forces, one composed of student physical education, exercise science, and sport majors; another of physical education faculty; and another of athletic department personnel. Each is charged with justifying why these programs should *not* be eliminated. (The city has offered to buy the existing physical education and athletic facilities, thereby eliminating the financial burden.) Form three groups representing these task forces and prepare responses. The task forces may proceed in any way they choose to collect pertinent data and information to justify the importance of these programs. Each task force should also prepare and present alternative strategies for the president to consider. Each task force will be chaired by a person responsible for delivering a five-minute defense during class.

REFERENCE

American Alliance for Health, Physical Education, Recreation and Dance: Reston, VA, 2000, the Alliance.

SUGGESTED READINGS

Bulger SM, Mohr DJ, Carson LM, Wiegand RL: Infusing health-related physical fitness in physical education teacher education, *Quest* 53(4):403, 2001. The authors describe how to prepare preservice physical education teachers to teach about and implement the concepts of health-related physical fitness.

Houston-Wilson C, Lieberman LJ: The individualized education program in physical education: a guide for regular physical educators, *JOPERD* 70(3):60, 1999. This practical article helps physical educators learn more about how to implement Individualized Education Programs and deal with problems associated with these programs.

Keating XD, Silverman S, Kulinna PM: Preservice physical education teacher attitudes toward fitness tests and the factors influencing their attitudes, *J of Teach in PE* 21(2):193, 2002. This article describes the importance of fitness tests to preservice physical education teachers.

Maeda JK: Teacher coaching in physical education: a review, *Phys Ed,* 58(3):140, 2001. In this review of the literature, the author describes the importance of coaching teachers, such as through constructive feedback to preservice teachers and professional development opportunities for in-service teachers, to help them enhance the quality of their instruction.

Pagnano K, Langley DJ: Teacher perspectives on the role of exercise as a management tool in physical education, *J of Teach in PE,* 21(1):57, 2001. The authors describe how physical educators perceive the use of exercise in managing their classes and students.

Sansom A: Preparing for the next 1,000 years: while the nation changes, we must adapt and serve, *Parks and Rec* 35(4):104, 2000. This article suggests that leisure time is becoming less available as the population expands and that leisure professionals must attract participants and adapt to changes.

Statt EH, Plummer OK, Marinelli RD: A circle of learning in sport instruction, *JOPERD* 72(3):34, 2001. The authors suggest that a comprehensive physical education program should be based on existing knowledge about learning styles and effective sport instruction strategies.

Stein JU: Physical education and special education: likely partners? *J of Educ* 180(2):77, 1998. This recognized expert in adapted physical education provides an extensive description of the relationships between physical education and special education.

Stiller C: Exploring the ethos of the physical therapy profession in the United States: social, cultural, and historical influences and their relationship to education, *J of Phy Ther Educ* 14(3):7, 2000. As the title suggests, this article examines the profession of physical therapy from various educational perspectives.

Woods AM, Lynn SK: Through the years: a longitudinal study of physical education teachers from a research-based preparation program, *Res Q for Exer & Sport* 72(3):219, 2001. This study of the career development of six physical education teachers found that students' skill development was a primary objective in their classes. Three teachers left the profession when their dedication to competency building and professional growth ebbed.

CHAPTER

4

PHILOSOPHY OF PHYSICAL EDUCATION, EXERCISE SCIENCE, AND SPORT

KEY CONCEPTS

- Philosophy is the pursuit of truth, knowledge, and values.
- Idealism, realism, pragmatism, naturalism, and existentialism have influenced the growth of physical education, exercise science, and sport programs.
- Ethics is a branch of philosophy that deals with moral values.
- The practical application of philosophical theories will help you develop a personal philosophy of physical education, exercise science, and sport.
- Philosophy, though often misunderstood and neglected, can provide focus, a communication bond, a clarity of vision and direction, and an opportunity to analyze the present to expand one's horizons for the future.

The pursuit of truth is as pervasive today as it was during the development of diverse philosophies in the past. This chapter examines the importance of philosophy, focusing on five of the traditional philosophies, with emphasis on how they have influenced physical education, exercise science, and sport. Other philosophies, especially ethics, are discussed because of their impact on today's programs. Based on the knowledge gained from this study, you are encouraged to develop a personal philosophy of physical education, exercise science, and sport.

WHY STUDY PHILOSOPHY?

Philosophy can be defined as a love of wisdom or, more broadly, as the pursuit of truth. Philosophy is both the developmental process and the resultant factors, theories, and values. Philosophy is an attempt to understand the meaning of life by analyzing and

> **philosophy:**
> a love of wisdom; the pursuit of truth

synthesizing *why;* simply having a purpose and objectives, as discussed in Chapter 1, is not sufficient. You must know why these are of value to yourself and to others, and you need to be able to articulate their importance.

What is the worth of physical education to a school child? What is the value of learning a lifetime sport? What constitutes a healthy lifestyle? What is the role of play? These are just a few of the questions that your philosophy can help answer.

Developing a personal philosophy can improve your teaching effectiveness, influence your behavior, provide direction in program development, contribute to society's awareness of the value of physical activity, and encourage a feeling of commonality among co-workers. How, you might ask, could a personal philosophy help accomplish all this? When you determine what goals you want your students or those with whom you work to attain, it will influence what you include in your curriculum or program and how you proceed. For example, if you value the development of physical fitness for your students, you will emphasize content and activities that can contribute to improving their fitness levels. Conversely, if you prioritize the development of movement and sport skills, you will focus on instructing and having students practice these skills. Another example of how a personal philosophy influences what is accomplished would be to consider whether you will emphasize fair play as a coach. If you believe in playing by the rules and living ethically, you can serve as a positive role model for your students, athletes, and co-workers. (See the Research View box below and on page 105 to help you in developing your personal philosophy.)

The discussion of the traditional philosophies that follows will challenge your thinking as you decide what you value and how to formulate your personal philosophy. By articulating what you believe in and what is important, you are laying the foundation for your personal philosophy.

RESEARCH VIEW

Developing a Personal Code of Conduct as a Physical Education, Exercise Science, and Sport Professional

What is the responsibility of the physical education, exercise science, or sport professional to each of the following?

- Program content relative to standards
- Delivery of instruction and dissemination of information
- Professional knowledge and expertise
- Treatment of individuals from various socioeconomic backgrounds, ages, genders, ethnicities, or ability levels
- Utilization of equipment and other resources
- Responsibilities relative to moral values
- Personal health and well-being

Research View (*Cont'd*)

The National Association for Sport and Physical Education's Code of Conduct (www.aahperd.org/naspe/pdf_files/pos_papers/resource-code.pdf) suggests eight principles to guide responsible ethical practice and provide a framework for the resolution of ethical dilemmas. Among these are maintaining the highest standards of ethical behavior, promoting activities that contribute to overall human welfare, emphasizing best practices and standards of excellence in programs, and completing responsibilities with competence and integrity.

The Coaches Code of Conduct developed by NASPE's Coaches Council can be found at www.aahperd.org/naspe/pdf_files/pos_papers/coaches.pdf. This document stresses that coaches must know and demonstrate expertise in coaching competencies such as injury prevention, care, and management; risk management; growth, development, and learning; training, conditioning, and nutrition; social-psychological aspects of coaching; and skills, tactics, and strategies. The code also emphasizes proper conduct of coaches who serve as role models for fair play, integrity, sportsmanship, and professionalism as well as focus on their athletes' development of skills and fitness in safe environments.

The National Strength and Conditioning Association (www.nsca-lift.org/Publications/posstatements.shtml#CodeofEthics) emphasizes in its code of ethics that fitness professionals should be nondiscriminatory, engage only in sportsmanlike conduct, guard against negligent techniques and practices that would result in injury, and be truthful when stating their education, training, and professional experience.

The Code of Ethics for the American Physical Therapist Association (www.apta.org/PT_Practice/ethics_pt/code_ethics) emphasizes maintaining and promoting ethical practice in the best interest of the client. Included among its 11 principles are respecting the rights and dignity of all individuals through the provision of compassionate care, acting in a trustworthy manner, exercising sound professional judgment, maintaining professional competence and high standards of practice, seeking only such remuneration as is reasonable, and protecting the public and the profession from unethical, incompetent, and illegal acts.

FIVE TRADITIONAL PHILOSOPHIES

Idealism, realism, pragmatism, naturalism, and existentialism provide the foundation for educational philosophy, including that of physical education, exercise science, and sport. These five traditional philosophies are defined in Box 4-1. A brief overview of the basic tenets of each philosophy and their application is provided. Table 4-1 delineates these five philosophies, and Table 4-2 applies their tenets to physical education, exercise science, and sport. Box 4-1 further clarifies specific characteristics of each philosophy. To assess your understanding of the five traditional philosophies, after you have studied them, take the philosophy quiz in Box 4-3 on page 115.

BOX 4-1   FIVE TRADITIONAL PHILOSOPHIES THAT HAVE INFLUENCED THE DEVELOPMENT OF PHYSICAL EDUCATION, EXERCISE SCIENCE, AND SPORT

Idealism: A philosophical theory advocating that reality depends on the mind for existence and that truth is universal and absolute.

Realism: The philosophical system stressing that the laws and order of the world as revealed by science are independent from human experience.

Pragmatism: An American movement in philosophy emphasizing reality as the sum total of each individual's experiences through practical experimentation.

Naturalism: A belief that the scientific laws of nature govern life and that individual goals are more important than societal goals.

Existentialism: A twentieth-century philosophy that centers on individual existence and advocates that truth and values are arrived at by each person's experiences.

Idealism

Idealism centers on the mind as critical to understanding, since only through reasoning and mental processes can truth emerge. Never-changing ideals, not things, constitute the ultimate reality. Idealists since the Greek philosopher Plato have stressed that only the reflective and intuitive individual can arrive at truth.

Ideals, virtues, and truths are universal and external, and remain the same regardless of how individual interpretations vary. As people develop and exercise their free will, they make choices through their intellectual powers. These decisions, whether right or wrong, do not alter the values important to the idealist.

The development of the total person is the objective of idealism as applied to physical education, exercise science, and sport. The individual is important and should be nurtured through an emphasis on the mind and its thought processes. Because reality is mental rather than physical, physical activity is sometimes

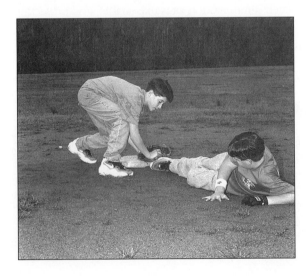

The mental side of sports, such as knowing when and how to slide or how to apply the tag to a sliding runner, is valued by the idealist. (Photo courtesy Bob Hilliard.)

TABLE 4-1

FIVE TRADITIONAL PHILOSOPHIES

	Idealism	Realism	Pragmatism	Naturalism	Existentialism
Source of Truth	Ideas	Scientific reality	Human experiences	Nature	Human existence
Most Important	People	Physical world	Society	Individual	Individual
How to Arrive at Truth	Reasoning and intuition	Scientific method	Experiencing changes	Laws of nature	Individual determination
Importance of the Mind	Emphasized	Reasoning powers and scientific method used	Learning by inquiring, observing, and participating	Physical and mental balance for the whole person	The individual's determination of the subject matter and the learning method
Importance of the Body	Simultaneous development with the mind	Emphasis on the whole individual	Variety of activities for effective functioning in society	Physical activity essential for optimal learning	Freedom to choose activity and to be creative
Curricular Focus	Teacher centered through examples for students; qualitative	Subject centered; quantitative	Student centered; based on individual differences	Individual readiness to learn	Individual centered; based on self-realization
Importance of the Teacher	Model and example	Orderly presentation of facts; drills and scientific method used	Motivator, especially through problem solving	Guide and helper	Stimulator and counselor
Importance of the Personality	Moral and spiritual values stressed	Learn for life adjustment	Development of social skills and meeting one's needs	Development of social skills important	Learning self-responsibility and knowing oneself
Education	Self-development	To meet realities of life	For social efficiency	Natural process	Teaching acceptance of individual responsibility

TABLE 4-2

APPLICATION OF FIVE PHILOSOPHIES TO PHYSICAL EDUCATION, EXERCISE SCIENCE, AND SPORT

	Idealism	Realism	Pragmatism	Naturalism	Existentialism
Objectives	Development of personality and mind	Training students to meet realities of life	Helping students to become better functioning members of society	Development of whole person	Assisting students to become self-actualizing, independent beings
Subject Matter	Utmost importance	Required; the focus of learning	Experiences in a wide variety of activities	Play; self-directed individual activity	Wide selection of alternatives, especially individual activities
Methodology	Lecture; question-answer; discussions	Use of real world; drills, lectures, and projects	Problem solving	Informal; problem solving	Questions raised, thoughts provoked, and freedom of action encouraged by the teacher
Teacher's Role	More important than process	Selects knowledge to learn	Guide	Guide; nature teaches	Guide
Student's Role	Development of the total person	Emphasizes the whole individual	Learning about the moral self	Individualized rate of learning	Self-realization
Evaluation	Subjective; qualitative	Quantitative; use of scientific means	Subjective and self-evaluation	Based on attainment of individual goals	Unimportant in the traditional sense
Weaknesses	Resistance to change; development of the physical secondary to the mind	Too narrow a view; everything must conform to natural laws or it is wrong	Lack of fixed aims to give students stability and direction	Too simple an approach for the complex world	Overemphasis on individuality precludes preparation for social life

relegated to a secondary status, even though optimally the mind and the body are to be developed simultaneously.

Since the curriculum focuses on ideas, teachers are more important than the process and free to use any methods that would help students achieve their optimal levels of personality and character development. Outcomes of the affective domain, such as creativity and fair play, are also values on which idealism places emphasis.

Relative to physical education, exercise science, and sport, the idealist requires students, athletes, and others engaged in physical activity to learn how and why any skill or movement is important and how it is executed. The idealist stresses that while there is one correct way to perform an overhead shot in tennis or to putt a golf ball, it is important that the participant understand *why* this is the proper technique. The teacher or exercise leader will model how to execute a specific movement and, through questions and answers, ensure that the participant conceptualizes how to execute the skill.

Realism

As a revolt against some of the tenets of idealism, the Greek philosopher Aristotle and today's advocates of realism state that the laws of nature, rather than existing truths, are in control. The scientific method provides the realist with the process for acquiring and applying truth (i.e., the knowledge that originates in the physical world but emerges through experimentation). Scientific investigation examines the material things of the world when seeking truth.

The role of education, according to the realist, is to train the student to discover and interpret the real things in life (i.e., things that can be shown by the

Skiers realize that the laws of nature, as believed by realists, influence how they deal with the demands of varying slopes and conditions.

scientific method) to ensure the individual's adjustment in the real world. Since the emphasis is on the whole individual, physical activity—including the traditional objectives of organic fitness, neuromuscular development, intellectual ability, and social and emotional development—makes a vital contribution.

An orderly progression in learning, extensive use of drills, and objective evaluation are important methodologies used by the realist teacher. Learning is subject centered. The curriculum includes activities and experiences that enable students to understand the laws of the physical world.

Relative to physical education, exercise science, and sport, the realist does not assume that physical fitness is developed just because this is a curricular or program focus. Rather, the realist administers fitness tests to verify that an increase in the fitness parameters, such as cardiovascular endurance or flexibility, has occurred. The realist presents factual information, such as how to execute a forearm pass in volleyball, uses a variety of drills so that all students can progress naturally in learning how to do this skill, and administers an objective test to assess skill development.

Pragmatism

Pragmatism states that experiences, not ideals, provide the key to seeking truth. Ultimate reality must be experienced and is not absolute. Circumstances and situations constantly vary from person to person; thus, pragmatism is characterized as dynamic and ever changing.

In seeking knowledge, the pragmatist looks for truth that works in a given situation. If it does, it is true at that moment. Truth is a function of the social and

The pragmatist learns through experiences, such as participating in a personal fitness program.

historical context, and is considered good if it is successful. Values are also relative and result from judgments about one's experiences as long as they are evaluated in terms of the good of the group, not selfishly. Pragmatists emphasize social responsibilities since it is essential that every individual function within, and hopefully contribute to, society.

The overall objective of a pragmatic education is the development of social efficiency in students, according to the most famous American pragmatist, John Dewey. That is, students need to have opportunities to experience solving the problems of life and to learn how to become better functioning members of society. Through the use of problem solving, the teacher focuses on the students' needs and interests. This student-centered curriculum encourages students to apply the scientific method and to experience a wide variety of activities. Team sports stress cooperation and the development of interpersonal skills, and movement activities provide opportunities for exploring numerous solutions to problems.

Relative to physical education, exercise science, and sport, the pragmatist loves to play sports and experience physical activities, especially with others. Pragmatists enjoy developing their social skills through sports and other activities because these interpersonal skills can help them in other situations in life. Self-pacing and self-evaluation activities, such as developing and implementing a personal weight-training program, lead to achieving the pragmatic goal of improved health and fitness.

Naturalism

The naturalist believes in things that exist within the physical realm of nature, which is itself the source of value. Since naturalism emphasizes the individual over society, education should focus on meeting each student's needs.

Stressing "everything according to nature," the eighteenth-century philosopher Jean-Jacques Rousseau echoed the oldest known philosophy of the Western world (dating back to certain pre-Socratic Greek philosophers). Rousseau advocated that education must use the physical world as the classroom and that teachers by example should guide students through inductive reasoning to draw their own conclusions. The laws of nature dictate to the teacher and to the student the logical pattern of growth, development, and learning. Rousseau also encouraged education of the mind and body simultaneously. Physical well-being should then enhance a readiness to learn mental, moral, and social skills.

Naturalism also declares the importance of individualized learning through self-education and self-activity. Exploration of one's capabilities and interests leads directly to greater skills and adjustments to nature. Noncompetitive team, individual, and outdoor activities provide play opportunities that benefit students physically, psychologically, and, especially, socially. Through physical activities, the individual develops in an all-around way.

Relative to physical education, exercise science, and sport, the naturalist prefers to use nature as the teacher, such as learning about preserving the environment while backpacking and learning about marine biology while scuba

A natural setting provides an excellent learning environment for developing social, intellectual, and physical skills. (Photo courtesy Aram Attarian.)

diving. The naturalist encourages students to explore how to execute a locomotor movement like jumping or to discover through trial and error the most effective technique for catching a ball. Through problem solving, individuals progress at their own rates to learn how to do a forward roll or hit a ball tossed to them. The naturalist in physical education uses the principles of movement education and individualized instruction.

Existentialism

According to existentialism, human experiences determine reality. Emerging in the 1900s as a reaction against societal conformity, this philosophy subjugated everything to the individual as long as acceptance of responsibility for oneself was recognized. Leaders of existential thought include Jean-Paul Sartre and Karl Jaspers.

For the existentialist, reality is composed of human experiences and is determined by the choices made. One's experiences and free choices result in truth and are uniquely personal. An individual's value system, while totally controlled by choice, must be tempered by an understanding of social responsibility. No values are imposed by society; instead, each person is free to think and to act as personal desires dictate.

The existentialist teaches acceptance of individual responsibility, such as self-motivation in designing and implementing a personal fitness program. (Photo courtesy Bob Hilliard.)

The self-actualizing person is the desired educational outcome, as each student is given freedom to choose. However, students must accept the consequences of their actions. In the curriculum, students are presented with a wide variety of activities, especially individual ones, through which to develop creativity, self-awareness, self-responsibility, and realization of individual essence. The teacher raises questions and provokes reflective thinking but leaves students free to choose their own courses of action.

Relative to physical education, exercise science, and sport, the existentialist emphasizes individuality so the curriculum or program will focus on individual activities. The existentialist allows students choices, such as in-line skating, aerobic dance, and self-challenging or adventure activities, so they can enjoy their experiences and will persist in their participation. The existentialist gives the individual tremendous self-responsibility for learning, such as through self-paced instruction and contract grading (see Box 4-2 for other comparisons). Box 4-3 provides an opportunity to assess your understanding of each of these philosophies.

Other Philosophies

Within physical education, exercise science, and sport studies, professionals also need to be knowledgeable about other philosophies that might help them respond to questions and deal with circumstances within their careers. Kretchmar (1994)

BOX 4-2   COMPARISONS OF THE FIVE TRADITIONAL PHILOSOPHIES RELATIVE TO PHYSICAL EDUCATION, EXERCISE SCIENCE, AND SPORT

Curriculum

- The idealist will select the curriculum without student input.
- The realist will allow students to select activities from various options.
- The pragmatist will pace each curricular offering based on students' individual differences.
- The naturalist will offer those activities that students indicate a readiness to learn.
- The existentialist will focus on each child's progress regardless of the activity.

Teaching Fitness and Sports Skills

- The idealist and the realist focus on content.
- The pragmatist and the existentialist emphasize experiencing a wide variety of activities.
- The naturalist advocates play and self-directed activity for students.

Teaching Methodology

- The idealist controls learning through lectures and some interactions with students.
- The realist maintains control using drills.
- The pragmatist uses a variety of instructional approaches because students have multiple learning styles.
- The naturalist encourages problem solving with the teacher as a guide.
- The existentialist guides by asking questions and offering challenges.

Evaluation

- The idealist's qualitative assessments always subjugate the physical to the mental.
- The realist overemphasizes testing, using scientific means for quantitative results.
- The pragmatist advocates subjective self-evaluation that, in the absence of specific goals, often leaves students without a sense of accomplishment.
- The naturalist focuses singularly on the attainment of individual goals.
- The existentialist views evaluation as nonessential because only self-realization is important.

suggests that the range of philosophical questions encompasses five other philosophies. We briefly describe four of these philosophies here and expand on the fifth

metaphysics:

a philosophy that refers to the nature of things, or how actions or events are related to one another

in the next section. **Metaphysics** refers to the nature of things, or how actions or events are related to one another. This philosophical study describes the qualities or characteristics of physical as well as nonphysical things. Metaphysical philosophers

BOX 4-3   PHILOSOPHY QUIZ

Fill in the blanks with one of the following: *existentialist, idealist, naturalist, pragmatist,* or *realist.*

1. The _____ advocates that students must indicate their readiness to attempt a cartwheel.

2. The _____ models or provides demonstrations of exactly how to serve a volleyball.

3. The _____ encourages students to use their reasoning powers to decide how to align defensive players to stop an opposing team that fast breaks.

4. Since a curriculum based on this philosophy focuses on the individual, the _____ focuses on teaching the acceptance of responsibility for self-discipline, cooperation, and fair play.

5. The _____ emphasizes learning team sports where social skills are developed.

6. An exercise scientist is sometimes called a/an _____ because he or she utilizes the scientific method of inquiry.

7. The _____ encourages students to select their own movement activities and to be creative, such as designing a new cooperative game or exploring playground apparatus.

8. The wholeness rather than duality (mind versus body) of people is stressed by the _____ and the _____ as they seek to achieve psychomotor, cognitive, and affective outcomes in all classes.

9. Since to the _____ experience is critical for learning, students are encouraged to experiment with their own techniques in executing body movements.

might answer questions such as "What is the nature of sport or play?" or "How does creativity play a role in sport, play, or dance?" **Axiology** deals with the value of things and discovering whether actions, things, or circumstances are good and virtuous. In seeking truth, the axiologist attempts to answer the question of how people should act in certain situations. Questions that relate to axiology include "What should be the value of competitive sports?" or "Is intentionally harming an opponent right?" **Epistemology** is the branch of philosophy that examines what people know and how and why they hold certain beliefs. This philosophy looks at various aspects of understanding. The epistemologist might ask, "Does being a former successful athlete make this person an effective teacher

axiology:
a philosophy that deals with the value of things and discovering whether actions, things, or circumstances are good and virtuous

epistemology:
the branch of philosophy that examines what people know and how and why they hold certain beliefs

of sport skills or a successful coach?" or "What understanding of a sport would a former athlete have that a nonathlete would not have?" **Aesthetics** is the philosophical area that focuses on the artistic, sensual, or beautiful aspects of anything, including movement. A person who values aesthetics is pleased more by the beauty of the human body in motion than by the outcome of a contest or the athletes' skills. Appealing questions might include "What is the beauty, not athleticism, of the movements of the figure skater?" or "What is the rhythm of the gymnast's movement during a floor exercise routine?" (See the reference for Kretchmar for a broader review of these other philosophies.) Finally, **ethics** refers to the study of moral values or the doing of good toward others or oneself. The ethical person would believe that it would be morally wrong to violate the rules of the game in order to win. Ethical questions might include "When, if ever, is it fair to take performance-enhancing drugs?" or "Is it morally wrong to violate the spirit of the rules?"

> **aesthetics:**
> the philosophical area that focuses on the artistic, sensual, or beautiful aspects of anything, including movement
>
> **ethics:**
> the study of moral values or the doing of good toward others or oneself

ETHICS

You be the judge:

- A high school defensive tackle sharpens the edges of the fasteners that hold his chin guard to his helmet. After he plays a few downs, several of the opposing players have been cut and are bleeding. Is this action ethical? Is suspending this player from the team and school ethical?

- An elementary school student in a physical education class records that she walked one mile each day to help her team win the special field trip to the zoo, even though she did not do all of this exercise. Is this action ethical? Is suspending this student from school ethical?

- An athletic trainer gives a track athlete amphetamines to help boost his energy level. Is this action ethical? Is this athletic trainer violating the National Athletic Trainers' Association Code of Ethics (see Box 4-6 on page 122)?

- A high school athlete cheats on a test to maintain his or her eligibility to play on a school team. Is this action ethical? Does it make any difference if other students (nonathletes) in the class cheated on the same test?

- An exercise scientist inaccurately reports data from a research study in a journal article. Is this action ethical? What action, if any, should be taken?

Ethical dilemmas are often associated with whether behaviors are within the spirit of the rules. (Photo courtesy Lisa Sense.)

These scenarios deal with ethics, which is the study of moral values. It deals with good and bad, right and wrong, obligation and choice, and principles of conduct. From the time of the ancient Greeks until today, educators have been held responsible for the nurturance and enhancement of ethical behavior. Character development, for example, has traditionally been a vital concern of educators, including physical educators, exercise scientists, and sports leaders. Drawing from the fields of religion, philosophy, and psychology, values serve as the foundation of a way of life: People are expected to conduct themselves in accordance with certain values.

Moral reasoning consists of determining what is the right thing to do. In this moral reasoning process, a person has to assess what he or she knows and values about a particular moral issue before acting on a decision. Kohlberg (1981) suggested that all people learn and develop morally in a six-stage sequence, organized into three levels:

Preconventional

- Stage One focuses on actions performed to avoid punishment.
- Stage Two emphasizes following rules for self-interest.

Conventional

- Stage Three suggests that people react to the expectations of parents, peers, and authority figures.
- Stage Four assumes that people conform to the social system and social order.

Postconventional

- Stage Five expects people to fulfill contract and individual rights.
- Stage Six posits universal ethical principles as the basis for all actions.

Kohlberg stated that the higher stages require more complex moral reasoning and that moral development can stagnate at any stage.

A moral reasoning strategy begins with what a person believes. These beliefs lead to the development of values about ourselves, society, and others. Values are the answer to the question of what is most important, or what has relative worth. Moral values can be described as the relative worth associated with something virtuous and good. Examples of these moral values include justice, honesty, responsibility, and beneficence.

Most ethical theories are based on teleology, deontology, or a combination of the two. **Teleological** theories focus on the end results or consequences of processes or occurrences. For the most prominent of these theories, John Stuart Mill's **utilitarianism,** the goal is the creation of the greatest good for the largest number of people. Since the benefit of the group or society as a whole is the goal, actions are judged to ensure that the good effects outweigh the bad. The utilitarian, however, lacks concern for how the results are produced and may have difficulty determining what society values most highly.

Immanuel Kant helped formulate the theory of moral obligation known as **deontology.** According to this ethical theory, actions must conform to absolute rules of moral behavior, which are characterized by universality, respect for the individual, and acceptability to rational beings. That is, deontology argues that regardless of the particular situation, moral action should make sense to each person and lead to the same behavior. Kant's **categorical imperative** states that moral duties are prescriptive and independent of consequences. Box 4-4 provides examples of how categorical imperatives relate to sport.

teleological:
refers to theories that focus on the end results or consequences of processes or occurrences

utilitarianism:
a theory that refers to the goal of creating the greatest good for the largest number of people

deontology:
an ethical theory advocating that actions must conform to absolute rules of moral behavior, which are characterized by universality, respect for the individual, and acceptability to rational beings

categorical imperative:
the belief that moral duties are prescriptive and independent of consequences

How to teach ethical standards most effectively has been a dilemma for educators and coaches for a long time. Since fair play is not an inherent characteristic of physical activities, how does it occur? When play, games, sports, and other physical pursuits are engaged in for their inherent pleasure, ethical problems seldom emerge. When the outcome becomes so highly significant that some or all participants employ whatever means possible to achieve success, questionable behavior is readily evident, to the detriment of values. A person's moral values do not preclude seeking to perform to the best of his or her ability. But doing so at the risk of impinging on what is good, on one's obligation to others, or on principles of proper conduct violates these values.

Sport participants often face ethical choices, such as whether to acknowledge touching the net during a volleyball match. (Photo courtesy Lisa Sense.)

BOX 4-4   EXAMPLES OF CATEGORICAL IMPERATIVES IN SPORT

- Fair play means playing within the letter and spirit of the rules.
- Seeking to win within the letter and spirit of the rules is acceptable, while winning "at-all-costs" is unacceptable.
- An opponent should be treated with respect and exactly as everyone would wish to be treated.
- Games are to be played as mutual quests for excellence where intimidation is inappropriate.
- Retribution for a violent or unfair action by an opponent or an official is never acceptable.

The consequences of bad ethical decisions may seem minimal or limited in impact only to the person making the choice. Too often, though, significant negative repercussions occur when individuals fail to act in morally responsible ways. A few examples in physical education, exercise, and sport settings illustrate how unethical behaviors can have harmful consequences:

- A sport manager at an intercollegiate sporting event ignores the rowdy and obscene behaviors of an intoxicated fan until a fight breaks out in the stands, leaving several individuals hospitalized, including a child who loses an eye from a thrown object and a man who appears to have had a heart attack.

- An exercise scientist prescribes an exercise program specifically forbidden by the physician, resulting in the death of the client.

- A volleyball coach emphasizes to his players that winning while looking feminine is most important. To meet weight requirements, one of his volleyball athletes severely curtails her food intake and becomes anorexic.

- A physical educator allows her students to tease and harass other students who are less skillful. A lawsuit is filed by the parent of a child with special needs.

- An individual alleges that he has a Health and Fitness Certification from the American College of Sports Medicine in order to get hired by a local fitness club. Several patrons of the club drop their membership due to injuries sustained in programs led by this unqualified person.

As these incidents show, unethical decisions can have serious and long-lasting consequences for others.

Can ethical decision making be taught and modeled by physical educators, exercise scientists, and sport leaders? In spite of our materialistic and pragmatic world, professionals have an obligation to teach and to perpetuate moral and ethical principles that are basic to society. Among these principles are sensitivity to individual needs and differences, responsibility for personal conduct, concern for others, and devotion to honesty, integrity, and fair play. Educators and leaders in all settings should exemplify ethical behavior and treat everyone fairly so that others are positively influenced. We must constantly be aware that our actions will teach character louder than our statements.

The 25 questions in Box 4-5 challenge you with several ethical choices. These can be discussed in class or with others. Each question may have multiple alternatives, or you may believe there is only one response. Your answer is a direct reflection of the ethical values that are uniquely yours. You should also realize that your attitudes toward and reactions to these and similar situations will influence those with whom you work in a physical education, exercise science, or sport career. Box 4-6 illustrates how the National Athletic Trainers' Association emphasizes the importance of ethical conduct through its code of professional practices.

BOX 4-5 ETHICAL CHOICES IN SPORTS

1. Should every child play in every contest in youth sports programs?
2. Should extrinsic awards (such as trophies, plaques, or money) be given to sports champions?
3. Should alumni be allowed to give money or tangible gifts to prospective college athletes during their recruitment?
4. Should athletes be allowed to befriend their opponents before or after a competition?
5. Should a coach be allowed to verbally abuse officials?
6. Should strikes (refusal to complete) for more benefits or rights by professional athletes be allowed?
7. Should males and females receive identical treatment in school and college sports?
8. Should all college students be required to pay fees to finance athletic teams?
9. Should a coach have the right to require that an athlete (at any age) compete in only one sport (i.e., specialize)?
10. Should an athlete be allowed to use drugs (such as amphetamines or anabolic steroids) to enhance performance?
11. Should sports competitions be open to individuals of both sexes playing together?
12. Should an athlete be required to pass all school subjects in order to play on an interscholastic team?
13. Should a coach teach athletes how to circumvent sports rules to their advantage?
14. Should college coaches who violate recruiting regulations be banned from coaching?
15. Should fans be protected from the misbehavior of other fans?
16. Should a coach have the right to verbally or physically abuse an athlete?
17. Should an athlete ever be allowed or required to play when injured?
18. Should children ever be cut when trying out for a youth sports team?
19. Should high school or college alumni or donors be able to influence the hiring and firing of coaches?
20. Should every child get an opportunity to play all positions in youth sports programs?
21. Should sports gambling be legalized?
22. Should fans have to pay to view major sporting events on television?
23. Should colleges be allowed to generate millions of dollars of revenues from their football and basketball programs, while the athletes who help generate these revenues are limited to grants-in-aid?
24. Should a television network be allowed to dictate the date and time of a college or professional competition?
25. Should athletes be punished for breaking team rules or federal or state laws during the season?

BOX 4-6   NATIONAL ATHLETIC TRAINERS' ASSOCIATION CODE OF ETHICS

Preamble

The Code of Ethics of the National Athletic Trainers' Association has been written to make the membership aware of the principles of ethical behavior that should be followed in the practice of athletic training. The primary goal of the Code is the assurance of high quality health care. The Code presents aspirational standards of behavior that all members should strive to achieve.

   The principles cannot be expected to cover all specific situations that may be encountered by the practicing athletic trainer, but should be considered representative of the spirit with which athletic trainers should make decisions. The principles are written generally and the circumstances of a situation will determine the interpretation and application of a given principle and of the Code as a whole. Whenever there is a conflict between the Code and legality, the laws prevail. The guidelines set forth in this Code are subject to continual review and revision as the athletic training profession develops and changes.

Principle 1

Members shall respect the rights, welfare and dignity of all individuals.

   1.1   Members shall not discriminate against any legally protected class.

   1.2   Members shall be committed to providing competent care consistent with both the requirements and the limitations of their profession.

   1.3   Members shall preserve the confidentiality of privileged information and shall not release such information to a third party not involved in the patient's care unless the person consents to such release or release is permitted or required by law.

Principle 2

Members shall comply with the laws and regulations governing the practice of athletic training.

   2.1   Members shall comply with applicable local, state, and federal laws and institutional guidelines.

   2.2   Members shall be familiar with and adhere to all National Athletic Trainers' Association guidelines and ethical standards.

   2.3   Members are encouraged to report illegal or unethical practice pertaining to athletic training to the appropriate person or authority.

   2.4   Members shall avoid substance abuse and, when necessary, seek rehabilitation for chemical dependency.

Principle 3

Members shall accept responsibility for the exercise of sound judgment.

   3.1   Members shall not misrepresent in any manner, either directly or indirectly, their skills, training, professional credentials, identity or services.

   3.2   Members shall provide only those services for which they are qualified via education and/or experience and by pertinent legal regulatory process.

   3.3   Members shall provide services, make referrals, and seek compensation only for those services that are necessary.

(continued)

BOX 4-6 NATIONAL ATHLETIC TRAINERS' ASSOCIATION CODE OF ETHICS (CONTINUED)

Principle 4

Members shall maintain and promote high standards in the provision of services.

4.1 Members shall recognize the need for continuing education and participate in various types of educational activities that enhance their skills and knowledge.

4.2 Members who have the responsibility for employing and evaluating the performance of other staff members shall fulfill such responsibility in a fair, considerate, and equitable manner, on the basis of clearly enunciated criteria.

4.3 Members who have the responsibility for evaluating the performance of employees, supervisees, or students are encouraged to share evaluations with them and allow them the opportunity to respond to those evaluations.

4.4 Members shall educate those whom they supervise in the practice of athletic training with regard to the Code of Ethics and encourage their adherence to it.

4.5 Whenever possible, members are encouraged to participate and support others in the conduct and communication of research and educational activities that may contribute knowledge for improved patient care, patient or student education, and the growth of athletic training as a profession.

4.6 When members are researchers or educators, they are responsible for maintaining and promoting ethical conduct in research and educational activities.

Principle 5

Members shall not engage in any form of conduct that constitutes a conflict of interest or that adversely reflects on the profession.

5.1 The private conduct of the member is a personal matter to the same degree as is any other person's except when such conduct compromises the fulfillment of professional responsibilities.

5.2 Members of the National Athletic Trainers' Association and others serving on the Association's committees or acting as consultants shall not use, directly or by implication, the Association's name or logo or their affiliation with the Association in the endorsement of products or services.

5.3 Members shall not place financial gain above the welfare of the patient being treated and shall not participate in any arrangement that exploits the patient.

5.4 Members may seek remuneration for their services that is commensurate with their services and in compliance with applicable law.

DEVELOPING A PERSONAL PHILOSOPHY OF PHYSICAL EDUCATION, EXERCISE SCIENCE, AND SPORT

Everyone who plans a career in physical education, exercise science, and sport needs to develop a personal philosophy as a guide to future actions. For example, if fair play is essential to your philosophy, you will stress this in your own behavior, your instruction of others, and the programs you lead. A personal philosophy forces you to think logically and analytically and to explain the worth and the value of what you do and how you serve others. This developmental process will help you relate physical education, exercise science, and sport to general education and will enhance your professional growth. Too frequently, professionals fail to develop definite personal philosophies, resulting in loss of career direction and purpose. Therefore, it is essential that you formulate principles, guidelines, and directions for your career. If you do not know where you are going, it is unlikely you will end up where you want to be (wherever that is!).

Some of the philosophical tenets discussed in this chapter differ significantly. For example, pragmatists advocate helping students become better functioning members of society, while existentialists focus on students becoming

 WEB CONNECTIONS

1. www.sportsethicsinstitute.org
   The Sports Ethics Institute encourages the exploration of ethical issues, an examination of the ethical dimensions of sports, and a heightened understanding of ethical behavior in sports.

2. www.nd.edu/~cscc
   The Mendelson Center at the University of Notre Dame seeks to build character and community in sports through educational programs, research, and services.

3. www.ets.uidaho.edu/center_for_ethics
   This site of the Center for ETHICS at the University of Idaho describes some of the leading research being conducted in the area of sport ethics.

4. www.sportsmanship.org
   The Citizenship through Sports Alliance is a coalition of professional and amateur athletic organizations that promotes fair play at all levels of sport and the development of character.

5. www.internationalsport.com/csp
   The Center for Sports Parenting provides guidance and information to parents, coaches, and others to help them work with young athletes dealing with the psychological and physical challenges in sports.

6. www.positivecoach.org
   By helping organization leaders, coaches, and parents ensure a positive playing environment, the Positive Coaching Alliance advocates for the development of life skills by young athletes that will serve them well beyond the playing field.

self-actualizing, independent beings. In light of this potential disagreement in values and knowledge, you must proceed logically and specifically.

Many educators and philosophers have adopted an eclectic approach rather than accepting all aspects of one particular philosophy. **Eclecticism** is a combination of theories and doctrines from several philosophies into a consistent and compatible set of beliefs. For example, you may believe that the teacher should model correct skill performance as the idealist would, yet encourage problem solving as the pragmatist and naturalist advocate. You may design your program to focus on individualized learning (naturalism) that allows for individuality (existentialism), yet also emphasizes developing social skills valued by pragmatists. You may choose to evaluate your students using subjective (idealist) and quantitative (realist) measures. Based on your experiences and established values, an eclectic philosophy may emerge as the foundation for your personal philosophy. Again, the key is to realize the importance of examining what you believe, why you believe it, and what your values mean (see Box 4-7, "Sample of a Teaching Philosophy"). Another example of a personal philosophy illustrates how a personal trainer lives out professional values (see Box 4-8).

> **eclecticism:**
> a combination of theories and doctrines from several philosophies into a consistent and compatible set of beliefs

Before developing your personal philosophy (and to show how your attitudes, beliefs, and values influence your moral reasoning process), read the following situations and give your responses. A composite of your opinions should help you better understand your values and knowledge and how they provide the foundation for your personal philosophy.

- *Situation 1:* During a basketball game, both player 44 (team A) and player 12 (team B) attempt to control a loose ball, but it goes out of bounds. You, the official, blow your whistle and award the ball to team A. Player 44 acknowledges touching the ball last. Do you change your call? If you were the player, would you have acknowledged causing the ball to go out of bounds? Why or why not?

- *Situation 2:* During a recreation league softball game, you, the field supervisor, learn that one of the teams is playing an individual not on the official team roster. That team is in last place in the league standings. What action, if any, do you take? Would your response differ if this team were in first place?

- *Situation 3:* As a coach, sporting goods distributors frequently offer you gifts, such as free golf clubs, or special incentives, such as clothing items, if your school purchases from their companies. Should you accept these personal gifts?

- *Situation 4:* As a collegiate football player, you are told by the coach to take anabolic steroids to help build muscle bulk. Do you take the drugs? Would this be cheating or gaining a competitive edge?

BOX 4-7   SAMPLE OF A TEACHING PHILOSOPHY

Student learning is my primary focus. I seek first to learn who my students are and what they know, because only then can we jointly work to help them learn what they need to know. This student-centered approach makes teaching a creative and complex journey as we challenge and stimulate each other to a deeper understanding of the content in the course.

I model a variety of instructional strategies and behaviors as I communicate information, attempting to integrate this with their existing knowledge as they enjoy the process of learning. In every class I demonstrate my personal enthusiasm for the course content, thereby helping students realize the importance of, excitement for, and continuous nature of learning. I seek to teach students collectively and individually the foundational concepts and skills in varied, innovative ways that will stimulate them to ask questions and to desire to learn more. Each class is organized to ensure sequential and clear presentations and complete student engagement. I ask questions and encourage dialogue to facilitate critical and creative thinking by involving every student, whom I seek to know by name. Questions are elicited from students to reinforce how valuable their active participation in the learning process is.

To engage students more actively in their learning, I use various groupings for discussing issues, solving learning problems, analyzing case studies, and helping each other learn concepts and applications. I challenge students to think critically, to reflect on what they are learning and how it is relevant to them, and to participate actively in the learning process.

A variety of authentic assessments are used throughout the course to ensure that students are monitoring their learning and demonstrating that they are progressing in the achievement of learning outcomes. Feedback that I seek and gladly receive from students enables me to reflect on and continually improve my instructional approaches as well as ensure the relevancy and application of course content to the learning process and students' knowledge base.

- *Situation 5:* Your soccer team of 9- and 10-year-olds is in the last game of the season. If your team wins, it will capture the league championship. Your best player twists an ankle just as the first half ends. The player is in pain, but there is seemingly no fracture and only slight swelling. Do you allow that player to participate in the second half? Should the player be allowed to decide whether to play?

- *Situation 6:* In applying for a position as an athletic trainer with a rehabilitation clinic, you are told that a preemployment drug test and annual random drug testing are required. Does this violate any of your beliefs or constitutional rights? Would you continue to seek this job?

- *Situation 7:* The health club at which you just took a position depends on enrolling at least 20 new members monthly to meet its expenses. In your first staff meeting, you are trained in how to sell memberships without explaining the required annual fee that is assessed after the first month. You are also told that selling memberships is more important than customer service. Does this policy contradict any of your values? Is this pragmatic approach offensive to you? Will you assist members less while working more diligently to convince guests to join the club?

BOX 4-8   SAMPLE PHILOSOPHY OF A PERSONAL TRAINER

I believe that every person should have the knowledge and skills to lead a healthy life. As a personal trainer, I am committed to helping each client learn how to eat right, exercise regularly, and practice healthy behaviors. These are the top seven areas in which I can help:

- Individualized instruction in exercise programs—Teach and guide through fundamental and advanced techniques and activities for the development of cardiovascular endurance, muscular strength and endurance, and flexibility
- Nutritional counseling—Guide clients in the selection, preparation, and consumption of nutritious foods that will lead to the maintenance of good health
- Motivation and positive reinforcement—Help clients develop an intrinsic motivation to enjoy healthy behaviors by providing positive comments about their effort, commitment, responsible actions, and persistence as well as their progress in achieving nutritional and fitness goals
- Safety—Ensure that clients complete each exercise, activity, and lifestyle change in a safe environment with appropriate supervision
- Specificity of training—Direct prescribed exercises and programs in congruence with personal goals, physical limitations, and physicians' directions
- Injury or disease rehabilitation—Assist clients in regaining levels of mobility and fitness commensurate with individual circumstances and within guidelines provided by physicians
- Education—Provide information and resources to help clients incorporate healthy behaviors into all aspects of their lives

Living this philosophy gives me great satisfaction in knowing that I have made a significant difference in the well-being of clients.

- *Situation 8:* For the recreation department where you serve as special events director, you are planning to conduct a family fun run, walk, and road race. The owner of a local hardware store who has pledged $1,000 to fund this event calls one week before the event to notify you that he will not be able to donate the money. You are distraught. Just then you receive a call from the new beer distributor in town offering to provide financial support ($1,000) for recreational activities in exchange for advertising. Do you accept this offer even though young people are participating in this event? Should the recreation department have a policy regarding the companies from which it can receive support? Is it better to cancel the event or accept the beer company's offer?

- *Situation 9:* As you assess the fitness of an employee at a corporate fitness facility, you are told by that person that several employees have been padding their expense accounts to pay for golf outings and sports tickets. Are you bound by any rules of confidentiality in this situation? Should you tell your supervisor? Is this action justified because everyone is doing it, or is it embezzlement?

- *Situation 10:* You, a local sportswriter, are given evidence that a 14-year-old just transferred to a public magnet school because of promised financial benefits. This student happens to be an outstanding athlete. Do you write this story?

Your responses to these real-life situations should help you understand the importance of developing a personal philosophy.

Your answers to the following questions can assist you in this developmental process:

- What is the basis for my ethical judgments personally, interpersonally, and programmatically?
  - Is the action honest, fair, responsible, and beneficent?
  - Will the action benefit me?
  - Will the action harm others?
  - Will the action violate a societal tradition, law, or expectation?
  - Will the action violate my personal values?
- Who and what are most important to me in my program?
  - Students
  - Participants
  - Employers
  - Parents
  - Taxpayers
  - Co-workers
  - Athletes
  - Fans
  - Teaching
  - Learning
  - Participation
  - Adherence to the program
  - Fun
  - Skill development
  - Fitness
  - Winning
  - Developing social skills
  - Fair play
  - Classroom management
  - Stress reduction
  - Safety
  - Critical thinking
- How do I determine what the program content should include?
  - Required state curriculum
  - National organization standards
  - Interests of participants
  - Traditional offerings

- Latest published research findings
- Popularity of new innovations
- Something learned at a recent workshop or conference
- Winning, using whatever means helps achieve this goal

- What instructional and operational approaches will I use?
  - Lecture
  - Problem solving
  - Guided discovery
  - Self-pacing
  - Mentor
  - Guide
  - Role model
  - Motivator
  - Counselor
  - Leader
  - Facilitator
  - Autocrat
  - Friend
  - Boss

- How will I know if program objectives and personal goals have been achieved?
  - Skills are learned.
  - Participants persist in lifetime activity.
  - Winning occurs.
  - Everyone, including me, has fun.
  - Fitness is developed and maintained.
  - Career advancement occurs.
  - Evaluations are positive.
  - Job security exists.

Hopefully, responding to these questions can start you on the way to developing a personal philosophy that will guide you into a career that matches what you value. A personal philosophy, though, is an evolving and changing perspective on how a person views those things of most value and the role each will serve in his or her life.

SUMMARY

As you progress in your education and enter your career, your philosophy may change. You may borrow concepts from idealism, realism, pragmatism, naturalism, or existentialism, or you may adopt an eclectic approach. You will face ethical decisions often. Regardless of the values chosen, having a philosophy is essential. It is your personal commitment to what you want to do and become. You can use your philosophy to help you think critically, to examine yourself, to resolve personal and professional issues, and to better understand your career.

CAREER PERSPECTIVE

SHARON KAY STOLL, PH.D.
Director, Center for ETHICS*
University of Idaho
Moscow, Idaho

EDUCATION
B.S. Ed., Physical Education, College of the Ozarks
M.Ed., Physical Education, Kent State University
Ph.D., History and Philosophy of Sport, Kent State University

JOB RESPONSIBILITIES AND HOURS
Sharon directs the Center for ETHICS* at the University of Idaho, which offers study, intervention, outreach, consultation, and leadership in developing and advancing the theory, knowledge, and understanding of character education, including moral and ethical reasoning, development, and application. She also teaches undergraduate and graduate classes in sport philosophy and sport ethics and advises master and doctoral students in sport ethics study. At the Center, professionals model ethical conduct; perform global research on competitive ethics, moral reasoning, and character development; develop and provide teaching methodologies and curricula supporting the practical application of moral reasoning in competitive communities; sponsor conferences through which participants utilize practical application of moral reasoning to confront problematic ethical reasoning and action; provide professional training programs to help decision makers navigate current ethical issues or trends; nurture a commitment to ethics, moral reasoning, and character development within competitive communities; and serve academic, professional, and public agencies in developing competitive moral excellence.

SPECIALIZED COURSE WORK, DEGREES, AND WORK EXPERIENCE NEEDED FOR THIS CAREER
An advanced degree in pedagogy and sport ethics is necessary for this career, as well as the good fortune to work in such an environment.

SATISFYING ASPECTS
Sharon believes she has the greatest job in the world. She works with young, intelligent people every day. She travels around the world helping others meet their needs, teaching ethics and moral reasoning. Her teaching, research, and service focus on moral reasoning. She is currently working or has worked with the United States Military Academy, the United States Naval Academy, the United States Air Force Academy, the football team at University of Georgia, the American Bar Association, the NCAA, and the Washington State University College of Veterinary Medicine, as well as at numerous colleges, high schools, and communities that aim to teach some aspect of ethics through their competitive programs.

JOB POTENTIAL

Jobs in this field are available but not abundant. There is an emerging career in Division I sport called the character coach. Most organizations have ethics as a required element, but most need help teaching their own ethical perspectives. There is also a need for good sports ethics teachers and professors. During your graduate work, make sure you are employable and take classes in many different fields, such as sport psychology and exercise physiology.

SUGGESTIONS FOR STUDENTS

First and most important, know yourself. What does it mean to be ethical? Take classes in ethics with physical education professors, and through formal study of ethics and moral development at your university. After graduation, attend an institution that offers an advanced degree in sport ethics or sport philosophy. Make contacts with individuals who work in the field of sport ethics, and develop a research profile that will support your employment with agencies and businesses.

REVIEW QUESTIONS

1. What does *philosophy* mean?
2. Using the philosophy of idealism, contrast the role of the teacher and the role of the student.
3. How do realists seek truth?
4. Which philosophy seeks to help students become better functioning members of society, and how is this accomplished?
5. Which philosophy focuses on self-realization for each student?
6. Which philosophies stress using a problem-solving approach?
7. How would a naturalist emphasize attaining individual goals?
8. How can a physical educator, exercise scientist, or sport leader teach ethics?
9. Why is a personal philosophy of physical education, exercise science, and sport important?
10. What is an eclectic philosophy?

STUDENT ACTIVITIES

1. Select one of the five traditional philosophies discussed in this chapter and write a two-page paper explaining how it applies to your physical education, exercise science, and sport experiences as a student.
2. The class is divided into five groups, with each group adopting one of the five traditional philosophies. Each group is to prepare and present a five-minute defense, based on their assigned philosophy, of the inclusion of required daily physical education classes in the schools.

3. Respond to each of the 10 situations listed on pages 125–128 and be prepared to discuss them in class. Be ready to justify your opinions.
4. Write your personal philosophy of physical education, exercise science, or sport.
5. Ask a person in a physical education, exercise science, or sport career to explain to you his or her personal philosophy.

REFERENCES

Kohlberg L: *The philosophy of moral development: moral stages and the idea of justice,* New York, 1981, Harper & Row.

Kretchmar RS: *Practice philosophy of sport,* Champaign, IL, 1994, Human Kinetics.

SUGGESTED READINGS

Bond JW: Applied sport psychology: philosophy, reflections, and experience, *Int J of Sp Psy* 33(1):19, 2002. This article describes the field of applied sport psychology from philosophical and experiential perspectives.

Brown DA: Pierre de Coubertin's Olympic exploration of modernism, 1894–1914: aesthetics, ideology and the spectacle, *Res Q for Exer & Sp* 67(2):121, 1996. This article explores the aesthetic ideas of the founder of the modern Olympic Games and how the symbols associated with Olympism might be conceptualized in the aesthetic movement known as modernism.

Capwell EM, Smith BJ, Shirreffs J, Olsen LK: Development of a unified code of ethics for the health education profession: a report of the national task force on ethics in health education, *Health Ed* 31(4):212, 2000. The members of this task force briefly describe the process of developing the code of ethics for the health education profession. The complete code and an abbreviated version are included.

Conn JH, Gerdes DA: Ethical decision making: issues and applications to American sport, *Phys Educ* 55(3):121, 1998. This article focuses on ethical decision making in the context of sport.

Lumpkin A, Cuneen J: Developing a personal philosophy of sport, *JOPERD* 72(8):40, 2001. This article asks readers to reflect on five questions and then follow five steps in the development of a personal philosophy of sport. This process can be enhanced by responding to some hypothetical dilemmas in sport.

Lumpkin A, Stoll SK, Beller JM: *Sport ethics—applications for fair play* (3rd ed.), Boston, 2003, McGraw-Hill. This book describes moral reasoning and fair play behavior as a foundation for chapters on elimination, eligibility, intimidation and sportsmanship, violence, ergogenic aids, commercialization, racial equity, and gender equity.

Malloy DC, Zakus DH: Ethical decision making in sport administration: a theoretical inquiry into substance and form, *J of Sp Mgmt* 9:36, 1995. A synthesis of four philosophical approaches to ethics and two psychological approaches to moral reasoning are presented as ways to understand the decision-making behavior of sport managers.

McCallister SG, Blinde EM, Weiss WM: Teaching values and implementing philosophies: dilemmas of the youth sport coach, *Phys Educ* 57(1):35, 2000. This study indicates that youth sport coaches generally have good intentions to provide a positive and wholesome learning environment for children playing baseball and softball, even though external pressures make this difficult.

Priest RF, Krause JV, Beach J: Four-year changes in college athletes' ethical value choices in sports situations. *Res Q for Exer & Sp* 70(2):170, 1999. Over four years, 631 male and female students attending the United States Military Academy who participated in intercollegiate team and individual sports decreased in making moral choices in sport. In addition, the athletes believed their coaches were more likely to make unethical choices than they were.

Panagiotopoulos D: The legal aspects of sports ethics and the protection of fair play, *Int J of Phys Educ* 35(3):99, 1998. The author suggests that a legislative approach to sports is necessary to safeguard the spirit of fair play and sports ethics and to punish those who violate sport rules.

CHAPTER

5

SELECTING A CAREER

KEY CONCEPTS

- Self-assessment inventories help identify individual characteristics and desired lifestyles that influence career choices.
- Numerious settings foster the teaching-learning process but differ in clientele, work hours, and related responsibilities.
- Programs for the development of fitness offer careers for those interested in helping others incorporate healthful habits and practices into their lives.
- Schools, colleges, nonschool agencies, and professional leagues expect coaches, administrators, trainers, officials, and other personnel to direct and provide quality athletic programs.
- Many schools and public and private organizations need individuals with sport management knowledge to direct their programs.
- Sport marketing has grown to be a multimillion-dollar business as it capitalizes on the nation's enthusiasm for fitness, sports, and leisure activities.

Career choices today are more complex decisions than ever before because of the obsolescence of some jobs, the burgeoning of technology, the demographic shifts in population, the acceptance of women and minorities in more jobs in the work force, and economic necessity. People seldom continue in their initial career choices; they change jobs several times during their working years.

The preceding chapters described the broad spectrum of physical education, exercise science, and sport, laying the foundation for the career options presented in this chapter. You should now be prepared to assess objectively your future career. This assessment is not a one-time event but an ongoing process. Your initial career choice is not necessarily a lifetime commitment, but it should be reevaluated periodically. As you read this chapter and assess your interests, abilities, and goals, remember that you are choosing a career pathway, not necessarily a single job.

Before embarking on this process, identify your attitudes and expectations. Your attitude toward a career greatly influences whether you will be successful

---

BOX 5-1   FACTORS INFLUENCING CAREER CHOICES

Using the scale below, indicate how you value each of the following in relation to your selection of a career:

5	4	3	2	1
Most highly valued	Strong influencing factor	Average consideration	Weak influencing factor	Not valued at all

_____ Influence of family and significant others
_____ Identification with role model(s)
_____ Knowledgeable about many aspects of this career
_____ Would personally enjoy this career
_____ Enjoy working with people
_____ Desire to serve others
_____ Ease of entrance into this career
_____ Monetary and other benefits from this career
_____ Time compatibility (work hours versus leisure time) meets expectations
_____ Job security available in this career
_____ Job location close to family and friends

From the list above, select the five that you think are most important to you in your career choice and write them (in descending order of importance) in the spaces below.

1. _____
2. _____
3. _____
4. _____
5. _____

Other factors influencing your career choice:
_____
_____

---

and happy. A major factor is your self-concept: How do you evaluate your abilities? Are you willing to listen to the advice of teachers, coaches, parents, and others? Can you objectively assess your personal strengths and weaknesses? Are you people oriented? Are you motivated to do your best?

Before considering available careers, analyze the relative importance of some personal and job-related factors. Two self-assessment inventories are provided in Boxes 5-1 and 5-2. Your responses to these inventories will help you determine which physical education, exercise science, or sport career best meets your needs and aspirations.

BOX 5-2　LIFESTYLE PREFERENCE ASSESSMENT

1. Where would you prefer to live (state or region)? _____
2. Do you prefer to work for yourself or for others? _____
3. Do you prefer a large or small work environment? _____
4. What ages would you prefer to interact with daily? _____
   _____
5. Do you prefer an outdoor or indoor work environment? _____
6. Do you prefer a sedentary or an active job? _____
7. How much travel (if any) would you want as a regular part of your work? _____
   _____
8. What days of the week would you prefer to work? _____
9. What hours of the day would you prefer to work? _____
10. What salary would you need now? _____ In 10 years? _____
11. How much vacation time would you want each year? _____
12. What fringe benefits would you want as part of your job? _____
    _____
    _____
13. How important to you is career advancement? _____
14. What other job characteristics do you think would be important to your job satisfaction?
    _____
    _____

FACTORS INFLUENCING CAREER CHOICES

Family influences regarding a career choice can be positive, negative, or both. Parents may overtly or subtly persuade you to pursue a career on which they place a high value. Many parents have forbidden their children to major in physical education because they view it as frivolous, nonacademic, or not prestigious enough. On the other hand, parents may push their children into a career in sports because of their own rewarding past experiences. Regardless of the situation, remember that your family will not be going to work for you each day or fulfilling the responsibilities of your chosen career. Although parents, siblings, and significant others can express their opinions and share their experiences, they should not decide for you.

Whether consciously or not, many people select a career because they respect and admire someone who is in a particular position, a role model whom they wish to emulate. This may be a parent, sibling, coach, teacher, or friend who has demonstrated enjoyment of and dedication to a career that you wish to share. One cautionary note: You may not be able to find the same type of position or may not possess the same abilities. Remember, you need to develop your own niche rather than trying to mimic another person.

The skills, knowledge, abilities, and experiences that you bring to your career will influence whether you are successful. This is not to imply that all career

One aspect of career satisfaction comes from maintaining personal fitness at the health club where you help others do the same.

preparation precedes employment; certainly considerable learning occurs while you are on the job. Your confidence in accepting an initial position is based on two factors, only one of which is prior formal preparation. Always remember the importance of the second factor: gaining experiences, including voluntary or internship experiences, that may enhance your chances of career change or advancement.

An important criterion for continuation in a job is the level of personal fulfillment and satisfaction. If you dread going to work, hate the day-to-day routine, and think the negative aspects far outweigh the positive gains, it is probably time for a change. It is not disastrous to sacrifice job security and material benefits to start a career that enhances self-worth and pleasure. One way to make a career change less traumatic is to prepare yourself for a broad physical education, exercise science, and sport career pathway that can offer you numerous alternatives.

Some people prefer a solitary setting; others need to interact frequently with people. If you are people oriented, you need to identify the ages of those with whom you find the greatest enjoyment and seek a career that includes these opportunities. It is also important to identify which aspects of working with people you enjoy most. Do you prefer to work with large groups, small groups, or one on one? Do you prefer constant or periodic interactions? Can you make decisions with others or concerning others?

Sometimes interaction with others is so highly valued that your personal needs become secondary to those of others. This characteristic is known as *altruism*. Teachers in various settings focus on helping their students develop healthy lifestyles, even though their own material benefits seem small compared to the hours spent in instruction.

Career opportunities in physical education, exercise science, and sport are expanding. Your expertise is needed because of increased leisure time, higher standards of living, and the emphasis on fitness. However, your ideal job in the exact location you wish and with the dreamed-for salary may not be available. After realizing that jobs are available for educated individuals who actively seek them, you must be willing to accept the probability of starting at the bottom. As a young professional, you can expect to work hard, volunteer for extra duties, learn new ideas, gain experiences, and accept less desirable responsibilities as a test of commitment to your field. If you do so successfully, you will advance.

You must weigh the importance you place on monetary and other material benefits as you choose a career. Your response on the Lifestyle Preference Assessment indicates the value that a certain salary has for you and how it relates to other aspects of your life, such as family, status, location, and travel. The importance that salary has for you is also shown in the hours and days that you prefer to work, as well as your desired vacation time. Money, however, is only one type of remuneration. Other benefits, including health insurance, retirement benefits, an expense account, travel, club memberships, and prestige, may offset a lower salary. Only you can decide the importance of money and other benefits, but you must do so honestly, since frequently these are pivotal factors in career selection.

A five-day, 8-to-5 workweek is unlikely in many physical education, exercise science, and sport careers. Your career choice could result in working any number of hours a week, nights, holidays, and weekends, and anywhere from 9 to 12 months a year. Only you can weigh your personal preferences versus each job's characteristics. Begrudging time spent working often results in negative feelings toward that task. How important are the amount and scheduling of leisure time for you? How do work hours relate to monetary benefits in importance?

Job security varies dramatically in physical education, exercise science, and sport careers. Competent fulfillment of job responsibilities in some careers results in retention of positions based on merit; careers in educational institutions require earning tenure for job security. Some careers carry no guarantee of future employment other than the demand for your services. Associated with the concept of job security is the potential for advancement. Relocation is often necessary for advancement because the position you qualify for or seek may not be available in the same city or with the same employer. Challenge and stimulation are important to many people for continuation in a career, as are recognition for a job well done and increased material benefits.

As you decide on a career, review and weigh all these factors. Take advantage of your institution's career services office, which can assist you in evaluating various career options. Only after evaluating the most influential considerations and your own personal preferences can you objectively select a career pathway. Regardless of your choice, the key is your commitment and motivation.

Box 5-3 provides a broad overview of career opportunities. The rest of this chapter describes these broad categories and some of the options, presenting educational requirements, job availability, and positive and negative aspects. After you have finished this chapter, refer to Figure 5-1 for sample questions to ask of professionals in any of the careers you are considering.

BOX 5-3   CAREER OPPORTUNITIES IN PHYSICAL EDUCATION, EXERCISE SCIENCE, AND SPORT

Teaching

Adapted physical education (K–12)
College/university (including research)
Corporate fitness
Cruise ship
Dance studio
Elementary public school (K–6)
Health club
Junior/community college
Middle public school (5–8)
Military
Private elementary school (K–6)
Private secondary school (7–12)
Recreation department
Resort
Secondary public school (7–12)
Senior citizens' program
Sport camp or school
Sport club

Fitness

Cardiac rehabilitation
Corporate fitness
Country club
Dance studio
Fitness and nutritional counseling
Health science professional
Health spa
Massage clinic
Private sport club
Protective services (police and fire)
Recreation department
Research laboratory
Sports medicine clinic
Stress management clinic
Therapeutic recreation
Weight control center

Athletics

Academic counseling
Athletic administration
Athletic training
Business management
Coaching
Facility management
Sports information
Sports marketing
Sport officiating
Sport psychology
Strength and conditioning coach
Ticket sales

Sport Management

Corporate fitness
Equipment research and design
Facility management
Intramurals/campus recreation
Program/department chair
Public fitness and recreation
Resort
Sport camp/school
Sport club
Sport hall of fame and museum
Theme park

Sport Marketing

Book sales
Clothing sales
Club membership sales
Equipment sales

Sport Communication

Sport broadcasting
Sport journalism
Sport photography

INTERVIEW OUTLINE—SAMPLE QUESTIONS ABOUT POTENTIAL CAREERS

Name: _____

Title: _____

Company or Institution: _____

JOB RESPONSIBILITIES AND HOURS

What are your primary job responsibilities?

_____

_____

_____

_____

_____

_____

What are your normal work hours? Are these typical?

_____

Is overtime or extra work required? If so, how often and for how long?

_____

What is the salary range for people in your career?

_____

SPECIALIZED COURSE WORK, DEGREES, AND WORK EXPERIENCES NEEDED FOR THIS CAREER

What specialized experiences were necessary as a prerequisite to being qualified for this career?

_____

_____

_____

What academic degrees, certifications, or licenses are required to do your job?

_____

_____

_____

_____

FIGURE 5-1

What course work that you completed is most useful in fulfilling your job responsibilities?

_____

_____

_____

SATISFYING ASPECTS OF YOUR CAREER

What are the most satisfying aspects of your career?

_____

_____

_____

_____

_____

Are there any aspects of your career that you dislike?

_____

_____

_____

_____

_____

JOB POTENTIAL

What are the opportunities for advancement (salary, responsibility, and promotion) in this career?

_____

_____

_____

_____

_____

SUGGESTIONS FOR STUDENTS

What suggestions and advice can you give students considering a career like yours?

_____

_____

_____

_____

_____

FIGURE 5-1 (continued)

TEACHING

Schools and Colleges

Employment for college graduates with majors in physical education has traditionally been in public and private schools. Teaching remains a viable choice for both beginning and lifelong careers. Teachers' salaries are determined by each state's salary schedule and local school district supplements. Additional stipends for extra responsibilities, like coaching, are possible. Base salaries for beginning teachers with baccalaureate degrees will be at least $20,000, with many school systems paying more and some offering signing bonuses due to teacher shortages. To find jobs, graduates may have to move to smaller communities, urban settings, or different states. In the last situation, a reciprocal agreement may exist between the certifying state and the new state, or additional course work may be required before full certification is granted.

Many states require *The Praxis Series: Professional Assessments for Beginning Teachers* for certification. This three-part series includes Praxis I (tests reading, writing, and mathematics skills needed by all teachers), Praxis II (measures prospective teachers' knowledge of their major fields of study), and Praxis III (judges actual teaching skill through the use of trained assessors).

Junior high and senior high physical educators in their first years sometimes teach classes outside their major fields. Preparing to teach in a second subject area through taking courses and obtaining certification will enhance the likelihood of securing a teaching position. Willingness to accept these teaching assignments may lead to full-time physical education positions in subsequent years. The physical educator, although perhaps not prepared to teach or interested in teaching health, frequently is assigned classes in this area as well. Some schools hire certified health educators and others have health consultants, but because of budget constraints many health classes are taught by physical educators in secondary schools. Physical education teachers work a minimum of seven hours at school, which usually includes one planning period and at least five classes. In addition, the teacher is expected to plan classes; grade papers; monitor the halls, lunchroom, and buses; and complete administrative reports. Some secondary teachers face discipline problems, apathetic students, student drug abuse, inadequate facilities and equipment, lack of administrative and community support, and sometimes even violent behaviors of students. On the other hand, professional involvement and educational enrichment are encouraged by supportive administrators. Low salaries deter some good candidates from choosing teaching careers, while opportunities to positively influence students' lives, retirement and health benefits, summer vacations, and job security are attractive job characteristics.

Adapted physical education specialists are hired most frequently by large systems and state departments of education so that many schools may share the expertise of one individual. This specialist helps classroom teachers and physical educators meet the needs of students with special needs or limitations who have been included in regular classes, or they may individualize instruction for students. Educational background and experience emphasizing adapted physical education is important for this career. Hours and salaries correspond with those of other teachers.

In some states, elementary school physical educators are in demand; in others, jobs are scarce. Their responsibilities vary from teaching daily classes for children at one school to conducting ten 30-minute classes at a different school each day of the week. The intrinsic satisfaction of helping children learn and develop is the reward these teachers cite most often. The benefits of positively influencing children's attitudes toward movement skills and encouraging healthy lifestyles outweigh problems like inadequate facilities and equipment and limited administrative support.

Teaching physical education in junior or community colleges or in four-year colleges and universities requires education beyond a bachelor's degree. In smaller institutions, faculty with master's degrees are expected to teach pre-major or major courses. Most institutions also require sports and activity instructors to have master's degrees. Since university activity instructors and small college teachers spend most of their time teaching rather than conducting research, job security or tenure is based primarily on teaching and service rather than on scholarly productivity. (These same teachers are often expected to advise students and to serve on departmental and university committees.) Beginning salaries range widely according to location and status of the institution, with benefits including health insurance, retirement programs, and summer vacations. In their activity and theory classes, these teachers enjoy helping adult students learn healthy lifestyles and relish the generalist approach to teaching physical education three to six hours per day and four to five days a week.

In larger institutions, exercise and sport scientists in specialties such as biomechanics, exercise physiology, sport and exercise psychology, and other

Teaching fundamental skills to children may lead to their continued participation in physical activity throughout life. (Photo courtesy Bob Hilliard.)

disciplines teach undergraduate and graduate courses in addition to conducting research. Research productivity, teaching effectiveness, and professional service are required for tenure, which is granted in five to seven years. For university professors, conducting research, writing articles for professional journals, and giving scholarly presentations are prerequisites for job security. Lack of time for research and class preparation is cited frequently as a problem by university teachers. Although their hours are somewhat flexible, committee meetings, student advising, and other departmental responsibilities besides teaching, research, and service extend the workweek well beyond 40 hours.

Other Instructional Settings

Opportunities abound for those who want to teach fitness and sports skills outside a school environment. Dance studios provide instruction in aerobic, jazz, ballet, tap, and modern dance for children and adults. Individuals with dance majors or specialized dance course work teach various dance forms to customers for fees (ranging from $5 per hour for group lessons to $25 per hour for private lessons) at these studios. Classes may be scheduled throughout the day and evening as well as on weekends.

Sport clubs focus on individual sports, such as tennis, aquatics, or racquetball, and need instructors for private and group lessons. Other clubs, which usually have expensive membership fees, may cater to several sports, such as country clubs that offer swimming, golf, and tennis. Vacation resorts are increasingly providing sports instruction for their guests. Health clubs usually offer fitness programs in aerobic conditioning and weight training; sports instruction, such as in racquetball; and sometimes classes in stress management and weight control. Because of the tremendous variety in clubs, salaries depend on location,

Teachers must be knowledgeable, organized, good communicators, enthusiastic, and respectful of others, as well as possess interpersonal skills and demonstrate professional integrity. (Photo courtesy Bob Hilliard.)

clientele, instructional expertise, and assigned responsibilities. Salaries for instructors may start at $8 to $10 an hour and increase as responsibilities grow.

Sport camps have become booming businesses related to commercial recreation. Both children and adults attend these highly successful ventures in the summer or on weekends and holidays. Sport camps provide excellent opportunities for gaining teaching experience and making valuable contacts that may lead to permanent positions. For school teachers looking for summer employment, opportunities abound in sport camps. Expertise in teaching one or more activities is important for employment, as is a desire to work with various age and skill levels. Responsibilities, such as those of an instructor or program director, determine salaries, which may vary widely. Day camp instructors may earn $25 to $50 per day, while residence camp instructors can expect salaries at about twice this level.

Golf instruction is popular in schools and colleges as well as in private and public clubs.

Concomitant with increasing lifespans in the United States is the critical need for professionals trained to provide recreational and leisure activities for senior citizens. Today approximately 20 percent of the population of the United States is 65 years of age or older. Federal programs, as well as private agencies, increasingly must provide physical activity programs in retirement homes, elder care centers, and senior citizens' apartment complexes. The job potential for individuals trained to prescribe and to direct activities for this clientele will expand rapidly in the years ahead.

Opportunities to teach and lead sport and fitness programs in the military abound because fitness training is highly valued by the various branches of the armed services. Instructional assignments in physical fitness programs are available to enlistees. Civilians instruct at the service academies, on military installations, and at special training facilities. Programs for the military vary widely, from basic conditioning drills for men and women to broad-based fitness and sport opportunities for career personnel to family-oriented recreational offerings. Highly competitive leagues in a variety of sports are commonplace on most military bases, since skilled, fit servicemen and servicewomen are valued. As an employee of the federal government, your pay would depend on classification, but benefits are excellent.

FITNESS, EXERCISE, AND SPORT SCIENCE

Many large corporations provide fitness centers for their executives. Concerns about work efficiency and loss of time and money from absenteeism have resulted in elaborate facilities to provide daily aerobic, strength, and flexibility workouts for more and more employees. The directors of these corporate fitness centers are usually individuals trained in one of the exercise sciences with a bachelor's degree. However, because of the attractiveness of these jobs and the in-depth knowledge needed, holders of master's degrees are often hired. Minimally, each individual should hold a certification as an exercise leader (such as that given by the American College of Sports Medicine), if not a higher certification such as an exercise specialist. Directors of corporate fitness centers are responsible for designing individually prescribed programs that include exercise sessions, nutritional changes, stress management hints, and other recommended lifestyle alterations. Close monitoring is required because for many people, these programs dramatically alter previous habits. Since lack of adherence is the primary reason goals are not achieved, these exercise scientists and leaders, along with their instructional staffs, must constantly motivate participants to adhere to their prescribed programs. In addition, personnel and program management skills are critical in these corporate settings.

Many companies have extended their fitness programs and recreational services to include all employees. Although these programs are not as elaborate as those for executives, management has realized the interrelationship between exercise and work efficiency; thus, graduates of physical education, exercise science, and sport studies programs are needed to provide the supervision and instruction for these programs. Working with people in a nonstructured setting appeals to many professionals in spite of the hours, which are frequently scheduled during workers' leisure time.

Fitness clubs offer several types of aerobic exercise machines, weight-training equipment, and usually personal trainers.

Many corporations have chosen to subcontract their fitness programs. In this arrangement, the business provides the site, but all daily administration and staff are provided by an outside supplier. This management firm hires fitness specialists to teach classes and to instruct one on one. Instructors can expect starting salaries of around $20,000, with significant variance depending on the location, number of clients served, and experience. Often corporate and commercial fitness centers contract with sports medicine clinics so that employees and members can receive treatment and rehabilitation services as needed.

Related to corporate fitness is the need for professionals to design and implement training programs for workers in the protective services (public safety officers). Exercise scientists are being hired to test the fitness levels of these workers and prescribe exercise programs to meet employees' individual needs and prepare them to meet the demands of their jobs. Observing positive lifestyle changes is rewarding.

The fitness emphasis pervading the United States has led to a proliferation of public facilities and programs promoting lifestyle changes for various groups. Directors and program coordinators organize and implement fitness programs, sport teams, and various social activities. Job security is good; however, few advancement opportunities exist unless management skills learned in this setting are transferred to a related career. The minimal wages earned in many part-time positions in public recreation are offset by the invaluable experiences gained.

Cardiac rehabilitation programs have grown out of the need to help heart attack and heart disease patients regain their health and develop fit lifestyles. Programs at universities, community centers, hospitals, private clinics, and many other settings provide the exercises and activities prescribed by physicians and implemented by individuals with degrees in physical education, exercise science, and sport studies.

LEISURE SERVICES

Programming and Instruction

Recreation and leisure services are allied fields with physical education, exercise science, and sport. Recreation and leisure services professionals provide activities and programs for individuals of all ages and ability levels. The private sector provides millions of jobs in commercial recreation. Many physical education and recreation graduates obtain their first jobs in the following areas:

- Lodging—management, operation, and programming for individuals associated with housing services, such as resorts, cruise ships, and camps
- Recreation—planning, management, and operation of recreational programs, facilities, and areas for agencies such as commercial/private, governmental, volunteer, industrial, outdoor, and therapeutic institutions
- Entertainment services—management, operation, and programming for such organizations as theme parks, racetracks, and toy and game manufacturers
- Culture services—management, operation, and programming for institutions that deal with the fine arts, such as museums and historical sites
- Sports—management, operation, and programming for athletic areas and facilities, such as racquetball and tennis complexes, health and fitness clubs, and professional athletic organizations

Although numerous opportunities exist in these areas, probably the sports sub-cluster appeals to most individuals, with instruction and program planning being the major types of jobs available. Tennis, golf, and swimming are among the popular types of specific sports clubs; multisport complexes also exist. Health and fitness clubs are examples of these general and specific types of leisure-service organizations.

All of these activity-related clubs or businesses require membership, thereby excluding a segment of the population. Most individuals who work for these organizations are encouraged, if not required, to sell memberships as one of their responsibilities. Hours vary by club but are usually in the afternoons, in the evening, and on weekends, since these are members' leisure hours. Job security varies with each person's expertise; however, potential for advancement into management and even ownership is good. Benefits include working with people and seeing their improvement, as well as having the opportunity to maintain your own healthy lifestyle in these settings. Social skills, sales ability, and sports

The thrill of activities like rock climbing attracts many enthusiasts to careers in recreation. (Photo courtesy Aram Attarian.)

expertise are more important than a college degree, although being knowledgeable about the components of physical fitness and having expertise in skill analysis are quite helpful. Attaining a national certification in exercise testing or as a personal trainer can increase career options and lead to a higher salary.

The lodging subcluster includes resorts, condominium complexes, and camps that are increasingly hiring specialists in golf, tennis, swimming, and other sports to organize and instruct groups and individuals. For these recreation directors, hours vary to meet the needs of the guests, but the pleasant work environment may compensate for not having a typical schedule.

City and county recreation departments offer a broad spectrum of activities, from instructional classes to league play to trips and special events. Teachers are especially needed early mornings, afternoons, and evenings, but also throughout the day. Recreational classes are offered in water aerobics, rock climbing, massage, cross-country skiing, karate, arts and crafts, parent and child aerobics, various types of dance, and racquetball. During the summers and evening hours, competitive and recreational leagues abound in basketball, baseball, football, volleyball, softball, soccer, tennis, and other popular sports.

Sponsored trips to museums, art events, state parks, zoos, and other attractions especially appeal to retirees and families. Fun runs, road races, and triathlons attract serious competitors as well as weekend athletes. The availability of facilities for a private swim, weight-training session, or workout on a stationary bike or for

a pickup basketball game also falls under the responsibility of recreation departments. Therefore, program supervisors and administrators have major responsibility for providing and scheduling facilities to ensure that events operate smoothly.
In the future, recreation departments will increasingly be charged with the preser-
vation of green space in cities to ensure that park areas are available for use during
leisure hours. Recreation professionals who teach can anticipate starting salaries
around $30,000. These salaries will grow as management responsibilities increase.

Rehabilitative

An outgrowth of the desire for a healthy lifestyle is the proliferation of specialized
clinics and counseling centers, including those for weight control, massage, nutrition, and stress management. Weight control centers sometimes promote a particular diet or system and usually provide information about nutrition and encourage
safe exercise. In massage, a method of tension release and relaxation, one manip-
ulates the body with various stroking, kneading, rubbing, or tapping motions.
Wellness programs emphasize the development of nutritional, exercise, and
attitudinal lifestyle changes through counseling and participatory sessions. The
proliferation of stress management classes, clinics, seminars, workshops, and
counseling centers reflects the demand for information and for preventive and corrective strategies. Since these are fee-based businesses, salaries vary dramatically.

In sports medicine clinics on college campuses and in hospitals, physicians,
physical therapists, and athletic trainers treat and rehabilitate sports-related injuries. Team physicians for professional, college, school, and community teams
must have earned medical degrees before specializing in this field. Physical therapists must be licensed.

ATHLETICS

Schools and Colleges

A second career aspiration of many secondary school and some elementary
school physical educators is coaching the numerous teams for boys and girls.
Many schools have coaching vacancies, but no teaching positions in physical education because of the resignations of some physical educators from coaching
but not from teaching and because of the increased number of girls' teams. If
certified in and willing to teach in a second subject area, the teacher/coach is automatically more marketable. Coaching positions in the more visible sports of
basketball and football are not as easy to obtain as those in other sports, and
more openings exist for coaches of girls' sports than for boys' teams (see the
Research View box "National Standards for Athletic Coaches").

In many schools, coaches are expected to work with more than one team
and sometimes may have to work with as many as three teams. Some states allow
nonteachers or substitute teachers to coach; others allow only employees of the
school system to be hired. Monetary supplements (ranging from $1,000 to
$10,000) are minimal compared with the long hours and innumerable demands

RESEARCH VIEW

National Standards for Athletic Coaches

The National Association for Sport and Physical Education published its National Standards for Athletic Coaches in 1995. The purpose of these standards is to provide coaches, athletic administrators, athletes, parents, and the public with the guidelines for the skills and knowledge that coaches should possess. These standards describe the basic competencies required of coaches, with the goal of ensuring enjoyment and skill development of athletes along with their health and safety. The 37 standards are grouped into 8 categories.

Injuries: Prevention, Care, and Management

Standard 1	Prevent injuries by recognizing and insisting on safe playing conditions.
Standard 2	Ensure that the protective equipment is in good condition, fits properly, and is worn as prescribed by the manufacturer; ensure that equipment and facilities meet required standards [American Society for Testing Materials (ASTM) and U.S. Consumer Product Safety Commission (USCPSC)].
Standard 3	Recognize that proper conditioning and good health are vital to the prevention of athletic injuries.
Standard 4	Prevent exposure to the risk of injuries by considering the effects of environmental conditions on the circulatory and respiratory systems when planning and scheduling practices and contests and implementing programs for physical conditioning.
Standard 5	Be able to plan, coordinate, and implement procedures for appropriate emergency care.
Standard 6	Demonstrate skill in the prevention, recognition, and evaluation of injuries and the ability to assist athletes with the recovery/rehabilitation from injuries that are generally associated with participation in athletics in accordance with guidelines provided by qualified medical personnel.
Standard 7	Facilitate a unified medical program of prevention, care, and management of injuries by coordinating the roles and actions of the coach and a National Athletic Trainers' Association (NATA) certified athletic trainer with those of the physician.
Standard 8	Provide coaching assistants, athletes, and parents/guardians with education about injury prevention, injury reporting, and sources of medical care.

(continued)

Risk Management

Standard 9   Understand the scope of legal responsibilities that comes with assuming a coaching position, i.e., proper supervision, planning and instruction, matching participants, safety, first aid, and risk management.

Standard 10   Properly inform coaching assistants, athletes, and parents/guardians of the inherent risks associated with sport so that decisions about participation can be made with informed consent.

Standard 11   Know and convey the need and availability of appropriate medical insurance.

Standard 12   Participate in continuing education regarding rules changes, improvements in equipment, philosophical changes, improved techniques, and other information in order to enhance the safety and success of the athlete.

Growth, Development, and Learning

Standard 13   Recognize the developmental physical changes that occur as athletes move from youth through adulthood and know how these changes influence the sequential learning and performance of motor skills in a specific sport.

Standard 14   Understand the social and emotional development of the athletes being coached, know how to recognize problems related to this development, and know where to refer them for appropriate assistance when necessary.

Standard 15   Analyze human performance in terms of developmental information and individual body structure.

Standard 16   Provide instruction to develop sport-specific motor skills and refer the athletes to appropriate counsel as needed.

Standard 17   Provide learning experiences appropriate to the growth and development of the age group coached.

Training, Conditioning, and Nutrition

Standard 18   Demonstrate a basic knowledge of physiological systems and their responses to training and conditioning.

Standard 19   Design programs of training and conditioning that properly incorporated the mechanics of movement and sound physiological principles taking into account each individual's ability and medical history, avoiding contraindicated exercises and activities and guarding against the possibility of over-training; be able to modify programs as needed.

Standard 20   Demonstrate knowledge of proper nutrition and educate athletes about the effects of nutrition upon health and physical performance.

(continued)

Standard 21   Demonstrate knowledge of the use and abuse of drugs and promote sound chemical health.

Social/Psychological Aspects of Coaching

Standard 22   Subscribe to a philosophy that acknowledges the role of athletics in developing the complete person.

Standard 23   Identify and interpret to co-coaches, athletes, concerned others, and the general public the values that are to be developed from participation in sports programs.

Standard 24   Identify and apply ethical conduct in sport by maintaining emotional control and demonstrating respect for athletes, officials, and other coaches.

Standard 25   Demonstrate effective motivational skills and provide positive, appropriate feedback.

Standard 26   Conduct practices and competitions to enhance the physical, social, and emotional growth of athletes.

Standard 27   Be sufficiently familiar with the basic principles of goal setting to motivate athletes toward immediate and long range goals.

Standard 28   Treat each athlete as an individual while recognizing the dynamic relationship of personality and socio-cultural variables such as gender, race, and socio-economic differences.

Standard 29   Identify desirable behaviors (self-discipline, support of teammates, following directions, etc.) and structure experiences to develop such behaviors in each athlete.

Skills, Tactics, and Strategies

Standard 30   Identify and apply specific competitive tactics and strategies appropriate for the age and skill levels involved.

Standard 31   Organize and implement materials for scouting, planning practices, and analysis of games.

Standard 32   Understand and enforce the rules and regulations of appropriate bodies that govern sport and education.

Standard 33   Organize, conduct, and evaluate practice sessions with regard to established program goals that are appropriate for different stages of the season.

Teaching and Administration

Standard 34   Know the key elements of sport principles and technical skills as well as the various teaching methods that can be used to introduce and refine them.

Standard 35   Demonstrate objective and effective procedures for the evaluation and selection of personnel involved in the athletic program and for periodic program reviews.

(continued)

Professional Preparation and Development

Standard 36   Demonstrate organizational and administrative efficiency in implementing sports programs, e.g., event management, budgetary procedures, facility maintenance, and participation in public relations activities.

Standard 37   Acquire sufficient practical field experience and supervision in the essential coaching areas to ensure an adequate level of coaching competence for the level of athlete coached. This would include a variety of knowledge, skills, and experiences.

placed on coaches. In some high schools, job security for football and basketball coaches does not exist unless winning teams are consistently produced. Victories are not as critical to job retention for coaches of other sports.

Other athletic opportunities within schools include athletic training, sport officiating, and administration. High school sport officials normally work at other jobs and umpire or referee only as a hobby or a second job. A former coach or current coach usually serves as the school's athletic director. This individual coordinates team schedules, budgets, and facilities, and supervises the overall athletic program.

Athletic programs vary dramatically depending on the size of a college. In junior or community colleges and small four-year colleges and universities, many coaches teach in physical education or in other departments, with coaching remaining a secondary responsibility. These individuals receive coaching supplements to their salaries and/or reduced teaching loads. Most sports at these institutions are non–revenue producing, although for some teams recruiting is expected, since athletic grants-in-aid are awarded. At larger universities, coaches of non–revenue-producing sports usually hold full-time positions in athletics, although some may also carry out assigned administrative responsibilities. Other coaches at larger institutions teach or coach only part time.

The teacher/coach, administrator/coach, part-time coach, or full-time coach frequently works day and night because of the increasing competitiveness of intercollegiate athletics (and the rewards that accrue to the victorious). Seldom is there an off-season or free time. While most college coaches have earned master's degrees, this is not a prerequisite, and the major field does not have to be physical education, although it often is. Ways of gaining entrance into college coaching vary. For example, you may volunteer to serve as an assistant or as a graduate student assistant coach, you may earn an assistant coach's position after a successful high school coaching career, or you may win a job because of outstanding achievements as a collegiate or professional athlete. In most cases, future head coaches, even those at small institutions and for non–revenue-producing sports, must get experience serving as successful assistant coaches.

Once jobs are obtained, most coaches, although not guaranteed tenure, retain them as long as they abide by the rules, keep their athletes content, maintain their desire to coach, and develop successful programs. In larger institutions, most football and basketball coaches have job security only when they win and show that they can handle the pressures of the job without violating institutional, sport governance organization, or other rules. For these coaches, the long hours and pressures are compensated for by the material benefits and the prestige. Most coaches take satisfaction in helping their athletes improve their skills and in seeing them mature as individuals.

Coaches' salaries depend on the sport; the competitive divisions in which their teams play; whether or not their sports are revenue producing; their years of experience; their past won–lost records; and additional benefits such as sport camp revenues, shoe contracts, and radio and television shows. Assistant coaches may receive no salaries, only tuition and fee waivers as graduate students, or may receive starting salaries around $30,000. Part-time coaches, who teach or hold other jobs, can expect stipends ranging from $2,000 to $10,000 depending on the factors listed above. Full-time, head coaches' salaries range from $30,000 to hundreds of thousands of dollars. Entire salary packages for a few coaches with winning records at large universities exceed $1 million.

At small colleges, coaches are often the directors of athletics. As larger universities' athletic programs grew, however, they enter the entertainment business and require administrators to direct them. Athletic directors, associate and assistant directors, fund-raisers, and ticket managers often have earned master's degrees in sport management to prepare them for these careers. Money and people management skills are crucial, as is expertise in public relations, since skyrocketing budgets have made fund-raising vital. When skillfully achieved, all of these factors mesh into a successful athletic program that brings prestige and lucrative benefits to their directors. Security is based on the institution's overall program rather than on one team's performance, although the successes of the revenue-producing sports are certainly most important.

Associated with intercollegiate athletics and vital to their programs are numerous career options. Assistant and associate athletic directors assume responsibility for facility management, compliance with rules such as those of the National Collegiate Athletic Association (NCAA), grants-in-aid, business affairs, fund-raising, and coordination of non–revenue-producing sports. These positions may be filled by coaches, former athletes, or people trained in sport management. Job security is not guaranteed; continuation is based on successful completion of assigned duties. A major benefit is the association with a successful athletic program and its reflected glamour. Individuals in these management positions earn from $30,000 to over $100,000, depending on level of responsibility, experience, and the institution served.

For individuals who wish to combine writing skills with athletics, sports information is an exciting career choice. This vital component of the athletic program is responsible for compiling statistics and personal information about athletes and teams to publicize upcoming events and provide postgame data. Press releases and team brochures further publicize the intercollegiate program. A degree in journalism or sport communication would be appropriate, but volunteer experience and a willingness to start at the lowest level and work upward may be necessary to gain entrance into this athletic career. Travel, personal contacts with players and coaches, and contributing to the success of a program are among the benefits.

Sports promotions specialists are responsible for filling the stadium through advertising and various promotional strategies. At a small college, one person

Sports promotions specialists work to attract fans to intercollegiate competitions. (Photo courtesy Lisa Sense.)

may handle both sports information and sports promotions, or each coach may have to accept these additional responsibilities for his or her team. Large institutions have promotions specialists who frequently share in activities to raise funds for grants-in-aid and facilities. Public relations skills are usually more important than a particular educational degree. These individuals' primary efforts are directed toward bringing money into the athletic department through gifts and donations. Salaries for these individuals are directly linked to their ability to market their teams, resulting in increased ticket sales and donations.

Strength and conditioning coaches design and implement training programs for all athletes. Frequently these positions are filled by exercise scientists with strong exercise physiology and biomechanics backgrounds and those who hold certifications from the National Strength and Conditioning Association. Helping athletes reach their athletic potential is a significant reward for these individuals.

Many professional teams and a few colleges hire sport psychologists to work individually with athletes. Because the athletic skills of all elite athletes are superior, many believe that the key to athletes' achieving optimal performances is mental. Sport and exercise psychologists use biofeedback, relaxation, imagery, and various coping mechanisms to help athletes handle the pressures of competition, achieve their potential, and enjoy their experiences.

Nonschool

More than 20 million children participate on youth sports teams sponsored by recreation departments, private clubs, community service organizations, national sport associations, and churches as well as in after-school physical activity programs. In most cases, the coaches are volunteers; the officials and the league, program, and association directors are usually paid. Many of these same groups also provide athletic competitions for adults, such as softball and basketball leagues, master's swimming events, and road races. Experience gained as a volunteer coach, program administrator or assistant, or official may lead to a full-time job in a recreation-related career.

Professional

Prior playing experience in college and as a professional is an asset for coaches of professional teams, although not necessarily a prerequisite. Coaches are hired on the basis of demonstrated success with high school, college, or professional teams and are fired for not producing winning teams. Lucrative salaries, some in excess of $1 million, help compensate for the pressures to win and constant media bombardment.

Professional sports require hundreds of people working behind the scenes to ensure that events take place as scheduled. A commonality of many of these positions is the need for experience in business and marketing. Responsibilities of the ticket sales staff include season ticket packaging, selling tickets for individual events, and arranging for complimentary seating. Correspondence and direct contacts with fans are extensive, with the greatest challenge always remaining that of trying to satisfy as many fans as possible. Customer satisfaction is essential. No formal educational background is required, but a sport management degree is highly desirable.

Business managers are responsible for planning budgets and administering the expenditures to support the program. Although accountants and secretaries may actually handle the daily transactions, business managers oversee multimillion-dollar budgets and the many personnel who work in this area. A business background is helpful, but on-the-job training in a small program or as an intern may be equally valuable in obtaining a job in this field.

The hours of practice and competition necessary for highly skilled athletes to develop and refine their talents may help qualify them for coaching careers later in life.

WEB CONNECTIONS

1. www.womensportscareers.com/default.htm
   Even though the sports industry is a tough industry to break into,
   Women Sports Services™ can assist you as it has over 100,000
   individuals in their pursuit of careers in sports.

2. www.ncaa.org
   Check out the official site of the National Collegiate Athletic
   Association for employment opportunities in college sports.

3. www.onlinesports.com/pages/CareerCenter.html
   Visit the Online Sports Career Center to learn more about a variety
   of sports careers and search for the right job for you.

4. www.sgma.com/jobs/index.html
   Find out more about sport-related careers in the sporting goods
   industry.

5. www.acsm.org/pdf/Careers.pdf
   Go to this site to learn about the variety of careers in athletic training
   and exercise science.

6. www.ymca.net/employment/ymca_recruiting/employment_frameset.htm
   Look for a job with the YMCAs nationally at this site.

Marketing directors serve various functions, depending on the situation. With teams needing to maintain or increase fan support, their primary responsibility focuses on public relations efforts to increase ticket sales. Radio or television commercials, newspaper advertisements, exciting upcoming events or opponents, or winning records may be used to generate greater spectator interest. Season ticket sales are keys to success, since they stabilize income and indicate increased and consistent fan support. Marketing directors may also help promote team emblems or merchandise. These marketing specialists are hired for their proven ability to fulfill job responsibilities rather than for any educational degree.

Professional sport officiating provides many part-time and some full-time careers (mostly in baseball and basketball). No specific educational background is required, but years of experience are necessary. As early as possible, such as in recreational youth leagues, anyone interested in officiating should start learning the rules and techniques while gaining experience and expertise. There may be some reflective glamour and prestige, but officials often are the "villains" and are only begrudgingly accepted as vital to professional games. After years of success in the high school and college ranks and completion of several training programs, the best-qualified officials may get opportunities to officiate in the professional leagues. Most officials, however, hold other jobs and officiate as a hobby or a second career. Unusual hours and travel are inherent characteristics, but salaries for professional officials are quite good.

SPORT MANAGEMENT

Business and Industry

Golf courses, bowling lanes, gymnastics schools, tennis camps, swimming centers, ice rinks, and health spas all require managers who have administrative skills in addition to knowledge about physical skills. Directors in each of these settings must possess budgetary skills, personnel management abilities, planning knowledge, and supervisory capabilities. Although these organizations are interested primarily in producing profits and thus maintaining high enrollments or large attendance, they must hire qualified instructional staff. These sport managers may earn $30,000 to $50,000 a year.

Corporate fitness programs also demand management, motivational, and supervisory skills. Exercise and sport science and fitness specialists who possess knowledge in public relations and marketing can advance more easily into management positions within corporate fitness programs. Since employers want the dollars spent for fitness programs to result in enhanced worker productivity, the goals are to motivate workers to adhere to fitness programs and increase their active participation.

Theme parks and resorts have become multimillion-dollar ventures providing leisure for people of all ages. Recreation administration and sport management backgrounds are essential for handling the massive budgetary, facility management, and personnel aspects of these businesses.

More than 150 sport halls of fame and museums each year host millions of people who view sports memorabilia and photographs and recall stars of the past. These tourist attractions highlight the achievements of former heroes and heroines, and periodically elect new enshrinees; some host events to promote their respective sports. Sport historians and administrative curators are needed for these careers.

Facility managers are associated with arenas and stadiums at universities, in communities, and with professional teams. To be cost efficient, large facilities must be multipurpose because audiences must be attracted to several different sporting events as well as to concerts, other types of entertainments, and conventions. Some specialized facilities, such as aquatic and ice arenas, are limited to competitive and recreational uses. Facility managers must have planning and organizational abilities as well as personnel management skills. Facility managers work for either a university, a governmental agency, a private corporation, or a professional team. They schedule events around the major team(s) or work for a municipality that rents time to teams. Depending on the size of the facility and the number of scheduled events, the individuals managing them may earn salaries of $40,000 to $80,000.

Schools and Colleges

Administration is another career possibility for physical educators in the schools. This position may be as a department chair who accepts management responsibilities, resulting in a reduced teaching load, or as a principal, headmaster, or superintendent. Advancement can result from successful service to the school, advanced education, or interest and demonstrated competence in these positions. In these jobs, increased salaries parallel longer hours and greater responsibilities.

Colleges and universities have many administrative positions, ranging from program director to department chair to college dean. These careers are open to individuals with doctoral degrees, years of experience, expertise in working with people, and management skills. Competition for these positions is strong. Administrative hassles, such as personnel problems, tight budgets, and day-to-day operational demands, are offset by opportunities to effect program change, lead faculty in the attainment of professional goals, and positively influence students' education.

Intramural recreational sports and campus recreation programs are popular components of collegiate life. Directors, assistant directors, facility supervisors, and program coordinators constitute the staff. Job responsibilities vary from publicity to facility management and from personnel to programming. These intramural and recreational programs are administered through either the physical education department or the office of student affairs. In the first context, the staff may also teach; in the second, they seldom do. Most intramural, recreational sports, or campus recreation professionals have earned at least master's degrees in physical education, exercise science, sport studies, or recreation. Increasingly, the trend is to make these positions nonfaculty, with job security based solely on fulfillment of assigned responsibilities. Rather than the usual school-day hours, these programs operate in the afternoons and evenings and on weekends, the leisure hours of the students they serve. Student interactions in nonacademic activities and the opportunities to administer fun-filled programs attract people to these positions. Entry-level program coordinators may earn $25,000 to $30,000; assistant directors' salaries range from $30,000 to $50,000; directors are paid between $50,000 and $100,000, depending on program size and scope.

SPORT MARKETING

Sporting attire is popular for everyone, whether for exercising, going out on the town, or working. From cross-training shoes to designer warm-up suits to team logo jackets, millions are wearing sports clothing. Billions of dollars of athletic and sports clothing and shoes are sold annually. Regardless of skill level, it seems only oversized tennis rackets, custom-made golf clubs, and autographed baseball gloves are good enough for aspiring athletes. Therefore, jobs are and will continue to be plentiful in the sales and marketing of sporting goods. Expertise in sports is an advantage for people in sales, marketing, and management. Individuals choosing sales may enjoy flexible hours, travel, rapid advancement, and job security if they are good at what they do.

Most administrators and many instructors in health and sports clubs are expected to sell memberships. Those who are especially adept at this task frequently

Sport marketing personnel promote sporting events to attract fans to purchase tickets to see their favorite teams.

advance into management positions with increased marketing responsibilities, such as initiating special promotions.

The design of new equipment and improved facilities requires a great deal of research. Some of this research involves exercise physiologists, biomechanists, and athletic trainers who, because of their expertise and experience, help improve and make safer new equipment and facilities. Safety and improved performance motivate these efforts to produce the best ball or surface. Inventors or innovative designers stand to reap financial benefits if their products gain the same kind of wide acceptance that the makers of specialized golf clubs, for example, have seen.

SPORT COMMUNICATION

The interdependence of the media and sports has created numerous opportunities in the glamour careers of sport broadcasting, sport journalism, and sport photography. Broadcasting opportunities vary from prime-time, national telecasts to special events coverage to sports reporting for a local network. On-the-air experience, expertise in play-by-play announcing, an aptitude for interviewing, and a smooth delivery in reading sports news overshadow an educational degree. Willingness to start in small markets at a salary just above minimum wage is a key to advancement. Cable networks provide another avenue for aspiring sport broadcasters on a variety of dedicated sport channels.

Since sports sell newspapers and magazines and increase television ratings, thereby selling commercial time, professional and college teams are especially sensitive to the media. The sportswriting field attracts a large number of people, although the percentage who succeed in it is small. Many sportswriters have earned college degrees in journalism, but some secure newspaper or magazine jobs because of their past experiences in college sports information offices, their own sports careers, or their background in physical education, exercise science, or sport studies. A sportswriter must possess an inquiring mind, a desire to talk with people, the ability to listen, and the willingness to work unusual hours while under the pressures of deadlines and space limitations.

A sport photographer may start by taking pictures for a college newspaper or yearbook and progress to assignments with a major publication. A thorough understanding of the intricacies of various sports provides a photographer with the insight necessary to capture the essence and meaning of sports as well as the outcome of a particular event. Long hours, low compensation, and little glamour may eventually be rewarded with extensive travel for a national publication.

OTHER RELATED CAREERS

In addition to the aforementioned broad categories of jobs open to physical education, exercise science, and sport studies majors, several other specific careers are available. Many of these, however, require specialized education, training, or certification. For the medical doctor with an interest in sports, there are specializations in exercise physiology, orthopedic surgery, and sports podiatry, as well as the option to serve as a team physician. Sport nutrition and sport and exercise psychology are growing fields for both private practice and consultation with college and professional athletes. Lawyers may choose to emphasize the ever-expanding area of sport law.

Dance careers include not only those of performing artists with national and regional companies but also those of artistic directors, managing directors, development officers, public relations agents, booking agents, dance journalists, and dance photographers. Limited jobs and long hours, though, deter some people from pursuing careers as dancers or in dance-related jobs. No educational degree is required for these positions or for those of studio teachers, yet all who pursue them have spent years developing their expertise.

Rather than viewing the sky as falling, a young professional should view the sky as the limit. Table 5-1 provides an overview of some potential careers, lists the necessary preparation, and indicates salary ranges. Knowing these alternatives

TABLE 5-1

JOB OPPORTUNITIES MATCHED WITH PREREQUISITE EDUCATION AND EXPERIENCES

Type of Career	Education and/or Experiences	Salary Range*
Athletic director in a college	Master's degree; past administrative experience	$50,000–$400,000
Athletic trainer in a college	Master's degree with NATA certification	$30,000–$100,000
Coach in a college	Master's degree; past coaching experience	$30,000–$1,000,000
Exercise scientist in a clinical setting	Master's degree in exercise science, plus certification in area of specialty	$35,000–$70,000
Intramural or campus recreation director	Master's degree, plus experience as a program director in some aspect of this field	$50,000–$100,000
Fitness instructor in a corporate or commercial setting	Baccalaureate degree with exercise science course work; internship and certification preferred	$20,000–$50,000
Personal trainer	Baccalaureate degree with exercise science course work; internship and certification preferred	$20,000–$100,000
Physical therapist	Doctor's degree in physical therapy; license	$40,000–$65,000
Professor in a college	Doctor's degree in area of teaching and research specialization	$45,000–$125,000
Public school coach	Baccalaureate degree; some states also require coach's certification	$1,000–$10,000
Public school (K–12) teacher	Baccalaureate degree with teacher certification	$20,000–$50,000
Recreation department program director	Baccalaureate degree in recreation, plus experience working with people and sports	$40,000–$70,000
Sport broadcaster	Baccalaureate degree, preferably with communication course work and public speaking experiences	$30,000–$100,000
Sport facility director	Master's degree, preferably in sport management	$50,000–$90,000
Sport information director in a college	Master's degree, preferably in sport communication or journalism; extensive experience as a writer	$40,000–$80,000
Sport instructor in a private club, camp, resort, or military installation	Experience with and expertise in sport being taught	$20,000–$50,000
Sport journalist	Baccalaureate degree, preferably with journalism course work, plus writing and publishing experience	Varies widely depending on media, position, and expertise
Sport marketer	Master's degree, preferably in sport management or business administration	$50,000–$200,000
Sport official	Experience at lower levels of competitive sports	$25 to $5,000 per game, plus expenses
Sport psychologist for a professional sports team	Doctor's degree in sport psychology, plus experience working with individuals and teams	$50,000–$100,000
Strength and conditioning coach in a college	Master's degree in exercise science, plus certification	$30,000–$80,000

*Salaries are based on education, experience, expertise, specific job expectations, and location. Almost everyone begins at the lower end of the salary range. Not everyone will advance during a career to the upper end of the salary range.

BOX 5-4   INFORMATION ON CAREERS IN SPORTS

Sport Careers (www.sportscareers.com/?AID=8195483&PID=111858), according to its website, has assisted thousands in finding a career in sports for over 20 years. A subscription includes over 1,000 listings each month in these categories: college athletics, sporting goods, health and fitness, broadcasting and media, recreation, sport venues, professional sports, sporting events, sports associations, professional services, and high schools.

At www.jobsinsports.com, if you choose to subscribe, you can search job databases, look for an internship, locate sports and industry contact information, and post your résumé.

Go to www.sportsemploymentnews.com, where, for the price of a subscription, you can find employment and internship opportunities in professional sports, broadcasting and print media, public relations, sports information, recreation and leisure, sport management, health and fitness, sports promotions, and sporting goods.

Search www.sportsworkers.com for job possibilities without the cost of a subscription.

According to www.workinsports.com/home.asp?referrer=72, by subscribing to Work in Sports, you have access to hundreds of current jobs and internships in sports, can submit résumés, and can obtain contact information of organizations in the sports industry.

Teachers in all settings should serve as role models for healthy lifestyles.

should help you focus on one or more broad areas of interest as you choose a career pathway.

Individuals choosing to enter a career in physical education, exercise science, and sport have the additional challenge of serving as positive role models for fitness and healthy lifestyles. The overweight, unfit person, who also may smoke, use other tobacco products, or abuse alcohol or other drugs, is a poor representative of the principles valued by those in physical education, exercise science, and sport careers. Rather, teachers, coaches, fitness specialists, recreation directors, exercise science professionals, athletic trainers, and sport managers should participate in sports and activities to maintain their fitness lifestyles.

See Box 5-4 for suggestions about how to locate more information about careers.

SUMMARY

In today's rapidly changing, technological world, career changes as often as every 10 years or less have become the norm rather than the exception. Instead of looking at one specialty, you need to become a multispecialist who can make different applications of your knowledge. Young people entering the work force need to bring creativity and imaginative reasoning to their jobs, as well as an adventuresome willingness to accept risks and failures while bouncing back to try again. Your first challenge is to assess your preferences and interests. Factors that influence your career choice(s) include family, role models, knowledge about career alternatives, opportunities to work with certain age groups, ease of entry, salary range, career advancement, time compatibility, job security, and location. Career opportunities abound in physical education, exercise science, and sport in teaching, inside and outside of educational institutions; in developmental and rehabilitative fitness; in school and college athletics; and in sport management, marketing, and communication. After matching your aspirations and abilities with career characteristics, you can select one or more as the focus for your college preparation and initial and subsequent careers.

CAREER PERSPECTIVE

PATRICIA ANN HIELSCHER
President
P.H. Enterprises of Apex, Inc.
Apex, North Carolina

EDUCATION
B.S., Physical Education, University of North Carolina at
Greensboro
M.S., Physical Education, University of North Carolina at
Greensboro

JOB RESPONSIBILITIES AND HOURS

Developing your own sports business permits absolute freedom to design it any way you
wish. Based on her interests and expertise, Pat's business initially offered five related yet
different services and products. While developing her business, Pat conducted volleyball
camps and clinics, marketed and sold volleyball uniforms and equipment, exhibited at
professional conferences, contracted for screen printing of T-shirts sold to various groups,
and offered a consignment program for summer sport camps. Once the business grew
sufficiently to become self-sustaining, she discontinued the volleyball camps and clinics to
focus on sales. Ordering, billing, selling, and stocking her product lines are vital parts of
her responsibilities. Generally Pat works from 8:00 A.M. to 5:00 P.M. and some evenings,
typical hours for this type of career. The amount of time worked determines the salary or
income. Pat has chosen to stay a one-person business because she wants to be able to
guarantee quality to her customers, most of whom she knows; getting rich is not her goal.

SPECIALIZED COURSE WORK, DEGREES, AND WORK EXPERIENCES
NEEDED FOR THIS CAREER

Pat recommends that students interested in forming their own sports products and
services businesses take physical education (with a coaching emphasis), psychology, and
business courses (such as marketing and accounting). Although no degree is absolutely
necessary, based on her experiences, a bachelor's degree in physical education
combined with a business minor and coaching experience would be ideal. Pat has
found her background in coaching, including administrative duties such as managing
a team, ordering equipment, and fund raising, and her master's degree in physical
education most helpful. Coaching, developing personal contacts with people in athletics,
having a general background in sales, and acquiring some work experience in business
are important prerequisites for this career.

SATISFYING ASPECTS

The popularity of sports and leisure activities provides a bountiful market for services
and products that anyone may wish to furnish as a career. Satisfaction comes both from
helping others select the equipment, shoes, and clothing that will enhance their pleasure
in sports participation and from teaching skills that can motivate people to start or
continue participating in a sport. Pat designed her business so she could enjoy a
continued association with female athletes and coaches and maintain involvement in
the promotion of women's sports.

JOB POTENTIAL

There are many jobs for men and women in athletic sales and services throughout the country, especially in urban areas. These opportunities include running one's own business or working for others. For Pat specifically, as owner of her own business, there is no security except that which comes from her belief in herself. While working for others may lead to greater job security, self-employment guarantees maximum freedom to design a custom-made career. Pat adds that her business is successful because 75 percent of it is with people she knows, her products are good quality and priced fairly, and she maintains a pleasant, trusting relationship with her customers.

SUGGESTIONS FOR STUDENTS

First, Pat suggests talking with people in this career and considering their advice. Second, she advocates working for someone else before starting a business to get vital training and experience, especially in marketing, sales, and accounting. Third, she recommends getting experience in athletics as a player, coach, and official to learn the needs and preferences of future customers as well as learn to communicate with them. Last, she cautions not to become discouraged by people who say that women's sports or a particular sport cannot provide a viable career.

REVIEW QUESTIONS

1. What are several factors that may influence one's career choice?
2. What factors may outweigh the importance of one's salary?
3. What are several careers that involve teaching?
4. What are several careers in professional sports?
5. What are the responsibilities of the sport marketing specialist?
6. What are three careers related to the media and sports?
7. What is the job potential for careers in recreational services for senior citizens?
8. In what types of careers would a sport management background be beneficial?
9. What are typical entry-level positions in coaching that may lead to a position as a college coach?
10. What are the major differences between the responsibilities of athletic directors at small colleges and those at large universities?

STUDENT ACTIVITIES

1. Complete the self-assessment inventories in Boxes 5-1 and 5-2 on pages 135–136.
2. Write a three- to five-page essay describing your professional and personal career goals.

3. Compile a list of the abilities and characteristics needed for success in your prospective career.

4. Talk with one person in each of the following careers: (a) one you think you definitely would like to pursue; (b) one you think you might like to pursue; (c) one you know little or nothing about.

5. Read any two of the suggested readings, and relate each article's concepts to your career choice.

6. Using the outline in Figure 5-1 on pages 140–141, conduct a formal interview of a person in a career that you are considering.

7. Using the Internet, find and briefly describe five career options discussed in this chapter or identify five emerging physical education, exercise science, and sport careers.

SUGGESTED READINGS

Carter L: The personal trainer: a perspective, *Stren & Cond J* 23(1):14, 2001. This article provides one person's insights into the role of a well-qualified personal trainer.

Gordon JA: Asian American resistance to selecting teaching as a career: the power of community and tradition, *The Teach Coll Rec* 102(1):173, 2000. The author examines why so few Asian Americans choose a teaching career in this country when this career pathway is recognized as one favored for upward mobility in Asia.

Guralnik JM, Leveille S, Volpato S, Marx MS, Cohen-Mansfield J: Physical activity and disability prevention—targeting high-risk older adults into exercise programs for disability prevention, *J of Aging & Phy Act* 11(2):219, 2003. The authors advocate for involving older adults in physical activity programs as an effective strategy for preventing disabilities.

Hays K, Chan C, Meyers AW, Coleman JK, Whelan JP, Mehlenbeck RS: Examining careers in sport psychology: who is working and who is making money? *Prof Psy, Res & Prac* 32(1):5, 2001. This article provides information about this emerging field within psychology.

Huettig C, Roth K: Maximizing the use of APE consultants: what the general physical educator has the right to expect, *JOPERD* 73(1):32, 2002. Teachers should tap into the resources that adapted physical educators can provide in helping them achieve the goals of individualized education programs for students with disabilities.

Kraus R: Leisure and recreation—careers in recreation: expanding horizons, *JOPERD* 73(5):46, 2002. Recreation careers in a great variety of fields are briefly described, including public recreation and park agencies; nonprofit organizations; commercial recreation; therapeutic recreation; armed forces recreation; employee services; private membership groups; campus recreation; sport management; and travel, tourism, and hospitality.

Neupauer NC: Take me out to the ball game: emphasizing sports broadcasting in the undergraduate curriculum for journalism/communication majors, *Com Abs* 24(3):29, 2001. The author suggests that colleges encourage students to pursue careers in sport broadcasting by providing undergraduate majors programs in this area.

Parks and Recreation and Promoting the Physical Activity Objectives in the Surgeon General's Report, *JOPERD* 70(1):21, 70(2):66, 70(3):36, 1999. This six-article series in the January, February, and March issues provides suggestions for how individuals in the leisure services area can provide opportunities for people of all ages, ability levels, ethnicities, and genders to participate in physical activities. Recreation professionals can help all of their clients develop and benefit from physically active lives through enjoyable leisure pursuits.

Rupp JC, Campbell K, Thompson WR, Terbizan D: Professional preparation of personal trainers, *JOPERD* 70(1):54, 1999. In this article, the authors describe the qualifications of the personal trainer, legal liability issues, and employment opportunities in this field.

Schafer SD: Three perspectives on physical therapist managerial work, *Phy Ther* 82(3):228, 2002. This study of physical therapists in hospitals and private practices examined the perceived importance of the managerial role and skills categories. Communication, financial control, entrepreneurial ability, resource allocation, and leadership emerged as the five most important areas of expertise.

CHAPTER

6

PREPARATION FOR A CAREER

KEY CONCEPTS

- Establishing short- and long-term goals helps in the process of career development.
- Course work required for a liberal arts education combined with a major in physical education, exercise science, or sport studies varies by institution and career choice.
- Extracurricular activities, internships, and volunteer work in physical education, exercise science, and sport offer important learning experiences and preparation for careers.
- Certifications in officiating, aquatics, first aid, exercise testing, athletic training, coaching, and other areas improve professional credentials for employment.
- Graduate programs provide opportunities for advanced study in various specialties.

Professionalism is based on knowledge. Thus far, you have learned about the objectives, disciplinary content, and professional structure of physical education, exercise science, and sport. You have begun to learn more about various careers through the career perspectives in each chapter. Now, with a career targeted, you are getting ready to learn more about your intended work. The information in this chapter should help you get the most out of your college years. As you grow in your knowledge of physical education, exercise science, and sport, take advantage of various activities in the field and obtain certifications. You are not just joining a profession; you are becoming a professional. This professionalism will demonstrate itself by your commitment to learning and your desire to develop your capabilities to the fullest.

While this chapter introduces you to various alternative careers, at this point you will want to focus on learning more about each career and as much as you can about those of greatest interest to you. The end of this chapter provides information about writing application letters, developing a résumé, and preparing for interviews.

THE CHALLENGE

Everyone's existence depends on self-worth. We all have varying degrees of this basic need that relate directly to our personal levels of happiness. Self-worth is developed by participating and achieving success in different activities. This may include feeling confident in one's sports skills, as well as in leadership skills acquired as a volunteer youth coach, a camp counselor, or an intern in a health and fitness club. An enhanced feeling of competency comes from taking on and completing responsible roles like team manager, lab assistant, Special Olympics or Senior Games volunteer, and sports reporter for a school newspaper. Most people want to feel satisfied with and successful in their lives. Each person, however, defines these concepts uniquely. Many factors contribute to this "satisfaction factor" in our lives. Listed below are some characteristics that people value personally. Select any of these that can help you establish a sense of direction for the personal, social, and professional goals you will be setting. It will help if you can identify one or more individuals who you think personify those traits you wish to emulate.

Analytical	Loyal	Respectful
Assertive	Organized	Responsible
Benevolent	Outgoing	Sensitive
Cautious	Patient	Serious
Competent	Persevering	Sincere
Considerate	Poised	Sociable
Cooperative	Polite	Spontaneous
Creative	Practical	Tactful
Determined	Progressive	Tenacious
Energetic	Prudent	Thorough
Enthusiastic	Quiet	Thoughtful
Friendly	Rational	Tolerant
Fun	Reflective	Trustworthy
Helpful	Reliable	Understanding
Honest	Resourceful	Versatile

Once you have observed some of these traits in others, you are encouraged to learn how you can adopt these characteristics. People who have been praised as good role models are usually willing to share how they developed their unique abilities. These same individuals are often eager to share strategies that have worked to make them successful.

Goal setting helps us assess abilities and interests and establish immediate and future expectations. Goal setting helps individuals establish their personal philosophies, as described in Chapter 4. Short-term goals are accomplishments that can occur within a day, week, month, or another not-too-distant time period.

BOX 6-1   PERSONAL AND PERFORMANCE GOAL SETTING

Personal

1. What is your personal long-term career goal or dream?
2. Is it possible to achieve this goal if you work hard and motivate yourself the next few years?
3. What intermediate goals must you fulfill in the next few months to progress toward your dream?
4. What are immediate (today/this week) goals that you can accomplish that will help you advance toward your long-term career goal?

Performance

5. What is one academic goal that you can achieve this semester?
6. How can you improve your academic performance during the following semester?
7. If you fail to meet this academic performance goal, how will you feel about yourself?
8. What is one athletic or fitness goal that you can achieve this semester?
9. How can you improve your athletic or fitness performance during the following semester?
10. If you fail to meet this athletic or fitness performance goal, how will you feel about yourself?
11. What is one leadership goal that you can achieve this semester?
12. How can you improve your leadership performance during the following semester?

Such goals could include attending a weekend workshop, starting a personal exercise program, or joining a professional association. It is important that short-term goals are readily achievable, positively reinforcing, and related to or leading to the attainment of long-term goals. Long-term goals are larger in scope and are often composed of numerous short-term goals. Continual self-assessment and reestablishment of goals are essential, since interests and aspirations change. Before establishing some professional goals, it may be easier to start with personal and performance goals. To facilitate this process, respond to the questions in Box 6-1.

Associated with developing positive character traits and goal setting is the skill of networking. As you decide what you want to do and determine the type of person you want to be, you can be helped by others who have experienced the same process through which you are progressing. Associating yourself with others who can serve as your mentors and who can introduce you to others in your chosen career can be valuable. These individuals can help you obtain internship experiences and possibly get an entry-level job. They are tremendous resources for information, guidance, and personal development.

EDUCATIONAL BACKGROUND

Academic success in college can greatly facilitate the achievement of your goals. Try to benefit as much as possible from these educational opportunities to learn and develop your skills and abilities. This does not mean that all you need to do is to study, but lifelong learning certainly is vital.

Everyone needs to develop basic academic competencies in reading, writing, speaking, listening, mathematics, critical thinking, studying, and computer literacy. Basic academic competencies and general education course work constitute most liberal arts programs through which institutions provide students with the broad knowledge base for their lives and careers. Advocates of a liberal arts education think that all students should be educated to function effectively in a culturally diverse world, regardless of their career choices. Such an education potentially helps the research scientist interact with the practitioner, assists the coach in understanding family backgrounds and pressures on their athletes, provides insights about other people and their languages in our multicultural society, and develops appreciation for the arts, history, and philosophy.

Some students may fulfill these core requirements by taking a conglomeration of courses without much thought or direction. Whether you take general education courses during the first two years at a junior or community college or throughout a four-year collegiate program, you should seriously consider your selection and sequence of course work to maximize career preparation. Your

Maintaining personal fitness is one vital aspect of preparing for a career in physical education, exercise science, and sport.

major or specialized studies normally hold greater interest because they tend to relate more directly to your chosen career. Nevertheless, you still need to make a serious commitment to learning the most that you can from each class.

Internships and fieldwork are valuable for career preparation. Some majors' programs require students to observe in the schools each week, complete an internship, design practicum experiences for their career choices through independent study courses, or take a laboratory course that offers practical experiences. Usually education courses for the prospective teacher require observation and mini–teaching experiences, many as early as the first year of college.

Several curricula allow students to earn college credit while receiving pay for work completed while learning, such as recreation leader for a community, camp counselor, sport club instructor, or personal trainer. An independent study option allows students to earn college credit for developing research projects or for work experiences specific to their areas of interest. Other curricula have experiential courses as a part of their requirements. Each of these options allows students opportunities to gain valuable experiences while they are selecting and preparing for their careers.

RELATED EXPERIENCES

Some people suggest that during the college years, considerable career-relevant learning occurs outside the classroom. It is certainly true that experiential learning is important. For example, by serving as a team manager, sport official, or event coordinator in intramural/recreational sports, you can learn about personnel management, scheduling, and rules. Working with a club sport, like karate or rugby, you may get an opportunity to coach and to manage the club's financial affairs. Of course, you can learn many things just by participating in various college activities or as a varsity athlete.

Volunteer Activities

While the knowledge gained in college courses introduces content and provides the foundation for a career choice, experiences and practical applications solidify learning. Participating in volunteer activities while a student offers valuable opportunities to gain experience. If athletic training interests you, volunteer to serve as a student trainer or shadow a physical therapist to learn more about these potential careers. If a career in fitness appeals to you, you may start by attending aerobics classes or joining a health club before volunteering to assist instructors in these classes or clubs. Later you may enhance your learning to become an instructor. Other volunteer possibilities in this field include conducting fitness classes for children in after-school programs, for senior citizens at retirement centers, or for students in your residence hall.

Exercise science majors often choose to volunteer to work in commercial or corporate fitness programs or a clinic setting. You could help exercise physiologists, fitness leaders, and physicians assess the fitness levels of clients, prescribe

Volunteer assistance with a track meet may provide valuable experience in learning how to manage sporting events. (Photo courtesy Barry Pennell.)

exercise programs, and monitor progress. You could observe and learn how to measure various fitness parameters and help participants adhere to their prescribed programs.

Exercise science students who aspire to earn graduate degrees should volunteer to serve as subjects in research studies. As undergraduate or graduate laboratory assistants working with your professors, you can gain tremendous experience using exercise physiology, biomechanical, and other scientific instrumentation. You will quickly learn whether the research process—hypothesis, design, data collection, statistical analysis, and interpretation—appeals to you.

The sport management major can seek out volunteer opportunities both on and off campus. Your college's intramural/recreational sports program needs students to serve as team managers for residence units, club sports officers, and facility and activity supervisors. Opportunities may also be available to organize special events, such as fun runs, orientation sessions, or all-night activities. Volunteers provide valuable assistance working with the Special Olympics, family recreational centers, Senior Games, private sports leagues, and State Games. After successfully completing minor tasks, you may qualify for the responsibility of coordinating sports competitions during these events. Volunteer coaches are needed in youth sport leagues and recreation programs. Experiences gained in these settings may lead to opportunities to serve as an assistant coach in a junior or senior high school.

Through volunteer officiating, students can gain experience and prepare for possible careers or part-time jobs. (Photo courtesy Maggie McGlynn.)

Officiating

Officiating opportunities abound in intramurals, within recreational leagues, and in junior high schools; some colleges offer classes in officiating. These learning experiences may result in advancement into the high school, college, and professional ranks. The National Federation of State High School Associations, through its state associations, requires interested individuals to attend clinics and take written examinations to become certified as sports officials. Following successful completion of these requirements, individuals earn ratings that qualify them to officiate high school athletic contests. The most proficient officials receive the top rankings, earn the honor of working in championships, and may get an opportunity to advance to the next competitive level. Several single-sport organizations, such as the United States Volleyball Association, have their own programs to train and certify officials for their sports.

Internship Opportunities

Many experiences as a volunteer provide greater knowledge and expertise to assist the aspiring teacher, exercise scientist, and sport manager in their internships. Most fields associated with physical activity require one or more internships, in which students enhance their skills and abilities and link the theory from their course work with actual practice in their future career. The aspiring sport manager has to participate in on-the-job experiences, such as in sport marketing and facility and event management, to help prepare for future jobs. Exercise scientists who aspire to prescribe exercise programs in a variety of settings need to experience through internships how to administer fitness assessments and assist individuals with personal programs to gain the knowledge and skills needed to succeed. In most programs, these internships are a part of the degree requirements, with associated academic expectations. Some internships permit students to receive pay; others must be completed without pay. The

Volunteering to work with children in an after-school program can help develop teaching skills. (Photo courtesy Bob Hilliard.)

Officiating is a popular part-time job for students and physical education, exercise science, and sport professionals.

Research View box "Importance of Internships" provides additional information about internships. One illustration is the American College of Sports Medicine's internship program for college students, which includes opportunities in sports administration, promotions/marketing, communication, and the health science career fields. For more information, go to www.acsm.org/textdocs/Intern2003.doc.

⌕ RESEARCH VIEW

Importance of Internships

In today's competitive job market, especially in physical education, exercise science, and sports careers, it is vital that students realize the value of internships and seek them out determinedly. According to numerous research studies, students who participate in internships during their undergraduate and graduate programs gain the following advantages:

- Get more extensive learning experiences
- Benefit from extensive hands-on experiences
- Obtain better preparation for employment
- Gain a competitive edge when seeking employment
- Develop networks with potential employers
- Learn from fellow employees and build good relationships with them
- Impress their internship employers, making them more likely to hire them as full-time employees
- Position themselves for more job offers
- Qualify for higher starting salaries
- Advance through more frequent promotions

Additional information can be obtained online using a favorite search engine, contacting departmental offices or university career services offices, or reviewing books such as *The National Directory of Internships, Peterson's Internships, The WetFeet Insider Guide to Getting Your Ideal Internship,* and *The Internship Bible.*

Internships Pay Off

Frequently students demonstrate their competence and enthusiasm for a career through their internships, resulting in being hired for a position in the same sport or setting. Mitch LaPoint completed the requirements for his bachelor's degree in exercise science (sport management) at the University of Kansas through an internship with the Kansas City Chiefs. Now employed by the Chiefs, Mitch evaluates college football players by visiting schools, interviewing coaches, evaluating athletes' performances in practice and through film, and filing reports on athletes' abilities. Mitch also coordinates players' meals and travel, manages the coaching and scouting budget, and attends to other operational details. The hours are long (for 10 months out of the year, Mitch works at least 12-hour days through the week and many weekends, too), but the personal sacrifices in time can lead to career advancement and salary increases from $35,000 to $100,000, depending on experiences and demonstrated expertise. In reflecting on his internship,

(continued)

Mitch learned the dedication and work ethic necessary to succeed in the sports industry. He also learned that he really enjoys being around the game and being involved with the players, coaches, and staff. Mitch advises students to work hard, put in the hours needed to get the job done each day, take on mundane tasks graciously, communicate well with people on the job, and share new ideas that may lead to doing things more effectively.

These experiences associated with your potential career choice may help confirm your interests or indicate that another field may be preferable. Another valuable learning experience is shadowing a person who agrees to mentor you as you learn more about a potential career. As a volunteer or intern, you will help others while developing your own abilities. Each time you participate in one of these activities, add this to a list of your extracurricular experiences. Later, when you apply for a job, you can include these activities on your résumé. Volunteer and internship experiences will help differentiate you from other applicants.

BEGINNING YOUR CAREER INVOLVEMENT

While you are a student, get involved in career-related activities. Most colleges and universities have majors' clubs in physical education, exercise science, and sport studies. Majors' clubs often sponsor faculty-student colloquia, invite leaders in the profession to give presentations, and interact academically and socially. These organizations also frequently organize trips to state, district, and national conferences or workshops where students learn about the profession, hear about current developments, and listen to research reports. Service projects, such as working with Special Olympics, holding Jump Rope for Heart programs, and officiating at sporting events to raise money for charities, are also popular ways for young professionals to help others by sharing their expertise; at the same time, they gain valuable experience. Following are some questions to assist you in your career development:

1. What would I like to do immediately following graduation? After five years? Ten years? Twenty years?

2. What experiences and learning opportunities can I take advantage of while in college to help me prepare for immediate, short-, and long-term career goals?

3. What resource people on my campus can help me prepare for immediate, short-, and long-term career goals?

4. What objectives and action plans have I established to help me explore various aspects of my career development while in college?

5. How will the development of a portfolio (describing work experiences, internships, volunteer experiences, and class activities) help demonstrate what I have learned in my career preparation?

6. How will my course work help me make better decisions in my career?

7. How are my personal, academic, and social strengths matched to the potential career for which I am preparing?

8. How can others help me evaluate and understand my abilities and develop strategies to work on areas in need of strengthening?

9. How will I use feedback from experiences and from others to better prepare myself to make decisions relative to my career choice?

10. How motivated am I to devote the time and effort needed to be successful in and satisfied with my career choice?

Certifications

An important demonstration of professional growth and development is the attainment of certifications. Certification is an important career step for the following reasons:

- Confirms the attainment of a high level of competence and the achievement of the standards of the profession, such as becoming a Certified Athletic Trainer by the NATA Board of Certification

- Demonstrates that the fundamental knowledge and skills associated with job responsibilities have been learned, such as being certified as a Physical Fitness Specialist by the Cooper Institute

- Shows a willingness and commitment on the part of certification applicants to enhance their career preparation, such as indicated by obtaining an Exercise Specialist certification from the American College of Sports Medicine

- Provides potential clients and the general public with a quality control measure that reassures them that the certified person possesses a level of competence, such as completing one or more levels of coaching certification through the American Sport Education Program

- Enables potential employers to differentiate among applicants based on a known standard of knowledge and skills, such as becoming a Certified Personal Trainer through the National Strength and Conditioning Association

The American Red Cross offers certifications for lifeguards and instructors in water safety, first aid, cardiopulmonary resuscitation, and other health and safety services courses. The YMCA of the USA also certifies lifeguards and swimming instructors. These certifications can lead to employment as pool and beach lifeguards and as swimming teachers.

In certifying health and fitness professionals, the American College of Sports Medicine (ACSM) requires a rigorous level of knowledge and skill in each of its

Exercise leaders can help individuals of all ages develop physically.

three programs. ACSM believes that certified professionals set the best possible performance examples, provide safe and caring environments, and show a greater incidence of client and patient success in achieving health and fitness goals. ACSM offers three types of certification.

- Health/Fitness Instructor
- Exercise Specialist
- Registered Clinical Exercise Physiologist

Table 6-1 provides information about these and other certifications in health, fitness, sport, and coaching.

The American Sport Education Program (ASEP) certifies coaches and officials for interscholastic and teenage sports programs (visit www.asep.com/learn/ PROF_professional.cfm). Coaches can advance through three levels of online

TABLE 6-1

CERTIFICATIONS

Certification	Description
American College of Sports Medicine	
Health/Fitness Instructor	A candidate must demonstrate comprehensive knowledge of exercise science and risk factor and health status identification, fitness appraisal, and exercise prescription, have work experience within the health and fitness field, be prepared to conduct fitness testing and implement exercise programs for low- to moderate-risk clients, and demonstrate the ability to effectively counsel individuals regarding lifestyle modification.
Exercise Specialist	A candidate must demonstrate extensive knowledge of functional anatomy, exercise physiology, electrocardiography, human behavior/psychology, gerontology, graded exercise testing and exercise prescription for healthy and diseased populations, exercise supervision/leadership, patient counseling, and emergency procedures related to exercise testing and training situations.
Registered Clinical Exercise Physiologist	A candidate must possess a master's degree in exercise physiology, exercise science, or physiology; have completed 1,200 hours of supervised clinical experience, including physical assessment, exercise testing, exercise prescription and counseling, exercise supervision, and client education; and demonstrate exercise competencies in cardiovascular, pulmonary, metabolic, immunological, inflammatory, and neuromuscular areas.
Cooper Institute	
Aquatics	A candidate learns rhythmical movements and calisthenic exercises for execution in water so clients can develop muscular strength with low impact.
Biomechanics of Resistance Training Specialty	A candidate learns about muscular structure and appropriate strengthening exercises and how to guide clients in all areas of strength training with safety and confidence.
Coaching Healthy Behaviors Specialty	A candidate learns scientific information, resources, tools, and assessment methods using real-life situations that can facilitate positive behavior change.
Fitness Specialist for Older Adults	A candidate learns about age-related conditions; assessing abilities; and determining appropriate exercises for clients with limitations due to health conditions, loss of muscular strength, compromised balance, or lack of self-confidence.
Group Exercise Leadership	A candidate learns leadership and technical skills needed to offer group exercise programs that are safe and effective.
Health Promotion Director	A candidate learns how to design the most effective health promotion program for an organization.
Indoor Cycling	A candidate learns how to provide instruction in a group stationary cycle class.
Master Fitness Specialist	A candidate learns in this advanced program the latest research findings, options for fitness testing, and specialized skills in fitness programming.
Optimal Performance Training	A candidate learns principles for increasing performance; how to improve strength, endurance, stability, mobility, speed, agility, and power for optimal performance; and concepts such as functional training, core development, corrective exercise, balance training, program design, and progression.
Physical Fitness Specialist	A candidate learns how to use fundamental scientific research in the field of physical activity to provide personal training and programs that are safe, effective, and motivational.
Pre/Postnatal Fitness Instructor	A candidate learns how to offer safe and effective exercise programming throughout each trimester of pregnancy and postpartum.
Providing Dietary Guidance	A candidate learns about the fundamental aspects of nutrition, as well as how to give dietary guidance and general nutritional information to healthy adults for reducing disease risk and enhancing sports and fitness performance.

TABLE 6-1 (CONTINUED)

CERTIFICATIONS

Certification	Description
Special Populations	A candidate learns about specialized fitness programming for individuals affected by illness, rehabilitation, or other limiting conditions.
Team Building Specialty	A candidate learns innovative methods of maximizing employee productivity, satisfaction, and commitment to the organization.

National Strength and Conditioning Association

Certified Personal Trainer	A candidate must hold a cardiopulmonary resuscitation certification and demonstrate on an exam the knowledge and skills needed to successfully train active and sedentary physically healthy individuals, as well as the elderly and obese.
Certified Strength and Conditioning Specialist	A candidate must possess a baccalaureate degree, hold a cardiopulmonary resuscitation certification, and demonstrate on an exam the knowledge and skills necessary to design and implement safe and effective strength and conditioning programs.

American Council on Education

Personal Trainer	A candidate must demonstrate knowledge in basic exercise science, nutrition, fitness assessment, exercise programming, and instructional and spotting techniques.
Group Fitness Instructor	A candidate must possess effective communication, instructional techniques, and motivational skills for groups and demonstrate knowledge in exercise science, exercise programming, instructional techniques, and professional responsibility.
Lifestyle and Weight Management Consultant	A candidate must demonstrate the requisite knowledge and skills to develop sound, balanced weight management programs, as well as pass an exam on client assessment, program planning, and professional responsibility.
Clinical Exercise Specialist	A candidate at this advanced level must demonstrate the ability to work with individuals with special needs, with physician's clearance, as well as pass an exam on screening and assessment, program design, and program implementation and management.

Aerobics and Fitness Association of America

Advanced Personal Training	A candidate must demonstrate knowledge of advanced training principles for performance and athletic-related goals and learn about research-based strength training techniques, sports nutrition, functional fitness, and advanced fitness assessment.
Fitness Practitioner	A candidate must have a baccalaureate degree and demonstrate the ability to provide assessment, nutritional education, one-on-one training, and counseling.
Kickboxing	A candidate must have group exercise teaching experience, hold the Primary Group Exercise Certification, and demonstrate familiarity with basic kickboxing techniques.
Personal Trainer	A candidate must demonstrate knowledge of basic exercise physiology, anatomy, and kinesiology, and learn practical applications of fitness assessments and the behavioral and physiological objectives of one-on-one fitness counseling.
Primary Group Exercise	A candidate must demonstrate knowledge of the basic exercise sciences and the ability to lead group exercise
Step	A candidate learns theoretical and practical knowledge and skills necessary for safe and effective instruction of step training, including a scientific background in physiology and biomechanics, step terminology, verbal and visual cueing skills, step pattern choreography and sequencing, and instructional skills and techniques.

education with coaching principles, sport first aid, and coaching sport-specific techniques and tactics courses comprising the entry level. Those completing the second level receive preparation in sport mechanics, sport physiology, sport psychology, teaching sport skills, and coaching advanced and sport-specific skills and strategies. Sport nutrition, risk management, social issues, and advanced coaching and practice planning are included in the third level. Officials learn the principles of officiating as well as the methods of officiating specific sports.

Thirty-five state high school associations utilize the National Federation of State High School Associations (NFHS) Coaches Education Program, in partnership with ASEP, so coaches can fulfill the coaching education requirements in their states. The first-level certification courses, coaching principles, sport first aid, and coaching sport-specific techniques and tactics serve to provide essential coaching education.

The Program for Athletic Coaches Education (www.mhsaa.com/administration/pace.html) was designed to serve the nonteacher coach in high schools. This program offers two levels of certification. The first includes legal responsibilities; insurance for coaches and athletes; emergency procedures; prevention, care, and rehabilitation of sports injuries; and essential medical records. The second level focuses on the role of the coach in interscholastic sports; planning, conducting, and evaluating effective instruction; physical conditioning; personal and social skills; positive coaching and motivation; effective communication; and maintaining discipline.

Some institutions offer students the option to complete course work in tracks, specializations, concentrations, or minors in addition to their majors. For example, students majoring in exercise science might choose to use their electives to specialize in a corporate fitness track. Students in physical education might choose to take a coaching minor to better prepare for a teaching/coaching position in a school. Other students might choose to major in sport management while completing a concentration in marketing through the business school. Although each institution uses its own terminology for these programs, each allows students to take undergraduate courses in areas directly relevant to their particular careers or as preparation for a graduate program for which both areas of emphasis would be beneficial.

GRADUATE EDUCATION

Your career objective may require advanced study in physical education, exercise science, or sport studies at an accredited institution. Master's degree programs usually take one to two years to complete; doctoral degree programs require two to four years beyond the master's degree. Master of Science (M.S.), Master of Arts (M.A.), Master of Education (M.Ed.), and Master of Arts in Teaching (M.A.T.) are the typical offerings. They normally require 30 to 36 semester hours for completion, although the actual course work taken varies from institution to institution. The M.S. and M.A. degrees generally emphasize more discipline-oriented study and may allow for specialization in athletic training, exercise science, sport

WEB CONNECTIONS

1. www.cooperinst.org

   At this site, you can learn more about the certification programs of the Cooper Institute, its health promotion products and services, the FITNESSGRAM, and internship opportunities.

2. www.acsm.org

   Learn more about the American College of Sports Medicine, including its certification programs, which promote scientific research and application of sports medicine and exercise science to enhance physical performance, fitness, health, and quality of life.

3. www.acefitness.org

   Check out this site for more information about fitness certifications, programs, and fitness facts.

4. www.nsca-lift.org/menu.asp

   Learn more about certifications, programs, and services offered by the National Strength and Conditioning Association.

5. http://ncaa.thetask.com/market/ads/index.html

   The Market is an online job listing service for college athletics taken from the *NCAA News*.

6. www.sportsjobboard.com

   This site provides an up-to-date listing of job openings. However, there is a cost for subscribing to this service.

management, or sport psychology, as shown in Table 6-2. Completion of these degrees usually requires a thesis, an original research project, or an internship in addition to a comprehensive examination or other summative assessment. Oriented toward education and teaching, the M.Ed. and M.A.T. degrees lead to advanced certification for individuals working in the schools and usually require a practicum experience (see Box 6-2). Many institutions offer certifications in advanced study beyond the master's degree in special education, supervision, counseling, and administration, as well as educational specialist degrees. Increasingly, schools expect teachers to obtain master's degrees or higher to continue their lifelong learning.

The highest academic degrees are the Doctor of Philosophy (Ph.D.) and the Doctor of Education (Ed.D.). The Ph.D. is oriented toward research in a specialty such as exercise physiology, sport history, sport management, motor learning, or sport and exercise psychology. The focus of most Ed.D. programs is advanced study in education, with physical education comprising one portion of the program.

TABLE 6-2

EXAMPLES OF COURSE WORK AND INTERNSHIPS ASSOCIATED WITH MASTER'S DEGREE PROGRAMS IN THE EXERCISE SCIENCES

Athletic Training	Sport Management
Care and Management of Athletic Injuries	Sport Organizational Behavior and Development
Clinical Methods in Athletic Training	Sport Law
Applied Statistics and Research Methods	Sport Finance and Business
Exercise Physiology	Social Issues in Sport
Psychological Considerations for Injury and Rehabilitation	Applied Statistics and Research
Issues in Sports Medicine	Sport Marketing
Nutritional Aspects of Exercise	Sport Ethics
Scientific Analysis of Human Motion	Sport Event and Facility Management
Advanced Orthopedic Assessment and Treatment	Applied Sport Marketing Research
Practicum in Athletic Training	Internship in Sport Administration

Exercise Physiology	Sport and Exercise Psychology
Exercise Physiology	Psychological Aspects of Sports
Applied Statistics and Research Methods	Applied Statistics and Research Methods
Assessment of Physiological Functions in Exercise	Motivation in Sport
Exercise Testing and Prescription in a Healthy Population	Sport and Society: Socioeconomic, Gender, Global, and Ethnic Relations
Nutritional Aspects of Exercise	Lifespan Sport Psychology
Planning Health Promotion in Medical and Worksite Settings	Issues in Sport and Exercise Psychology
Cardiovascular Disease Epidemiology	Counseling and Interviewing Skills
Clinical Exercise Testing and Prescription	Social Cognition
Seminar in Exercise Physiology	Personality Assessment and Research
Practicum in Exercise Physiology	Practicum in Sport Psychology

Before deciding whether to enroll in a prospective graduate program, determine whether advanced education is needed for your career. If so, you may want to find out which accredited universities offer the type of program that meets your needs. For example, only a few institutions offer a specialization in athletic training at the master's degree level. Although some institutions require an area of specialization for a master's degree, others offer a general physical education, exercise science, or sport studies program.

Most admission requirements include an undergraduate degree in physical education or related exercise or sport science emphasis, a minimum of a 3.0 (on a 4.0 scale) grade point average, and a better-than-average score on the Graduate Record Examination (GRE) or Miller Analogies Test (MAT). Since institutions are free to set their own admissions standards, review the institutions that offer the

BOX 6-2   TYPICAL COURSE WORK FOR MASTER'S DEGREE EMPHASIZING PHYSICAL EDUCATION

Curriculum

Educational psychology

Educational research

Educational statistics

Issues and trends in physical education

Legal issues in education

Motor learning in physical education

Internship or fieldwork experience

School and program management

Scientific foundations of physical education

One important component of graduate education is participation in research projects.

program you desire. Libraries house catalogs of most leading institutions, or you may write for information. Another way to check out multiple institutions and their programs is to visit their websites, some of which offer online applications. Applications should be completed during the middle of the senior year or at least six months prior to the expected entrance date. Required admissions materials include college transcript(s), letters of recommendation, application forms, and test scores (such as GRE or MAT results).

For careers that do not require advanced degrees, additional and ongoing education is beneficial. Employers sometimes provide this on the job; otherwise, employees need to attend workshops, conferences, or continuing education classes. Keep current with and stimulated by career changes and developments. These often result in greater job productivity and can lead to career advancement. Remember, career development is a lifelong process.

GAINING EXPERIENCE

While you are still a first- or second-year college student, it is important to investigate the job market by talking with older students, faculty members, or individuals in the career(s) you are considering, maybe by asking them the questions listed in Box 6-3. Reflect on their responses as you continue to narrow or broaden

---

BOX 6-3   POSSIBLE QUESTIONS TO ASK ABOUT YOUR PROSPECTIVE CAREER

1. What is the educational background required?
2. How much prior experience is needed?
3. What are the typical work hours?
4. What is the daily routine and the average time spent on each part of these activities?
5. What is the starting salary and salary range?
6. How much vacation time is provided?
7. What are the fringe benefits?
8. To what extent will this job affect my personal life?
9. What are the requisite skills and knowledge for this job?
10. What personal characteristics, such as creativity, problem-solving ability, or enthusiasm, are necessary for this job?
11. What is the potential for employment in this career?
12. In what regions or states is this job available?
13. What is the potential for advancement in this career?
14. Is on-the-job training or advanced education required to maintain employment or to advance in this career?
15. What are the specific work responsibilities of this type of job? How much time is spent doing each?
16. What criteria are used to evaluate job performance?
17. What are the most satisfying or advantageous aspects of this job?
18. What are the most frustrating or disadvantageous aspects of this job?
19. Ask someone in this career, "What has been your biggest disillusionment?"
20. Ask someone in this career, "What has been your most rewarding or enjoyable experience?"

your career possibilities and make the most of your education. By carefully selecting your elective courses, you may be able to obtain a double major or specialize in some area, such as corporate fitness. Through certain courses you may qualify for an internship, a summer work experience, or a part-time job, or you may have an opportunity to gain valuable experience as a volunteer in intramurals or intercollegiate athletics.

During your college years, be sure to take advantage of your institution's resources. Most college libraries have materials on market trends, career guidance, and opportunities for advanced education. Counseling or guidance personnel offer career aptitude testing, assistance in résumé writing, and hints for interviews. Tables 6-3 and 6-4 show sample résumés, and Boxes 6-4 and 6-5 show sample application letters (for full-time or part-time positions). You should visit

---

TABLE 6-3

SAMPLE RÉSUMÉ FOR A PROSPECTIVE TEACHER

LEWIS RAY KNIGHT

School Address:	**Permanent Address:**
1234 Drake Lane Columbus, FL 38281 Phone: (915) 437-4921	567 Swinging Bridge Boulevard Norlina, TX 72802 Phone: (173) 548-2183

Career Objective:	To teach physical education in a junior high school and to coach basketball
Education:	University of South Miami, Miami, Florida, May, 2005 Bachelor of Science in Physical Education Major GPA: 3.7; Overall GPA: 3.1
Experiences:	Student Teacher, East Junior High School, Miami, Florida (Spring 2005) Teacher's Aide, West Junior High School, Miami, Florida (Fall 2004) Miami Boys' Club volunteer basketball coach (2001–2005) Counselor at Norlina, Texas, summer sports camp (2002–2004)
Honors and Awards:	Residence Hall Intramural Manager of the Year (2003) Dean's List (2002–2004)
College Activities:	Chairperson of the Physical Education Majors' Club Social Committee (2002–2003) Intramural and Boys' Club basketball official (2001–2005) Intramural participant in basketball, touch football, softball, and tennis (2001–2005) Student member of the American Alliance for Health, Physical Education, Recreation and Dance
Availability:	Available for employment, August, 2005
References:	Will be furnished upon request

TABLE 6-4

SAMPLE RÉSUMÉ FOR A PROSPECTIVE CORPORATE FITNESS LEADER

MARY ANN SMITH

School Address:	***Permanent Address:***
8923 Amigo Drive	7421 Langley Road
Northridge, CA 90324	San Antonia, CA 97181
Phone: (412) 901-4413	Phone: (433) 821-0431

Career Objective: To develop and implement a corporate executive fitness program utilizing skills in exercise prescription

Education: California State University, Northridge, California, May, 2005
Bachelor of Science in exercise and sport science
Major GPA: 3.8; Overall GPA: 3.5

Experiences: Intern exercise leader with Jones & Jones Company in Newark, New Jersey (summer 2004)

- Designed an aerobics program for 125 employees
- Organized a family-oriented fun run
- Initiated a company-wide incentive program for weight reduction

Volunteer at Redwood Convalescent Center, Northwest, California (2002–2003)

- Developed a recreation program for non-ambulatory patients

Sales person, The Sports Shop, Northwest, California (2000–2002)

College Activities: Vice President of the university's Racquetball Club (2004–2005)
Member of Exercise Science Majors' Club (2002–2003)
Volunteer assistant in department's exercise physiology laboratory (2003–2005)

Special Skills: Certified as a Health/Fitness Instructor (American College of Sports Medicine)
Certified in first aid and cardiopulmonary resuscitation

Affiliations: Student member of the American College of Sports Medicine
Student member of the American Alliance for Health, Physical Education, Recreation and Dance

References: Will be furnished upon request

---

your college's placement center to learn about the services they offer. They can help you get a summer job as well as your first job after graduation.

It has been said that "it's not what you can do, but whom you know" that determines whether or not you get certain jobs. Many good jobs are obtained through personal contacts. Why not let this work for you? Notify friends, relatives, former employers, and other people you have met that you are looking for a

BOX 6-4   SAMPLE APPLICATION LETTER FOR A PART-TIME JOB

Ms. Terry Ann Cowan   October 1, 2004
Manager, Sports Unlimited
1902 Smithfield Road
Helena, MO 61102

Dear Ms. Cowan:

As a sophomore at Western State University majoring in sport management, I am interested in finding a part-time job related to my prospective career. Specifically, I would like to learn about retail sporting goods sales by working 10 to 12 hours per week, in the evenings and on weekends.

My previous work experience includes three summers as a camp counselor, teaching racket sports to boys and girls ages 6 to 16, and 9 months as a clerk in a fast-food restaurant. My immediate supervisors for these two jobs have agreed to provide you with an evaluation of my work.

At the university, I am a member of a social sorority, the jazz dance club, and the Sport Management Majors Club. My commitments to these would not interfere with whatever hours you might assign me to work. I have enclosed my résumé, which provides you with additional information about my work experiences and campus activities.

If you have an opening for a sales clerk or anticipate one in the near future, I would appreciate your calling me at 371-9882. In the event that you cannot reach me within one week, I will call you to follow up on this inquiry. Thank you for your consideration.

Sincerely,

Mary Sue Markam

---

part-time or summer job or an internship. Follow up on all leads, because sometimes getting a good job results from "being in the right place at the right time." Initiate contact with anyone you think can help you. Networking is extremely important. You can begin to establish a network of acquaintances in physical education, exercise science, and sport careers through your extracurricular activities, internships, volunteer experiences, and summer jobs, and by attending workshops and conferences. The people whom you meet, interact with, and impress can help you get your initial or a subsequent job. Networking includes expanding your number of friends in the field and building positive relationships with them.

Another way to lead potential employers to view your job application favorably is to provide them with a portfolio that describes and illustrates your educational accomplishments, work experiences, and unique abilities. This portfolio could be provided in a looseleaf notebook for the interviewer to review, shared on a compact disk submitted at the time of application for review prior to the personal interview, or via a webpage that you design and maintain. Box 6-6 provides an outline for a portfolio.

BOX 6-5 SAMPLE APPLICATION LETTER FOR A TEACHING/COACHING POSITION

1742 Maple Avenue
Cary GA, 37938

March 1, 2005

Dr. Raymond C. Van Meter
Personnel Director
Guilford City Schools
Guilford, GA 37941

Dear Dr. Van Meter:

In May, 2005, I will graduate from the University of South Miami with a bachelor's degree in physical education and probably with a 3.1 G.P.A. (out of a possible 4.0). I am writing to inquire about current or potential vacancies for a physical education teacher and coach in Guilford.

I have benefited from a strong liberal arts and in-depth professional education at South Miami. With the completion of my current student teaching experiences, conducted under the supervision of John R. Williams, at East Junior High School in Miami, I will be eager to continue to enjoy helping students learn. I am committed to and enthusiastic about teaching as a career.

As a volunteer coach, an intramural and Boys' Club official, and an intramural participant for four years and a former varsity player in high school, I believe that I have both the technical knowledge and the personal qualities to coach basketball at the junior high school level. I would also welcome the opportunity to serve as an assistant coach in football, baseball, or softball because of my past experiences in these sports.

Other items on my enclosed résumé indicate my potential to be involved professionally and to contribute as a staff member at a school in Guilford. If a vacancy currently exists, I would appreciate being considered a candidate. If no positions are available at this time, please keep my application on file in the event one becomes available. I may be contacted at my school address through May 7 and thereafter at my permanent address.

Thank you very much for considering my application. I hope that we will meet someday to discuss the possibility of my teaching in the Guilford City Schools.

Sincerely,

Lewis Ray Knight

Enclosure

SUMMARY

As you prepare for your career, you need to begin to set short- and long-term goals. These will help you make incremental progress toward the achievement of your career aspirations. As an undergraduate, your choices of courses to fulfill requirements, your selection of a major, and your use of electives will determine the quality of your education and career preparation. The quantity, quality, and

BOX 6-6   OUTLINE FOR A PORTFOLIO

Professional Philosophy
- Provide a brief profile about yourself.
- Describe your personal values.
- Share your short-term professional goals specifically as they relate to this career.

Educational Background
- List colleges attended, degrees earned, and majors.
- Describe academic honors earned and recognitions received.
- Explain how your collegiate studies prepared you for a career in this field.
- Identify memberships held in professional organizations, and describe how your past participation has helped enhance your professional development.
- List any professional certifications and explain their significance relative to the position sought.

Work Experiences
- List all work experiences that have helped prepare you for the position sought.
- Describe the scope of your work responsibilities in each job.
- Include commendations and illustrations of the quality of your work.

Extracurricular Activities
- Describe your participation in nonacademic clubs and organizations and how what you learned and experienced helped increase your abilities and knowledge.
- Explain the importance of each aspect of your volunteer work.

Examples of Your Professional Abilities
- Include copies of awards, dean's list citations, and thank-you letters for service.
- Illustrate your competence, such as through publication of student research, a videotape of a professional presentation, samples of lesson plans, or internship evaluations.
- Provide examples of your commitment to lifelong learning.

Professional Goals
- Share your long-term career aspirations and your current plans for achieving them.

diversity of your extracurricular activities will enrich your college years and possibly assist in your career choice. Internships and volunteer activities, especially those that enable you to gain invaluable experiences related to your interest area, are important additions to your undergraduate years. Obtain certifications prior to seeking your first job, since many positions require these for employment. In addition, completing advanced degrees in an area of specialization will enhance your knowledge and marketability. The process of getting a job begins with the courses you take, the experiences you gain, and the abilities you demonstrate as a young professional. Build on this base of knowledge and experience by examining various career options, developing a résumé, writing application letters, and interviewing for a part-time or summer job.

CAREER PERSPECTIVE

SUSAN B. JOHNSON
Vice President and Director of
Education and Certification
The Cooper Institute
Dallas, Texas

EDUCATION
B.S., Physical Education, Memphis State University
M.Ed., Physical Education, Memphis State University
Ed.D., Teacher Behavior in Physical Education, University of
North Carolina at Greensboro

JOB RESPONSIBILITIES AND HOURS
Susan and her staff develop and conduct certification workshops for exercise instructors, law enforcement agencies, military instructors, and a variety of other health and fitness professionals such as physicians, fitness specialists, and personal trainers. Her division provides products, consulting services, and training for Health Promotion, particularly at the worksite. She also writes articles, initiates research, develops new materials, teaches workshops, and consults with agencies, businesses, and organizations in regard to physical fitness programs. Susan works from 7:00 A.M. to 5:00 P.M. Monday through Friday and 10:00 A.M. to 2.00 P.M. most Saturdays, typical hours for this career.

SPECIALIZED COURSE WORK, DEGREES, AND WORK EXPERIENCES NEEDED FOR THIS CAREER
Management is a major function of this job, so administrative courses are important. Because teaching is also a primary responsibility, education courses are critical. It is highly recommended that individuals wishing to pursue this career possess specialized knowledge in health promotion, exercise physiology, psychology, kinesiology, nutrition, and sociology. Susan states that her doctorate has provided a vital background for her specific responsibilities, although other corporate fitness careers may require only master's degrees. In addition, a medical background, statistical skills, and research methodology complement this work. New initiatives include distance learning and home study courses that are video, audio, and web based. Therefore, videography and computer programming are excellent skills to develop as a student. Also, it is very useful to know how to create PowerPoint slides and import artwork and graphics to make slides visually attractive. Other abilities needed include competence in speaking before groups, writing skills, leadership abilities, and administrative skills. Jobs that involve teaching and research will best prepare students for this type of career. Also, administrative jobs can help students acquire the necessary organizational and management skills.

SATISFYING ASPECTS
One reason health and fitness professionals are needed is the growth in corporate fitness programs. Leaders in business and industry are realizing that taking care of their number one asset, their employees, is cost efficient as well as an excellent fringe benefit for the participants. Many physical educators are attracted to working with adults in the fitness field, where the major challenges are developing motivational and adherence strategies.

Susan especially enjoys training fitness leaders to implement safe, effective, and enjoyable programs. She also takes pleasure in seeing individuals make lifestyle changes that lead to healthier and happier lives.

JOB POTENTIAL

Susan predicts that the fitness boom will continue to expand and will affect all phases of life: work, home, school, business, and community. In the twenty-first century, the availability of jobs for training health and fitness professionals will expand dramatically. Businesses and industries will continue to provide fitness programs for executives and will offer more programs for blue-collar workers, too. Urban areas with larger companies will have more jobs, although businesses in small cities may jointly offer programs for their employees. Occupational groups, such as police officers, will begin to set health and fitness standards for their members, and the general public will seek out qualified professionals to help them regain and maintain health. The salary range is $100,000–$125,000 a year for this type of fitness management position.

SUGGESTIONS FOR STUDENTS

Susan suggests that students study the field and all its related subdisciplines, and acquire as much knowledge as possible from current leaders in the field and from their writings. Students should become involved in professional organizations and develop professional networks and contacts. On an emotional level, she recommends that students find a special area of interest or study that appeals to their sense of commitment. In the field of physical fitness, Susan stresses the importance of functioning as a role model. Credibility is lost if fitness leaders smoke, are overweight, use drugs, or practice other unhealthy habits. Susan believes that working as a team player and being willing to do a variety of tasks to reach an ultimate goal are important. She also recommends that physical educators learn to think futuristically and to act progressively and productively to make valid plans come to life.

REVIEW QUESTIONS

1. What are the values of establishing long- and short-term goals?

2. Why is an internship important?

3. Give four examples of internship possibilities for an exercise science or a sport management major.

4. Give four examples of volunteer experiences that can enhance your undergraduate years and make you more marketable in your job search.

5. What are the various types of graduate degree programs? What is the emphasis of each?

6. What are five important questions you should ask about your prospective career?

7. Name several types of certificates you can obtain to prepare you for working in the health and fitness industry.

8. What should a résumé include?

STUDENT ACTIVITIES

1. Talk with other students who have completed internships in intramurals, in athletics, with a community group, in a corporate fitness program, or with a sports business. Ask them about the positive and negative aspects of their experiences.

2. Get involved in one professionally related extracurricular activity for at least one semester. Evaluate your experiences to determine what you learned and how they could help you in the future.

3. Find out about your institution's majors' club in your field of study and become actively involved with it.

4. Select a certification, such as one in health and fitness, and set short- and long-term goals for achieving it.

5. Interview individuals in a career that interests you. Ask their advice about how best to prepare to enter that career.

6. Write a letter of application for a position in your chosen career. In one paragraph, highlight your most significant qualities.

7. Using the Internet or library resources, obtain information about three graduate programs that may interest you.

8. Conduct a debate in class about the pros and cons of doing volunteer activities.

9. Find three articles about the value of either networking, volunteering, or internships. Write a one-page paper reporting on your choice.

SUGGESTED READINGS

Ammon R, Ming L, Delpy L: Careers in sport management: part II, *Strategies* 11(5):13, 1998. This article provides information about various career possibilities in the field of sport management.

Campbell K, Kovar SK: Fitness/exercise science internships: how to ensure success, *JOPERD* 65(2):69, 1994. The authors identify four potential areas associated with an internship—academic preparation, intern accountability, supervisor's skills, and appropriateness of the internship site—and suggest possible solutions.

Cardinal BJ: Role modeling attitudes and physical activity and fitness promoting behaviors of HPERD professionals and preprofessionals, *Res Q for Exer & Sp* 72(1):84, 2001. This research note described the activity and fitness behaviors of professionals in the field to better understand their attitudes toward serving as role models for fitness and found positive relationships between body mass index and physical activity.

Cono J: Middle and high school officiating: crisis or opportunity, *Coach & Ath Dir* 70(5):10, 2000. This article examines issues confronting officiating in schools, such as meeting the increasing demand for more officials, ensuring the quality of their officiating, and the cost of officiating. The author suggests that athletic directors must address and resolve each of these concerns.

Dils AK: The application of teacher education curriculum to theory of interscholastic coaching education: learning outcomes associated with a quality interscholastic athletic program, *The Phy Educ* 57(2):88, 2000. This article describes how coaching education programs in college should prepare coaches of interscholastic athletes to teach, model, and reinforce outcomes associated with educational objectives.

Gilbert WD, Trudel P: Learning to coach through experience: reflection in model youth sport coaches, *J of Teach in PE* 21(1):16, 2001. The authors stress that valuable learning occurs when individuals volunteer to coach youth sports teams. One important aspect of this learning occurs when the volunteer coach reflects on the experiences and thereby gains insights about future actions to take.

Job shadowing—career exploration at work, *Techniques* 76(8):30, 2001. This article describes how job shadowing can enhance learning through work-based experiences as well as provide a valuable opportunity for career exploration.

Michno D: Gotta get a plan: setting and reaching goals, *Career World,* 25(3):14, 1996. This special feature focuses on setting goals and working to achieve those goals to establish the direction of your career.

Nnadozie E, Ishiyama J, Chon J: Undergraduate research internships and graduate school success, *J of Coll Stud Dev* 42(2):145, 2001. The authors examine the relationships between involvement in research studies while an undergraduate student and the transfer of these experiences and learning into graduate educational programs.

Stier WF: Sport management internships: from theory to practice, *Strategies* 15(4):7, 2002. This article suggests that through internships, sport management students learn to apply what they have learned in their college courses in a very practical sense.

UNIT 2

HISTORY AND DEVELOPMENT OF PHYSICAL EDUCATION, EXERCISE SCIENCE, AND SPORT

CHAPTER

7

SPORT IN THE ANCIENT WORLD AND OUR EUROPEAN HERITAGE

KEY CONCEPTS

- Early civilizations, including the Greeks, valued physical development to varying degrees.
- The Greek Ideal stressed the unity of the "man of action" with the "man of wisdom."
- Training to become a knight was the primary physical development valued during the Middle Ages.
- A search for knowledge and an emphasis on "a sound mind in a sound body" emerged during the Renaissance.
- Naturalism focused on teaching children when they were ready to learn and on meeting their individual needs.
- European gymnastics programs developed to train soldiers for nationalistic purposes and later influenced school curricula.
- The British popularized and spread their love of sports and games.

Throughout history, people have participated in various physical activities. Integral to the early civilizations' survival tasks of seeking food, clothing, shelter, and protection were the utilitarian skills of running, jumping, throwing, wrestling, climbing, and swimming. Before formal educational programs emerged, tribal leaders and parents mandated that children learn and practice survival skills through imitation. Communal requirements stressed physical prowess for both aggressive and defensive purposes.

Modern programs of physical education in the United States borrowed primarily from the philosophies, activities, and developments of Europeans from prehistoric times through the 1800s. The Greeks revered optimal physical prowess, and Greek athletics laid the foundation for subsequent physical education and sport programs. Military training in many countries served utilitarian purposes and sometimes supplanted religious ideals. After social conditions stabilized, the philosophy of naturalism stressed development of the body to help educate the whole child. Gymnastics that stressed nationalistic goals borrowed the apparatus and activities of the earlier naturalistic programs. Sports and games in England offered an alternative to these formalized gymnastics systems.

EARLY CULTURES

The Egyptians (2000 to 30 B.C.) have been recognized more for their alphabet and their scientific, agricultural, and engineering prowess than for their educational achievements. Although the Egyptians did not have health objectives related to physical activity, they showed interest in physical development if it achieved a vocational, recreational, or religious objective. The warrior class physically trained for hunting, charioteering, warfare, and wrestling. For recreation, people of all classes swam, hunted, and played ball games. Dancing, like wrestling, was a form of entertainment. Dancing was also important in religious rituals.

Between 2500 B.C. and A.D. 1200, the Chinese adhered to an entrenched social system based on reverence for the aged scholar. Although in earlier eras physical training was somewhat valued, the religions of Taoism, Buddhism, and Confucianism emphasized the contemplative life. The defense-minded Chinese maintained a military class who participated in archery, boxing, chariot racing, football, and wrestling, but these activities were never popularized for the masses. Many Chinese flew kites, played chess, practiced light exercises called *Ku fu,* hunted, and fished. For the Chinese, literary studies and moral and religious training were valued most.

In India (2500 B.C. to A.D. 500), the Hindu religion imposed an unchanging social caste system on the people. This dogma renounced pleasure and individualism and advocated asceticism in preparation for the next life. Spiritual well-being led to healthful practices and to participation in physical exercises such as yoga, a system of meditation and regulated breathing. Buddhism, which deemphasized physical activities, sought to reform the excesses of the Indian caste system.

For various reasons, the Egyptians, Chinese, and Indians engaged minimally in physical activities. Not until the Greeks did a civilization openly stress physical prowess and prescribe organized methods for its development.

Greece, regarded as the birthplace of Western civilization, produced a rich heritage of art, drama, history, mathematics, oratory, philosophy, poetry, science, and sculpture, as well as the earliest recorded athletic or sports activities. This progressive society, which recognized the importance of educating the whole individual, evolved through four eras: (1) the Homeric era, from prehistoric times until the first recorded Olympic Games in 776 B.C.; (2) the era of the totalitarian city-state of Sparta, from 776 B.C. to 371 B.C.; (3) the early Athenian era, which emphasized democracy and individual freedom, from 776 B.C. to the end of the Persian Wars in 480 B.C.; and (4) the later Athenian era, from 480 B.C. until 338 B.C., which grew out of heightened intellectual curiosity (Van Dalen & Bennett, 1971).

THE HOMERIC GREEKS (BEFORE 776 B.C.)

The Homeric era was named for the Greek poet Homer, who is credited with writing the *Iliad* and the *Odyssey,* which include the earliest records of athletic competitions. Book XXIII of the *Iliad* describes the funeral games held in honor of Patrocius, Achilles' friend who was killed in the Trojan War. The contests included a chariot race, boxing, wrestling, a footrace, a duel with spears, a discus throw, archery, and a javelin throw. Athletes of the period competing in individual events fought fiercely to win. In the *Odyssey,* Homer chronicled the wanderings and return of Odysseus from the Trojan War. Illustrative of these adventures was one episode in Book VIII in which Odysseus, taunted by the Phaeacians, responded by throwing the discus beyond the distances achieved by their athletes.

The predominant philosophy that developed during the Homeric era became known as the **Greek Ideal,** which stressed the unity of the "man of action" and the "man of wisdom." This all-around mental, moral, and physical excellence was called **arete** and was believed to be personified by the Greek gods. Revered as part deity and part human, the 12 major gods of the Olympic Council were worshiped as the personifications of the Greek Ideal, with superior intellectual and physical capacities, such as strength, endurance, agility, and bravery. In funeral games held in honor of both respected soldiers killed in battle and the gods, Greek warrior-athletes competed to prove their arete. Success, or winning to prove one's athletic superiority, was valued more highly than prizes. Prior to competing, many athletes sought the favor of the gods.

> **Greek Ideal:**
> unity of the "man of action" and the "man of wisdom"
>
> **arete:**
> all-around mental, moral, and physical excellence valued by the Greeks
>
> **agoge:**
> an educational system for Spartan boys that ensured the singular goal of serving the city-state

THE SPARTANS (776 B.C. TO 371 B.C.)

The Greeks organized themselves into small governmental units known as city-states. The two dominant, though dramatically contrasting, city-states were Sparta and Athens. By the eighth century B.C., Sparta had begun its military conquests. As Sparta conquered land and took captives, a strict code of discipline, rather than adherence to the Greek Ideal, was imposed on its people. The **agoge,** an educational system that ensured the singular goal of serving the city-state, evolved. Mandating complete submission, the Spartan civilization became static because everything, including education, was controlled exclusively by the government.

At birth, a child was examined by a council of elders. If healthy and strong, the child was spared. Weak or sickly children were exposed to the elements to die. The mothers' roles in raising children resembled those of state nurses; they had to suppress all tender and maternalistic feelings. While sons were taught to value their roles as obedient soldiers, daughters learned about their responsibility to bear healthy children.

To prepare themselves physically for this duty, girls participated in state-prescribed gymnastics in addition to wrestling, swimming, and horseback riding. Dancing was also important in the education of girls and boys as a means both of physical conditioning and of honoring the gods.

The boys' educational system, the agoge, was highly structured and formalized. Boys were conscripted by the state at seven years of age and remained in military service until death. Spartan boys began their military training with running and jumping for conditioning. They progressed to swimming, hunting, wrestling, boxing, playing ball, riding horses bareback, throwing the discus and the javelin, and competing in the **pancratium,** a contest combining wrestling and boxing skills. Young boys were trained to endure hardships and pain. Discipline reigned supreme; youths who failed to develop valor, devotion to the state, and military skill were punished, often severely.

> **pancratium:**
> an event in Panhellenic festivals that combined wrestling and boxing skills into an "almost-anything-goes" combat

Beginning at 20 years of age, youths engaged in intensive military maneuvers and actual warfare. These Spartan soldiers, who had been conditioned to fight until death, repeatedly demonstrated their superiority over neighboring city-states and other foes. Not only did the Spartans dominate militarily during this time, but they also won more Olympic victories than athletes from any other city-state. Spartan men, at the age of 30 years, qualified for citizenship and were expected to marry; however, their obligation to the state continued as they trained youth in the public barracks. The Spartan military machine, with its singular focus on physical prowess and disregard for intellectual development, contributed to its inability to rule its innumerable captives and lands. Although they made excellent soldiers, the people were trained not to think for themselves but to perform on command. The Spartans were also few in number due to their strict practices. These factors led to the end of their domination as a city-state.

THE EARLY ATHENIANS (776 B.C. TO 480 B.C.)

Athens differed sharply from Sparta. The Greek Ideal became the Athenian Ideal as this city-state sought to provide an educational system that encouraged boys to develop their physical and mental abilities. Within this framework of democracy, liberalism, and the popularization of various philosophies, physical prowess flourished as an integral part of the preparation of boys for war and as a means through which to depict beauty and harmony.

Girls remained at home under the care of their mothers and received little or no education. Once married, they lived secluded lives. Unlike the physically trained women in Sparta, the Athenian women's social role typically was very different from the men's role. Boys in the lower classes, though, were as uneducated as girls.

The Athenian educational system, which valued the all-around citizen, dominated the lives of upper-class boys, who, under the guidance of their fathers, learned about their future responsibilities. Usually beginning at age 7 and lasting until 14 to 18 years, young boys were formally educated at privately owned schools. The time when each boy started, the length of time he attended, and the time when he ended this phase of his education were determined solely by the father, since no governmental regulations existed. Not all boys could attend these schools, since fathers had to pay for their sons' education.

The importance attached to the all-around-development ideal was evident in each boy's attendance at two schools. A music school provided instruction in arithmetic, literature, and music, while at a **palaestra**, called a wrestling school, boys trained physically. Both schools were equally valued, as the unity concept prevailed. Palaestras were owned and directed by **paidotribes**, the first physical education teachers. They were not elaborate athletic facilities but varied from sparse rooms to simple buildings. There the boys practiced wrestling, boxing, jumping, and dancing. Some palaestras also included playing fields and a place for swimming.

palaestra:
a Greek school where boys learned wrestling, boxing, jumping, dancing, and gymnastics

paidotribes:
the first physical education teachers, who taught Greek boys wrestling, boxing, jumping, dancing, and gymnastics at a palaestra

gymnasium:
a site for intellectual and physical activities for Greek citizens

At the age of 18 years, Athenian boys became eligible for citizenship. For two years thereafter they were subject to military service, if the state needed them, although no mandatory conscription existed. From 20 years of age onward, upper-class Athenian men did not work but instead spent their days at government-furnished **gymnasiums**, sites for intellectual and physical activites for Greek citizens. There they practiced athletics to maintain their readiness as warriors in case they were needed by the state. Intellectual discussions, governmental decisions, and social interactions were equally important facets of life at the gymnasium.

Greek dancing provided one means of honoring the gods as part of religious worship. It also enhanced physical conditioning and demonstrated the symmetry and beauty adored by the Athenians. Athletics played a similar role, as festivals honoring the gods gave Greek men the opportunity to display their physical prowess and aesthetically pleasing bodies. The importance of honoring the gods eventually led to a proliferation of festivals throughout Greece.

THE LATE ATHENIANS (480 B.C. TO 338 B.C.)

The Athenian-led victory over the Persians in 480 B.C. set the stage for several cultural changes. Economic expansion, self-confidence, increased leisure time, intellectual curiosity, and expansion of political power combined to shift educational goals away from devotion to the state and toward a heightened pursuit of individual happiness. This rampant individualism led to a deemphasis of the physical aspects of education because, as members of the dominant city-state, citizens no longer saw the need to train as soldiers. The Athenian warrior-athletes were replaced by mercenaries and professional athletes.

The gymnasiums became more like pleasure resorts than places for exercise. They provided sites for philosophical discussions and the training of professional

 WEB CONNECTIONS

1. www.minbar.cs.dartmouth.edu/greecom/olympics
   This site provides a plethora of historical facts and interesting information about the history and events of the ancient Olympic Games.

2. www.perseus.tufts.edu/Olympics
   Students visiting this site can learn more about ancient Olympic sports, tour ancient Olympia, gain an understanding of the context and spirit of the ancient Olympic Games, and read stories from Olympic athletes of that time.

3. www.sunsite.tus.ac.jp/olympics/classical/other_festivals.html
   This site briefly describes the other Panhellenic festivals—Pythian Games, Isthmian Games, Nemean Games, and other Panhellenic Games.

4. www.roman-empire.net
   Learn more about the Roman Empire through the brief descriptions of the early and late Republic, the Emperors, the army, society, and religion, as well as through the pictures provided on this site.

5. www.kyrene.k12.az.us/schools/brisas/sunda/ma/mahome.htm
   This site, developed by school students, provides brief overviews and pictures of life in the Middle Ages.

6. www.learner.org/exhibits/renaissance/middleages.html
   After visiting this site, you will know more about the major aspects of the rebirth of knowledge (Renaissance) as Europe emerged from the Dark Ages.

athletes. The Golden Age of Athens (443 B.C. to 429 B.C.) was highlighted by a flowering of democracy and intellectual curiosity led by the Sophists, a class of teachers of rhetoric, philosophy, and the art of successful living, and by philosophers such as Plato. Warning cries from some philosophers about the undermining of the Athenian society went largely unheeded. As a result, the Athenians were militarily unprepared and fell to the Macedonians in 338 B.C.

THE PANHELLENIC FESTIVALS (776 B.C. TO A.D. 400)

Festivals honoring the gods during the Homeric period led to the establishment of regular celebrations, which expanded dramatically in the fifth century B.C. The warrior-athletes, who were expected to perfect their skills for warfare, used these religious festivals to demonstrate their physical prowess, especially since this proved their allegiance to the Greek Ideal as personified by the gods. Some of these **Panhellenic** (meaning "for all Greeks") **festivals** also included musical events and aquatic displays. The Panhellenic festivals were exclusively for men with one exception: the Heraean Games, which were held for maiden women who competed in a footrace.

> **Panhellenic festivals:**
> festivals open to all Greeks in which athletic contests were a focal point

The ancient Olympic Games were unmatched in prestige among these festivals. They were held every four years at Olympia, in honor of Zeus, the chief Greek god. These events began at least by 776 B.C. (the date of the earliest existing artifact of a victory at Olympia), but probably started much earlier. The sacrifices to Zeus, feasting, and athletic contests lasted five days in August and attained such prestige that the perennially warring city-states would guarantee safe passage to travelers to the games. Box 7-1 lists when it is believed that each event became a part of the games at Olympia and provides a probable outline of how events were organized during the five days. This sequence of events, with sacrifices and other tributes to Zeus, reinforced the link between religious service and athletic competition.

To be eligible for the games at Olympia, a prospective athlete had to be male, Greek born, and free (not a slave), and had to train for 10 months before the contests (with the last month of training at Olympia under the guidance of the judges). Although the games were open to men from all social classes, the training requirement precluded participation by most poor Greeks, who had to work. Athletes were required to take an oath of fair play. Victors received a wreath of olive branches to symbolize their highly respected victory. Accorded a hero's welcome when returning home, a victor reveled in triumphal processions and banquets, special privileges, and monetary rewards. Initially Olympia provided no accommodations for either spectators or athletes, as neither a stadium nor a site for the contests existed. The games were scheduled in open spaces with spectators sitting wherever they could. Later construction of a stadium (for footraces) and the hippodrome (for horse and chariot races) provided space for about 40,000 spectators.

BOX 7-1   ANCIENT OLYMPIC GAMES

Chronology

776 B.C.	Stade race
724 B.C.	Added the two-stade race
720 B.C.	Added the longer distance races
708 B.C.	Added pentathlon and wrestling
688 B.C.	Added boxing
680 B.C.	Added chariot race
648 B.C.	Added pancratium and horse race
632 B.C.	Added events for boys
580 B.C.	Added the race in armor
472 B.C.	Festival set as a five-day event and the sequence of events set as follows:

First Day
Oath-taking ceremony
Contests for heralds and trumpeters
Contests for boys
Sacrifices, prayers, singing of hymns, and other religious observances

Second Day
Chariot race
Horse race
Pentathlon (discus, javelin, long jump, stade race, and wrestling)

Third Day
Main sacrifice to Zeus
Footraces

Fourth Day
Wrestling
Boxing
Pancratium
Race in armor

Fifth Day
Prize-giving ceremony
Service of thanksgiving to Zeus
Banquet

The **stade race,** so named because it was a footrace the length of the stadium (about 200 meters), was probably the only event in the first games at Olympia. A two-stade race, a longer race of about 12 laps, and a race in armor were later added to this phase of the athletic contests. Marble slabs

stade race:
a footrace in Panhellenic games run the length of the stadium

with toe grooves may have served as starting blocks, and either a trumpet blast or a starting gate was probably used to start these events. In the longer distance races, the athletes rounded posts at the opposite end of the stadium.

Hand-to-hand combat events included boxing, wrestling, and the pancratium. Since no weight categories existed, boxing pitted two athletes of any size against each other until one raised a hand to admit defeat. No gloves were worn; the boxers' hands were wrapped with pieces of leather. Blows were confined primarily to the head, often resulting in severe injuries. Wrestling was one of the most popular events because its competitors displayed agility, gracefulness, and strength. The objective was to throw the opponent to the ground three times. The pancratium borrowed from boxing and wrestling to become an "almost-anything-goes" combat. Except for biting and gouging, an athlete could employ any maneuver, such as tripping, breaking fingers, and strangle holds, to force an opponent's admission of defeat.

Chariots, two-wheeled vehicles pulled by four horses, raced, as did horses, at the hippodrome, a narrow field about 500 meters long. These races were limited to the wealthy, who could afford to maintain the horses and hire the charioteers. The victors were the owners, not the charioteers or jockeys. The chariot race consisted of 12 laps.

The winner of the **pentathlon** was recognized as the best all-around athlete. Although the order of events and the method of determining the victor have been lost in antiquity, the discus throw, the javelin throw, the long jump, the stade race, and wrestling constituted the pentathlon. Like the long jump and the javelin throw, the

pentathlon:
a five-event competition that included the discus throw, javelin throw, long jump, stade race, and wrestling

Greek sprinters in the stade race—one of the five events in the pentathlon as well as an individual event.

Javelin throw—one of the five events in the pentathlon.

Long jump—one of the five events in the pentathlon.

discus throw existed only as a pentathlon event. In the discus throw, the athlete hurled a circular piece of stone or bronze about 1 foot in diameter and weighing 4 to 5 pounds. In the long jump, which was probably similar to today's triple jump, legend recorded that one athlete jumped a distance of more than 55 feet. Jumpers were aided by handheld weights, called **halteres,** which were swung to enhance their performances. The javelin was thrown for both distance and form as a test of skill and strength. A leather thong was wrapped around the 8- to 10-foot javelin, giving it a rotary motion

halteres:
handheld weights used by jumpers to enhance their performances

Discus throw—one of the five events in the pentathlon.

Wrestling—one of the five events in the pentathlon, as well as an individual event.

upon release, thereby increasing accuracy. The stade race and the wrestling match probably concluded the pentathlon, although these may not have been held if one athlete had already won the first three events.

Two developments ushered in a change in attitude toward the Panhellenic festivals. Beginning in Athens, intellectual curiosity and a search for knowledge

The ancient stadium at Delphi, site of the Pythian Games.

TABLE 7-1				
PANHELLENIC FESTIVALS				
Name	*Frequency*	*Honoring*	*Location*	*Wreath for Victor*
Olympic Games	Every four years	Zeus	Olympia	Olive leaves
Pythian Games	Every four years (third year of each Olympiad)	Apollo	Delphi	Bay leaves
Isthmian Games	Every two years (second and fourth years of each Olympiad)	Poseidon	Isthmia	Pine
Nemean Games	Every two years	Zeus	Nemea	Wild celery

replaced the Greek Ideal and hence lessened interest in physical development. Within the games themselves, lucrative prizes increasingly overshadowed the earlier motive of honoring the gods through displays of athletic prowess (see Table 7-1). Professional athletes who trained under coaches at the gymnasiums and who specialized in certain events became prominent in the contests. Expensive prizes led to cheating, corruption, and bribery. Although officially ended by Roman decree around A.D. 400, the Olympics had lost association with their former values much earlier.

Pancratium.

THE ROMAN REPUBLIC (500 B.C. TO 27 B.C.)

Roman civilization began as a small tribal community near the Tiber River during the height of the Greek civilization. By extending its rule over neighboring tribes, the Roman nobles, who were landowners, succeeded in establishing a republic around 500 B.C. Soon the common people, who had been given land for their military service, demanded and received greater voice in the government. Thus, through this democratization process, many Romans attained a higher degree of political and economic freedom.

Roman life during this era focused singularly on serving the state, even though the home provided education for youths without government involvement. Fathers and mothers taught their sons to become citizen-soldiers, including in their education a mental and physical readiness for war, respect for the law, and reverence for the gods. Accompanying their fathers to the Campus Martius or other military camps, boys learned military skills such as archery, fencing, javelin throwing, marching, riding, running, swimming, and wrestling; they developed bodily strength, courage, and obedience to commands as they trained. Conscripted into the military at 17 years of age, men were available for active duty, if needed, until age 47. During these 30 years, men were expected to fulfill their business and political duties as well.

Daughters were educated to assume a vital role in raising children and were expected to instill in their sons the importance of fighting, and even dying, for the state. Roman women were more highly respected and socially active than Athenian women.

Religious festivals honoring the gods held as prominent a place in the Roman society as they had during Greek times. However, the Romans did not

TABLE 7-2

COMPARISON OF ATHLETIC PROGRAMS

Early Athens	Late Athens	Roman Republic	Roman Empire
Participants			
Aristocratic citizens	Professional athletes	Citizen-soldiers	Professional gladiators and charioteers
Motivation			
All-around development	Profit	Preparation for war	Profit
Training			
Gymnasiums and palaestras	Gymnasiums under trainers	Military camps and fathers	Specialized schools
Events			
Archery, boxing, chariot races, discus, footraces, javelin, and wrestling	Boxing, chariot races, footraces, horse races, pancratium, pentathlon, and wrestling	Archery, fencing, javelin, marching, riding, running, swimming, and wrestling	Chariot races and gladiatorial contests
Organization			
Festivals	Scheduled games and festivals	Festivals	Frequent, organized festivals
Number of Stadiums or Arenas			
Few	Many	Few	Many
Number of Spectators			
Limited	Thousands	Limited	Thousands
Professionals or Amateurs			
Amateurs	Professionals	Amateurs	Professionals
Awards			
Some, but not most important	Lucrative benefits	Limited awards	Lucrative prizes

participate in athletic contests or dance; rather, they offered sacrifices to their gods and then watched horse and chariot races or gladiatorial contests. These festivals provided leisure-time relief from strenuous military training, but served no educational purposes. Table 7-2 compares Greek and Roman athletic programs.

THE ROMAN EMPIRE (27 B.C. TO A.D. 476)

The economic and political freedoms gained by citizens during the Republic eroded during the century before the Empire was established in 27 B.C. under Augustus Caesar. The hardy peasants, who had received land in exchange for military service, were ravaged by years of war and subsequent debts and mortgages. Powerful landowners seized this opportunity to expand their estates and gain greater political influence. The poorer citizens, who were forced off their land, migrated to Rome, where they lived off the public dole. Replaced by a professional army and denied political freedoms and personal dignity, the common people spent their days attending the festivals and games sponsored by corrupt, upper-class senators or the emperors. Gambling on the outcomes of these contests became a favorite pastime.

At least 200 days per year were public holidays and provided opportunities for festivals. Up to 260,000 spectators watched chariot races at the Circus Maximus, attesting to the popularity of these contests. Professional charioteers hired by the teams (the blues, the greens, the reds, and the whites) raced their low, lightweight chariots drawn by four horses in seven-lap races, for a distance of about 3 miles. The Colosseum became the favorite site for the gladiatorial contests, where, to the pleasure of as many as 90,000 spectators, animal fights featured elephants, bulls, tigers, lions, panthers, and bears. Condemned criminals, social undesirables, and Christians were forced to combat lions, tigers, and panthers. Massive sea battles in the Colosseum provided additional bloody, gory entertainment. Gladiators, armed with shield and sword, buckle and dagger, or net and spear, fought each other for freedom or for money.

Gladiators and charioteers trained physically, but most other Romans lost interest in developing their own bodies because they were no longer expected to serve as soldiers. Instead, **thermae,** for baths of varying water temperatures, provided leisure for both men and women (with separate hours reserved for the women). At the numerous thermae, Roman men participated in health gymnastics or ball play to overcome indolent lifestyles that featured gluttonous feasts and drinking bouts.

thermae:
facilities in Rome for contrast baths of varying water temperatures and other leisure activities

Claudius Galen, born in Pergamum in Greece and educated in Alexandria in Egypt when it was the greatest medical center in the ancient world, became a physician to emperors and gladiators. His public demonstrations of anatomy enhanced his stature as a physician, despite the prevailing taboo against human dissection that resulted in his conducting most of his anatomical studies using animals. Galen's writings were circulated widely during his lifetime, with translations of his original Greek manuscripts forming the basis of medical education in medieval universities.

The moral fabric and physical abilities of the Romans dissipated rapidly during an era characterized by governmental upheavals, power struggles, and an apathetic and dependent populace. In A.D. 476, with the deposition of the last Roman emperor by the Visigoths under Odoacer, the domination of the Roman Empire came to an ignoble end. As was true of the demise of the city-state of Athens, a lack of emphasis on physical development contributed to the decline of a once powerful civilization.

MEDIEVAL EUROPE (500 TO 1500)

The years following the fall of the Roman Empire represented a low point physically and intellectually. During the Middle Ages, many church leaders, such as St. Augustine, spoke against dancing because it had degenerated from its earlier religious purpose. Church leaders also opposed frivolous activities that might detract from piety, proper commitment to worship, and godly living. The Catholic church, in seeking a higher level of morality than displayed by most Romans, regarded the body and anything that benefited it as sinful. **Asceticism,** a doctrine that renounces the comforts of society and espouses austere self-discipline, especially as an act of religious devotion, was practiced by many monks during medieval times.

> **asceticism:**
> a doctrine that renounces the comforts of society and espouses austere self-discipline, especially as an act of religious devotion
>
> **knight:**
> warrior during the medieval period

The only schools that existed during this time were at the monasteries, which restricted intellectual education to those who served the church. The common people were dominated by concerns for survival rather than education. The monks, however, preserved the Greek philosophies. Later these philosophies would again be studied and valued by a broad range of people.

European society in the eleventh to the sixteenth centuries was feudalistic; that is, the economic, political, and social aspects of life centered around ownership of land and the military power to maintain or expand territory. The monarch, at least theoretically, owned the land. Unable to rule diverse properties successfully, the king divided the territory among nobles who, in turn, promised military service. As vassals to the king, they similarly divided their holdings among lesser vassals, with the same reciprocal protection guarantees. At the bottom of this pyramidal structure were the serfs, or peasants, who toiled in the fields. Their labors were meagerly rewarded with protection provided by those they served.

The vassal landowners, who were **knights,** were the only ones in feudal society to value physical training, although the peasants engaged in various recreational pursuits. At 7 years of age, the sons of nobles left their homes to go to the manors of other knights. Under the guidance of the ladies of the castles for the

Medieval knights prepared for battle.

next seven years, these **pages** were educated through stories about chivalry, with its code of moral and social duties of knighthood. **Squires,** beginning at 14 years of age, learned the arts of archery, climbing, dancing, fencing, jousting, riding, swimming, tourneying, and wrestling. As a valet for a knight, the squire served meals, cleaned armor, cared for the knight's horse, played chess and backgammon, and accompanied the knight into battle. Following seven years of extensive training as a squire, the youth became eligible for knighthood. Once knighted, these nobles engaged in hunting and hawking and continued their training for battle.

page:
term used for the boy during the first seven-year training period (ages 7–14), under the guidance of the lady of the castle, to become a knight

squire:
term used for the boy during the second seven-year training period (ages 14–21), under the direction of a knight

In the isolation of the manorial system of the Middle Ages, few opportunities existed for social interaction and entertainment, so tournaments grew in popularity to fill this void. Although festive occasions, these tournaments focused on combats between knights, who divided into two teams and fought under conditions similar to war in the **grand tourney,** or **melee.** Although strict rules and blunt weapons supposedly limited the injuries, fatalities frequently occurred in the melee, leading to its demise. Another event at the tournaments was **jousting,** which pitted two mounted knights armed with lances in a head-on attempt to unseat each other. Since weapons were blunt and the objective was not to kill the opponent, the joust gradually became the primary event of the tournaments.

> **grand tourney** or **melee:**
> combats fought under conditions similar to war between two teams of knights
>
> **jousting:**
> an event at medieval tournaments in which two mounted knights armed with lances attempted in a head-on charge to unseat each other
>
> **Renaissance:**
> a period from the fifteenth to seventeenth centuries marked by a renewed appreciation for classical culture

Because war served as an adventurous solution to boredom, and because service to God was required of the knights, many willingly volunteered for the eight Crusades between 1096 and 1270. Instigated by the church, these military expeditions attempted to expel Moslems and Turks from the Holy Lands and to establish papal control in that region. The knights profited from the captured spoils of war, and some took part mainly for this reason.

Interaction with people from other civilizations through the Crusades contrasted markedly with the isolated lifestyle of the feudalistic period, which peaked between 1250 and 1350. As the importance of the knights lessened because of the invention of gunpowder, towns became established as trade centers. The emergence of a strong merchant class in these towns started the transition to a period of intellectual, cultural, and social reawakening.

THE RENAISSANCE AND THE REFORMATION (1450 TO 1650)

A renewed appreciation for classical culture grew out of the intellectual void of the Middle Ages. Intellectual curiosity and creativity were encouraged rather than stymied as education came to be highly valued by people of all social classes. During the Middle Ages, several allied yet diverse philosophies developed; these blossomed from the fifteenth to seventeenth centuries, marked by a renewed appreciation for classical cultural called the **Renaissance.** They directly influenced attitudes toward physical education, although most often the mind and the body were viewed as two separate entities. Scholasticism, based on the authority of church leaders and the writings of the Greek philosopher Aristotle, placed intellectual development in a revered position alongside a fixed religious dogma.

Humanistic education in Italy stressed the harmonious and holistic development of human beings, embracing the Greek Ideal of unity. A sound mind in a sound body described this philosophy, which implemented the principles of humanism and emphasized the physical as well as the intellectual development of students. Humanists stressed the importance of a healthy body as preparation for intellectual endeavors rather than stressing a dichotomous relationship between mind and body.

Realism, which grew out of humanism, emphasized the importance of understanding the Greek classics and of educating for life. The development of health (through exercise and play) and scientific thinking became critical educational outcomes for the realists. Realism and the other philosophies of this era directly or indirectly influenced the philosophies discussed in Chapter 4.

During the Protestant Reformation of the 1500s and 1600s, educational moralism developed as religious fervor combined with nationalism. Although initially wanting only to purify the Catholic church, reformers such as Martin Luther and John Calvin became catalysts for widespread religious and cultural change. Their doctrines stressed personal salvation, moral responsibilities, and state duties. Most of the Protestant sects deemphasized physical development as a distraction from these objectives. One religious group, the Puritans, was especially vehement in its opposition to frivolous activities and tried to enforce its strict doctrines on others. While humanism and realism furthered the Renaissance theme of a sound mind in a sound body, moralism hindered its acceptance as an educational goal.

Throughout the Renaissance, the 1700s, and most of the 1800s, education was valued for boys, especially those from the upper class, who attended boarding schools or were taught privately by tutors. Seldom was education provided for girls.

THE AGE OF ENLIGHTENMENT (1700s)

The Renaissance set the stage for the Age of Enlightenment, during which two additional philosophies influenced physical education. Englishman John Locke wrote about educational disciplinarianism. He said that character, especially valued for upper-class boys, requires a sound mind in a sound body, and developed best through moral and physical discipline. Jean-Jacques Rousseau, a French philosopher, led the rebellion against the devaluation of the individual. In his book *Emile,* Rousseau described the ideal way to educate a boy, stressing **naturalism,** or everything according to nature. That is, each child possesses a unique readiness to learn in a natural developmental process that should dictate when a child is exposed to various types of knowledge. The child, free to explore nature while recreating, thus

naturalism:
a belief that the scientific laws of nature govern life and that individual goals are more important than societal goals; everything according to nature

prepares physically for later intellectual pursuits and therefore will learn optimally. The Age of Enlightenment provided additional insights into how to educate a child, thereby laying the foundation for European gymnastics programs. Before examining these programs, however, it is important to frame the 1400s to 1800s into an educational context by describing some of the leaders in education.

EDUCATIONAL PROTAGONISTS (1400s TO 1800s)

Vittorino da Feltre (1378–1446) has been acclaimed as the greatest humanist schoolmaster and teacher of the Renaissance. As a teacher in the Italian court (private) schools supported by wealthy patrons, as well as in his school La Giocosa, da Feltre stressed the importance of intellectual, moral, and physical development, elevating physical education to a place of prominence. In his curriculum, he used archery, fencing, riding, and martial exercises to help create the complete citizen.

François Rabelais (1490–1553) helped provide a bridge between Renaissance humanists and seventeenth-century realists. He believed that physical education should focus on teaching skills to prepare young gentlemen for war. Especially valuable were the knightly exercises of the medieval era.

Michel de Montaigne (1533–1592) held that the body and soul are equal and inseparable. Thus, the mind and body are to be educated simultaneously, as the Greek philosopher Plato had stated centuries earlier. Montaigne's plan for education stressed thinking, learning by doing, developing the whole person, and preparing students for life. His *Essays* advocated a human-centered morality.

John Comenius (1592–1670), in *The Great Didactic,* set forth a comprehensive methodology for teaching. A body/mind dualist, like John Locke, he regarded play as essential for children's development, especially for ensuring healthy, vigorous bodies.

John Locke (1632–1704), despite his preoccupation with the education of gentlemen, valued physical exercise for its health benefits for all. His phrase "a sound mind in a sound body," taken from *Some Thoughts Concerning Education* (1693), became the motto for physical educators who supported his belief in the development of the healthy body as a primary function of education.

Jean-Jacques Rousseau (1712–1788) in *Emile* (1762) described an ideal education that continues throughout life. Physical activity within a natural setting should occur when the child is ready to learn.

Johann Pestalozzi's (1746–1827) ideas, as expressed in his book *Leonard and Gertrude,* established the foundation of modern educational theory. He advocated empirical education whereby children become adept at using their senses to make accurate observations. He also stressed the progression of learning from the simple to the complex, the importance of developmental readiness to learn, and the use of children's interest as an indicator of ability to understand. Daily physical exercise aided his students in achieving full unity and harmony between the body and intellect.

	TABLE 7-3		
	EDUCATIONAL PROTAGONISTS		
Individual	*Philosophy*	*Focus*	*Program/Setting*
Vittorino da Feltre	Humanism	Physically sound youth with alert intellect	Ball games; riding; running; fencing; dancing
François Rabelais	Verbal realism	Prepare gentlemen for war	Horsemanship; swordsmanship; swimming
Michel de Montaigne	Social humanism	Shape aristocratic youth for integrated life as a gentleman	Running; wrestling; dancing; hunting; riding
John Comenius	Sense realism	Play is essential to the natural educational process	Children's games; playing with toys
John Locke	Educational disciplinarianism	A sound mind in a sound body	Swimming; dancing; riding; fencing
Jean-Jacques Rousseau	Educational naturalism	Everything in education according to nature	Jumping; leaping; climbing; ball playing
Johann Pestalozzi	Educational developmentalism	Children learn progressively and in harmony with the body and mind	Games; gymnastics; outdoor activities
Friedrich Froebel	Educational developmentalism	Connect interest in learning with pleasure	Games in the open air; play

Friedrich Froebel (1782–1852) believed in play as the highest phase of child development. The efficacy of play could bring children to a realization of the internal and external unity of the world.

Table 7-3 compares these educational protagonists.

NATURALISM (1770 TO 1830)

Although the French were not receptive to Rousseau's educational theories, Johann Basedow, a German teacher, was. In establishing a school for boys called the Philanthropinum in 1774, Basedow sought to implement naturalistic principles that focused on meeting individual needs; he also stressed the importance of readiness to learn. At his school, he allotted three hours each day to instructional and recreational activities, such as gymnastics, sports, and games, and two hours to manual labor. While Basedow advocated dancing, fencing, riding, and vaulting, the teacher hired to direct the program, Johann Simon, introduced Greek gymnastics, consisting of jumping, running, throwing, and wrestling. Simon utilized natural settings to provide the needed apparatus, such as balance beams, high-jumping poles, jumping ditches, and tree swings. Johann Du Toit, Simon's successor, added archery, skating, swimming, marching, gardening, and woodworking to Basedow's original curriculum.

In 1785, Christian Salzmann patterned the program at the Schnepfenthal Educational Institute after Basedow's naturalistic lessons in games and gymnastics. Johann GutsMuths, who taught at Schnepfenthal for 50 years, was strongly influenced by Basedow's writings and provided similar activities and pieces of apparatus. GutsMuths' three- to four-hour daily program consisted of the following:

- Natural activities, such as jumping and running
- Greek gymnastics, such as throwing and wrestling
- Military exercises, such as fencing and marching
- Knightly activities, such as climbing and vaulting
- Manual labor, such as gardening and woodworking.

GutsMuths influenced many people with two significant books: *Gymnastics for the Young,* which not only described Schnepfenthal's program but also laid the theoretical foundation for modern programs, and *Games for Exercise and Recreation of the Body and Spirit,* which described the skills developed in 105 games or activities and provided illustrations of the apparatus used, such as climbing masts, hanging ladders, rope ladders, and wooden horses.

Examples of various German gymnastics movements on the horse.

NATIONALISM (1800s)

Friedrich Jahn, a German educator and an ardent patriot, visited the Schnepfenthal Educational Institute and borrowed many aspects of GutsMuths' program. Jahn's purpose in promoting physical development was nationalistic rather than naturalistic. He sought to develop fitness and strength in German youth for the eventual unification of all German people. After encouraging his students to climb trees, jump over ditches, run, and throw stones on half-holiday excursions from classes, he established the first turnplatz near Berlin in 1811. A **turnplatz** was an outdoor exercise area where boys, who became known as **turners,** trained using balance beams, ropes and ladders for climbing, high-jumping standards, horizontal bars, parallel bars, pole-vaulting standards, broad-jumping pits, vaulting horses, a figure-eight-shaped track, and a wrestling ring. Jahn also promoted **nationalism** through patriotic speeches and stories and group singing of patriotic songs. This theme of nationalism stressed promotion and defense of Germany. First boys and then, as the turner system of gymnastics expanded, males of all ages and social classes participated in the increasingly popular gymnastic exercises. Jahn explained his program in his book *German Gymnastics.*

turnplatz:
an outdoor exercise area established by Friedrich Jahn

turners:
individuals who exercised at a turnplatz

nationalism:
a pervasive theme stressing promotion and defense of one's country that was the desired outcome of several European systems of gymnastics in the 1800s

The turners vigorously advocated for a unified Germany, and many local turnplatz sites initially received government subsidies. After the Congress of Vienna realigned Germany into a confederation of 38 independent states in 1815, the turners' single-minded goal of a unified nation was viewed as threatening. Finally, in 1819, government leaders succeeded in banning turner gymnastics. Not until 1840 was it again legal to participate in turner gymnastics, although underground programs continued during the intervening years. Turner gymnastics never gained widespread popularity in other nations because of its nationalistic appeal and emphasis on strength.

In the 1840s, Adolph Spiess borrowed from his training in turner gymnastics to devise a system of German school gymnastics. Approval of his program in the public schools hinged on his defense of gymnastics as a subject equal to all others, one that had progressions for various ages, for boys and girls, and for all ability levels, and that required trained teachers and equipped indoor and outdoor facilities. Although influenced somewhat by Jahn's and GutsMuths' programs, Spiess devised a school system that stressed discipline and obedience and included diverse activities such as marching, free exercises, and gymnastics with musical accompaniment.

Class of female students exercising on a Swedish boom at the Royal Gymnastics Central Institute. Note stall bars on left-side wall.

Nationalism dominated Danish gymnastics in the early 1800s, too. Fitness, strength, and military competence emerged as the goals of Franz Nachtegall. In 1799, he established a private gymnasium in Copenhagen, the first of its kind. Nachtegall's curriculum, which borrowed extensively from the apparatus and exercises of GutsMuths, gained popularity and, in 1809, helped Denmark initiate the first European school program in physical education for boys. His *Manual of Gymnastics,* published in 1828, provided the curriculum for the schools. Teachers for the schools were initially educated alongside military men at the Military Gymnastic Institute, founded in 1804 by the king of Denmark, with Nachtegall as its director. Danish gymnastics in the military and in the schools was based totally on command-response exercises, with rigid, mass drills associated with the nationalistic theme.

Patriotism raged in Sweden in the late 1700s and early 1800s due to Sweden's loss of territory to Russian and Napoleonic forces. This nationalistic fervor initially influenced Per Henrik Ling to study and write about the Scandinavian heritage. While pursuing this objective in Denmark for five years, he learned gymnastics from Franz Nachtegall and engaged in fencing, through which he improved an arthritic arm. The personal therapeutic benefits Ling experienced led him to promote gymnastics throughout his career. Returning to his homeland in 1804, Ling became a fencing master and an instructor of literature and history, while also teaching gymnastics.

Ling's theory that the knowledge of Norse literature and history combined with gymnastics training could make Sweden a stronger nation influenced the king. As a result, the Royal Gymnastics Central Institute was established in Stockholm in 1814, under Ling's direction. As a training program for military men, this program allowed Swedes to stress precise execution of movements on command, mass drills, posture-correcting movements, and specific exercises on specially designed exercise apparatus. England, Denmark, Belgium, Greece, and other countries adopted Swedish gymnastics for military training. Ling initiated therapeutic, or medical, gymnastics to restore health through exercises, and is credited with devising a system of massage to treat ailments involving joints and muscles. He also promoted gymnastics for pedagogical (educational) and aesthetic purposes. Swedish apparatus developed by Ling, such as stall bars, booms, vaulting boxes, and oblique ropes, were always subordinated to the exercises and to students' needs.

When Hjalmar Ling, Per Henrik Ling's son, began teaching at the Royal Gymnastics Central Institute, he initiated the development of Swedish school gymnastics. Borrowing from his father's program the principles of progression and

An example of one rigidly held position in a Day's Order of Swedish school gymnastics.

TABLE 7-4

COMPARISON OF EUROPEAN GYMNASTICS SYSTEMS

System	Theme(s)	Participants	Program	Apparatus
German	National regeneration; physical activities used to develop strong, sturdy fearless youth	Working and lower-middle classes; first boys, then men too	Individualized under Jahn and vorturners (teachers)	Vaulting horses; parallel bars; ropes and ladders for climbing; balance beams; running track
Danish	Nationalism	Soldiers; teachers	Formalized exercises on command; no individual expression	Hanging ladders; rope ladders; masts and poles for climbing; balance beams; vaulting horses
Swedish	National preparedness; therapeutic healing; pedagogical or educational; aesthetics	Soldiers; teachers	Movement on command; posture correcting	Stall bars; vaulting boxes; climbing poles; oblique ropes; Swedish booms

precise execution of movements on command, Hjalmar Ling devised the **Day's Order,** systematized, daily exercises that progressed through the whole body from head to toe. These lessons were appropriately graded for the age, ability, and gender of each child and used apparatus designed for children. Mass drills under a teacher's direction remained paramount.

Day's Order:
systematized, daily exercises that progressed through the whole body from head to toe

Table 7-4 compares the three major gymnastics systems in Europe. The timeline in Table 7-5 lists the various activities in which people of each era participated, along with the primary purpose of each activity. Figure 7-1 illustrates how European philosophies and innovators influenced subsequent programs. The

TABLE 7-5			
ANCIENT WORLD AND EUROPEAN HERITAGE TIMELINE			
Dates	*People*	*Popular Activities*	*Purpose*
Pre–776 B.C.	Homeric Greeks	Chariot racing; boxing; wrestling; footracing; throwing the discus and javelin	Preparation for war; honoring the gods
776 B.C. to 371 B.C.	Spartans	Running; jumping; wrestling; boxing; horseback riding; throwing the discus and javelin; pancratium; hunting; swimming	Military supremacy
776 B.C. to 480 B.C.	Early Athenians	Wrestling; boxing; jumping; throwing the discus and javelin; dancing	Preparation for war; honoring the gods
500 B.C. to 27 B.C.	Romans during the Republic	Archery; fencing; throwing the javelin; marching; riding; running; swimming; wrestling	Preparation for war
A.D. 500 to 1500	Knights	Archery; climbing; dancing; fencing; jousting; riding; swimming; wrestling; hunting; hawking	Preparation for war
1450 to 1650	Educational protagonists	Archery; fencing; riding; games; play; gymnastics	Education of the whole child
1770 to 1830	Naturalists (Germans)	Dancing; fencing; riding; vaulting; jumping; running; throwing; wrestling; manual labor; gymnastics; games	Meeting individual needs
1800s	German turners	Climbing; vaulting; jumping; wrestling; running	National regeneration
1800s	Danish	Vaulting; climbing; jumping; gymnastics exercises	Nationalism
1800s	Swedish	Vaulting; climbing; gymnastics exercises	Nationalism; therapy

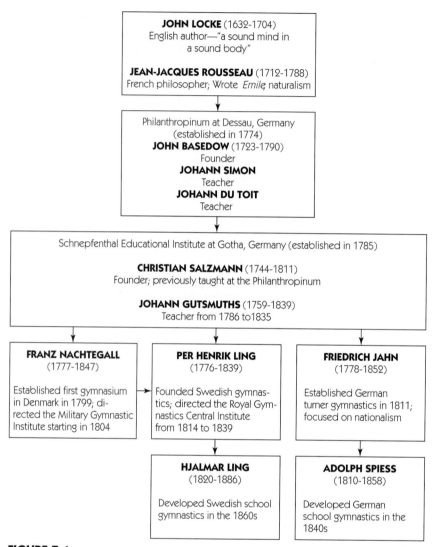

FIGURE 7-1
Significant European influences on physical education and sport programs in the United States.

Research View box on page 227 adds information about the influence of early cultures on strength training.

SPORTS IN GREAT BRITAIN (1800s)

The nationalistic fervor for European gymnastics never gained prominence in Great Britain other than through minimal usage of Ling's program by the British military. As the dominant world power, Great Britain had not faced territorial

⌕ RESEARCH VIEW

Strength Training

Long before strength training became a scientific discipline, soldiers and others in ancient China, India, and Egypt lifted weights to develop strength. Greeks and Romans also exercised with weights. According to Mel Siff in *A Short History of Strength and Conditioning* (available online at www.dolfzine.com/page515.htm), the first books on weight training were published in the sixteenth century in Europe. Weight training was included in some educational programs in England, France, and Germany. As espoused by Per Henrik Ling, muscular exercise was believed to offer therapeutic benefits. Building on these concepts in the mid-nineteenth century, Archibald MacLaren developed a system of physical training with barbells and dumbbells for the British Army.

decimation as so many other nations had; therefore, nationalism failed to undergird a gymnastics program in that country. Instead the British legacy to both European and worldwide physical education has undoubtedly been its sports and games.

The Greek Ideal paralleled Englishman John Locke's sound mind and sound body concept. The Greek love for athletic supremacy, rather than lucrative benefits, in the Panhellenic festivals is remarkably similar to the **British Amateur Sport Ideal** of "playing the game for the game's sake." The Greek Ideal as displayed by upper-class males in Great Britain dramatically influenced Frenchman Pierre de Coubertin, who founded the modern Olympic Games.

> **British Amateur Sport Ideal:** concept espoused by upper-class males in Great Britain that values playing sports for fun and competition and not for remuneration

Sports and recreational pastimes have traditionally been divided along class or socioeconomic lines in Great Britain. Given few alternatives due to their socioeconomic status, working-class males were especially attracted to pugilism (bare-knuckle boxing), blood sports (such as cockfighting), and varieties of football (soccer). These "poor man's sports" required little equipment, usually encouraged gambling, and were often banned by the church.

British upper-class sports, such as cricket and rugby, were popularized at private boys' boarding schools, called public schools, in the 1800s. Thomas Arnold, headmaster at Rugby School, praised the role of sport according to Thomas Hughes in *Tom Brown's Schooldays*. Arnold regularly advocated sports participation as a means for boys to learn moral virtues such as cooperation, leadership, loyalty, self-discipline, and sportsmanship. Sport within these public schools

The British popularized rugby in boys' boarding schools in the 1800s.

stressed participation in a variety of sports rather than specialization in one, playing the game rather than training in skills and fitness, and competition between boys in various residences. Public school boys often demonstrated greater learning through sport than in their scholastic efforts. Since graduates of these public schools were the future leaders of the nation, lessons learned in sports were acclaimed for preparing better citizens.

Cricket, rowing, association football (soccer), track and field athletics, rugby, and field hockey became the most popular sports at Oxford and Cambridge Universities despite faculty disfavor. The British Amateur Sport Ideal of playing the game for the game's sake rather than for remuneration prevailed in these sports competitions, especially since these upper-class men did not need to play for money.

The emergence of the philosophy of **muscular Christianity,** the teaching of moral values through sport, influenced British sports and subsequently those in the United States. Most Protestants viewed participation in sports and games as sinful. However, when people refused to

muscular Christianity:
the philosophy that moral values can be taught through sport

TABLE 7-6		
SELECTED SPORTS AND THEIR ORIGINS		
Wrestling	China	1788 B.C.
Boxing	China	850 B.C.
Track and field	Greece	776 B.C.
Rugby	Great Britain	900 A.D.
Golf	Scotland	1457
Cricket	Great Britain	1679
Gymnastics	Germany	1816
Baseball (rounders)	Great Britain	1846
Soccer	Great Britain	1859
Badminton	India	1870
Tennis	Great Britain	1873
Water polo	Great Britain	1885
Field hockey	Great Britain	1886
Table tennis	Great Britain	1889

conform to rigid prohibitions, attitudes gradually softened to permit sporting diversions as long as moral values could be taught and reinforced. Religion and sport peacefully coexisted whenever ethical virtues remained foremost. Fair play, honorable victories, respect for the opponent, and sports for fun rather than winning at all costs characterized British upper-class and schoolboy sports.

Many sports started in Great Britain spread throughout the world during their years of colonization (see Table 7-6). Sometimes these sports were welcomed by indigenous people; at other times they were rejected outright. Horse racing, tennis, golf, soccer, badminton, field hockey, and rugby are among the most prominent of these sports. Most sports in the United States were introduced by British colonists.

SUMMARY

The European legacy of athletics, gymnastics, and sports laid the foundation for physical education and sport programs in the United States (as depicted in Figure 7-2). The Greeks provided a rich heritage of mind/body unity and glorified the aesthetically developed, all-around athlete. Varying dramatically from this ideal were the Spartan soldiers and the specialized, professional athletes of the later Athenian era. The Roman Republic illustrated the utilitarian goal of a fit military force. During the next thousand years, mostly the knights developed their bodies, but they did so primarily for military conquest rather than for any inherent value. Church leaders discouraged frivolous activities. During the

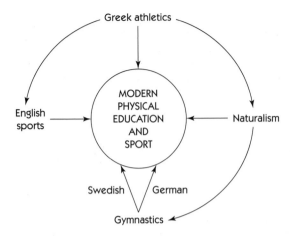

FIGURE 7-2

Relationships among European programs as they influenced physical education and sport programs in the United States.

Renaissance, philosophers and educators emphasized physical development for overall education and grappled with whether the mind and body should be educated separately or simultaneously. Naturalism and nationalism directly influenced the development of gymnastics systems in Germany, Denmark, and Sweden. British sports and games, with their associated emphasis on moral values, laid the foundation for physical education and sport programs in the United States.

CAREER PERSPECTIVE

KELLY ECKOLS
Physical Therapist
Fort Worth, Texas

EDUCATION
B.S., Exercise and Sports Science, Texas Tech University
M.S., Physical Therapy, Texas Woman's University

JOB RESPONSIBILITIES AND HOURS

Kelly is committed to providing the best possible care to her patients between 7 A.M. and 6 P.M. daily, with the goal of helping them return to work, activity, and other normal aspects of life. In addition to providing total patient care and service, Kelly's primary job responsibilities include supervising other staff, completing insurance utilization reports, marketing to physicians, building a reputation in the area for complete physical therapy care, maintaining a positive flow of daily tasks and duties, ordering equipment and supplies for the clinic, and keeping up with Medicare guidelines. She also prepares discharge notes and progress notes, calls patients who have missed appointments, supervises and evaluates one or two physical therapy students, and volunteers by providing physical therapy services or high school game coverage. The starting salary for physical therapists is around $40,000, increasing to $55,000 to $65,000 after four to six years of experience, depending on employment setting and responsibilities.

SPECIALIZED COURSE WORK, DEGREES, AND EXPERIENCES NEEDED FOR THIS CAREER

Each physical therapy school has specific admission and academic coursework requirements. Since becoming a physical therapist requires a master's degree, the Graduate Record Exam is usually required, as well as a strong score, such as a combined 1,000, on any two sections. Given the competition for admission into a physical therapy program, the grade point average during a baccalaureate program usually must exceed 3.5 (on a 4.0 scale). In addition, admission requirements typically include previous volunteer work in physical therapy settings, letters of recommendation, certification in cardiopulmonary resuscitation, completion of prerequisite courses, and an interview. In her studies, Kelly found studying gross anatomy and the student rotations most fulfilling. While her program of study was very difficult, she would not eliminate or change the requirements because everything she learned was relevant to and helpful in the fulfillment of her job responsibilities.

SATISFYING ASPECTS

Kelly especially enjoys helping people learn what their bodies can and cannot and should or should not do. She is committed to getting people back to all aspects of their lives with a caring attitude and being that person whom they have faith in and trust to make them better. She takes great satisfaction in analyzing physical problems and helping clients address and resolve them. She is disappointed when she cannot help lessen someone's pain and get the person back to a fully functioning life. She is frustrated when trying to help those who do not want to get better or who are unwilling to learn how to work toward their recovery.

JOB POTENTIAL

Within a large corporation such as HealthSouth, advancement can be limitless as long as there are vacancies, such as in administrative positions to supervise clinics, oversee continuing education, or work in marketing. Individuals moving into these administrative positions can earn as much as $95,000, depending on the number of clinics supervised and scope of responsibilities. A physical therapist can also teach educational seminars, write for newsletters or other publications, and conduct research with university faculty. Physical therapists have the opportunity to work in numerous settings, such as hospitals; sports rehabilitation clinics; neurological rehabilitation, traumatic brain injury, and spinal cord programs; pain management clinics; pediatrics and geriatrics; aquatic therapy; schools; and research centers.

SUGGESTIONS FOR STUDENTS

Kelly recommends that students decide on a career in physical therapy early during their college years so they can take the classes required for admission into a graduate program in this field, volunteer in various physical therapy settings, and assess whether this is the right profession based on their interests and abilities. It is very important, she suggests, that students have a strong commitment to this career choice before deciding to dedicate themselves to spending volunteer hours and completing difficult course work.

REVIEW QUESTIONS

1. What is the Greek Ideal?

2. How did the education of girls and boys in Sparta differ from that in Athens?

3. What took place at an Athenian gymnasium during both the early and later eras?

4. Why did the Olympic Games start, and how did they attain such a prestigious status?

5. Why were the Romans a nation of spectators?

6. How and why did the Renaissance serve as a transitional period between the Middle Ages and the Age of Enlightenment?

7. How did naturalism influence the early development of European gymnastics?

8. How did nationalism influence the development of European gymnastics?

9. What were the similarities and differences among the school gymnastics programs of Adolph Spiess in Germany, Franz Nachtegall in Denmark, and Hjalmar Ling in Sweden?

10. What outcomes were stressed to justify sports and games for boys in the public schools in Great Britain?

STUDENT ACTIVITIES

1. As a class project, reenact the ancient Olympic Games by having each student participate in an appropriate athletic contest. Each student is expected to research the specifics about the assigned or selected event before competing against classmates.

2. Select one activity or area of training for a page or squire during medieval times. Prepare a five-minute oral report and demonstration of how the boys were taught and how they practiced the necessary skills.

3. Along with several classmates, prepare a demonstration of German, Swedish, or Danish gymnastics, and then lead the rest of the class in a five-minute lesson.

4. Write a five-page paper about the early history and development of any sport that is associated with the British Amateur Sport Ideal or was founded in Great Britain.

5. Challenge yourself to find 16 people, ideas, or terms from the medieval era forward in the history puzzle below. Define or describe each one found.

```
E R H S I L B U F J A H N E H T M O R F N O I T N I R W G O R O E S I W N G R
T H A V S T E S W I N L E T A R P U Y O S B N Y L A O L A Z C X U D E S U E U
D H E T A R K A G E S E S D I C S O M S T Y P O L Q E N Z V B K S A J M U B G
S F E I R B S M E T I A I D E M H E G D E L W O N K T A N R H C E A Q O S L B
P R E R U T C E L D S A S P I R T I D N I F H L C R I C K E T U T I W O P L Y
I Z X C V T U R N V E R I E N S O L V J U Z X P R E W Z S D H I Y O P C V B U
E N M B V C X Z L K J H G F D S A B N A E W Q A T Y L R O U S S E A U O P U X
S F N A T U R A L I S M E S Y T E I R A L E W Q J I O P L M Y H N R F L S C U
S Q P O I U T R E W L K J H G F D S U I O R E W Q J I O P L M Y H N R Y S X C
Y U I O P T Y B A S E D O W Q W E R T Y I F Y O P L K J H G F D S A M M B V P
P C V X B N M J I K L A G Y T F D E S G U T S M U T H S L M H Y I A U P U R E
S Z G H S W C D C R U S A D E S S B G T N H M Y J U K I P O Z A G W S I Y I O
C B V X J I F O N O S D F G H J O Q O N A C H T E G A L L O L U P T R C O E B
O Z P X A O C I V U B Y N A T W E R E N A I S S A N C E O K L Y U G C S V B A
P E R H E N R I K L I N G A M S N A T I O N A L I S M C H X J Z L Q E J H R G
```

6. Conduct a class debate about the similarities and differences among the early and later Athenians, the Roman Republic and Empire, and modern-day sporting activities and competitions.

7. Identify 20 contributions to or influences on American physical education and sport as described in this chapter.

REFERENCE

Van Dalen DB, Bennett BL: *A world history of physical education,* 2nd ed., Englewood Cliffs, NJ, 1971, Prentice-Hall.

SUGGESTED READINGS

Corrick JA: *Life of a medieval knight,* Farmington Hills, MI, 2001, Gale Group. This book discusses feudalism, chivalry, knight training, the Crusades, tournaments, and other aspects of the lives of knights.

Crowther N: Visiting the Olympic Games in ancient Greece: travel and conditions for athletes and spectators, *The Internat J of the Hist of Sp* 18(4):37, 2001. This article decribes Low the travel circumstances and accommodations for athletes and spectators at the ancient Olympic Games were quite different from the arrangements and plush stadiums of today.

Crowther NB: Qualifying for the Olympic Games in ancient Greece, *J of Sp Hist* 23 (Spring):34, 1996. This article explains the requirements for eligibility in the most popular of the Panhellenic festivals.

Finkelberg M: Time and arete in Homer, *Classical Quar* 48(1):14, 1998. This article presents information about the all-around mental, moral, and physical excellence valued by the ancient Greeks.

Golden M: *Sport and society in ancient Greece,* Cambridge, 1998, Cambridge University Press. The author draws distinctions among social classes, genders, and ages in this examination of the role of sport in ancient society.

Harris HA: *Sport in Greece and Rome,* Ithaca, 1972, Cornell University Press. This classical scholar comprehensively examines athletics, ball games, and chariot racing in both Greece and Rome and helps the reader understand the role of each in the cultures of these early civilizations.

Kennell NM: *The gymnasium of virtue: education and culture in ancient Sparta,* Chapel Hill, NC, 1995, University of North Carolina Press. This book expounds on the unique characteristics of the city-state of Sparta, with an emphasis on education.

Kyle DG: Winning and watching the Greek pentathlon, *J of Sp Hist* 17:291, 1990. Based on a reexamination of the archaeological evidence, the author suggests how the winner of the Greek pentathlon was determined. Some comments on Greek sport and spectating are offered.

Nardo D: *Life of a Roman gladiator,* Farmington Hills, MI, 2003, Gale Group. The author describes the recruitment, training, weapons, and tactics of gladiators.

Thompson-Noel M: Not so far from Mount Olympus: comparison of modern and ancient Olympics, *New Statesman* 125:31, 1996. This article compares the corruption and crass commercialization of the ancient and modern games, concluding that the ancient Greeks would have felt at home in Atlanta in 1996.

EARLY AMERICAN PHYSICAL EDUCATION AND SPORT

8

KEY CONCEPTS

- Participation in sporting activities was a valued part of Native Americans' lives.
- Colonists coming to the New World, especially those from Great Britain, brought with them a love for sports and games.
- Early physical education programs in the United States promoted calisthenics, light gymnastics, hygiene, and strength development.
- German and Swedish gymnastics formed the basis for many early physical education programs.
- Teacher training institutes and a professional organization provided the educational foundation and a forum for the future development of physical education and sport programs.
- Play became recognized as an essential aspect of healthy child development.
- Amateur sports in clubs and on college campuses were organized and became competitive.

Individuals arriving in the New World found Native Americans playing sports. The early colonists brought with them a love for sporting pastimes. Once survival was assured, time was spent bowling, racing horses, skating, wrestling, and playing various ball games. Formalized exercises comprising the German gymnastics and Swedish gymnastics systems appealed to a few, but neither won full acceptance as a unified, national approach to physical education appropriate for people in the United States. People from Great Britain, through worldwide colonization (including North America), spread their love of sports and games. **Hygiene,** the science of preserving one's health, was the focus of many early school programs in the

> **hygiene:**
> the science of preserving one's health

United States. These programs were often called *physical culture* or *physical training* because of the beneficial effects of exercise. Emphasizing health, strength, and bodily measurements, physical training programs in the 1800s were added to school and college curricula primarily under the direction of physicians. Leaders established teacher training institutes that offered course work in the theoretical aspects of the emerging profession of physical education. Sports and play activities drawn from a European heritage continued to grow in popularity as college students and upper-class clubs sponsored contests. Many towns also provided playgrounds, further stimulating interest in physical education and sport.

Before examining the major programs and developments that contributed to early American physical education programs, it is important to explain their significance. The emerging field of physical education was built on a heritage of hygiene, medicine, strength development, formalized exercises, play, and sports. Early leaders in physical education developed organizations to govern their myriad activities. Many individuals contributed to the sound foundation laid prior to the twentieth century that led to subsequent developments in physical education, exercise science, and sport, described more fully in Chapter 9.

PHYSICAL ACTIVITIES IN THE COLONIES

Sports, physical activities, and dance occupied a prominent role in the traditional life of most Native Americans when colonists from other countries arrived in North America. These events were associated with religious ceremonies, festive celebrations, and social relaxation. However, differences in language, lifestyles, geographic regions, livelihoods, and overall cultures verify that one cohesive image did not exist. Most tribes' outlook on life contributed to the popularity of their preferred sporting pastimes.

According to Oxendine (1988), some of the most important factors characterizing traditional Native American sports include the following:

- A strong connection between sport and other social, spiritual, and economic aspects of daily life
- The serious preparation of mind, body, and spirit of both participants and the community as a whole prior to major competition
- The assumption that rigid adherence to standardized rules and technical precision was unimportant in sport
- Strong allegiance to high standards of sportsmanship and fair play
- The prominence of both males and females in sport activity, but with different expectations
- A special perspective on team membership, interaction, and leadership styles
- The role of gambling as a widespread and vital component in all sports
- The importance of art as an expression of identity and aesthetics (pages 3–4).

The most popular Native American sport was lacrosse, also called baggataway, meaning ball game or the game of ball. The competitors displayed grace, adroitness, and dexterity, often in honor of their gods. The courage, rugged-ness, skill, speed, and endurance required to play this game helped train males for war. The rules, size of the playing field, equipment, and clothing varied by tribe.

Native Americans, including many females, played shinny, a ball-and-stick game similar to modern field hockey. Women also actively participated in double ball, in which a stick was used to propel two balls attached by a string.

Footraces, especially among Native Americans, served as a source of motiva-tion and pride. Besides children's play and ceremonial uses by adults, running skills benefited tribes in war, the pursuit of game animals, and the delivery of messages. The sacred ball race combined kicking a ball along a prescribed 25-mile course and running after it.

Other sports of major interest to Native Americans included archery, swim-ming, fishing, canoeing, and snow snaking, which involved sliding a pole a great distance across a frozen path. Ritualistic dances and games of chance were also popular.

In the late 1500s, the first colonists came to the New World in search of a new life, adventure, and religious freedom. During that century, the prime motivator for physical activity was survival: Men hunted, fished, and grew crops, while women performed domestic chores. What little time existed for relaxation was frequently spent in work-related recreation, such as barn raisings, corn huskings, or quilting bees. Dancing and games were often a part of these gatherings, al-though some religions forbade dancing.

The sporting heritage brought to this country by Europeans became in-creasingly popular in the 1700s. In spite of Puritan-initiated laws forbidding gam-bling, card playing, and mixed dancing, New Englanders relaxed by bowling, fishing, fowling, or playing cricket, rugby fives (a game similar to handball), or marbles.

Led by the Dutch in New York, the settlers in the middle colonies, free from many of the religious prohibitions imposed on their northern neighbors, eagerly engaged in merriments such as pulling the goose (snapping off the head of a greased goose while riding horseback or while standing in a moving boat); played games, such as skittles (in which a ball or flat disk is thrown down an alley at nine skittles, or pins); and participated in outdoor amusements, such as boat-ing, fishing, hunting, horse racing, and sleighing. These activities were enthusias-tically pursued by the upper class. Interestingly, when nine-pin bowling was prohibited by law because of its association with gambling, a tenth pin was added to allow bowlers, and hence gamblers, to participate legally in their favorite pastime. The Quakers of Pennsylvania favored fishing, hunting, and swimming as diversions while banning many other leisure pursuits.

Virginia, strongly influenced by the British, emerged as the leading Southern colony. Emulating the gentry across the ocean, the Southern plantation owners sought to acquire all the trappings befitting their aristocratic status, including sporting pastimes. Cockfighting, bowling, card playing, and horse racing were pursued vigorously at taverns, which initially were exclusively for men. Fox hunt-ing, hawking, and watching boxing matches found many enthusiasts.

Participation in various physical activities increased throughout the 1770s as an emerging nationalism placed emphasis on the development of health and strength. Benjamin Franklin, Noah Webster, and Thomas Jefferson were among those who supported physical activities for healthful benefits. At the same time, sports involvement continued to win new adherents because sports offered competition, freedom, and fun.

In the late 1700s, as the colonists prepared for a confrontation with the British, military days provided opportunities for marching and drilling with weapons, but also offered opportunities for social interaction and game playing. The military training was utilitarian in purpose, though, and did not lead to an emphasis on physical fitness in the post–Revolutionary War years. This trend repeated itself throughout the history of the United States as each war signaled a need to have trained soldiers; aside from these times of emergency, there was little emphasis by the military on physical fitness programs.

Many immigrants traveled to the New World in search of religious freedom. Mostly Protestants, they valued labor and education as long as the latter contributed to the development of the highest type of Christian manhood. Latin grammar schools and a few universities educated the intellectually and financially elite. Dame schools offered mostly boys the basics of reading, writing, and arithmetic (the three Rs).

Following the War of 1812, nationalism burst into popularity, setting the stage for a gradual extension of democratic rights to more people and for the provision of education to more children. Beginning in the 1800s, free, public education for boys and girls consisted primarily of the three Rs. These public schools initially showed little interest in physical education, although in 1853 Boston became the first city to require daily exercise for children. In private academies and schools in the early 1800s, though, the belief that physical activities contributed to health led to children's participation in sports. Prior to the Civil War, few colleges provided for their students' physical development; however, academies and private schools for boys and occasionally for girls (such as Mt. Holyoke Female Seminary beginning in 1837) included physical exercises in their curricula.

Early experiences in physical activities and sport for minority groups in this country could be described as either isolation or assimilation influenced by an emerging nationalist spirit. Most African Americans, whether enslaved or free, valued their cultural heritage in music and dance but, due to prejudicial attitudes, remained largely excluded from organized programs. Paul Robeson became an All-America football star at Rutgers and the Walker brothers played professional baseball in the late 1900s, but they were notable exceptions to segregated sport. German, Irish, Italian, Jewish, and other European immigrants during this time engaged in dances, games, sports, and gymnastics brought from their homelands. Other immigrants chose to pursue sports like baseball and boxing as a way to become more like their American playmates.

Early American physical education and sport was influenced by European systems of exercises (called gymnastics), the development of normal schools and a national organization, the provision of play for children, and amateur sports for men and women. Each of these contributed to the content and structure of twentieth-century physical education and sport programs, which are an amalgam of a variety of exercises, gymnastics, formalized educational curricula, play, and sports.

EARLY GERMAN GYMNASTICS IN THE UNITED STATES

The most significant private school to initiate required physical education in the United States was the Round Hill School, founded in 1823 in Northampton, Massachusetts. Table 8-1 lists this school's establishment, along with other highlights in the development of physical education in the nineteenth century. The founders of Round Hill School scheduled time each day for sports and games even before they employed Charles Beck, a German turner, to instruct boys in the German system of gymnastics. Beck established an outdoor gymnasium, taught the first turner exercises on apparatus in this country, and translated Friedrich Jahn's treatise on gymnastics into English. In addition, Harvard students and Bostonians were taught turner gymnastics by German immigrants in the 1820s. The interest in turner gymnastics dissipated when these instructors ceased to teach and because this system's emphasis on strength-developing work on apparatus failed to appeal to sports-minded Americans.

When a second wave of political refugees fled Germany beginning in 1848, they too brought their love of gymnastics to the United States, where they established turner societies (beginning in 1848 in Cincinnati) and turner festivals (in 1851). These **turnfests** featured thousands of turners who exhibited their physical prowess on German apparatus and through running and jumping activities. In 1866, they founded the Normal School of the North American Gymnastic Union in New York City to prepare teachers of German

turnfests:
festivals for the exhibiting of German (turner) gymnastics

German gymnastics in the United States in the late 1800s.

TABLE 8-1

SIGNIFICANT EVENTS IN EARLY AMERICAN PHYSICAL EDUCATION

1823	Round Hill School established with physical education in its curriculum
1824	Hartford Female Seminary, directed by Catharine Beecher, included calisthenics in its curriculum
1825	Charles Beck became an instructor of German gymnastics at Round Hill School
1825	New York City high schools offered gymnastics
1826	Charles Follen organized gymnastics classes for students at Harvard College
1831	John C. Warren's *The Importance of Physical Education* published
1832	Catharine Beecher's *Course of Calisthenics for Young Ladies* published
1837	Mount Holyoke Female Seminary opened, with calisthenics listed as part of its school program
1837	Western Female Institute founded by Catharine Beecher
1848	Friedrich Hecker organized the first American turnverein in Cincinnati
1851	First national turnfest held in Philadelphia
1853	Boston became the first city to require daily exercise for school children
1855	Cincinnati, Ohio, first offered physical education using German gymnastics in its public schools
1856	Catharine Beecher's *A Manual of Physiology and Calisthenics for Schools and Families* published
1859	A. Molineaux Hewlitt, an African American, appointed gymnasium instructor at Harvard College
1861	Normal Institute for Physical Education founded by Dioclesian Lewis
1861	Edward Hitchcock, M.D., became director of physical education at Amherst College
1862	Dioclesian Lewis's *New Gymnastics for Men, Women, and Children* published
1865	First women's physical education program started at Vassar College
1866	California passed the first state physical education law
1866	Normal School of the North American Gymnastic Union established
1869	First YMCA gymnasiums opened in New York City, San Francisco, and Washington, DC
1872	Brookline, Massachusetts, became the first community in America to vote for the establishment of a playground using public funds
1879	Harvard College's Hemenway Gymnasium opened under the direction of Dudley Sargent, M.D.
1883	Hartvig Nissen started teaching Swedish gymnastics in Washington, DC
1885	Nils Posse started teaching Swedish gymnastics in Boston
1885	Association for the Advancement of Physical Education founded in Brooklyn, New York
1885	YMCA Training School established in Springfield, Massachusetts
1886	Brooklyn Normal School established by William Anderson, M.D.
1886	Chautauqua Summer School of Physical Education established
1887	Harvard Summer School established
1889	Boston Normal School of Gymnastics established
1889	Boston Conference on Physical Training held
1890	Posse Normal School founded
1890	Edward Hartwell, M.D., became director of physical education for the Boston public schools
1892	Ohio became the second state to pass a physical education law
1893	Harvard became the first college to confer an academic degree in physical education
1894	American Association for the Advancement of Physical Education established departments of interest, including the Department of Anthropometry and Statistics under the leadership of Edward Hitchcock, M.D.
1896	American Association for the Advancement of Physical Education began publication of *American Physical Education Review*
1897	American Association for the Advancement of Physical Education established a committee on School Anthropometry with Henry Bowditch, M.D., of Harvard Medical School as chairman
1897	Society of College Gymnasium Directors founded

gymnastics. When most German immigrants migrated to the Midwest, they settled in isolated communities and maintained their national identity, including their gymnastics programs. Gradually their turner societies broadened their programs to include social functions and exercises appropriate for the entire family. Later in the 1800s, they introduced the turner system into several schools, although it was modified with Adolph Spiess's school gymnastics principles. The influence of German gymnastics on programs in the United States was limited because of its regional nature and the emphasis on strength development and nationalism. However, during the late 1800s and early 1900s, many schools and colleges incorporated exercises on German apparatus into their programs. Some of these apparatus, such as the parallel bars, rings, and balance beam, remain vital parts of the sport of gymnastics.

EARLY AMERICANS WHO INFLUENCED PHYSICAL EDUCATION PROGRAMS

Catharine Beecher, the first American to design a program of exercises for American children, tried to get daily physical activity into the public schools. As director of the Hartford (Connecticut) Female Seminary beginning in 1824 and later, when she founded the Western Female Institute in Cincinnati in 1837, she introduced girls to **calisthenics.** At the latter school, she set aside 30 minutes per half-day for this program of exercises, which was designed to promote health, beauty, and strength. Beecher's objective was to aid girls in improving their vitality so they could better fulfill their missions in life as wives and mothers. She expanded her concepts from a *Course of Calisthenics for Young Ladies,* which she wrote in 1832 primarily for girls, to *A Manual of Physiology and Calisthenics for Schools and Families,* published in 1856, in which she advocated the introduction of physical training in American schools for all children. Borrowing from the therapeutic concepts of Swedish gymnastics as developed by Per Henrik Ling, Beecher, through her writings and school programs, emphasized exercises that could be executed at home without a teacher, using diagrams from her books as guides.

> **calisthenics:**
> the term used in the 1800s to describe Catharine Beecher's program of exercises designed to promote health, beauty, and strength
>
> **light gymnastics:**
> Dioclesian Lewis's program based on executing Beecher's calisthenics along with handheld apparatus

Although Beecher's efforts did not achieve widespread results, she did influence another American. Dioclesian Lewis was a promulgator of causes for the day, including the abolition of slavery, temperance, women's rights, and health. At the convention of the American Institute of Instruction in 1860, Lewis had the opportunity to bring his concept of **light gymnastics** to the attention of educators from around the country and, especially, Boston. For his program, Lewis borrowed from Beecher's calisthenics, adding light apparatus such as bean bags, dumbbells,

Indian clubs, and wands. He also borrowed from Swedish gymnastics its special emphasis on treatment of curvature of the spine and other chronic maladies. As a result of his promotional efforts, Boston adopted his system in its elementary schools. To prepare teachers to instruct children in light gymnastics, he founded the Normal Institute for Physical Education in 1861, the first institute of its kind. A **normal school** was a specialized institution for preparing students to become teachers in one or more subjects.

normal school:
a specialized institution for preparing students to become teachers in one or more subjects

The 10-week program of study at the Normal Institute for Physical Education included instruction in anatomy, physiology, hygiene, and gymnastics. Seemingly ahead of his time, Lewis believed in equity between the genders, cardiovascular conditioning, and conducting measurements to demonstrate the success of his program in improving the health of students. He also emphasized that exercises done to the accompaniment of music would result in more activity and more enjoyment.

In 1860, the first required college physical education program began at Amherst College because its president was concerned about the health of the students. This paramount concern led to the hiring of Edward Hitchcock, a physician. As director of the Department of Hygiene and Physical Education, Hitchcock gave health lectures, served as college physician, and supervised the required physical exercises for all students. As was true of most of the early physical educators, Hitchcock's primary credential for the job was a medical degree.

Examples of movements and handheld apparatus used in Dioclesian Lewis's light gymnastics program.

Borrowing from Lewis's light gymnastics, Hitchcock's program, led by squad captains, included class exercises to the accompaniment of music. Students had class four days per week and were allowed to use a portion of their class time to practice sports skills or exercise on the horizontal bars, rings, ropes, and vaulting horses. Hitchcock also administered a battery of bodily, or **anthropometric,** measurements, such as height, weight, chest girth,

anthropometrics:
bodily measurements used to evaluate physical size and capacity

and lung capacity, to evaluate the effects of the program on students and compare their progress from year to year.

A second noteworthy college physical education program was developed by Dudley Sargent at Harvard College beginning in 1879, when he was hired to direct the newly opened Hemenway Gymnasium. Since no required physical education program existed at Harvard, Sargent, who was also a physician, used an individualized approach to encourage students to exercise. Based on numerous anthropometric measurements, Sargent prescribed a series of exercises to meet each student's physical needs, using chest expanders and developers, leg machines, rowing machines, and other apparatus that he had designed. Opposed to strict German gymnastics and light gymnastics programs, Sargent encouraged students to participate in baseball, bowling, boxing, fencing, rowing, and running in addition to their individual conditioning programs.

Box 8-1 provides a brief summary of the contributions of the early leaders in physical education in the United States. The Research View box describes the contributions of the "father of physical culture."

Class exercises at Amherst College. Note the dumbbells used along with the class leader.

BOX 8-1   EARLY LEADERS IN PHYSICAL EDUCATION IN THE UNITED STATES

Charles Follen (1796–1840)
Established gymnasium in Boston (1826)
Taught German gymnastics to Harvard College students (1826–1828)

Charles Beck (1798–1866)
Hired as first physical education teacher in the United States (1825)
Taught at Round Hill School (1825–1830)

Catharine Beecher (1800–1878)
Taught at the Hartford Female Seminary (1824)
Started the Western Female Institute (1837)
Promoted calisthenics in American schools for boys and girls

Dioclesian Lewis (1823–1888)
Developed light gymnastics with handheld apparatus
Started the Normal Institute for Physical Education (1861)

Edward Hitchcock, M.D. (1828–1911)
Served as Professor of Hygiene and Physical Education at Amherst College (1861–1911)
Elected first president of the Association for the Advancement of Physical Education (1885)
Led in development of anthropometric measurements of males

Amy Morris Homans (1848–1933)
Directed the Boston Normal School of Gymnastics (1889–1909)
Directed the Department of Hygiene and Physical Education at Wellesley College (1909–1918)
Founded the Association of Directors of Physical Education for Women (1915)

Dudley Sargent, M.D. (1849–1924)
Directed the Hemenway Gymnasium at Harvard College (1879–1919)
Led in development of anthropometric measurements of males
Founded the Sargent Normal School (1881)
Founded the Harvard Summer School (1887)

Edward Hartwell, M.D. (1850–1922)
Instructed (1882) and directed (1885–1890) the gymnasium at Johns Hopkins University
Directed physical training for the Boston public schools (1890–1897)

William Anderson, M.D. (1860–1947)
Initiated the meeting that led to the formation of the Association for the Advancement of
   Physical Education (1885)
Founded the Chautauqua Summer School of Physical Education (1886)
Founded the Brooklyn (Anderson) Normal School (1886)

(continued)

BOX 8-1   EARLY LEADERS IN PHYSICAL EDUCATION IN THE UNITED STATES (CONTINUED)

Hartvig Nissen (1856–1924)

Introduced Swedish gymnastics at the Swedish Health Institute in Washington, DC (1883)

Served as assistant director (1891–1897) and then director (1897–1900) of physical training for the Boston public schools

Taught at the Harvard Summer School and the Sargent Normal School and directed the Posse-Nissen School

Nils Posse (1862–1895)

Graduated from the Royal Gymnastics Central Institute

Led in instruction of Swedish gymnastics in the United States (1885–1895)

Taught at the Boston Normal School of Gymnastics (1889)

Started the Posse Normal School (1890)

Delphine Hanna (1854–1941)

Taught at Oberlin College (1885–1920)

Became the first female professor of physical education (1903)

Initiated anthropometric measurements of females

Taught Luther Gulick, Thomas Wood, Jay Nash, and Jesse Williams

RESEARCH VIEW

The Father of Physical Culture

Bernarr Macfadden (1868–1955) has been called the "Father of Physical Culture." He was a lifelong advocate of physical fitness, eating fresh, all-natural food and promoting bodybuilding and outdoor exercise. He advocated the natural treatment of disease and stressed the avoidance of drugs and stimulants. Macfadden wrote over 100 books and became a millionaire publisher of *Physical Culture,* a magazine for women called *Beauty & Health,* and other magazines and newspapers that inspired millions to live healthy, vigorous lives. Although only 5960 and weighing around 145 pounds, he developed amazing physical strength, including powerful upper body muscles, a strong chest, and incredible stamina and energy. After reading William Blaikie's *How to Get Strong and How to Stay So* (published in 1879), Macfadden became a highly skilled gymnast, champion wrestler, and showman who liked to demonstrate his muscles, which he did by illustrating and posing (wearing limited or no clothing) for his books and magazines. *Physical Culture,* begun in 1899, focused on bodybuilding but also became the most popular health magazine of the time and was the forerunner of today's health and bodybuilding publications. MacFadden advocated bodybuilding for men and women. He conflicted with societal standards of his time by encouraging women to exercise, participate in outdoor sports such as tennis and swimming, and discard restrictive clothing. For more about the enigmatic life of Bernarr Macfadden, visit www.bernarrmacfadden.com.

EARLY SWEDISH GYMNASTICS IN THE UNITED STATES

The first American introduction to Swedish gymnastics as a complete system occurred in 1883, when a Norwegian, Hartvig Nissen, opened a Swedish Health
Institute in Washington, DC. Two years later Nils Posse, a graduate of the Royal
Gymnastics Central Institute in Stockholm, introduced Swedish gymnastics in
Boston. Impressed by Posse's program, philanthropist Mary Hemenway volunteered to furnish the Boston School Committee free teacher training in Swedish
gymnastics if the schools would offer this program to children. This led Hemenway to finance the establishment of the Boston Normal School of Gymnastics in
1889. Hemenway selected Amy Morris Homans for its director; Nils Posse became
the first instructor. The graduates of this school taught in the Boston schools
and nationally, especially in women's colleges, spreading Swedish gymnastics.
Edward Hartwell, director of physical training for the Boston public schools beginning in 1890, was also a strong supporter of Swedish gymnastics. Previously
he had directed the Johns Hopkins University gymnasium, where he experi-
mented with many of the principles that Dudley Sargent advocated.

THE BATTLE OF THE SYSTEMS

Between 1885 and 1900, a leading topic for discussion among physical educators
was which system of gymnastics could provide a unified, national program for the United States. This raging controversy became known as the **Battle of the Systems.** Although there was some overlap between programs, in general the

> **Battle of the Systems:**
> a controversy raging in the 1800s over
> which system of gymnastics was most
> appropriate for Americans

German and Swedish systems and those advanced by various Americans developed and vied for supporters (see Figure 8-1 and Table 8-2).

In an attempt to introduce Swedish gymnastics to the general public and
to leaders in physical training and thus gain its acceptance as *the* program for
American schools, Mary Hemenway financed the Boston Conference on Physical
Training in 1889. Under the direction of Amy Morris Homans, this conference was
highly successful and was one of the most important conferences in physical education ever held in the United States. Its significance can be attributed to the exposure given to the various programs existing at that time. German gymnastics,
Swedish gymnastics, Hitchcock's program, Sargent's system, and others were explained, and the merits of each were discussed. After explaining his program,
Sargent proposed an answer to the search for an American system:

> What America most needs is the happy combination which the European nations
> are trying to effect: the strength-giving qualities of the German gymnasium, the
> active and energetic properties of the English sports, the grace and suppleness
> acquired from French calisthenics, and the beautiful poise and mechanical precision
> of the Swedish free movement, all regulated, systematized, and adapted to our
> peculiar needs and institutions. (Barrows, 1899, page 76)

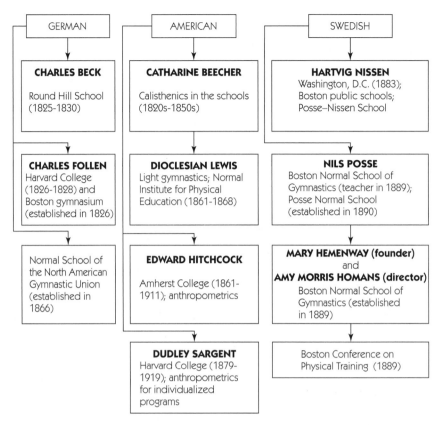

FIGURE 8-1

Leaders in early American physical education.

Although the leaders in physical education at this conference were exposed to the various systems, no one system was found to meet completely the needs of American programs because each seemed to have its weaknesses. Still, the Boston conference provided an opportunity for leaders to learn about the various systems and to exchange ideas for the future promotion of American physical education.

Although German gymnastics in the Midwest and Swedish gymnastics in the Northeast were widely accepted, few states mandated physical education. In 1866, California passed a law providing for twice-a-day exercises for a minimum of five minutes to promote health and bodily vigor, but it was short-lived. Ohio's 1892 law was the first lasting physical education law. Louisiana (in 1894), Wisconsin (in 1897), North Dakota (in 1899), and Pennsylvania (in 1901) passed similar legislation. In the late 1800s, most colleges included German and Swedish gymnastics in their physical education programs, but they also borrowed from Hitchcock's program and Sargent's principles and apparatus.

TABLE 8-2

BATTLE OF THE SYSTEMS

System	Purpose	Advocates
German gymnastics	Developed individual abilities and healthy, strong youth for war or emergencies using apparatus	German turners, including Carl Betz, C.G. Rathman, George Brosius, and William Stecher
Swedish gymnastics	Promoted health, correct expression, and beauty of performance using exact movement patterns	Hartvig Nissen; Nils Posse; Amy Morris Homans; Edward Hartwell; women's colleges
Hitchcock's system	Emphasized hygiene through required exercises with light apparatus	Edward Hitchcock
Sargent's system	Advocated hygienic, educative, recreative, and remedial aims through individualized exercises on apparatus	Dudley Sargent; Delphine Hanna; women's colleges
Association gymnastics	Contributed to the development of the all-around person	YMCA directors

ESTABLISHMENT OF NORMAL SCHOOLS FOR PHYSICAL EDUCATION

One means by which the various programs were promoted was the development of normal, or teacher training, schools. The 1880s were especially noteworthy: Six institutions were established to prepare physical education teachers either in a specific system or in an eclectic program that borrowed from several systems. In 1881, Dudley Sargent began teaching women from Harvard Annex and other women and men who were interested in his apparatus and methodology. At the resultant Sargent Normal School, he provided a general curriculum based on a theoretical, scientific foundation, along with various activities of a practical nature.

Delphine Hanna took courses from Dioclesian Lewis, Nils Posse, and Dudley Sargent; she attended both the Sargent Normal School and the Harvard Summer School of Physical Education. The program she initiated at coeducational Oberlin College in 1885 closely resembled Sargent's. Besides using many pieces of apparatus that he designed, Hanna emphasized anthropometric measurements of female students to assess their individual development. The scope of her work included teaching a class to train men to instruct their male classmates. Among her first students were Thomas Wood and Luther Gulick, later luminaries in physical education.

Harvard College's Hemenway Gymnasium was equipped with exercise apparatus designed by Dudley Sargent.

A class at the Sargent Normal School performing an Indian club routine.

Table 8-3 summarizes the early teacher training institutions in the United States and their curricula.

A unique normal school established in 1885 in Springfield, Massachusetts, was the Young Men's Christian Association (YMCA) Training School. The YMCA's goal, through its association gymnastics, was to develop the all-around man and send him out as a physical director to the increasing number of YMCAs, both

TABLE 8-3

EARLY PROFESSIONAL PREPARATION INSTITUTIONS OR NORMAL SCHOOLS IN THE UNITED STATES

Years	Founder	Name	Program
1861–1868	Dioclesian Lewis	Normal Institute for Physical Education	Light gymnastics
1866–1951	Turners	Normal School of the North American Gymnastic Union	German gymnastics
1881–1929	Dudley Sargent	Sargent Normal School	Theoretical and practical curriculum
1885–today	Young Men's Christian Association	YMCA Training School (Springfield College)	Association gymnastics
1886–1920s	William Anderson	Chautauqua Summer School of Physical Education	Advanced theoretical and practical curriculum
1886–1953	William Anderson	Brooklyn (Anderson) Normal School	Theoretical and practical curriculum
1887–1932	Dudley Sargent	Harvard Summer School of Physical Education	Advanced theoretical and practical curriculum
1889–1909	Mary Hemenway and Amy Morris Homans	Boston Normal School of Gymnastics	Swedish gymnastics
1890–1942	Nils Posse	Posse Normal School	Swedish gymnastics

nationally and internationally. (The first YMCA gymnasiums had opened in 1869 in New York City, San Francisco, and Washington, DC.)

In 1886, William Anderson established two additional institutions. While teaching in New York, he started the Brooklyn Normal School; later, when he became the director of the Yale College gymnasium, he moved this school to New Haven, Connecticut, and renamed it the Anderson Normal School. Anderson, along with Jay Seaver, also worked with leaders in the Chautauqua movement to set up the Chautauqua Summer School of Physical Education. The curricula at both schools focused on a generalized approach with theoretical and practical course work.

In 1887, Dudley Sargent gained approval to open the Harvard Summer School of Physical Education, which provided opportunities for teachers already in the field to start or continue their professional training in physical education. This summer school was particularly important in the expansion of knowledge in physical education, since at this time no graduate programs existed. The diversity and breadth of the offerings, along with its outstanding faculty, made attendance at the Harvard Summer School prestigious; a certificate from the school was highly respected.

Swedish gymnastics was initially taught at the Boston Normal School of Gymnastics in 1889 and continued to be taught following the school's affiliation with

WEB CONNECTIONS

1. www.ymca.com/about/cont/history.htm
   Check out this site for more information about the Young Men's
   Christian Association and its heritage in the promotion of sports.

2. www.ncaa.org
   In addition to extensive information about the rules and governance of
   intercollegiate athletics, this site provides some historical information
   as well as a virtual tour of the NCAA's Hall of Champions.

3. http://aausports.org/exec/aau/index.cfm?publicationID=12
   The Amateur Athletic Union, one of the largest multisport volunteer
   sports organizations in the United States, offers amateur sports and
   physical fitness programs.

4. www.northnet.org/stlawrenceaauw/timeline.htm
   Check out this site for an extensive timeline of the significant events in
   women's sports.

5. http://inventors.about.com/library/inventors/blsports.htm
   This site describes the history of sports, from football and basketball
   to windsurfing and paintball, as well as the invention of sports
   equipment, through extensive information and associated links.

6. www.hickoksports.com/history/collfhof.shtml
   This site provides a wealth of historical information about men's
   college sports.

Wellesley College beginning in 1909. Amy Morris Homans directed the programs at both these institutions. In 1890, Nils Posse established the Posse Normal School, which also promoted Swedish gymnastics.

Beginning in the late 1800s, normal schools were replaced with teacher preparation programs that offered undergraduate college degrees. In 1885, Delphine Hanna initiated a physical education teacher curriculum for women students at Oberlin College; it became a four-year degree program in 1900. Only programs at Stanford University, the University of California, the University of Nebraska, and Harvard College preceded it.

This country's first degree program in physical education (a Bachelor of Science in Anatomy, Physiology, and Physical Training) was established in 1891 at Harvard College. Carl Fitz, a physician, worked with Dudley Sargent in the development and delivery of this program, which was designed to prepare gymnasium directors to teach and to provide general preparation for individuals wishing to pursue the study of medicine. Working at the Physiological Laboratory, which was associated with the Lawrence Scientific School, Fitz focused on the importance of research in the relatively new field of physical education and was one of the foremost researchers in the experimental study of physiology of exercise in the 1890s.

FOUNDING OF THE NATIONAL ASSOCIATION

In the late 1800s, physical education programs offered a potpourri of activities reflecting the philosophies and interests of their leaders. As a young teacher, William Anderson recognized this diversity and the fact that few opportunities existed for the exchange of curricula and philosophical ideas among individuals interested in physical development. After seeking support from two recognized leaders in the field, Edward Hitchcock and Dudley Sargent, Anderson invited gymnastics teachers, ministers, journalists, school principals, college presidents, and others engaged in the promotion of physical training to meet at Adelphi Academy in Brooklyn, New York, on November 27, 1885, to discuss their various programs and decide whether sufficient interest existed to regularly provide a forum for professional interchange. Of the 60 people who attended, 49 responded positively, resulting in the formation of the Association for the Advancement of Physical Education, today's American Alliance for Health, Physical Education, Recreation and Dance. (Table 8-4 traces its various name changes.)

Edward Hitchcock of Amherst College was elected the first president. Dudley Sargent, who was selected as the first vice president, later served as the third, fifth, and eighth president. William Anderson served as the first secretary. Other recognized leaders in attendance included Dioclesian Lewis; Henry Ward Beecher, clergyman and brother of Catharine Beecher; Helen Putnam, head of the Vassar College Gymnasium, who was elected a vice president; and William Blaikie, author of the acclaimed book *How to Get Strong and How to Stay So* and the second president of the association. This organization's objectives, established in 1886, were "to disseminate knowledge concerning physical education, to improve the methods, and by meetings of the members to bring those interested in the subject into closer relation to each other" (Lee & Bennett, 1960, page 27). Discussions in the early meetings focused on the strengths and attributes of the various programs or systems, methods of teaching, anthropometric measurements, military drills, athletics, and

TABLE 8-4	
THE CHANGING NAMES OF THE NATIONAL ORGANIZATION	
1885	Association for the Advancement of Physical Education
1886	American Association for the Advancement of Physical Education
1903	American Physical Education Association
1937	American Association for Health and Physical Education
1938	American Association for Health, Physical Education and Recreation
1974	American Alliance for Health, Physical Education and Recreation
1979	American Alliance for Health, Physical Education, Recreation and Dance

hygiene. To provide another forum to share professional knowledge and experiences, the *American Physical Education Review* was published, beginning in 1896.

The American Association for the Advancement of Physical Education's (AAAPE) first contact with the National Education Association (NEA) occurred in 1893. The NEA asked Edward Hartwell, 1891–1892 AAAPE president, to chair a departmental conference on physical education and hygiene at the International Congress on Education held in connection with the 1893 Chicago World's Fair. Two years later, the NEA established a permanent Department of Physical Education; in 1924, this became the Department of School Health and Physical Education. The American Association for Health and Physical Education merged with this department when it became affiliated with the NEA in 1937.

PROMOTION OF PLAY FOR CHILDREN

While organized school programs were being established, the play movement outside the schools gained support and momentum. The industrialization of the United States directly influenced this development. Immigration and the massive influx of Americans into urban areas resulted in overcrowded cities with miles and miles of brick tenements. In an effort to provide suitable play space for children in this environment, the first sand boxes were built in Boston in 1885. In 1888, New York passed the first state legislation that led to an organized play area for children. By 1899, the Massachusetts Emergency and Hygiene Association sponsored 21 playgrounds.

Play is a child's favorite activity.

Jane Addams' Hull House, a Chicago settlement house started in 1894, included a model playground. Boston constructed the Charlesbank outdoor gymnasium in 1889. Religious leaders, school administrators, philanthropists, and social workers worked together or alone in the late 1800s to ensure that children were provided both places and opportunities to play. In part, these efforts demonstrated a genuine concern for the welfare of children and for society as a whole. These playgrounds also served as a method of social control; that is, the early leaders in the playground movement sought to use play to "Americanize" the myriad immigrants pouring into the cities.

DEVELOPMENT OF AMATEUR SPORTS

Americans' love for sports preceded the founding of the United States but blossomed after the Civil War as baseball became the national sport for men of all ages and for amateurs as well as professionals. Races between cyclists, horses, runners, and yachts, with associated gambling, were especially attractive to the upper class. Normally these races, as well as sports such as cricket, golf, and tennis, were organized or played by members of elite social clubs. The New York Athletic Club, founded in 1868, led the formation of the Amateur Athletic Union (AAU) in 1879. This organization sought to promote amateur sports for upper-class males, similar to the British ideal of the pure amateur who played sports for the love of the game. Paid, professional athletes were disdained because they played for the money; hence, the AAU sought to check the evils associated with professionals playing sports. In 1853, Scottish immigrants, through their Caledonian games, began to promote their native sports, such as hammer throwing, putting stones, and tossing the caber (lifting a large wooden pole and flipping it end over end). The Czechoslovakian Sokols also promoted physical activities through mass displays in national festivals, such as the first held in 1879 in New York City. Table 8-5 lists many of the sports organizations that helped promote amateur sports during the late 1800s.

Frenchman Pierre deCoubertin, through persistent efforts, revived the Olympic Games and the spirit of amateurism that honored the integration of mind, body, and spirit. The classical restoration of the Panathenaic Stadium, in pure white marble, provided an awe-inspiring setting for the opening of the Athens Olympic Games on April 5, 1896. Male athletes (311) representing 13 countries competed. While track and field athletics occupied center stage, athletes also competed in cycling, fencing, gymnastics, lawn tennis, shooting, swimming, weight lifting, and wrestling.

Jim Connolly, one of the 13 athletes representing the United States, captured the first victory in the hop, step, and jump (triple jump) and was honored by the hoisting of an American flag while the national anthem played. Athletes from the United States dominated the track and field events, with silver first-place medals in the 100-meters, 400-meters, 110-meters, hurdles, broad jump, high jump, pole vault, shot put, and discus throw. Greek athletes placed in swimming, cycling, fencing, gymnastics, and shooting, and won the marathon. Germans captured most of the gymnastics medals.

The YMCA developed and promoted two sports. In 1891, at the YMCA Training School, Canadian James Naismith developed the rules for basketball and

TABLE 8-5	
AMATEUR SPORTS ORGANIZATIONS	
1871	National Rifle Association
1875	National Bowling League
1878	Cricketer's Association of the United States
1879	National Archery Association
1879	Amateur Athletic Union
1880	League of American Wheelmen (cycling)
1880	National Canoe Association
1881	United States National Lawn Tennis Association
1882	National Croquet Association
1884	United States Skating Association
1887	American Trotting Association
1892	United States Golf Association

initiated the first game. This game was designed as an indoor sport to fill the void between football and baseball seasons. Five years later, William Morgan, at a YMCA in Holyoke, Massachusetts, originated volleyball as a less vigorous indoor game for businessmen. Both sports met a need and found more early adherents in the YMCAs than in private clubs and colleges. The YMCA promoted both sports internationally and especially urged American youth to play basketball.

Gambling had been associated with sports since colonial times when owners and spectators bet on the outcomes of horse races. Americans from all levels of society wagered on cockfights, wrestling bouts, boxing matches, walking contests, and baseball games throughout the 1800s. One of the evils the AAU sought to eliminate in its promotion of amateur athletics was gambling. Baseball promoters had to overcome the perception that all players and fans bet on the outcomes of professional games. Nevertheless, college students enthusiastically gambled on their sports competitions, especially football.

COLLEGIATE SPORTS FOR MEN

Sports on college campuses were initially organized by students as extracurricular activities, to the displeasure of administrators and faculty, who viewed them as extraneous to the mission of higher education. The first intercollegiate event, in 1852, matched Harvard and Yale in rowing. The two early favorites in collegiate sports were baseball, which first matched Amherst against Williams in 1859, and football, which actually began as a soccerlike game between Princeton and Rutgers in 1869. Students founded organizations to standardize rules for competitions in rowing, baseball, football, and track.

College faculties paid little attention to sports until they began to infringe on students' academic work. Missed classes, decreased academic performance, injuries, gambling, property damage on campus and in nearby towns during victory

Men's intercollegiate basketball was a slower-paced game years ago when a center jump followed each basket scored.

The University of Virginia versus the University of North Carolina in baseball in 1895. (Photo courtesy North Carolina Collection, UNC Library at Chapel Hill.)

celebrations, playing against professional teams, commercialization, and a general overemphasis on athletics compelled faculties to take action. In 1882, a group of Harvard faculty members recommended that a committee of three faculty members oversee athletics. Three years later, this committee was expanded to include two students and one alumnus. In 1888, it again expanded to an equal representation of three faculty, three students, and three alumni. In 1883, representatives of nine eastern colleges met, established the Intercollegiate Athletic Conference, and proposed that colleges should not compete against professional teams; no professional athletes should coach college teams; students should be permitted only four years of participation in athletics; contests should take place only on campuses; and faculties should control athletics. Because only three colleges ratified them, these regulations failed to take effect.

In 1895, the Intercollegiate Conference of Faculty Representatives (today's Big Ten Conference), composed of one faculty member from each of seven midwestern institutions, adopted rules requiring all players to be enrolled in college, all transfer students to wait six months before being eligible to play on a team, and all athletes to maintain the required academic standards to be eligible to play. These efforts, however, did not control the overwhelming growth of student-initiated and student-administered intercollegiate athletics in the late 1800s. Table 8-6 chronicles the initiation of collegiate sports organizations and competitions (primarily for men).

TABLE 8-6
DEVELOPMENT OF COLLEGIATE SPORTS FOR MEN AND WOMEN

1843	First collegiate rowing club started at Yale
1844	Harvard forms a rowing club
1852	First intercollegiate sports competition in rowing occurs as Harvard defeats Yale by four lengths
1859	College Union Regatta Association established by Harvard, Yale, Brown, and Trinity
1864	Haverford beats Penn 89–60 in first intercollegiate cricket competition
1869	Rutgers outscores Princeton (6–4) in the first intercollegiate football game
1871	Rowing Association of American Colleges formed
1873	First intercollegiate track and field competition held in conjunction with the intercollegiate rowing regatta
1876	Intercollegiate Football Association established
1876	Intercollegiate Association of Amateur Athletes of America formed to govern track and field
1877	Harvard shoots 20 points better than Yale in the first intercollegiate rifle competition
1877	New York University defeats Manhattan (2–0) in the first intercollegiate lacrosse contest
1883	Intercollegiate Lawn Tennis Association founded
1883	Harvard's J. S. Clark wins the singles and the doubles (with P. E. Presbrey) events during the first intercollegiate tennis tournament
1883	Intercollegiate Athletic Conference established by Harvard, Princeton, and Cornell
1884	Penn defeats Wesleyan (16–10) in the first intercollegiate polo contest
1890	First intercollegiate cross-country saw Penn beat Cornell
1894	Harvard outscores Columbia (5–4) in the first intercollegiate fencing meet
1895	Brown beats Harvard (4–2) in the first intercollegiate ice hockey game
1895	Intercollegiate Conference of Faculty Representatives formed by midwestern colleges
1896	Yale beats Columbia by 35 holes in the first intercollegiate golf event with six-man teams
1896	First intercollegiate swimming meet held with Penn defeating Columbia and Yale
1896	First intercollegiate sports competition for women in basketball occurs as Stanford defeats California (2–1)
1899	Penn surpasses Columbia (2–0) in the first intercollegiate water polo contest
1899	Intercollegiate Cross Country Association of Amateur Athletes of America established
1899	Yale's gymnastics team defeats competitors from 19 institutions in the first intercollegiate gymnastics meet

COLLEGIATE SPORTS FOR WOMEN

In the late 1800s, archery, croquet, and tennis were among the first sports to attract female participants because these activities did not require revealing clothing and were nonvigorous. Male and female attitudes about proper feminine behavior and medical opinion that vigorous activity would irreparably harm women's reproductive capabilities combined to prevent women from engaging in aggressive and highly competitive sports. Bicycling introduced a radical change in attire with the bloomer costume, or divided skirt, which allowed freedom from the appropriate attire of the day, which included voluminous skirts and petticoats and tightly laced corsets. Bloomers and middy blouses became the accepted costume for gymnastics and other physical activities; students at the Sargent Normal School were among the first to wear them.

Societal attitudes toward women in the 1800s closely paralleled the Victorian perception that females were weak, objects to be placed on pedestals for admiration but not to be taken seriously because they were incapable of mental achievements. Females who sought schooling, especially college attendance, encountered ridicule and suspicions about their femininity. Their roles as wives and mothers were viewed as contradictory to the development of their minds.

Catharine Beecher's calisthenics and Swedish gymnastics, with their therapeutic emphasis, became acceptable because they complemented the feminine role. When college women enthusiastically participated in baseball, basketball, and rowing, many physicians and some women strongly opposed such vigorous exertion. They argued that although mild activity such as walking, gardening, or moderate exercise could benefit women, an overexpenditure of energy might leave them infertile, hopelessly depleted of the energy needed to survive childbirth or motherhood. Not until medical opinions gradually changed in the twentieth century did these restrictive opinions dissipate as women began to be viewed as capable of physical and mental achievement.

Women in the upper socioeconomic strata shared their husbands' and fathers' desires to engage in conspicuous consumption. In flaunting their wealth, the rich popularized sports such as archery, golf, tennis, and yachting. In each case, these sports were organized at private clubs or in settings where social interaction between the sexes usually was a desired outcome. Following the lead of men, upper-class women began to compete nationally in archery (1879), tennis (1887), and golf (1896). Because of societal expectations, they always dressed in the latest fashions, many of which severely limited their mobility and skill development.

Women eagerly adopted basketball but adapted and modified its rules to make the game less strenuous and rough. The Committee on Women's Basketball was established by the American Association for the Advancement of Physical Education to standardize these rules. In 1896, the first intercollegiate contest between women, from the University of California and Stanford University, occurred. In addition to basketball, field days for track events and a few other sports became popular in women's colleges in the 1890s.

SUMMARY

Early physical education in the United States evolved from recreational sports and games into organized school and college programs that either emphasized one system of gymnastics or combined exercises from various systems. Swedish and German gymnastics had their advocates, but neither found widespread national acceptance. Health and strength were favored outcomes, but even these did not fully satisfy Americans' needs. Prior to 1900, teachers of physical education had completed programs in normal schools; a fledgling national association existed, but a unified, national program had not yet emerged. With the popularization in the late 1800s of children's play and of sports in amateur clubs and on college campuses, the stage was set for the development in the 1900s of an American program based primarily on playing sports and games.

Senda Berenson (in the long skirt) with Smith College students in Northampton, Massachusetts, where women played in their first public basketball game on March 22, 1893. (Photo courtesy Basketball Hall of Fame.)

CAREER PERSPECTIVE

RON M. LANG

Secondary School English Teacher and Coach
Lawrence Public Schools
Lawrence, Kansas

EDUCATION

B.S.E., Physical Education, University of Kansas
M.S.E., School Administration, University of Kansas

JOB RESPONSIBILITIES AND HOURS

Ron is a teacher of English during the normal school day. As a coach during the season, his normal work day expands substantially. Frequently this means being at work by 7 A.M. and staying until after 8 P.M. In addition, he often takes scouting trips and attends staff meetings. As a coach, he is responsible for the analysis of athletes' performance, including determining their strengths and weaknesses so he can help them improve their skills. He plans and directs the physical conditioning of his athletes. To plan game strategy, Ron evaluates opponents' capabilities and prepares scouting reports. During his coaching career, he has seen the extra-duty contract for coaching increase from $300 for an assistant coach and $800 for a head coach to over five times those amounts today.

SPECIALIZED COURSE WORK, DEGREES, AND EXPERIENCES NEEDED FOR THIS CAREER

In order to teach, Ron must have earned at least a bachelor's degree in his content field within education, as well as a teaching certificate. While there is no required educational level for coaching, Ron, as a scholarship athlete at the University of Kansas, credits his college playing experiences as well as his opportunity to work as an assistant coach for preparing him to coach. He believes his coaches served as excellent role models as he developed his abilities in this field. Although he did not identify a specific class, Ron believes the self-discipline, time management, and organizational fundamentals that he learned as a student through all of his classes helped him succeed as a coach in football, track, and basketball. His student teaching experiences were the most helpful in preparing him for his teaching responsibilities.

SATISFYING ASPECTS

Ron has found that creating long-term bonds with former players and fellow coaches is the most satisfying aspect of his coaching career. The most difficult aspect of coaching for Ron is having to reduce the number of participants to achieve a workable unit. Ron also finds it somewhat disconcerting that others sometimes measure his worth as a coach contingent on the performance of teenage athletes.

JOB POTENTIAL

In coaching, advancement is usually tied to one's winning record. Although opportunities for advancement are flexible, they often depend on the capabilities of students who attend your school.

SUGGESTIONS FOR STUDENTS

Ron challenges students to commit their expertise to performing their best not only as coaches on the court and field but also as teachers in the classroom. Serving as a role model for his athletes and students has always been a high priority for Ron.

REVIEW QUESTIONS

1. What types of physical activities were considered recreation by the colonists in the 1700s? How did these activities differ by region of the country?

2. Why did German gymnastics fail to gain wide acceptance in the United States in the 1820s and between the 1850s and 1880s?

3. What constituted the program of hygiene and physical education at Amherst College?

4. What were the basic principles of Dudley Sargent's program for Harvard College students?

5. Why was the 1889 Boston Conference on Physical Training significant?

6. Why were normal schools for physical education established, especially in the 1880s?

7. Why was the Association for the Advancement of Physical Education founded?

8. What events or developments led to the playground movement?

9. Why did faculty get involved in men's intercollegiate athletics?

10. What types of physical activities were considered appropriate for females in the 1800s, and why?

STUDENT ACTIVITIES

1. As a class, reenact a portion of the Boston Conference on Physical Training (1889) by having each student report on one of the following systems: Swedish, German, Edward Hitchcock's, or Dudley Sargent's.

2. Read about the founding of the first professional organization in physical education (today's American Alliance for Health, Physical Education, Recreation and Dance), and report your findings to the class orally or in a three-page paper.

3. By examining histories of your state or region, find the most popular sport or recreational activity for one of the following groups:

   Native American adult males
   Native American adult females
   Native American children
   Early male colonists
   Early female colonists
   Children of early colonists

Upper-class males in the 1800s
Upper-class females in the 1800s
Upper-class children in the 1800s
Middle-class males in the 1800s
Middle-class females in the 1800s
Middle-class children in the 1800s
Lower-class males in the 1800s
Lower-class females in the 1800s
Lower-class children in the 1800s

4. Research the name(s) and starting date(s) of the oldest normal school(s) for physical education for males and for females in your state.

5. Investigate which college(s) in your state offered the first intercollegiate athletic competitions for men and for women. In which sports did these competitions occur?

6. Research any one of the individuals, events, or topics discussed in this chapter. Write a five-page paper about the major contributions of this individual, event, or topic to the history and growth of physical education and sport.

REFERENCES

Barrows IC: *Physical training,* Boston, 1899, George H. Ellis Press.

Lee M, Bennett BL: This is our heritage, *JOHPER* 31(4):27, 1960.

Oxendine JB: *American Indian sports heritage,* Champaign, IL, 1988, Human Kinetics.

SUGGESTED READINGS

Borish LJ: The sporting past in American history, *OAH Mag of Hist* 7(1):3, 1992. This article reviews the role of sports from the Puritans to today and suggests how primary sources and scholarly articles about sport can be integrated into history courses.

Cazers G, Miller GA: The German contribution to American physical education: a historical perspective, *JOPERD* 71(6):44, 2000. This article recounts the origins of German gymnastics and its impact on programs in this country.

Cronin M: Playing games? The serious business of sports history, *J of Cont Hist* 38(3):495, 2003. The author provides an extensive description and defense of the importance of studying the history of sports.

Davenport J: A legacy of leaders, *Quest* 51(1):55, 1999. In this Amy Morris Homans Lecture, a historian of physical education and sport pays tribute to many giants in the field.

Davenport J (ed.): The normal schools: exploring our heritage, *JOPERD* 65(3):25, 1994. This seven-part feature describes the contributions made by seven normal schools to the profession. Those described include Dioclesian

Lewis's Normal Institute for Physical Education, the Sargent School for Physical Education, William Anderson's Brooklyn Normal School, the Harvard Summer School of Physical Education, the Boston Normal School of Gymnastics, the Posse Gymnasium, and the H. Sophie Newcomb Memorial College.

Lee M, Bennett B: Alliance centennial: 100 years of health, physical education, recreation and dance, *JOPERD* 56(4):17, 1985. This article reprints the *This Is Our Heritage* historical series in 15-year thematic sections that highlight significant occurrences related to the activities of today's American Alliance for Health, Physical Education, Recreation and Dance. It also chronicles the profession's major developments between 1960 and 1985.

Overman SJ, Baker WJ: The influence of the Protestant ethic on sport and recreation. *J of Sp Hist* 25(2):340, 1998. In this article, the authors describe the influence of values associated with the Protestant work ethic on recreation and sport.

Park RJ: Physiology and anatomy are destiny!?: brains, bodies and exercise in nineteenth century American thought, *J of Sp Hist* 18:31, 1991. Using the biomedical literature of the 1800s, the author concludes that one's physiology and anatomy—that is, the body as an icon for gender—dictated athletics for men and modest exercise for women.

Smith RA: History of amateurism in men's intercollegiate athletics: the continuance of a 19th century anachronism in America, *Quest* 45:430, 1993. The myth of amateurism in intercollegiate athletics is analyzed and dispelled in this comprehensive history.

Todd J: The strength builders: a history of barbells, dumbbells and Indian clubs, *The Interna J of Hist of Sp* 20(1):65, 2003. With a focus on the importance placed on strength development, this article examines the early use of light apparatus in physical training programs.

9

TWENTIETH-CENTURY PHYSICAL EDUCATION, EXERCISE SCIENCE, AND SPORT

KEY CONCEPTS

- The new physical education emphasized play, sport, games, outdoor activities, and educational developmentalism.
- Programs developing from the play movement, the rise of teacher training, the growth of women's physical education, the increasing emphasis on fitness, the focus on physical movement, principles of the scientific movement, educational developmentalism, and social education contributed to twentieth-century physical education, exercise science, and sport.
- Leadership from the national association and efforts to establish standards for teachers led to the recognition of physical education as a profession.
- Men's intercollegiate sports expanded from their interclass origins into commercialized businesses.
- Women's intercollegiate sports featured mass participation until the early 1970s, when competition, aided by federal legislation, became a primary goal.
- The children's play movement began with a recreational emphasis and evolved into a focus on fitness.
- Starting in the 1950s, youth sports expanded from value-oriented programs to adult-controlled leagues.
- The federal government mandated equal educational opportunities (including physical education) for individuals with disabilities and special needs.

Professional discussions concerning which system of gymnastics would best meet the needs of students in the United States continued into the early twentieth century. Beginning in the 1920s, school physical education moved from formalized exercise programs to curricula that included sports, games, aquatics, and outdoor activities with educational outcomes stressed. Two themes emerged in the middle of the twentieth century: Education "through" the physical and education "of" the physical vied for advocates and influenced school physical education and sport curricula. Since the turn of the century, the popularity of athletics at all levels and for both sexes has expanded tremendously. Nonschool programs from mid-century until today have offered sports competitions for individuals of all ages and skill levels, lifetime recreational activities, and fitness alternatives. Federal legislation mandating equal opportunity for participation in sports and physical activities for females and individuals with disabilities led to dramatic changes in school and nonschool programs. Today people participate in physical activities to develop and maintain fitness and in lifetime sports for fun, fitness, and competition.

THE NEW PHYSICAL EDUCATION

By the end of the nineteenth century, no one gymnastics system had been adopted. The formal nature of the alternatives had failed to appeal to a broad base of physical educators and their students, who were seeking activities that offered competition, fun, and more freedom of expression.

Speaking at the International Congress on Education sponsored by the National Education Association in 1893, Thomas Wood articulated his vision for a new physical education:

> The great thought in physical education is not the education of the physical nature, but the relation of physical training to complete education, and then the effort to make the physical contribute its full share to the life of the individual, in environment, training, and culture. (page 621)

The **new physical education** focused on developing the whole individual through participation in play, sports, games, and natural, outdoor activities. The curriculum and philosophy of the new physical education was heavily influenced by and consistent with educational and psychological theory that was developing at that time.

> **new physical education:**
> a curriculum focused on developing the whole individual through participation in play, sports, games, and natural, outdoor activities

Psychologist G. Stanley Hall made Clark University a center for child study after publishing his landmark book, *Adolescence,* in which he defined the educational significance of children's developmental stages. Other leaders in the study of the individual, many of whom influenced one another's work, included William James, Edward Thorndike, William Kilpatrick, and John Dewey. They successfully integrated scientific education, educational developmentalism, and social education. Educational developmentalism, also known as the psychological movement, used children's play and other natural activities for learning. Teachers College of Columbia University nurtured the development and popularization of the latter two educational themes through faculty members Thorndike and Dewey, who were close associates of Hall.

Teachers College also contributed to the integration of educational developmentalism and social education into the new physical education. Thomas Wood taught there for 31 years. Rosalind Cassidy took a Teachers College degree, as did hundreds of physical educators in the middle decades of the 1900s. For 27 years, Jesse Williams influenced Teachers College students to advocate for education through the physical as proposed by Wood and Cassidy. Williams was the primary advocate for seeking to achieve social outcomes through physical education and sport.

LEADERS IN THE NEW PHYSICAL EDUCATION

Luther Gulick and his roommate, Thomas Wood, discussed their mutual interest in physical education while at Oberlin College, where they were influenced by Delphine Hanna. In 1887, Luther Gulick became an instructor at the YMCA Training School in Springfield, Massachusetts, and, two years later, was named superintendent. While at the YMCA Training School, he emphasized sports in the physical directors' curriculum and started the YMCA's Athletic League to promote amateur sports. Stressing unity in the development of body, mind, and spirit, he designed the YMCA triangle (Figure 9-1), emblematic of the all-around man. He then moved to New York and taught before accepting the position of director of physical training for the New York City public schools. Although Gulick supported gymnastics as the basis of school curricula, he founded the Public Schools Athletic League to provide after-school sports opportunities for boys, especially in track and field activities.

Another Gulick legacy was his promotion of play. In 1906, he helped establish the Playground Association of America and served as its first president. He also advocated for the provision of playgrounds and public recreation in this country, initiated (with his wife) the Campfire Girls in 1913, and led in the camping movement. In *A Philosophy of Play,* he articulated the importance of play as an educational force and helped begin the play movement within physical education.

For two years, Thomas Wood directed the gymnasium work for men at Oberlin College. After receiving a medical degree at Columbia, he developed the undergraduate teacher training curriculum in physical education at Stanford University, beginning in 1891. Ten years later, he joined the faculty of Teachers College of Columbia University, where he led in the establishment of the first master's (1910) and doctor's (1924) degree programs in physical education. He was also instrumental in the development of health education as a separate field

FIGURE 9-1
YMCA emblem designed by Luther Gulick.

of study. *The New Physical Education,* which he co-authored with Rosalind Cassidy in 1927, provided the philosophical foundation for refocusing school programs from gymnastics to sports, games, dance, aquatics, and natural activities.

Rosalind Cassidy helped broaden and clarify the tenets of the new physical education during her professional career at Mills College in California. She helped develop and promote **education through the physical,** a leading theme for understanding physical education as the field that could uniquely contribute to the education of the whole person through physical activities. Through her voluminous writings, she also redefined physical education as the study of human movement.

> **education through the physical:**
> a belief that physical education should uniquely contribute to the education of the whole person through physical activities; promoted educating children to live in a democratic society through social and intellectual interactions within physical education

Clark Hetherington was taught and greatly influenced by Wood at Stanford University. This influence is evident from Hetherington's coining of the term *new physical education* and from his advocacy of organic, psychomotor, character, and intellectual development as descriptive of physical education's objectives. G. Stanley Hall, a second mentor for Hetherington, also emphasized educational developmentalism, which paralleled Hetherington's philosophy that play is a child's chief business in life. At the University of Missouri, the University of Wisconsin, New York University, and Stanford University, Hetherington helped establish undergraduate physical education programs. At New York University, he led in the development of graduate degree programs.

One of the first graduates of New York University's Ph.D. program in physical education was Jay Nash. Nash had served as the California assistant supervisor of physical education under Hetherington before joining the faculty at New York University in 1926 as Hetherington's replacement. Nash stressed that recreational skills should be learned early in life and could provide enjoyment throughout life. Fearing an overemphasis on spectating in the United States, Nash stated that school programs should teach carryover, or lifetime, sports to encourage people to adopt active lifestyles; that is, people should be educated for leisure.

Influenced by Wood and Cassidy's concept of complete education through the physical and John Dewey's social education theories, Jesse Williams believed the development of physical skills in the schools could be justified only if such activities helped to educate the total child. Williams' theories of education through the physical, which prompted educating a child to live in a democratic society through social and intellectual interactions within physical education, became a part of the standard curriculum in the schools. Through his 41 books and the students he influenced in the highly regarded graduate physical education programs at Teachers College of Columbia University, Williams became one of the most influential leaders in physical education, especially between 1930 and 1960.

Figure 9-2 summarizes the influence of these new physical educators on one another. It is interesting that Nash signaled a change in the professional training

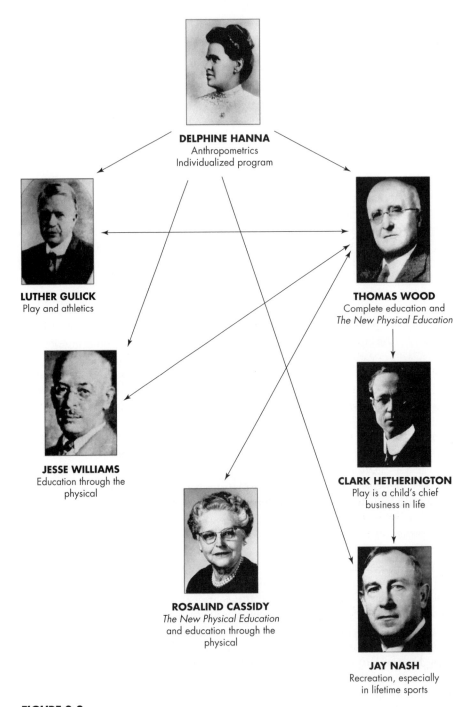

FIGURE 9-2

New physical educators.

of physical educators: Whereas Gulick, Wood, and Williams held medical degrees, Nash earned a Ph.D. in physical education.

MAJOR DEVELOPMENTS IN PHYSICAL EDUCATION AND EXERCISE SCIENCE

Several parallel movements built on the advances of the new physical education, expanding this educational curriculum even further. These developments included the play movement; the rise of teacher training; the growth of women's physical education; the education of the physical movement; the emergence of exercise science; the growing emphasis on fitness; the focus on human movement; and the influence of the scientific movement, educational developmentalism, and social education in the schools. Box 9-1 highlights many of the leaders in these developments.

The Play Movement

Luther Gulick proclaimed the importance of play for children, especially outside the schools. In New York, he established the Public Schools Athletic League's (PSAL) sports competitions for boys and the Girls' Branch of the PSAL, which provided opportunities for girls to participate in folk dancing. Elizabeth Burchenal directed the Girls' Branch of the PSAL before founding and presiding over the American Folk-Dance Society.

As supervisor of physical culture in the Detroit public schools for 14 years, Ethel Perrin stressed informal, coeducational classes that emphasized play rather than formalized gymnastics. Under her leadership, Detroit led the nation in the provision of specially trained physical educators at all levels of instruction.

The play movement also influenced nonschool programs. Following the passage of child labor laws, children were taken out of the sweat shops and returned to their neighborhoods, where playgrounds and parks were provided for them. Children of immigrants were assimilated into the American culture, made friends, learned social skills, and learned how to win and lose as they perfected their baseball, basketball, football, softball, and ice hockey skills. Cities and towns prioritized offering sports competitions and recreational activities, first for children and later for adults, to meet this inherent need to play.

Teacher Training

When physical education gained stature as a recognized subject by the National Education Association in 1891, it began to move from its association with medicine to allegiance with educational philosophies and curricula. Whereas many early physical educators, like Hitchcock, Sargent, Wood, and Williams, held medical degrees, after 1900 several universities offered professional preparation courses in physical education. Oberlin College, the Universities of Nebraska, Missouri, and California, and Stanford University developed the initial programs.

Most states established teacher training institutes, or normal colleges, to replace the private schools that had predominated in the late 1800s. While the state

BOX 9-1   TWENTIETH-CENTURY LEADERS IN PHYSICAL EDUCATION IN THE UNITED STATES

Luther Gulick, M.D. (1865–1918)
Served as instructor (1887–1900) and superintendent (1889–1900) of the Department of Physical Training at the YMCA Training School
Directed physical training for the New York City public schools (1903–1908)
Established the Public Schools Athletic League in New York City (1903)
Helped establish the Playground Association of America (1906)
Influenced by Delphine Hanna and Thomas Wood

Thomas Wood, M.D. (1864–1951)
Taught at Stanford University (1891–1901)
Taught at Teachers College of Columbia University (1901–1932)
Helped formulate the philosophical cornerstone for the new physical education
Appointed first professor of health education at Teachers College of Columbia University
Influenced by Delphine Hanna, Luther Gulick, and Rosalind Cassidy

Clark Hetherington (1870–1942)
Directed physical training and athletics at the University of Missouri (1900–1910)
Established a Demonstration Play School at the University of California at Berkeley (1913–1917)
Taught at the University of Wisconsin (1913–1918)
Served as state supervisor of physical education for California (1918–1921)
Taught at New York University (1923–1929)
Taught at Stanford University (1929–1938)
Influenced by Thomas Wood and G. Stanley Hall

Jay Nash (1886–1965)
Taught at New York University (1926–1953)
Promoted recreation and carryover sports
Influenced by Clark Hetherington and extended his theories as well as those of Luther Gulick and Thomas Wood

Jesse Williams, M.D. (1886–1966)
Taught at Teachers College of Columbia University (1911–1916; 1919–1941)
Stressed educational values, social education, and education through the physical
Became a dominant influence in physical education (1930–1960)
Influenced by John Dewey

Rosalind Cassidy (1895–1980)
Taught at Mills College, California (1918–1947)
Taught at the University of California at Los Angeles (1947–1962)
Led in writing about and promotion of the new physical education, education through the physical, and physical education as human movement
Influenced by Thomas Wood

(continued)

BOX 9-1   TWENTIETH-CENTURY LEADERS IN PHYSICAL EDUCATION IN THE UNITED STATES (CONTINUED)

Elizabeth Burchenal (1876–1959)

Served as executive secretary of the Girls' Branch of the Public Schools Athletic League (1906–1916)

Founded and served as first president of the American Folk-Dance Society (1916–1929)

Became first chairperson of the Committee on Women's Athletics of the American Physical Education Association (1917)

Influenced by Luther Gulick and Melvin Gilbert (in dance)

Ethel Perrin (1871–1962)

Supervised physical culture in the Detroit public schools (1909–1923)

Provided leadership with the executive committee of the Women's Division of the National Amateur Athletic Federation (1923–1932)

Served as assistant/associate director of health education for the American Child Health Association (1923–1936)

Influenced by Amy Morris Homans

Tait McKenzie, M.D. (1867–1938)

Taught (1891–1904) and served as medical director of physical education (1896–1904) at University Medical College (Canada)

Taught as professor on medical faculty and directed physical education (1904–1931) and served as professor of physical therapy (1907–1931) at the University of Pennsylvania

Depicted hundreds of athletic events in works of sculpture that showed the aesthetic harmony of bodily proportion and expression

Mabel Lee (1886–1985)

Directed physical education for women at the University of Nebraska (1924–1952)

Elected first woman president of the American Physical Education Association (1931)

Led the profession as a proponent of wholesome sport for women

Influenced by Amy Morris Homans

Charles McCloy (1886–1959)

Worked for the YMCA in the United States and internationally (1908–1930)

Served as a research professor in physical education at the State University of Iowa (1930–1954)

Stressed the development of skills and organic vigor (education of the physical) as the primary objectives of physical education

Eleanor Metheny (1908–1982)

Taught at Wellesley College and at the Harvard Fatigue Laboratory (1940–1942)

Taught at the University of Southern California (1942–1971)

Led in the study of meaningful movement experiences

Influenced by Charles McCloy

normal colleges became comprehensive regional universities, most retained their commitment to teacher education, including physical education.

The impact of teacher training has extended to nonschool settings as well. Physical educators, who were educated to use physical activities to teach sports skills and physical fitness, have moved into other careers. For example, physical educators have been leaders in training military personnel during wartime and times of peace. Physical educators have directed public and private recreational programs, coached sports teams for youth and adults, taught lessons in swimming, tennis, and golf at private clubs, and managed commercial and professional sporting events. Most of these individuals received their education at one of the teacher education institutions with a physical education program.

Women's Physical Education

Not until the 1970s did most college physical education programs end their practice of separation by gender. Throughout most of the 1900s, women's physical education focused on preparing teachers, with strict disassociation from competitive athletics. Curricula remained somewhat formalized, were centered on minimal skill development for all rather than on enhancement of the abilities of the highly skilled, and focused on value development rather than winning, through sport.

Only gradually did women gain acceptance as equals within the physical education profession, possibly because most early male leaders were physicians and few females had the opportunity to pursue medical degrees in the early years. Exceptions were Eliza Mosher and Helen Putnam, who served as vice presidents in the national organization. Mabel Lee was elected the first woman president of the American Physical Education Association (APEA) 46 years after it was established. Within the APEA, Lee, Burchenal, and other women worked to preserve an educational model for women's participation in sport.

Education of the Physical

Charles McCloy led the campaign against a primary emphasis on educational outcomes as advocated by Wood, Cassidy, and Williams. Instead of supporting Williams's claim that physical education merited inclusion in the schools because it helped attain social, emotional, and intellectual goals, McCloy affirmed his

Mabel Lee, the first female president of the American Physical Education Association.

commitment to **education of the physical,** a belief that physical education's unique contribution within education should be to develop individuals' physical fitness and sport skills. During his more than 20 years with the YMCA, and especially during his tenure at the State University of Iowa, McCloy stressed organic and psychomotor development as the most important objectives for physical education. He stated that the uniqueness of physical education depended on the development of physical skills. He also encouraged the teaching of sports skills and the measurement of progress through standardized tests.

> **education of the physical:**
> a belief that physical education's unique contribution within education should be to develop individuals' physical fitness and sport skills

An extension of this philosophical approach to physical education was the growth in the use of tests and measurements, which paralleled the scientific movement in education. Built on the importance of anthropometric measurements in the late 1800s, early twentieth-century physical educators developed numerous physical tests. The Public Schools Athletic League initiated achievement tests to reward boys' successful performances. College achievement tests measured cognitive knowledge, motor ability, endurance, and sports skills. David Brace's Motor Ability Test, Frederick Cozens' test of general athletic ability, Frederick Rogers' Strength Index and Physical Fitness Index, and Charles McCloy's Motor Quotient were among the most notable measures developed.

Exercise Science

Dudley Sargent, a leader in anthropometrics (discussed in the previous chapter), included measurements of the strength and power of his students at Harvard in his prescriptions for individualized programs. His use of dynamometers and the various exercise machines that he designed made him a pioneer in combining data of physical performance with exercise prescription and sport involvement. Through the Harvard Summer School and Sargent Normal School, his influence was pervasive. In 1892 George Fitz, who, like Sargent, held an M.D., established the Physiology Laboratory as a part of the Lawrence Scientific School at Harvard. Advanced students completed physiological, research, some of the first conducted in this country. The Harvard Fatigue Laboratory (interestingly, located within the School of Business) was directed by David Dill during its operation from 1927 to 1947. The breadth of the exercise and environmental research included clinical studies in physiology as well as investigations involving nutrition, physical fitness, and heart and lung function. Researchers in this laboratory, as well as the Institute for Environmental Stress at the University of California at Santa Barbara, the Laboratory for Physiological Hygiene at the University of Minnesota, and the Human Physiology Laboratory at Indiana University, became prolific publishers of their research findings, providing the foundation for today's exercise science programs.

In the 1900s, four researchers were particularly noteworthy for translating exercise physiology research into practice for the enhancement of physical fitness.

At the YMCA's George Williams College in Chicago, Arthur Steinhaus trained students for laboratory-based research and was a prolific author. Peter Karpovich at Springfield College helped link physical education with exercise physiology. Thomas Cureton at Springfield and the University of Illinois became a leading spokesperson for the importance of physical fitness through his writings and the students he taught. Kenneth Cooper, an Air Force physician, developed the aerobics fitness scoring system that helped spawn the popularity of jogging and other fitness activities in the 1970s. Cooper established a research institute in Dallas that continues to promote scientifically based educational and certification programs.

Fitness

Historically, fitness as a curricular emphasis surfaced during wartime or times when peace was threatened. Certainly this characterized physical education during the years surrounding World Wars I and II. One of the greatest advocates for physical training for the war effort was Tait McKenzie. Although recognized more for his outstanding sports sculptures, McKenzie used his training as a physical

Fitness activities, such as water aerobics, are offered by recreation departments, YMCAs and YWCAs, and health clubs.

educator and physician in England, his native Canada, and the United States to re-habilitate soldiers injured during World War I. Many male and female physical educators served as physical training instructors or consultants to the armed forces.

During World Wars I and II in schools and colleges, mass calisthenics and the development of fitness formed the basis of the curricula. In peacetime, fitness was seldom emphasized in the educational curriculum.

However, during the Cold War years of the late 1950s, all that changed. First, many people felt threatened by the rising prominence of the Union of Soviet Socialist Republics (USSR). Second, the United States was embarrassed by the 1953 results of the Kraus-Weber Minimal Muscular Fitness Test, which indicated that American children were inferior to European children in terms of fitness. This test included six items:

- In supine position, execute one straight leg sit-up.
- In supine position, do one bent-knee sit-up.
- In supine position, hold extended legs above the floor for 10 seconds.
- In prone position, pull the head, shoulders, and chest off the mat and hold for 10 seconds.
- In prone position, raise the extended legs off the mat and hold for 10 seconds.
- From a standing position, bend until fingertips touch the floor without bouncing or bending the knees and hold this contact for three seconds.

As an immediate response to this report and following a national conference on the topic, President Dwight Eisenhower established the President's Council on Youth Fitness. This council promoted a minimum of 15 minutes a day of vigorous activity for all children and distributed thousands of copies of *Youth Physical Fitness: Suggested Elements of a School-Centered Program.* The American Association for Health, Physical Education and Recreation (AAHPER) stimulated fitness through its 1958 Operation Fitness project, which included the AAHPER Youth Fitness Test. (See also the Research View box, which lists a few misconceptions about fitness that have been dispelled.)

Human Movement

Rosalind Cassidy and Eleanor Metheny helped revolutionize the conceptual base of physical education. Metheny, a student of Charles McCloy, was acclaimed for her insightful writings and inspirational speeches on this topic.

movement education:
a child-centered curriculum that emphasized presenting movement challenges to students and encouraging them to use problem solving and guided discovery to learn fundamental skills

Movement education, especially as influenced by Rudolf Laban in England, significantly influenced elementary school curricula. Movement education, a child-centered curriculum, emphasized presenting

RESEARCH VIEW

Dispelling Myths through the Exercise Sciences

Date	Misconception	What the Research Has Shown
1900s–1950s	Endurance exercise is harmful to females.	Activities that increase cardiovascular endurance are important for females' health.
1900s	American children are physically fit.	American children are increasingly obese, and many participate in no regular physical activity.
1930s–1940s	Weight training will slow an athlete and should be banned.	Strength training is highly effective in enhancing performance as well as helping to prevent injury.
1930s–1940s	Endurance training is bad for the heart.	Cardiovascular training strengthens the heart and increases its capacity.
1950s	Diseases are not related to inactivity.	Heart disease, high blood pressure, obesity, and some types of cancer are directly related to a lack of regular physical activity.
1950s	Exercise is not useful for older individuals.	Older individuals can greatly enhance the quality of their lives through cardiovascular, muscular, and flexibility activities.
1970s	Water should not be consumed during vigorous physical activity.	Fluid replacement is essential to prevent heat-related illness.
1980s	Anabolic steroids are harmless and may have only a minimal effect on the development of strength.	Anabolic steroids have many harmful and irreversible health risks even though they significantly contribute to strength development.

movement challenges to students and encouraging them to use problem solving and guided discovery to learn fundamental skills. Some educators believed the developmentally appropriate subject matter for children should focus on their free expression of movements in response to challenges or problems. Advocates favored individualized learning of locomotor, nonlocomotor, and perceptual-motor skills.

Other Influencing Factors

In the 1900s, public school physical education was directly influenced by the scientific movement, educational developmentalism, and social education. Athletic and motor ability achievement tests, measurements of posture, and the use of statistical analyses are three examples of techniques resulting from the scientific movement. The justification of play for children led the way for the playground and recreation movement that carried over into the schools. Educational developmentalism influenced the passage of state laws requiring physical education as an integral part of each child's school experiences. The popularity of sports within physical education curricula contributed to achievement of social education outcomes, including development of cooperation, good citizenship, and ethical conduct.

In more recent years, however, school physical education programs have experienced numerous attacks, partially as a result of administrators, faced with limited resources, cutting any program viewed as nonessential. Such attacks increased when physical educators were unable to demonstrate the achievement of educational standards. Another causal factor was the national call to reform education in response to the belief that the economic predominance of this country was threatened. An examination of *AMERICA 2000: An Education Strategy*, released in 1991, verified the lack of centrality of physical education. The health and physical well-being of children was not valued enough to receive mention.

Throughout the 1990s, politicians and parents consistently advocated raising academic standards for all students and demanded that educators be held accountable for improved student learning. Despite significant increases in the diversity of student populations and the guaranteeing of the educational rights of children with special needs, educators are increasingly being judged on how their students perform on norm-referenced, high-stakes tests. In the 1990s, the National Standards for Physical Education were developed to articulate what students should know and be able to do in terms of physical education. The challenge, however, was how to achieve the six content standards in physical education in the wake of decreased funding, reduced programs and personnel, and renewed emphasis on so-called academic subjects.

Understanding the history of physical education, exercise science, and sport as a field can help professionals respond to such difficulties. Certainly these major developments in school physical education have shaped today's programs.

LEADERSHIP FROM THE NATIONAL ASSOCIATION

In the early 1900s, the American Physical Education Association (APEA) was dominated by easterners who attempted to build a strong profession through the exchange of ideas and shared projects. James McCurdy, who served as editor of the APEA's *American Physical Education Review* for 23 years, was one outstanding leader during the early years.

In the early 1900s, dancing and athletics were frequently added to school and college programs, challenging the former supremacy of gymnastics. Besides these two subjects, frequently discussed topics at the annual meetings of the APEA included school hygiene, the value of gymnastics, skill and fitness testing, and standards for teacher preparation and graduate education. There was a proliferation of professional preparation in physical education between 1920 and 1927, during which 70 new college programs were begun.

WEB CONNECTIONS

1. www.aahperd.org/naspe/template.cfm
   Visit the homepage of the National Association for Sport and Physical Education, an association of the American Alliance for Health, Physical Education, Recreation and Dance, to learn about services, publications, position statements, and latest news and to link to other professional organizations and sport and physical activity sites.

2. www.womenssportsfoundation.org
   The Women's Sports Foundation, as described on this site, is an advocacy organization on behalf of girls and women in sports and physical activity.

3. www.americanfitness.net/Fitnessgram
   At this site, you will find comprehensive information about the FITNESSGRAM and Physical Best educational materials.

4. www.ed.gov/offices/OSERS/OSEP/Products/IEP_Guide
   A Guide to the Individualized Education Program can be read or downloaded at this site.

5. www.ed.gov/pubs/TitleIX
   At this site, the Department of Education provides a 25-year description of the progress achieved through Title IX of the 1972 Education Amendments.

6. www.heartofachampion.org
   The Heart of a Champion Foundation promotes positive character development through sport in schools and communities.

Following the merger of the Midwest Society (a regional group of physical educators) into the national APEA in 1930, Elmer Mitchell assumed the editorship of the profession's two major publications, the *Journal of Health and Physical Education* and the *Research Quarterly;* he served in this capacity for 13 years. In 1937, the Department of School Health and Physical Education of the National Education Association merged with the APEA to become the American Association for Health and Physical Education (*Recreation* was added to its name in 1938). The national organization was subsequently configured into six geographical districts.

After World War II, AAHPER sponsored numerous conferences focusing on facilities, undergraduate professional preparation, graduate professional preparation, fitness, and other interest areas. In 1974, it was restructured into an alliance composed of seven (now six) associations (see Chapter 3) to allow greater autonomy in providing leadership and programs for the diverse interests of its members. The addition of dance and to its current acronym, AAHPERD, occurred in 1979.

In 1985, AAHPERD's centennial celebration focused on recalling its service and leadership in health, physical education, recreation, dance, and sports. The April 1985 issue of the *Journal of Physical Education, Recreation and Dance* traced 100 years of the profession, highlighting special events and notable leaders. The message conveyed in this publication and through the centennial convention was that AAHPERD, through its membership, had enriched programs for diverse populations. Today the six national associations focusing on health, leisure and recreation, dance, active lifestyles, physical education, and sport serve the unique needs of their members.

TEACHER PREPARATION

A perennial concern of AAHPERD and its preceding organizations has been the inconsistencies among professional preparation programs for teachers. Each normal school, as it developed, was free to pursue its own course of study, with little relationship to what was being taught at the others. When four-year degree programs were developed in colleges and universities, each institution had the latitude to design and implement its own curriculum. Since there were no accreditation procedures or standards in the early 1900s, great program diversity resulted. In the 1930s, the Department of School Health and Physical Education of the National Education Association established a committee to evaluate teacher education curricula and establish standards. In 1948, the National Conference on Undergraduate Professional Preparation in Health Education, Physical Education, and Recreation recommended standards and programs in teacher preparation. In 1960, AAHPER voted to accept the National Council for Accreditation of Teacher Education (NCATE) as the official accrediting agency in its fields of study. This led to many state departments of education certifying only teachers who graduated from NCATE-approved institutions. In the 1970s, many state departments began to require that certain competencies be met in professional course work before future teachers would be certified. Each of these developments enhanced the quality of the graduates of teacher education programs.

In the 1980s, many people expressed concern about the lack of standards for and credentials of individuals engaged in various sports and fitness programs. For example, there was no national certification for aerobic dance instructors. Seemingly anyone who could enthusiastically motivate people to exercise to the resounding beat of the latest hit tunes could teach. Knowledge about human anatomy, exercise physiology, first aid, cardiopulmonary resuscitation, psychology, and teaching progressions was not a prerequisite. This lack of standards led to repeated injuries, some serious; high dropout rates; and a general lack of accountability on the part of instructors and sponsoring groups. Certification programs for fitness instructors and leaders, such as through the American College of Sports Medicine, have filled the gap in this area, but such training still is often optional rather than mandatory. Unless sports like scuba diving, weight training, karate, and racquetball regulate their own instructors' training, anyone is free to teach these or other activities outside the schools.

AMATEUR AND COLLEGIATE SPORTS

The popularization of sports in the twentieth and twenty-first centuries has been phenomenal. In addition to becoming the nucleus of physical education programs, sports are organized for competition inside and outside schools and colleges.

Intramurals

In the late 1800s and early 1900s, most college athletic teams and some physical education programs evolved out of interclass competitions organized by male students. As athletics and physical education developed their own separate programs, a need still existed for recreational activities for students. In 1913, the University of Michigan and The Ohio State University appointed the first intramural directors. At Michigan, beginning in 1919, Elmer Mitchell led in the development of sports opportunities for students who were not varsity athletes but wanted more competition than was available in physical education classes. Originally in the colleges and after the mid-1920s in the schools, intramurals offered league and class (or homeroom) competition in individual and team sports. In the 1940s, coeducational activities were introduced and became popular. The greatest expansion in combined male and female activities occurred in the 1970s.

Today many intramural programs operate as campus recreation programs, having greatly expanded the scope of their activities. In addition to competitive leagues and coeducational recreation, club sports, extramural competitions, faculty/staff programs, instructional clinics, fitness classes, special events and tournaments, and free-play opportunities have been offered. Over the years, many of these intramural and recreational sports programs have moved from receiving funds first from athletic departments and then from physical education departments to being supported by students' fees. At the school level, where intramural activities vary from traditional competitions to a variety of leisure-time events and are scheduled throughout the day and night, physical educators normally provide the expertise while school budgets provide the equipment.

Outside the schools, the same concept of intramurals, or sports competition within the walls, has provided innumerable opportunities for physical activity. Many corporations offer sports leagues and competitions in volleyball, bowling, softball, and many other sports for their employees at all levels of the organization. These leisure-time activities help build camaraderie among employees as well as help them live healthier lifestyles.

Collegiate Sports for Men

In the early 1900s, concerns in collegiate sports focused on football, primarily because of the injuries and deaths that occurred with shocking regularity. While President Theodore Roosevelt expressed concern, college presidents threatened to ban intercollegiate football. As a direct result of football injuries and deaths, the National Collegiate Athletic Association (NCAA) was formed in 1906. Although composed of a small group of faculty representatives with power only to make recommendations, the NCAA attempted to control the roughness and brutality of football by revising its rules. Gradually football overcame these problems and emerged as the major collegiate sport. Baseball in colleges, though rivaled by the professional major leagues, retained a degree of popularity secondary to the pros and to football, while intercollegiate competitions in boxing, golf, tennis, track and field, and wrestling have never seriously challenged the supremacy of football. Basketball emerged as the second leading collegiate sport, but not until the 1950s.

The NCAA continued as the sole voice of and controlling organization for college athletes until 1938, when the National Junior College Athletic Association (NJCAA) was founded to provide competitive opportunities for students in two-year institutions. Then, in 1952, the National Association of Intercollegiate Athletics (NAIA) began to sponsor championships for small colleges (it sponsored an annual basketball tournament for men starting in 1940). Table 9-1 lists these and other major sports organizations for men and women.

Today collegiate athletics for men are very different from what they were in the 1940s. Under faculty control by representative vote, the NCAA remained primarily an advisory organization during its first 40 years. Control rested with each institution, where most frequently athletic councils composed of alumni, faculty,

College football in the 1930s. (Photo courtesy North Carolina Collection, UNC Library at Chapel Hill.)

TABLE 9-1

SPORT GOVERNANCE ORGANIZATIONS

Boys and Men

1888	Amateur Athletic Union (AAU)
	*1879—National Association of Amateur Athletes of America
1910	National Collegiate Athletic Association (NCAA)
	*1906—Intercollegiate Athletic Association of the United States
1922	National Federation of State High School Associations (NFHS)
1938	National Junior College Athletic Association (NJCAA)
1952	National Association of Intercollegiate Athletics (NAIA)
	*1940—National Association of Intercollegiate Basketball

Girls and Women

1974	National Association for Girls and Women in Sport (NAGWS)
	*1917—Committee on Women's Athletics
	*1927—Women's Athletic Section
	*1932—National Section of Women's Athletics
	*1953—National Section for Girls and Women in Sport
	*1958—Division for Girls and Women in Sport
1971	Association for Intercollegiate Athletics for Women (AIAW) (ceased in 1982)
	*1966—Commission on Intercollegiate Athletics for Women

First Championships Offered for Girls and Women

1916	Amateur Athletic Union
1976	National Junior College Athletic Association
1980	National Association of Intercollegiate Athletics
1981	National Collegiate Athletic Association

*Earlier name of the same organization.

and students exercised authority over athletics. Institutions that held membership in conferences agreed to follow additional regulations and guidelines. Other than standardizing the rules and providing championships, the NCAA had not been granted power by the institutions to legislate or to mandate rules. Beginning with the national acceptance of athletic grants-in-aid in 1952 and throughout the following decade, the role of the NCAA changed dramatically as institutions became willing to relinquish some of their autonomy to the NCAA to ensure that other institutions would comply with the regulations governing grants-in-aid and recruiting. A second development began with the first negotiation of a television contract in 1951, thus providing the NCAA with enforcement leverage. Subsequently, the NCAA could penalize an institution economically by disallowing television appearances. With a budget in the hundreds of millions of dollars, the NCAA has become the most powerful amateur sports organization in the United States and possibly the world.

During the last quarter of the twentieth century, the NCAA once again experienced dramatic change. In its Division III programs, students without grants-in-aid continued to compete for the love of the sport, cheered on by a handful of friends and family and with minimal hope of continuing their athletic careers beyond graduation. While students competing in Division II programs received grants-in-aid, most realized that their talents were limited and therefore focused more on the educational opportunities provided them. It was at the Division I level that highly commercialized sports emerged. Corporate sponsorships, donations from enthusiastic fans (in return for priority seating and other perks), and television contracts became essential to funding the multimillion-dollar budgets needed to support athletic programs at the highest level. Athletic administrators at the approximately 100 "big-time" football and basketball programs finally admitted to being in the entertainment rather the education business. Coaches with multimillion-dollar contracts were hired to win and fired for losing. Athletes received an educational opportunity that was too often discounted, while universities reaped millions for their performances in bowl games or for coming away with a win during a Final Four game. Gamblers influenced the outcomes of some games; the media exploited every angle; many athletes, coaches, and others associated with intercollegiate athletics sought ways to gain personal advancement and financial benefits. The NCAA seemingly made every attempt to solidify its control over intercollegiate sports with apparent disregard for the raging controversies over gambling, drug abuse, commercialization, professionalism, and other issues.

Collegiate Sports for Women

During the early 1900s, sports for women were strictly controlled by women physical educators, who consistently followed the societal expectations for their gender. Caution about a potential overemphasis on competition or on "unladylike" behavior led to modified rules in several sports. Mass participation in class exercises, field days, play days, and sports days, rather than competitive athletics, became the norm. Because of its healthful benefits, physical education was stressed for girls in schools and for women who attended colleges. Outfitted in middy blouses and bloomers, the traditional gymnasium costume of the day, women exercised in mass drills, engaged in therapeutic Swedish gymnastics, and enjoyed sports such as archery, basketball, field hockey, rowing, and tennis. Some girls and women competed on teams, especially in basketball, until these teams were eliminated by physical educators who believed competitive sports were harmful to females physically, emotionally, and mentally.

In women's colleges, field days were normally conducted once or twice a year on campus, and all students were urged to participate. Play days, beginning in the 1920s, provided for social interaction as women students met and formed teams composed of representatives from several institutions. These teams played one or more sports before reassembling for a picnic or other social event. Evolving from these play days were sports days, during which college teams competed, frequently in only one sport, but still with the emphasis on social interaction and fun.

Female archers in 1890s attire.

Basketball, played in bloomers, was the most popular college sport for women in the 1890s and early 1900s. (Photo courtesy Basketball Hall of Fame.)

Photos on pages 284–285 show the changes in women's sports attire.

A women's play day in the 1920s.

Softball was a popular industrial recreation sport in the 1940s.

In 1917, the Committee on Women's Athletics was established by the American Physical Education Association (today's AAHPERD) to implement standards and policies that advocated mass participation while vigorously opposing varsity competition. Between 1923 and 1942, the Women's Division of the National Amateur Athletic Federation also opposed highly competitive sports, including those in the Olympic Games, claiming they were inappropriate for women.

In the late 1960s, a gradual change in societal attitudes regarding women in sports paralleled a liberalized philosophy displayed by women leaders in physical education. As long as the athletes' welfare was guaranteed and high standards were maintained, competitions were permitted and even encouraged, especially beginning in 1969, when the Commission on Intercollegiate Athletics

The All-American Girls Professional Baseball League provided competitive opportunities in the 1940s and 1950s.

for Women began sponsoring national tournaments. Two years later, the Association for Intercollegiate Athletics for Women (AIAW), an institutional membership organization, assumed this responsibility. During the next 11 years, the AIAW sponsored championships and established standards and policies governing women's intercollegiate athletics. With equal opportunity mandated by Title IX of the 1972 Education Amendments, colleges and schools financed increased sports competitions for girls and women. In 1976 the NJCAA and in 1980 the NAIA began offering championships for college women; smaller institutions benefited financially from having one membership fee, one governance structure and set of rules, and similar sport schedules for all athletes.

The NCAA initially opposed Title IX of the 1972 Education Amendments, claiming that its requirement for equal opportunity in all educational programs would end men's intercollegiate athletics. The NCAA lobbied the Department of Health, Education and Welfare for exclusion of athletics from Title IX; they campaigned in support of the Tower Amendment in the Senate to exclude revenue sports from Title IX jurisdiction; and they turned to the courts, arguing the inapplicability of Title IX to athletics on constitutional grounds. Each of these approaches was unsuccessful (see "A Brief History of Title IX" in Table 9-2).

Claiming Title IX mandated that the NCAA govern both men's and women's athletics, the NCAA began in 1981 to offer championships for women in what amounted to a hostile takeover of women's intercollegiate athletics. Even though in the previous decade the AIAW had grown to 960 members and sponsored 42 championships in three competitive divisions in 19 sports, it could not match the NCAA's large financial base, out of which it covered the expenses for women's teams participating in NCAA championships. The NCAA also waived its membership dues for women's athletic teams if its institution was already a member for its men's programs, and it contracted to televise the women's basketball finals

TABLE 9-2

A BRIEF HISTORY OF TITLE IX

"No person in the United States shall, on the basis of sex, be excluded from participation in, be denied the benefits of, or be subjected to discrimination under any education program or activity receiving Federal financial assistance."

1972	Congress enacts Title IX of the Education Amendments of 1972	Prohibits sex discrimination in any education program or activity in an institution receiving federal financial assistance
1974	Attempt to exclude revenue-producing sports from Title IX	Senator John Tower introduces an amendment (which was not adopted) to exempt revenue-producing sports from inclusion in determining whether an institution was in compliance with Title IX; other, similar attempts fail in 1975 and 1977
1974	Javits Amendment	Senator Jacob Javits' amendment (which was adopted) requires the Department of Health, Education, and Welfare (HEW) to issue Title IX regulations that include specific reference to particular sports
1975	HEW issues final Title IX regulations	Higher education institutions and secondary schools have three years to comply with Title IX
1979	HEW issues final policy interpretation on Title IX and intercollegiate athletics	This policy interpretation requires institutions to provide equal opportunity and specifies three areas required for compliance: financial assistance (athletic grants-in-aid); programs areas such as coaching, facilities, travel and per diem, and tutoring); meeting the interests and abilities of male and female students
1980	Department of Education (DOE) is established	DOE is given oversight of Title IX through the Office for Civil Rights (OCR)
1984	*Grove City vs. Bell*	The Supreme Court rules that the applicability of Title IX in athletics programs is limited to only those programs or activities that receive direct federal financial assistance
1988	Civil Rights Restoration Act	This congressional act overrides *Grove City vs. Bell* and mandates that all educational institutions receiving federal financial assistance, whether direct or indirect, must comply with Title IX
1992	*Franklin vs. Gwinnett County Public Schools*	The Supreme Court rules that under Title IX, plaintiffs may receive punitive damages when noncompliance with Title IX is intentional
1992	Gender Equity Study	National Collegiate Athletic Association publishes its Gender Equity Study
1996	Policy clarification	OCR issues clarifications about how institutions can provide effective accommodations in intercollegiate athletics
1996	First EADA report due	The Equity in Athletics Disclosure Act requires all institutions to make available specific information about their intercollegiate athletics programs

(directly opposite the AIAW's title game). Despite the AIAW's educational model for athletics, which was specifically designed to avoid the problems associated with the male sports model, the AIAW ceased to exist in June 1982. Although a few women have gained some status in the NCAA, such as Judith Sweet, the first female to serve as president, the NCAA is governed predominantly by men. Men hold most coaching and administrative positions in women's athletics within the NCAA as well as in the NAIA and NJCAA.

Amateur Sports

The amateur sports scene in the United States outside the colleges remained largely under the direction of the AAU through the 1970s, since this organization sponsored diverse sports competitions for people of all ages. Basketball, boxing, swimming, and track and field especially attracted thousands of participants. Because championships in these sports were offered by NCAA institutions, the two organizations frequently clashed. Repeatedly, when the time arrived for the selection of Olympic teams, controversies raged. In 1922, the National Amateur Athletic Federation was formed to mediate this dispute, with few positive results. The conflicts inevitably affected the athletes because the two associations often refused to sanction events, certify records, or permit athletes to participate in each other's events. The Amateur Sports Act, passed in 1978, resolved some of these problems by requiring that each Olympic sport have its own governing body and establishing guidelines governing the selection of these organizations.

For the most part, the spirit of the Olympics promoted by Pierre de Coubertin, founder of the modern games, and perpetuated by the governing International Olympic Committee, prevailed during the first half of the twentieth century. The five interlocking rings symbolized friendship among the athletes of the world. Competitive superiority remained the ideal until the Olympic Games became the stage for displaying the supremacy of one's national ideology. This was certainly the case in the 1952 Helsinki Games, where professionally trained athletes from the USSR entered Olympic competition. It would seem that nationalism's intrusion into Olympic competition, where winning demonstrates the

Jim Thorpe, a Native American, won gold medals in the 1912 Stockholm Olympic Games in the pentathlon and decathlon.

superiority of one's political or ideological system, has signaled the beginning of the end for amateurism as the foundation of the Olympic Games. The boycotts of 1980 and 1984 certainly confirmed the power of politics in international sports competition.

Commercialism, with its product displays and lucrative television contracts, has forever changed the image of these competitions. Media attention and the potential for leveraging medals into endorsements have also played significant roles in the demise of amateur competition in the Olympics. While the 1984 Los Angeles Games were the first to be commercially successful, the 1996 Atlanta Games hosted mostly professional athletes who were also paid by their countries when they won medals. Scandals associated with site selection and perks for International Olympic Committee members substantiated the influence of money on these games.

The original events of the modern Olympic Games paralleled the popular activities of the turn of the century, such as track and field, gymnastics, fencing, and tennis. These and other Olympic sports had minimal impact on school curricula. While many Olympic sports were associated with elitist clubs for men, including shooting, rowing, yachting, and equestrian clubs, the entry of college males in track and field, swimming, and wrestling broadened the composition of the teams from the United States and thus may have attracted participants from throughout society. Few women, primarily in swimming (starting in 1912) and track and field (starting in 1928), competed in the Olympics, until the number of sports opened to them increased. The popularity of gymnastics, basketball, and figure skating certainly has been enhanced through the showcasing of Olympic competitions. However, only the growth in gymnastics can probably be linked specifically to the Olympics.

Mildred (Babe) Didrikson won gold medals in the 800-meter hurdles and the javelin throw and a silver medal in the high jump in the 1932 Los Angeles Olympic Games.

PLAY TO RECREATION TO FITNESS

Play

The playground movement continued apace in the early 1900s as the Playground Association of America (PAA), founded in 1906 by Luther Gulick and Henry Curtis, provided the necessary leadership. Gulick was instrumental in the publication of its monthly magazine, *The Playground*. The provision of adequate playgrounds throughout the country was also enhanced by the support of President Theodore Roosevelt. Clark Hetherington supervised the writing of *The Normal Course in Play* in 1910, the book used to prepare recreation leaders. Joseph Lee, president of the PAA, helped expand the play concept to include the value of play and recreation for all ages, leading to the reorganization of the PAA in 1911 and its new name, the Playground and Recreation Association of America (PRAA).

Recreation

In 1930, the PRAA became the National Recreation Association (which became the National Recreation and Park Association in 1965), verifying the importance and worth of leisure time for people of all ages. The Depression years suddenly gave people large amounts of leisure time, but many had limited financial resources. The federal government helped in two ways. Federal agencies, such as the Works Progress Administration, provided jobs by funding construction of camping sites, golf courses, gymnasiums, playing fields, and swimming pools.

Many states offer amateurs competitive opportunities through State Games. (Photo courtesy Maggie McGlynn.)

Once completed, these were opened for mass recreational use. Especially popular sports during the 1930s were bowling and softball.

Wartime production brought the United States out of the Depression. At the same time, sports competitions and recreational programs were initiated to revive the spirits and bodies of soldiers and factory workers. While the armed services used sports for training and conditioning soldiers, industries began to provide sports teams and competitive opportunities for employees, realizing that such activities positively affected productivity and morale. Industrial recreation continued to expand, even after the war ended.

Outdoor education emerged as the recreational thrust of the 1950s. As the country became more mechanized and technological, the appeal of camping, hiking, and similar back-to-nature activities provided people with the chance to get away from daily routines and stress. Some schools and colleges began to offer backpacking, rock climbing, spelunking, winter survival, ropes courses, and orienteering, all of which have maintained their popularity.

As early as the 1930s, Jay Nash promoted carryover, or lifetime, sports within the curriculum. By the 1960s, this philosophy had gained numerous supporters and affected programs. Led by the Lifetime Sports Foundation with joint sponsorship of AAHPER, archery, badminton, bowling, golf, and tennis were introduced into many schools. Slowly programs expanded from offering only team sports to the inclusion of these and other lifetime sports.

Backpacking is one of several popular outdoor activities. (Photo courtesy Jim Kirby.)

Fitness

The fitness mania began in the 1970s, with joggers leading the craze. In 1970, the lonely runner was suddenly joined by thousands of marathoners and road racers of all ages and both genders, while tennis participants multiplied and swimming became more popular. The pervasiveness of this fitness mania was evident not only by the sport paraphernalia that enthusiasts used and wore but also by the popularity of sporting attire for everyone. This fitness phenomenon has continued as verified by the rise in health club memberships. However, the people most involved in getting and keeping in shape have come from the middle and upper classes rather than being drawn equally from all economic levels. Also, many school-age children, rather than becoming fitness advocates, have preferred to watch television, play video and computer games, surf the Web, or become sports spectators.

Fitness for Children   When the results of the Kraus-Weber Minimal Muscular Fitness Test were published in 1953, European children demonstrated greater fitness (only 9 percent failed) than children in the United States (57.8 percent failed). Since the six-item Kraus-Weber test measured primarily flexibility and abdominal strength (and thus received criticism that it inaccurately assessed overall fitness), the physical education profession developed the AAHPER Youth Fitness Test. To the dismay of professionals, the 1958 results of this eight-item test battery showed that children in the United States had low levels of fitness. This test included pull-ups (for boys), flexed-arm hang (for girls), straight-leg sit-ups, the shuttle run, the standing broad jump, the softball throw, the 50-yard dash, and the 600-yard run/walk. Between 1958 and the second national administration of this test in 1965, teachers promoted fitness through daily physical education classes, periodic testing, and an increased emphasis on the importance of fitness. These efforts were rewarded with improvement by all age groups in all skills, except for 17-year-old girls in the softball throw. Unfortunately, these vigorous efforts lapsed, so poor fitness levels among school-age children were reported in the 1980s.

In response to widespread criticism that the AAHPER Youth Fitness Test failed to measure the major components of fitness, the AAHPERD introduced the Health-Related Lifetime Physical Fitness Test in 1981. Its items measured strength with sit-ups, flexibility using a sit-and-reach, cardiovascular endurance in

Muscular strength and endurance can be measured using sit-ups.

a 1.5-mile or 12-minute run, and body composition by taking skinfold measurements. While more accurately measuring the recognized components of fitness, these test norms only reconfirmed the lack of fitness among school-age children in the 1980s.

In 1994, the AAHPERD joined the Cooper Institute in a collaborative and comprehensive physical fitness education and assessment program. Physical Best, the educational component of the program, helps students develop the knowledge, skills, and attitudes for a healthy and fit life, and tries to motivate them to engage in regular, enjoyable physical activity. Physical Best seeks to educate all children about health-related fitness concepts, regardless of their athletic talent and physical and mental abilities (or disabilities). FITNESSGRAM, the fitness test component of this program, was designed to allow physical education teachers to easily report their students' fitness levels to parents. This three-part assessment compares each student's fitness to age and gender standards, not to other children. Following are the three health-related fitness components and assessment options:

- Aerobic Capacity (select one)
  - The Pacer—a 20-meter progressive, multistage shuttle run set to music
  - One Mile Walk/Run
  - Walk Test—available for secondary students
- Body Composition (select one)
  - Percent Body Fat—calculated from triceps and calf skinfold measurements
  - Body Mass Index—calculated from height and weight
- Muscle Strength, Endurance, and Flexibility
  - Abdominal Strength—curl-up test
  - Trunk Extensor Strength and Flexibility—trunk lift
  - Upper Body Strength (select one)—90-degree push-up; pull-up; flexed-arm hang; modified pull-up
  - Flexibility (select one)—back-saver; sit-and-reach; shoulder stretch

Students use the ACTIVITYGRAM assessment to complete a three-day recall of their physical activity in 30-minute blocks of time between the hours of 7 A.M. and 11 P.M. Students are asked to enter three pieces of information about each activity:

- Type and Name of Activity—rest; muscular activity; flexibility activity; aerobic sports; aerobic activity; lifestyle activity
- Intensity of Activity—rest; light; moderate; vigorous
- Length of Activity—some (1–10 minutes); most (11–29 minutes); all of the time (30 minutes)

The latest data on the fitness of American youth come from the National Children and Youth Fitness Study I (1985) and II (1987). These studies revealed that the fitness levels of American youth still need improvement. The need for improvement in youth fitness comprises a part of *Healthy People 2010* goals as discussed in Chapter 1.

Although some local and state assessments of children's fitness levels have been conducted, there has not been a replication of the national study since the 1980s. Available data, however, show that the youth fitness goals in Healthy People 2010 have not been achieved. In the wake of the 1996 publication of the surgeon general's *Report on Physical Activity and Health* and the identification of physical inactivity as a primary risk factor contributing to coronary heart disease, the nation's interest in the physical well-being of parents and children alike has never been stronger. Increased concern has been expressed about the rising incidence of obesity in children. Schools, public recreation programs, and private businesses need to combine their efforts to provide greater opportunities for physical education and sport activities for children. Increased funding is needed to provide daily physical education classes for all children, as well as to purchase equipment such as aerobic machines and heart rate monitors.

Fitness for All Ages   The emphasis on aerobic fitness for individuals of all ages was aided by the 1968 publication of Kenneth Cooper's *Aerobics*. This book outlined a program for helping every individual attain and maintain physical fitness by compiling a certain number of points each week while participating in favorite activities. Since the 1970s, many Americans have renewed regular physical activity by playing tennis, racquetball, and golf; running road races and marathons; engaging in skating, wind surfing, and skiing; and purchasing millions of dollars' worth of home exercise equipment. Women, many for the first time, have joined classes in aerobic dance, step aerobics, water aerobics, and several other variations of exercise combined with music. Health and fitness clubs now offer aerobics classes; individualized weight-training programs; aerobic machines such as elliptical machines, stair climbers, treadmills, stationary bikes, and rowing machines; and instruction in tennis, racquetball, and golf. Many clubs also offer various sports leagues and tournaments, massage, sports medicine consultation, and nutritional counseling. Some people have suggested that such clubs have replaced social events and bars as the preferred places for meeting and interacting with others. The appearance of fitness is certainly apparent in fashions; many Americans are trying to achieve a level of fitness that both looks and feels good. Unfortunately, this glamorizing of ideal body images may be pushing females into unhealthy exercise and diet habits that can lead to amenorrhea, anorexia, and osteoporosis.

YOUTH SPORTS PROGRAMS

In the 1920s, the popularity of sports in the United States led many people to expect the schools to provide competitive sports for children. Some junior and most senior high schools assumed this responsibility because physical educators believed that students in these age groups were physiologically and psychologically prepared for competition. For elementary-age children, educators widely believed that the negative outcomes from competitive sports outweighed the benefits. This belief did not prevent the development of youth sports programs, however. Communities, private associations, and civic organizations stepped in to fill the void, seeing sports as a deterrent to delinquency, a tool for social control, a means of developing self-discipline and cooperation, and an outlet for exercise and fun. Local as well as national programs, such as Little League Baseball, Pop Warner Football, and Biddy Basketball, expanded to the point that today they involve millions of young athletes and adult organizers and billions of dollars.

Although many physical educators philosophically disagree with highly competitive youth leagues, these sports enterprises are deeply entrenched in American society. Parents have favored youth sports programs for several reasons:

- Their children have fun through participation.
- The programs offer opportunities for learning sports skills.
- These experiences enhance socialization abilities such as cooperation and teamwork and development of values.
- Sports involvement contributes to physical development and fitness.
- Youth sports programs provide children with wholesome alternatives for the use of their time, thus lessening misbehavior or unattended hours at home watching television or surfing the Web. In addition, many value youth sports because the whole family can participate together—as players, coaches, and cheerleaders, and in various other volunteer capacities.

Children have varying reasons for participating in youth sports. Mostly they want to have fun, learn or improve sports skills, stay in shape or get exercise, associate with friends, or merely have something to do. Unfortunately, some youth join a team or participate in individual youth sports just to please their parents. After years of success as a young athlete, winning, seeking valued rewards or awards, maintaining popularity, or even qualifying for college grants-in-aid or professional careers may become the primary motivations for participating in sports.

When youth sports programs remain focused on the children's aspirations, and when parents' attitudes and behaviors are kept in perspective, millions benefit. When winning surpasses all other goals, exploitation of young athletes and an erosion of values reign. For example, exposure to the media, such as the televising of the Little League World Series, has served only to intensify the pressures on young competitors as well as raise the expected levels of performance to adult and even professional levels. As a result, children are no longer allowed to be children or to play just for the fun of it. When adults rudely dispute officials' calls and berate their children for not performing well enough, they become part of the problem. These adults rob children of the many benefits of playful participation in sport. Adult domination also prevents children from learning in and through sport the art of negotiation, how to make decisions, communication skills, and how to lead and follow.

Numerous occurrences in youth sports call attention to the prevalence of exploitation. Pressures to win, commercialization, elimination of less competitive players, injuries resulting from excessive play or practice, violence, overspecialization, cheating, and lack of value development are but a few examples. As more and more educators promote and provide coaching education programs, these problems may be reduced. Parent orientation sessions are also important deterrents to adult misbehavior and placing excessive pressures on children.

FEDERAL LEGISLATION

Although early leaders of this country, such as Benjamin Franklin and Thomas Jefferson, were promoters of physical education, the federal government has not become involved in physical education issues until recent years. Legislation that directly influences physical education includes mandates for equal opportunity for both genders and for students with special needs.

Coeducational Physical Education

Title IX of the 1972 Education Amendments required equal opportunity in all educational programs and stated as its basic principle that "no person in the United States shall, on the basis of sex, be excluded from participation in, be denied the

An increasingly popular school elective in physical education is weight training. (Photo courtesy Bob Hilliard.)

benefits of, or be subjected to discrimination under any education program or activity receiving federal financial assistance." In relation to physical education, this statement meant it was illegal to discriminate against either gender in curricula content, equipment and facility usage, teacher quality, or other program areas. One specific impact of this legislation was to make school physical education classes coeducational. Boys and girls could be separated by gender for contact sports (like wrestling). They could also be taught separately in sex education units within health education classes. (See Chapter 11 for other ways in which this legislation affected sports.)

Although equitable treatment (except in sex education and contact sports) was the law, some schools and colleges resisted change. Often this resistance was due to teachers' refusal to instruct students of the opposite gender or to the administration's lack of insistence on compliance. Many institutions maintained class rolls of boys and girls but offered gender-segregated instruction and activity. As attitudes and behaviors gradually changed, some teachers instructed mixed classes but refused to allow girls and boys to compete with and against each other.

Despite such resistance, Title IX has led to substantial changes. Elementary school children accept classes composed of both girls and boys as the norm. As they participate with and against each other during the developmental years, the differences in their levels of performance lessen. Teachers assess abilities and evaluate performances to ensure fair standards and groupings. Increasingly, students in the secondary schools are accepting combined classes, learning respect for the capabilities of members of the opposite gender. Gradually acceptance and appreciation of girls and women actively participating in sports have led to recreation and fitness programs that welcome all who seek to enjoy activity and develop their physical capabilities.

Adapted Physical Education Programs

Historically, students with disabilities were not given opportunities to participate in activity classes or were assigned to corrective or remedial classes, with a resulting social stigma. The development of adapted programs led to a more individualized approach. *Adapted physical education* is intended for exceptional students who are so different in mental, physical, emotional, or behavioral characteristics that, in the interest of quality of educational opportunity, special provisions must be made for their proper education. Yet not all schools made such provisions for students' special needs; therefore, the federal government became involved.

Section 504 of the Rehabilitation Act of 1973 specified that "no otherwise qualified handicapped person shall, on the basis of handicap, be excluded from participation in, be denied the benefits of, or otherwise be subjected to discrimination under any program which receives or benefits from Federal financial assistance." Thus, every student was guaranteed access to the entire school program, including physical education. The Education Amendment Act of 1974

Inclusion places physically challenged children into regular education classes.
(Photo courtesy Bob Hilliard.)

mandated that all children must be placed in the least restrictive environment, or the setting in which their optimal learning and development could occur.

The Education for All Handicapped Children Act of 1975 (Public Law 94-142) was the first law to specifically mandate physical education in its guidelines. Generally, it required that physical education, specially designed if necessary, be provided for every child with a disability in the public schools within regular physical education classes, unless the student has unusual restrictions; any unusual restrictions are to be provided for through the development of an Individualized Education Program (IEP).

The basic tenets of the Individuals with Disabilities Education Act (IDEA) have remained intact since the original passage of the law in 1975, even though each set of amendments has strengthened the original law. This legislation has fostered significant changes in the lives of children with disabilities and their families, and in the roles of schools and teachers who educate children with disabilities. The six principles of IDEA include free, appropriate public education; appropriate evaluation; an Individualized Education Program; the least restrictive environment for each child; parent and student participation in decision making; and procedural safeguards. Special education and related services, including the initial evaluation, must be provided at public expense, under public supervision and direction, and be delivered by appropriately trained personnel. (In addition, the Americans with Disabilities Act [passed in 1990] sought to eliminate barriers that have prevented individuals with special needs from fully participating in society.)

The IEP (see the sample in Table 9-3) must be a written plan designed by a representative of the public agency (school) who is qualified to provide or to

TABLE 9-3

INDIVIDUALIZED EDUCATION PROGRAM

Student: <u>Chris Miller</u> Age: <u>9</u> Grade: <u>3</u>
School: <u>Eastwood Elementary</u> Height: <u>42"</u> Weight: <u>62</u>
Placement: <u>Least Restrictive Environment</u> Date of annual review: <u>August, 2004</u>

Present level of performance: Chris is mildly mentally retarded and lacks balance and eye–hand coordination skills; prefers sedentary to vigorous activity; can toss and catch a rubber ball thrown from 12 feet, 3 times out of 10; can do two bent-knee sit-ups and comes within 6 inches of touching toes with legs slightly flexed.

Annual goals:

1. Increase abdominal strength
2. Increase flexibility
3. Increase eye–hand coordination
4. Increase balance

Sample Performance Objectives	Sample Activities	Evaluation Measure	Completion Date
1. Perform 10 bent-knee sit-ups without stopping	1. Teacher-assisted sit-ups daily; leg lifts held for 1 to 10 seconds	1. Observation	1. December, 2004
2. Touch toes with fingers without bending knees and hold for 2 seconds	2. Lower and upper leg stretches; teacher-assisted toe touches	2. Observation	2. December, 2004
3. Toss and catch a 20-inch rubber ball, at 20 feet, 6 times out of 10 times	3. Self-toss, wall toss, and partner toss from 10, 15, and 20 feet	3. Observation	3. March, 2005
4. Walk 6 feet on a 4-inch balance beam placed 6 inches off the floor	4. Walk on a 4-inch line on the floor; teacher assistance while on balance beam	4. Observation	4. March, 2005

Date: _____ Teacher: _____

supervise special education, and may include the input of the child's teacher, one or both of the child's parents, the child (when appropriate), and other individuals selected at the discretion of the parent or school. One problem in the development of IEPs has been the frequent failure to involve physical educators, even though IDEA specifies that the child's physical needs must be met.

Each IEP must contain the following:

- A statement of the child's current levels of educational performance
- A statement of measurable annual goals, including short-term objectives or benchmarks

- A statement of the specific special education and related services to be provided to the child
- A statement of the extent (if any) to which the child will not participate with nondisabled children in regular class and other school activities
- A statement of any individual modifications in the administration of statewide or districtwide assessment of student achievement
- A statement of when services will begin, how often they will be provided, where they will be provided, and how long they will last
- A statement of transition services needs (beginning at age 14) and transition services needed to prepare for leaving school (beginning at age 16)
- A statement of any rights that will transfer to the child at the age of majority (at least one year prior)
- A statement of how the child's progress will be measured and how parents will be informed of this progress

Inclusion refers to the integration of children with disabilities into classes with nondisabled students. *Full inclusion* means that even though there may be individual adaptations in class assignments, a child with a disability is placed in a regular educational setting if this is believed to be the best placement. Advocates of full inclusion emphasize that being near and interacting with nondisabled peers, primarily to foster social skills and build self-esteem or self-image, far outweigh any liabilities. The principles of full inclusion rest on the rights of children to attend their local schools instead of being isolated in special programs. Critical to the success of inclusion classrooms are well-prepared teachers, supplementary aids and services, and support personnel.

Another approach that complies with federal legislation is the use of the least restrictive environment. Each child is placed into the educational setting most appropriate for his or her learning and development. Placement and curricular decisions are based on individuals' abilities and needs, with a continuum of alternatives available from full inclusion to one-on-one instruction. Special classes, such as adaptive physical education, should be provided, if needed, to enhance the learning of each child. Although students may learn from one another, students with disabilities may also negatively affect the academic environment of other students by increasing class sizes or making the teachers' job more difficult. Rather than automatically including all children with special needs in a regular classroom, each child should be placed in the setting where optimal learning can occur. This least restrictive environment varies from child to child. Whether mentally retarded, learning disabled, emotionally disturbed, or physically handicapped, all children can benefit from programs that are appropriate for their developmental levels.

Usually children with special needs are placed into physical education classes with their peers in support of an inclusive or least restrictive environment approach to meeting their educational needs. These children, with the support of their families and appropriate educational services, desire and deserve to have the opportunity to develop friendships with classmates without disabilities. Too often, though, physical educators lack the preparation to appropriately modify the curriculum to meet the individual needs of each child. Also, special education teachers also may lack the background to provide instruction in motor skill development and health-related fitness activities as specified in each IEP. Most schools lack adaptive physical educators who are well prepared to provide guidance in this area because of the shortage of professionals in this field. Because the physical needs of children with disabilities must be met, schools should enhance the professional development opportunities for classroom, physical education, and special education teachers in this important area.

SUMMARY

Today's curricula in physical education provide a blend of gymnastics, play, fitness, health, intramurals, recreation, and sports. The new physical education, beginning in the 1920s, led in this transition, demonstrating that physical education contributes to the complete education of students. Table 9-4 highlights many of the significant occurrences in physical education and sport in the twentieth century, including the play movement, the rise of teacher training, the growth of women's physical education, the education of the physical movement, the growing emphasis on fitness, the focus on human movement, and the influence of the scientific movement, educational developmentalism, and social education, as well as the establishment of standards and accountability. Intramural programs were developed to meet the needs of students desiring sports competition outside of physical education classes but at a lower level than varsity athletics. Leadership from the national association, such as through professional journals or at conferences, and standards for teacher preparation helped solidify physical education into a recognized profession.

Collegiate sports for men expanded from their student-organized status into multimillion-dollar business enterprises with extensive regulations and media exposure. Women's sports in the colleges focused on a philosophy of mass participation until the 1970s, when the AIAW encouraged competition and Title IX mandated equality of opportunity. The most visible amateur sports competitions were the Olympic Games. The play movement for children expanded into recreational activities and then fitness for workers and families.

Despite sporadic emphasis on fitness, throughout the twentieth century many American children did not achieve optimal fitness. Nevertheless, instilling in children a commitment to health-related fitness should be a primary goal of education in the twenty-first century. Youth sports programs can also benefit the participants, although adult-controlled leagues may threaten the intended outcomes. The federal government has attempted to ensure that all Americans have equal educational opportunities by legislating that all school children, including those with disabilities, have the right to physical education.

TABLE 9-4

SIGNIFICANT EVENTS IN TWENTIETH-CENTURY PHYSICAL EDUCATION, EXERCISE SCIENCE, AND SPORT

1900	Grammar School Athletic League of Philadelphia created
1903	Public Schools Athletic League formed in New York by Luther Gulick (Girls' Branch began in 1905)
1906	Playground Association of America founded
1910	Teachers College of Columbia University offered the first master's degree with a specialization in physical education
1913	First departments of intramural sports started at the University of Michigan and The Ohio State University
1916	New York became the first state to appoint a Director of Physical Education, Thomas Storey
1924	National Association of Physical Education of College Women started
1924	Teachers College of Columbia University conferred the first Ph.D. with a specialization in physical education
1926	American Academy of Kinesiology and Physical Education founded
1927	Harvard Fatigue Laboratory established
1927	American School Health Association established
1930	First publication of the *Journal of Health and Physical Education* and the *Research Quarterly*
1931	Mabel Lee elected first woman president of the American Physical Education Association
1937	The American Physical Education Association merged with the Department of School Health and Physical Education of the National Education Association to form the American Association for Health and Physical Education
1950	National Athletic Trainers' Association established
1950	National Intramural-Recreational Sports Association established
1953	Results of the Kraus-Weber Minimal Muscular Fitness Test published
1954	American College of Sports Medicine established
1956	President's Council on Youth Fitness established
1958	Administration of the AAHPER Youth Fitness Test began
1965	Lifetime Sports Foundation established
1967	North American Society for the Psychology of Sport and Physical Activity established
1971	Association for Intercollegiate Athletics for Women established
1972	Title IX of the Education Amendments passed
1973	North American Society for Sport History established
1975	The Education of All Handicapped Children Act passed
1978	Amateur Sports Act passed
1978	North American Society for the Sociology of Sport established
1978	National Strength and Conditioning Association established
1985	North American Society for Sport Management established
1986	Association for the Advancement of Applied Sport Psychology established
1996	Surgeon General's *Report on Physical Activity and Health* published

CAREER PERSPECTIVE

SHIRLEY ANN HOLT/HALE
Elementary Physical Education Specialist
Linden Elementary School, Oak Ridge Schools
Oak Ridge, Tennessee

EDUCATION
A.B., Elementary Education, Berea College, Berea, Kentucky
M. Ed., Physical Education, Eastern Kentucky University, Richmond, Kentucky
Ph.D., Early Childhood Education, Peabody College of Vanderbilt University, Nashville, Tennessee

JOB RESPONSIBILITIES AND HOURS
Shirley teaches nine daily classes of elementary physical education in kindergarten through grade 4. Her normal work hours are 7:30 A.M. to 4:00 P.M. These hours include conducting before-school jogging and jump rope clubs and supervising students during after-school bus duty. The work required by the school system beyond the normal school day is limited to an occasional request to attend city council or school board meetings. However, to be prepared for classes, as a veteran teacher Shirley spends another two hours at night writing lesson plans and doing professional reading. The salary range for teachers in her school system is from $32,000 for beginning teachers to over $50,000, depending on years of experience and advanced degrees.

SPECIALIZED COURSE WORK, DEGREES, AND EXPERIENCES NEEDED FOR THIS CAREER
An undergraduate degree in elementary education, with minors in physical education and music, coupled with the student labor program at Berea, provided Shirley with a rich combination of "competency in the many movement forms of dance, gymnastics, and games/sports" and a focus on the teaching of children. That focus on the teaching of children in physical education has been central to Shirley's teaching, writing, and consulting endeavors throughout her career. It has also served her extremely well in communicating with classroom teachers and integrating various curricula within the elementary school classes. Also valuable were her experiences in field placements and student teaching in schools, as well as the opportunity to serve as a teaching assistant in the physical education department. Thus, Shirley graduated with teaching experiences in primary, middle school, and secondary physical education, as well as in college-level classes. As a public school teacher, she must hold state certification in physical education, which her academic degrees prepared her to obtain.

SATISFYING ASPECTS
To Shirley, teaching children is a satisfaction beyond measure. Having taught children in elementary physical education for 30 years, she has experienced daily "highs" from teaching children as well as treasured the joys of seeing a number of her students succeeding in their chosen careers in physical activity and health; their adoption of

healthy, active lifestyles; and, most importantly, watching them grow into confident, contributing citizens of the community and nation.

JOB POTENTIAL

Salary increases come from advancement steps on the index, advanced degrees, and state incentives for merit pay. Certification by the National Board for Professional Teaching Standards provides financial incentive in many states. Opportunities for responsibility are always available; they are, however, added to the normal workload with no reduction in teaching duties. Promotion, if desired, can come through leaving the teaching of students and moving into administration.

SUGGESTIONS FOR STUDENTS

When named National Teacher of the Year several years ago, Shirley stated, "I consider the teaching of children the greatest career one can choose and the ability to do so the greatest gifts one can be given." Shirley emphasizes that there are a few requirements for success in this career: an absolute love of physical education/activity, a joy in being with children, an abundance of energy, the ability to laugh at oneself and to laugh often, and knowing "Monday is my favorite day of the week!"

REVIEW QUESTIONS

1. What were the philosophies of the new physical educators of the 1920s? How are these philosophies different from or similar to those of your teachers?

2. What was the significance of any two developments in physical education, other than the new physical education, during the 1900s? Who were the key leaders in these developments?

3. What is the difference between Jesse Williams' education *through* the physical and Charles McCloy's education *of* the physical?

4. What are several programs for which the American Alliance for Health, Physical Education, Recreation and Dance has provided leadership?

5. Why were intramural programs begun? Why did they flourish in the colleges?

6. How is the National Collegiate Athletic Association's power different today from what it was in its earlier years and why?

7. Why were the sports opportunities provided for girls and women from the 1920s to the late 1960s different from those provided for boys and men?

8. What recreational developments have highlighted each decade since the 1930s? How popular has each been?

9. What have been the major developments in the promotion of youth fitness since the 1950s?

10. What major changes resulted from passage of the following federal legislation: Title IX of the Education Amendments of 1972, Section 504 of the Rehabilitation Act of 1973, and the Education for All Handicapped Children Act of 1975 (IDEA today)?

STUDENT ACTIVITIES

1. Interview someone in the sports information office, athletic department, library, or news bureau who can help you learn about the earliest intercollegiate men's and women's sports programs at your institution. Based on this and on information you can obtain from other sources, write a two-page description of each program.

2. Write a three-page comparison of the philosophies and major contributions of the "new physical educators."

3. Learn about the test items of the FITNESSGRAM. Divide into groups and administer these test items to one another.

4. Ask your professors who they think were the most important physical educators of the twentieth century. Based on their responses and your reading, summarize the career and contributions of one of these individuals in a two-minute class presentation.

5. Select one personality from a decade of the twentieth century. Write a three-page description of his or her contributions to physical education, exercise science, and sport.

6. Conduct a class debate about whether the most appropriate theme for physical education should be "education *through* the physical" or "education *of* the physical."

7. Select one theme each for school and for nonschool physical activity programs for the first half and second half of this century. Develop a position statement to explain the value and impact of each on the field of physical education, exercise science, and sport in the twenty-first century.

8. Write a five-page paper comparing the major developments in men's and women's intercollegiate sports in the twentieth century.

REFERENCE

NEA Proceedings, 32:621, 1893, National Education Association.

SUGGESTED READINGS

Bandy S: Clark Wilson Hetherington: a pioneering spirit in physical education, *JOPERD* 56(1):20, 1985. Throughout his many years of service at Missouri, Wisconsin, New York University, and Stanford and in other professional positions, Clark Hetherington stressed achieving educational objectives and reinforced his advocacy of play.

Block ME, Conatser P: Adapted aquatics and inclusion. *JOPERD* 73(5):31, 2002. The authors discuss areas such as teaching styles, collaboration, goal setting, placement, and curricular adaptations in the context of inclusive aquatics programs.

Davenport J: Thomas Denison Wood: physical educator and father of health education, *JOPERD* 55(8):63, 1984. Stressing educational outcomes, Thomas Wood, at Stanford and Teachers College, initiated bachelor's degree programs in physical education. At the latter institution, he also started master's and doctor's degree programs in physical education and undergraduate health education programs.

English EB: Charles H. McCloy: the research professor of physical education, *JOPERD* 54(4):16, 1983. Charles McCloy led in producing a scientific body of knowledge for physical education, especially in the areas of strength tests, cardiovascular measures, classification indices, anthropometric scores, and character/social traits.

French R, Henderson H, Kinnison L, Sherrill C: Revisiting Section 504, physical education, and sport, *JOPERD* 69(7):57, 1998. The authors provide an overview of the implications of IDEA for physical education and sport programs.

Hall AE, Kuga DJ, Jones DF: A multivariate study of determinants of vigorous physical activity in a multicultural sample of college students, *J of Sp & Soc Issues* 26(1):66, 2002. This study found no significant differences between race and physical activity levels among African American, Asian, and Hispanic students. African Americans engaged in more regular physical activity than other students, while males reported more vigorous physical activity than females.

Miller SE: Inclusion of children with disabilities: can we meet the challenge? *Phy Educ* 51(1):47, 1994. This article describes the impact of the Education for All Handicapped Children Act on physical education classes, along with the challenges presented in inclusion classrooms.

Motley ML, LaVine ME: Century marathon: a race for equality in girls' and women's sports, *JOPERD* 72(6):56, 2001. This article provides a brief overview of the achievements in sports for females during the twentieth century, including information associated with progress gained through Title IX.

Stein JU: Total inclusion or least restrictive environment? *JOPERD* 65(9):21, 1994. This article describes the principles of total inclusion and the least restrictive environment (LRE). It includes an explanation of the basic legislative requirements relevant to the LRE.

Thorngren CM (ed.).: Women in sport leadership, *JOPERD,* 64(3):33, 1993. This seven-article feature emphasizes the leadership roles women physical educators have played and continue to play in coaching, sports officiating, conducting research, and changing societal attitudes.

Wiggins DK: Edwin Bancroft Henderson—physical educator, civil rights activist, and chronicler of African American athletes, *Res Q for Exer & Sp* 70(2):91, 1999. This article describes many of the outstanding accomplishments of a physical educator who, personally and through his dynamic speeches and prolific writings, fought racial discrimination, including in professional organizations, and helped provide sports opportunities in segregated Washington, DC, and the larger society.

3

THE CHANGING NATURE OF PHYSICAL EDUCATION, EXERCISE SCIENCE, AND SPORT

© PhotoDisk
Website

10

OPPORTUNITIES AND CHALLENGES IN PHYSICAL EDUCATION AND EXERCISE SCIENCE

KEY CONCEPTS

- A major health need Americans of all ages face is to attain and maintain a level of fitness that contributes to a positive quality of life.
- The expansion of research by specialists in physical education and exercise science, along with technological advances in research methods and measurements, has contributed to a broader and deeper knowledge base.
- School programs include the concepts of movement education, a renewed emphasis on fitness, and a focus on the development of lifelong fitness behaviors.
- Increasingly, professionals are being held accountable for their students' and clients' learning through a variety of assessments.
- Greater competencies expected of professionals have led to significant changes in certification requirements and accreditation standards.
- Teachers of physical activity in all settings must understand and meet their legal obligations.
- Career burnout can be alleviated by recognizing the signs, counteracting the causes, and providing appropriate rewards for excellent performance.
- Physical educators face several instructional challenges, but these can be overcome through a comprehensive and relevant curriculum, excellent instruction, varied assessments, lifelong learning, and leadership.

Being physically active is an important key to an enhanced quality of life for individuals of all ages. Providers of recreational and leisure services must adapt to changing demographics, family structures and schedules, work patterns, and economic realities while enhancing the quality of their programs. Fitness specialists and exercise scientists in various settings work with adults to help them establish and maintain lifelong activity programs. Specialization, research, technology, and the scholarly pursuit of knowledge are significant factors in the expansion and recognition of careers associated with physical activity. Changes in school programs should guarantee opportunities for all people to meet their unique needs while engaged in progressively challenging experiences. Daily physical education for students, changes in certification requirements, increased teacher competencies, and accreditation standards are all related efforts to improve the quality of education for students. The threat of lawsuits and the high risk of injuries mandate that individuals working in physical activity settings avoid negligent behavior by acting responsibly. Challenges confronting school physical educators include limited equipment and facilities, lack of parental support for education, and discipline problems.

THE VALUE OF PHYSICAL ACTIVITY FOR EVERYONE

Physical activity is for everyone. But convincing people of this fact remains a major challenge. However, as listed in Box 10-1, significant and lasting values result from participating regularly in physical activity.

BOX 10-1   VALUE OF PHYSICAL ACTIVITY

According to the American Heart Association (AHA), physical inactivity is a major risk factor for coronary artery disease and contributes to obesity, high blood pressure, high triglycerides, a low level of HDL ("good") cholesterol, and diabetes. The AHA recommends moderately intense physical activity, such as brisk walking, for a total of 30 minutes or longer on most days.

The AHA stresses the importance of physical activity because it

- Plays a role in both primary and secondary prevention of cardiovascular disease
- Helps reduce or eliminate some of the risk factors associated with high blood pressure
- Reduces some of the risk factors associated with obesity
- Reduces some of the risk factors associated with diabetes
- Reduces the risk of colon cancer
- Lowers the risk of stroke
- Helps reduce or eliminate some of the risk factors associated with blood lipid abnormalities
- Reduces feelings of depression and anxiety
- Improves mood
- Promotes a sense of well-being
- Increases cardiovascular endurance
- Builds muscular strength and endurance
- Improves flexibility
- Builds healthy bones, muscles, and joints
- Increases capacity for exercise

The objectives of physical education in the schools include learning and applying fitness concepts, learning motor and fundamental sports skills, encouraging lifetime fitness, gaining knowledge about sports rules and strategies, and enhancing social and emotional development. As discussed in Chapter 1, teachers can meet these objectives only by making them a central focus of their work and teaching them consistently, to ensure their achievement. Teachers must provide quality programs and promote their value to school administrators, legislators, and parents.

Children and youth must learn healthful living habits while in school because many will not attend college or be able to afford sports club memberships or expensive private exercise equipment. During the critical elementary years, students need to learn how to develop cardiovascular endurance, with a focus on frequency, intensity, and duration of exercise. They need to learn to walk, jog, swim, cycle, and jump rope as alternative ways to develop aerobic endurance. They need to learn how to attain and maintain muscular strength, endurance, and flexibility because these health-related fitness components will enhance not only how they feel but also their ability to study, work, and play more easily and productively. Closely aligned with these needs is the importance of teaching children sports skills they can use throughout life. Basic throwing, catching, striking, and locomotor movements are easily transferable to tennis, golf, bowling, dance, and other lifetime activities. Teachers should demonstrate and positively reinforce development of cooperative behavior, teamwork, fair play, and the ability to be a follower and a leader. Individually, students will nurture self-confidence and self-worth by successfully achieving personal goals. Concurrent with these psychomotor and affective outcomes, teachers should ensure that children are provided information about nutrition, diseases, environmental concerns, and the harmful effects of drugs.

After ensuring that quality experiences are offered to their students, teachers should invite school administrators, legislators, and parents to observe what physical education really is. Hosting PTA/PTO programs, parents' nights, mall demonstrations, and other special events shows that physical education is vital to the health and well-being of students. In addition, parents should be encouraged to participate more fully in their children's education.

At the high school level, the emphasis on fitness development, lifetime sports, and health issues such as smoking, drugs, sex education, and nutrition should continue. At this level, it is especially important to give students some options for what sports and activities they want to learn. Although some consumer information may be relevant at an earlier age, the teen years lend themselves well to consumer education. Adolescents need to learn how to differentiate between the facts and fallacies of fitness ads. Although some home exercise equipment, such as rowing machines or exercise bicycles, can improve one's fitness if used properly, machines that supposedly help a person lose weight without effort blatantly misrepresent the truth. What are the caloric and nutritional components of the average fast-food meal? Are any diet centers or diet programs safe or worth the money? Should a person smoke cigarettes or marijuana? What are the effects of alcohol on the body and its fitness? Where can a person find a qualified aerobics instructor? Given the need for answers to these questions and the potential benefits of school physical education, it is imperative that schools fund physical education and health curricula.

Tennis is a favorite lifetime physical activity. (Photo courtesy Department of Physical Education and Recreation, State University of West Georgia.)

Opponents of such funding claim that physical education is nonessential. But the poor fitness levels of American school-age children, which currently may be the worst ever, say otherwise. Others argue that community programs and inter-scholastic athletics can provide students with adequate sports opportunities. However, due to the cost and additional time, many students (especially those who drop out of school) will never participate in these programs. And most community-sponsored programs stress competition rather than instruction.

Parents who realize the importance of living fit lifestyles can demand that the schools help their children learn these habits. But they must be convinced of the importance of developing the fitness parameters themselves; by making lifestyle changes at home, they can reinforce their children's learning in school. Again, the involvement of parents in the education of their children is vital.

Fewer than half of the colleges and universities have retained their required physical education programs. Many other colleges and universities have reduced their requirements because of budget limitations and an increasing emphasis on general education and major course requirements. In many of the programs at institutions where physical education is an elective, these programs have had to become entirely self-supporting. Students may elect any activity course available, but then they must pay instructional, facility usage, and equipment rental fees. On other campuses, this pay-as-you-participate approach applies only to certain off-campus or nontraditional courses. This type of program is limited to those who are genuinely interested in a particular activity or sport and who can afford to enroll in it. Unfortunately, at universities with elective programs, those who need physical education the most may not choose to enroll.

In 1992, the American Heart Association added physical inactivity to high blood pressure, smoking, and high blood cholesterol as a significant contributor to heart disease. To counteract the effects of these risks, many inactive, over-weight adults are changing their habits. As middle-aged and senior citizens join the millions of others who are walking to stay fit, these segments of the population reinforce being physically active. To help avoid becoming the next coronary statistics, many older Americans are quitting smoking, reducing alcohol consumption, ridding their diets of many sources of cholesterol, and exercising. Popular exercise and recreational activities include walking, swimming, fishing, camping, aerobics, and bowling. For those with physical limitations, many retire-ment homes, recreation departments, churches, and hospitals are providing appropriate opportunities for movement, sports, and recreational pastimes.

Exercise and sport scientists may prescribe walking as part of an aerobic conditioning program for clients.

BOX 10-2   PROGRAM ADHERENCE FACTORS

- Set realistic goals.
- Implement an individualized and progressive program that is safe.
- Ensure proper supervision that includes education and motivation.
- Be patient—developing fitness takes time.
- Ensure convenient access to facilities.
- Provide periodic assessments and feedback.
- Provide family and peer group encouragement and reinforcement.
- Participate in fun and satisfying activities.

BOX 10-3   PHYSICAL ACTIVITY TIPS

- Schedule a time for daily physical activity of at least 30 minutes.
- Vary your physical activities to maintain enthusiasm and interest.
- Find a partner to join you in your physical activity program so you can help each other adhere to your physical activity program.
- Set realistic goals so you can achieve success.
- Include physical activities that contribute to all-around physical fitness, such as cardiovascular endurance, muscular strength and endurance, and flexibility.
- Use time engaged in physical activity to socialize with others.
- Use time riding a stationary bicycle or using other aerobic equipment to read (intellectual benefits).
- Make sure your equipment and exercise areas are safe.
- Combine physical activity with healthier eating patterns.
- Have fun and enjoy!

Providing for the leisure needs of older Americans may become the largest segment of new physical activity–related jobs in this century.

Once people are convinced that regular exercise is not only important but essential, the next challenge is how to get those who have begun exercise programs to continue them. Adherence is a pervasive problem for everyone who prescribes exercises and activities. Whether a corporation or an individual is paying for the exercise program, the goal is positive, lasting outcomes. Box 10-2 lists several factors that contribute to activity adherence. Most adult exercise programs emphasize similar strategies to enhance lasting and positive lifestyle changes. Most important, all people need appropriately designed programs that they can understand; goals that are feasible, measureable, and monitored; and positive experiences that will encourage them to adhere to the programs.

Physical activity should be a part of everyone's life regardless of age or capability. Some physical activity suggestions are provided in Box 10-3. The earlier you can teach others the value of being physically fit, the greater the quality of their lives. You are challenged to serve as an advocate who never ceases to proclaim and demonstrate through your own life the value of physical activity.

RECREATION AND LEISURE SERVICES

Demographic changes, altered family and work patterns, environmental concerns, and shifts in the economy have transformed contemporary recreation and leisure services. An increasingly diverse ethnic mix in the population of the United States makes business as usual no longer acceptable. African Americans, Native Americans, Asian Americans, Hispanics, and other ethnic groups are demanding recreational and artistic programs that appeal to their unique cultural backgrounds. The former melting pot concept has given way to an appreciation and promotion of diversity throughout society, which means these changes must be reflected in leisure programming.

Demographics indicate a graying of America. The older segment of the population possesses considerable political clout and financial resources. As life expectancies increase, older adults want to have their recreational needs met along with those of younger groups. Senior citizens are often physically vigorous. While some may require only passive activities in a retirement center, other retirees robustly play golf and tennis, walk and hike, travel and tour, and swim and cycle. In this century, serving the recreational and leisure needs of this population will become more widespread and demanding. Seniors want more opportunities for

- Masters competitions in sports like tennis, swimming, golf, and running
- Senior Games in numerous sports
- Age- and ability-appropriate activity classes at health and fitness clubs
- Age- and ability-appropriate activity programs sponsored by recreation departments
- Walking clubs
- Sport leagues, such as in bowling, golf, and softball
- Therapeutic programs sponsored by senior citizen programs, retirement centers, and hospitals
- Intergenerational after-school activity programs for children and grandparents

The traditional 1950s family of a working father, a homemaking mother, and two or three children characterizes fewer than half of today's families with school-age children. Divorced parents, broken homes, and absent fathers leave approximately one out of every two children in single-parent homes before they reach adulthood. The cost and quality of child care have become major issues for these parents. Meeting the developmental play needs of preschool children challenges those who offer in-house or commercialized child care services. Currently schools, churches and synagogues, and public centers offer after-school care for children, which may or may not include developmentally appropriate play opportunities.

Many adolescents (and some preadolescents) have become latchkey kids—children who come home from school to empty houses. These unattended children often have to lock themselves in their houses because playing outside is considered unsafe. This setting seems to foster unending hours of watching television and eating junk food. Lack of supervision may also permit youthful experimentation with alcohol, tobacco, illegal drugs, sex, and law-breaking activities.

In most cities and towns, the schools, recreation departments, and private clubs provide numerous alternatives to unsafe, inactive, and delinquent behaviors. Competitive youth sports teams, children's fitness clubs and programs, adventure activities, cooperative games, and creative playground opportunities are just a few of the options available. While some parents can afford to enroll their children in private dance, gymnastics, swimming, or tennis lessons, many rely on public programs for facilities, equipment, and instruction.

Threats to the environment also jeopardize the resources available for recreation and leisure. Outdoor enthusiasts are increasing their efforts to protect natural resources and open spaces from abusive individuals and encroaching real estate developers. Rock climbers, hikers, and campers are expected to leave nature exactly as they found it. Industries are expected to stop polluting the air, water, and land. Despite limited resources, cities and states continue to acquire land to meet the recreational needs of present and future generations.

Like many public programs, recreation and leisure services have experienced increased budgetary constraints. Although people are taxed for municipal services, including recreation, there never seems to be enough money, space, or programs. To meet their budgets, many recreation departments must charge entry or participation fees, which excludes those unable to pay. In addition to the rising cost of programming, these agencies have increased expenses due to vandalism, lawsuits, and security. In addition, bringing programs and facilities into compliance with the Americans with Disabilities Act is costly. To adequately serve individuals with limitations, facilities must be handicapped accessible, have specialized recreational equipment, and have qualified, trained personnel.

Recreation and leisure services are among the human services industries that have proliferated in recent decades. Individuals pursuing careers in national and state parks, boys' and girls' clubs, commercial and corporate fitness, sports clubs, and recreation must focus on customer or client satisfaction. To accomplish this, they must determine the personal goals of those they serve. For example, those who choose careers in backpacking, rock climbing, and canoeing may have the following goals in mind for program participants:

- To learn outdoor skills
- To challenge the limits of one's ability
- To enjoy risk-taking achievements
- To develop cooperative or self-reliant behavior
- To appreciate nature

Outdoor education activities, such as rock climbing, can be practiced in safe situations. (Photo courtesy Department of Physical Education and Recreation, State University of West Georgia.)

Knowing these goals, professionals can propose suitable programs to meet participants' goals or help them design a customized individual or group program. (See the Research View box for an overview of the competencies needed by sport managers.)

Recreation and leisure services professionals may choose to seek national certification through the National Recreation and Park Association. To be certified, applicants must meet educational and experience requirements as well as demonstrate a high level of professionalism in their work. As with other certifications, the Certified Park and Recreational Professional has enhanced credibility and contributes to the status of the field. The challenge for recreation and leisure services specialists is to create programs with activities that match each person's interests and needs.

⌕ RESEARCH VIEW

Competencies of Sport Managers

As an emerging field of study, sport management is continuing to define itself and the role it should play in the pervasive area of sport in society. Because sport is a multibillion-dollar business in this country, including professional, intercollegiate, interscholastic, youth, and recreational sport, professionals in this field are responsible for upholding sport in the public trust. That is, sport managers are expected to fulfill their duties in accordance with the highest level of professional conduct. The ethical standards of this field, such as those found in codes of ethics, require accountability for meeting the performance expectations of the public being served, such as demonstrated through integrity, honesty, and the equitable and respectful treatment of all individuals.

In addition to these personal traits, sport managers must be competent in carrying out their jobs. Toh and Jamieson* conducted an extensive review of the literature in this area as they constructed and validated a survey instrument to determine the competencies essential in a sport management competency model. They labeled the resultant six-factor model of competencies for sport managers as follows:

- Governance
- Sport foundations
- Budgeting
- Risk management
- Computer skills
- Communications

While certainly not a definitive listing, these factors and the associated 31 competencies parallel the findings of other studies concerning what sport managers should know and demonstrate in accomplishing their job responsibilities.

---

*Toh KL, Jamieson LM: Constructing and validating competencies of sport managers (COSM) instrument: a model development, *Recreational Sports Journal* 24(2):38, 2000.

EXERCISE SCIENCE

More and more students are pursuing careers related to physical activity that are outside educational settings. Many prepare for these noneducational careers by studying exercise science, where one studies human movement along with the body's adaptations to movement. The exercise scientist seeks to understand the scientific foundations of exercise's physiological responses. This field has grown more specialized as the quantity and quality of knowledge have expanded.

In the 1970s and 1980s, colleges and universities responded to the decrease in physical education majors preparing to teach by offering specializations. Students were attracted to these majors because they sought careers in the emerging fields of athletic training, corporate and commercial fitness, exercise physiology, and sport management. Most of these graduates sought positions that allowed them to work with adults participating in fitness and sports programs. The diversity of career options and opportunities for advancement, travel, economic security, research, and management also appealed to many.

In recent years, career options in exercise science have increased due to the media-reinforced appeal of cosmetic fitness; concern about health conditions related to lifestyle, such as coronary heart disease and obesity; and skyrocketing health care costs. Those most likely to participate in fitness programs are upper-income individuals, young adults, males, whites, suburban residents, and the more highly educated, although fitness enthusiasts occupy every demographic stratum. Fitness specialists find their greatest challenge in trying to motivate individuals to initiate and maintain activity programs through self-discipline. The two most frequent explanations for not exercising are lack of time and poor motivation or self-discipline.

Fitness programs have expanded in private and public health and sports clubs, recreation departments, retirement homes, work sites, rehabilitation clinics, hotels, and resorts. Many people have joined clubs specifically to receive instruction and encouragement from fitness leaders in aerobics and weight training. Besides teaching, individuals in these careers are expected to prescribe safe exercise programs, monitor members' progress, provide nutritional guidance, manage the facility, and sometimes supervise other personnel. Fitness specialists and exercise scientists are expected to conduct smoking cessation classes, provide information about injury prevention and care, teach exercises to reduce low back pain, conduct assessments of various fitness parameters, prescribe exercise programs for rehabilitation, and conduct clinical research. Undergraduate students need to be prepared to handle these diverse responsibilities. Increasingly, graduates of exercise science curricula are working with adults (and sometimes children) in health and fitness programs. As described in previous chapters, these professionals are challenged to direct and manage programs that help unfit Americans develop and maintain personal fitness, to provide recreational opportunities in a wide variety of sports and games, and to offer leisure-time activities that may include spectator events, cruises, and trips to theme parks.

Since exercise scientists must understand the scientific basis underlying exercise-induced physiological responses to movement, they frequently work in clinical settings. These include sports medicine facilities, biomechanical and exercise physiology research laboratories, cardiac rehabilitation clinics, hospitals, health promotion and wellness education centers, and therapeutic programs. Following are a few examples of the types of services exercise scientists provide in these settings:

- Prevent, diagnose, and treat injuries
- Investigate how muscles, bones, and joints are injured under certain conditions

Exercise scientists can help athletic teams improve their flexibility, strength, and endurance, which in turn can help improve performance. (Photo courtesy State University of West Georgia Sports Information Office.)

- Recommend ways to improve work or sports performance using motion analysis techniques
- Administer exercise testing and training sessions
- Prescribe appropriate exercises based on age, ability, and medical condition
- Provide for rehabilitation of individuals who have had a heart attack or have emphysema
- Supervise stress management and nutrition education programs
- Provide employee fitness programs to employees with cardiac, pulmonary, or musculoskeletal problems
- Study acute and chronic physiological responses and adaptations resulting from physical activity
- Improve the performance of workers by enhancing their health, preventing or rehabilitating work-related injuries, and redesigning the work environment to fit individual employees
- Help people recover from injuries or diseases of the muscles, joints, nerves, or bones
- Conduct basic research studies at the cellular and molecular levels, such as how organ systems function, adapt, or respond to various factors

College graduates may need to obtain certifications and licensure to work in exercise science positions. More and more health and fitness clubs are expecting their employees to hold certifications as personal trainers, aerobics leaders, and fitness program directors. Almost all individuals responsible for providing emergency care to athletes in sports competitions are expected to have training in basic first aid and cardiopulmonary resuscitation. Athletic trainers must hold such certifications. States and employers are increasingly requiring higher levels of expertise to ensure that only qualified individuals work in physical activity situations. Exercise scientists working in clinical settings, such as hospitals, research laboratories, and rehabilitation clinics, need to demonstrate competencies in areas such as the following:

- The structure and function of the human body and its systems
- The operation of muscles and joints through various movements, such as supination, pronation, flexion, extension, adduction, and rotation
- The major components of motor fitness, including agility, speed, balance, coordination, and power, and the biomechanical principles underlying these components
- The biomechanical principles associated with striking, throwing, catching, running, walking, and jumping
- The ability to accurately measure body fat, blood pressure, heart rate, and oxygen consumption during exercise
- The ability to explain, demonstrate, and prescribe the physiological principles associated with warm-ups and cool-downs
- The ability to explain, demonstrate, and prescribe appropriate cardiovascular endurance activities
- The ability to explain, demonstrate, and prescribe exercises designed to increase muscular strength and endurance
- The ability to explain, demonstrate, and prescribe appropriate flexibility exercises
- The care and prevention of common exercise injuries
- The genetic and cellular basis of disease
- The prevention and treatment of chronic illnesses
- The determinants of oxygen consumption under differing conditions of exercise

Most people who solicit the services of an exercise scientist want to develop all-around wellness. Physical activity is only one component of all-around wellness; increasingly, people are also seeking emotional, spiritual, intellectual, and social benefits along with fitness. Many want to find balance through their workouts, leading to the management of stress reduction, increased self-esteem, friendships, and peace of mind. This means that program and exercise leaders must prepare themselves to address the whole person, not just the body. The expansion in program offerings in health and fitness clubs to include massage, yoga, Pilates, nutrition counseling, stress management workshops, and musical and artistic outings along with personal fitness plans reflects this broadening focus.

GENERALISTS REPLACED BY SPECIALISTS

Traditionally physical educators were generalists who could teach a dozen or more sports, coach two or three teams, and still make time to sweep the gymnasium floor. They proudly considered themselves generalists who focused on the practical field of teaching. Students majoring in physical education in previous generations were exposed to the breadth in this field. Today students are more likely to specialize in one of the exercise sciences.

The knowledge explosion in recent years has influenced all subject areas. Expanded research efforts, technological advances, and computer-assisted data analyses have aided this proliferation. The quality and quantity of information have led to increasing specializations for two primary reasons. First, the sheer volume of books, research, reports, resources on the Internet, and scholarly papers makes it difficult for individuals to gain exhaustive knowledge in any one discipline, let alone several. Second, a greater understanding of a subdiscipline encourages people to specialize in an area of particular interest in order to create and disseminate new knowledge. In turn, this greater understanding may lead to enhanced sport performances or strategies to improve health. For example, the coach who prefers treating athletic injuries and helping to rehabilitate athletes could become a full-time athletic trainer. The physical education generalist who teaches a wide spectrum of courses but really enjoys teaching weight training might choose to become a personal trainer. A person who wants to help highly skilled individuals enhance their performances may become a sport psychologist, biomechanist, or exercise physiologist.

The popularity of physical activity and sport throughout society has created numerous, diverse career options. Colleges and universities have responded by broadening the types of majors offered. Most students today choose to specialize in athletic training, sport management, fitness, or exercise science because these areas interest them and provide a greater availability of jobs. When hired, they will be expected to remain knowledgeable in their specialties.

Graduate degree programs at the master's and doctor's levels are becoming increasingly specialized. For example, graduate students with career goals of becoming exercise physiologists or sport psychologists study specific content areas, such as biochemistry and experimental psychology. Corporate fitness directors, club managers, athletic trainers at universities or on staff with professional teams, and facility managers are often required to have master's degrees because of the scope of their responsibilities.

College faculty are required to have the minimum of a master's degree, while university professors must have earned doctorates. Both groups are usually expected to teach in their areas of specialization. Most universities also require scholarly productivity of faculty, including research-based presentations at professional conferences and publications in peer-reviewed journals. Most of this scholarship is narrowly focused, reflecting areas of specialization, faculty interests, and current research.

PROLIFERATION OF RESEARCH

Within the past decade, the quantity of scholarly publications and presentations in physical education and exercise science has been increasing. Responding to university mandates, specialists with Ph.D's are dedicating themselves to expanding knowledge in their areas of specialization. They pursue research questions such as how to improve athletic performance, how to enhance the process of teaching and learning movement skills, and how to maximize muscle mass and flexibility using certain types of exercise equipment. Physical education and exercise science professionals in clinical settings, corporate fitness centers, recreation programs, and fitness and health clubs are also conducting research on various fitness programs, training regimens, and success rates among their clientele.

A growing area of research in physical education focuses on pedagogy. Pedagogical studies include teaching observations such as analyses of time-on-task and academic learning time, student performance, and teacher expectations, and how these factors are interrelated. Research in this specialization has the potential to dramatically affect the quality of instruction in all settings.

Technology has also contributed to the proliferation of research in physical education and exercise science. Athletes can now recover from injuries faster through advanced surgical techniques and computer-monitored rehabilitation programs. Data collection on the incidence and causes of injuries has been used to redesign conditioning and practice drills to both reduce injury and enhance rehabilitation. Sport psychologists use biofeedback and relaxation techniques to positively affect performance. Biomechanists apply computer technology to skill execution to both improve technique and reduce the risk of injury. Computer analyses of blood lactates, oxygen exchange, workloads, and drug effects are invaluable to the exercise physiologist's understanding of how the body functions under the stress of exercise.

Library retrieval systems and CD-ROMs help researchers in all disciplines keep abreast of current research, trends, and experimental data. Access to such information allows researchers to attempt to replicate studies or build on the findings of their colleagues. Electronic mail also helps researchers collaborate in a timely manner. Without the use of personal computers for word processing, data analyses, and information retrieval through the Internet, the productivity of today's university, corporate, and community researchers would be tremendously hampered. Increasingly physicians, sport psychologists, sport biomechanists, exercise physiologists, and athletic trainers will share their expertise and research electronically to the benefit of students, world-class athletes, and the general public.

Physical education and exercise science researchers are frequently criticized for their failure to apply their findings. Technology can partly alleviate this

WEB CONNECTIONS

1. www.kidsrunning.com

   This innovative site sponsored by *Runner's World* includes ideas about recreational and competitive running activities for children, including news events, writings by kids, advice on setting up programs, and school curricular suggestions.

2. www.acsm-msse.org

   This site for *Medicine and Science in Sports and Exercise* provides abstracts of articles (and full text to members of the American College of Sports Medicine [ACSM]) and full-text position stands of the ACSM that have been published in this professional journal. Among these are "Progression Models in Resistance Training for Healthy Adults," "The Recommended Quantity and Quality of Exercise for Developing and Maintaining Cardiorespiratory and Muscular Fitness," and "Female Athlete Triad."

3. www.aoa.dhhs.gov/aoa/pages/agepages/exercise.html

   At this site, the National Institute on Aging provides information about exercise as well as helpful links to other sites that focus on physical activity and health issues.

4. http://chid.nih.gov/welcome/welcome.html

   The combined Health Information Database available at this site provides a comprehensive bibliography of the health-related agencies of the federal government with links to titles, abstracts, and other health information and resources.

5. www.ncate.org

   This site of the National Council for Accreditation of Teacher Education describes the performance-based standards for teacher education programs and provides links to the content standards in all fields.

6. www.ncbi.nlm.nih.gov/PubMed

   Check out the PubMed site of the National Library of Medicine to gain access to over 11 million citations in MEDLINE and related databases, with links to participating online journals.

problem by emphasizing practical as well as theoretical studies, disseminating new information more widely, and focusing on specific situations in need of change. For example, those participating in various weight loss programs could be outfitted with heart rate monitors to ensure they are exercising within their target heart rate zones. By careful recordkeeping with regard to heart rates, diets, frequency and duration of exercises, and types of exercises, exercise scientists, along with athletic trainers, aerobics instructors, and fitness program directors, would not only add to the base of knowledge concerning weight loss but also have one more scientific measure by which to compare various weight loss programs. Physical educators and exercise scientists who could benefit from such findings also have a responsibility to work with researchers in applying new information in a timely fashion. This will help close the research-to-practice gap.

It is incumbent on fitness and exercise professionals to remain current with the latest research. Regardless of position held, the knowledge explosion has made the "half-life" of information learned in college, graduate school, or certification courses short-lived. That is, the relevancy and even accuracy of information that you acquire while obtaining your physical education or exercise science degree may be wrong, dangerous, or of questionable validity a decade after you graduate. A few examples follow. Once-popular exercises such as squat thrusts are now contraindicated. Withholding fluid replacement from athletes, which was once thought to build stamina or toughness, is very dangerous; such an action today would be the basis for a wrongful-death lawsuit if an athlete died after being denied fluids. Some drugs taken to enhance performance or build muscular strength may be legal today but banned tomorrow if new research determined they were harmful to the body. Thus, lifelong learning is imperative, particularly with regard to research in your specialty.

ELEMENTARY SCHOOL PROGRAMS

Since the early 1900s, elementary school physical education programs have focused on teaching fundamental skills that lead directly to the ability to play sports and games (see Chapter 9). As the curricula evolved, greater stress was placed on a balanced and varied range of activities that progressed from the simple to the complex (in keeping with developmental skills to the various grade levels). These activities included stunts, tumbling, simple games and relays, rhythmic activities, basic sport skills, lead-up games, and game play. Professional preparation courses and textbooks suggested the importance of progressions, certain allotments of time for each major category of activity, and instructional methodology.

In the 1960s, an alternative elementary physical education curriculum, called *movement education,* was introduced in the United States. It was based on the concepts of spatial and body awareness; movement qualities of flow, force, space, and time; and relationships to others or to objects. Students learned about their own space relative to body size, movement task, and equipment, thereby gaining insights into their own capabilities and becoming more skilled movers. Movement education stressed the following:

- Lessons were to be both activity centered and student centered.
- Specific movement patterns were to be determined by each child within parameters established by teachers, emphasizing experimentation through movement rather than simply following instructions.

- Children were encouraged to explore and analyze space, their bodies, and various uses for pieces of equipment, with a focus on self-directed or individualized learning.

- Problem solving and guided discovery were incorporated into fun and games, using open-ended challenges and goals.

- The teacher was to guide students through movement experiences by imaginatively and creatively involving both their minds and their bodies.

- Independently and at their own rates of development, children were to be given time to think about the challenges and then move in response.

- Each child was to be evaluated on an individual basis.

- Informality in class structure allowed children to create freely and to learn at their own levels of achievement.

Today, in addition to selecting elementary physical education curricula that match their own philosophies, teachers must be aware of state standards and district curricular requirements. Each elementary school child should learn competency in several movement forms, learn to express and communicate through movement, and be able to demonstrate movement principles while learning motor skills. In addition, children can begin to achieve a high level of physical and health-related fitness, gain greater self-understanding and acceptance of themselves and others, and learn how to handle winning and losing.

Elementary school students should be encouraged to learn fundamental movement skills. (Photo courtesy Bob Hilliard.)

TABLE 10-1

DEVELOPMENTALLY APPROPRIATE AND INAPPROPRIATE PHYSICAL EDUCATION PRACTICES FOR CHILDREN

Appropriate Practice	*Inappropriate Practice*
Curricular Decisions	**Curricular Decisions**
The physical education curriculum has an obvious scope and sequence based on goals and objectives that are appropriate for all children. The curriculum includes a balance of skills and concepts in the areas of games, educational gymnastics, and rhythmical activities and dance. Teachers design experiences and select benchmarks to enhance the psychomotor, cognitive, and affective development of all children.	The physical education curriculum lacks age appropriate, developmental goals and objectives and is based primarily on the teacher's interests, preferences, and background rather than those of the children. For example, the curriculum consists primarily of large group and competitive team games. Activities are the same for all grade levels.
Physical Fitness Testing	**Physical Fitness Testing**
Teachers use fitness assessment as part of the ongoing process of helping children understand, enjoy, improve, and/or maintain their physical fitness and well-being. Test results are shared privately with children and their parents as a tool for developing personal goals and strategies for maintaining and increasing the respective fitness parameters. As part of an ongoing program of physical education, children are physically prepared in each fitness component so they can safely complete the assessments.	Teachers administer the physical fitness test once or twice each year for the purpose of identifying children to receive awards or to meet a school district or state development requirement. Children complete physical fitness test batteries without understanding why they are performing the tests or how the tests relate to their activity levels and individuals goals. Results are interpreted based on comparison to norms rather than in terms of how they apply to children's future health and well-being. Individuals scores are publicly posted, comparisons are made between student scores, and/or grades are based on fitness scores. Children are required to take fitness tests without adequate conditioning.
Forming Groups/Partners	**Forming Groups/Partners**
Groups/partners are formed in ways that preserve the dignity and self-respect of every child. For example, a teacher privately forms groups or teams by using knowledge of children's skill abilities in ways that will facilitate learning. Groups or teams may also be formed by grouping clothing colors, birthdays, and favorite activities.	Groups or teams are formed by student "captains" publicly selecting one child at a time, sometimes with a system of alternating gender, and always exposing the lower skilled children to peer ridicule or embarrassment. Groups/teams are formed by pitting "boys against the girls" emphasizing gender differences rather than cooperation and working together. Students are regularly asked to select partners without strategies to assure that no children are left out.
Facilitating Maximum Participation	**Facilitating Maximum Participation**
Teachers organize small games, e.g., 2–3 per team that allow numerous practice opportunities for children while also allowing them to learn the various aspects of the game being taught. Equipment is provided to permit active participation and practice for every child. A variety of equipment is selected to accommodate the size, confidence, and skill levels of the children. Teachers make sure that equipment is kept up-to-date and routinely inspected for safety.	Teachers organize full-sided or large-sided games (e.g., the class of 30 is split into two groups of 15 that play against each other), thereby limiting practice opportunities for individual students. An insufficient amount of equipment is available to maximize practice repetitions. "Adult-size" equipment is used, which may inhibit skill development, injure, and/or intimidate the children. Teachers use outdated and potentially unsafe equipment.

Each elementary physical education program should be centered on the concept that movement is a child's first expressive opportunity. Since it is through movement experiences and challenges that the world is discovered, these must be developmentally appropriate for the age, size, and maturational level of each child. For example, parallel and cooperative activities are developmentally appropriate for five- to seven-year-olds, whereas team sports are not. Dodgeball, relays, musical chairs, and kickball are contraindicated games for this age group because they emphasize hitting classmates with balls, stress speed over technique, involve too little activity, and eliminate rather than include student participation. NASPE's document "Developmentally Appropriate Physical Education Practices for Children" describes these concepts in greater detail (see Table 10-1 for some examples).

MIDDLE SCHOOL PROGRAMS

Middle schools emerged in response to the unique developmental needs of students during this transitional period of physical, social, emotional, and intellectual growth. Students between ages 10 and 14 should have already been taught fundamental movement skills and basic fitness concepts. If they have, they are ready to learn lead-up games, specific sports skills, and cooperative and competitive games and sports. Interest and ability grouping, rather than gender-role stereotyping, are essential during these years.

At the middle school level, time should be spent on developing responsible personal and social behavior, respecting differences among people, and using physical activity for enjoyment, challenge, self-expression, and social interaction. Although seasonal team sports like volleyball, basketball, and softball may comprise a portion of the curriculum, these young people need instruction in the skills of throwing, catching, striking, and running independently and within lead-up games. Inclusion of various dance forms, tumbling, outdoor adventure activities, and games chosen by students will enrich the curriculum. Despite limited facilities and equipment, skill heterogeneity, and large class sizes, physical educators need to creatively design and implement broad curricula that meet the interests and needs of their students.

Vital components of middle school curricula are health-related physical fitness and sport skill-related fitness. Students in this age group are capable of taking greater responsibility for establishing personal goals to enhance their cardiovascular endurance, muscular strength and endurance, and flexibility as well as skill-related fitness. School programs should creatively reinforce the achievement of these goals using honor rolls on bulletin boards, schoolwide announcements, newsletter features, assembly recognitions, "I'm Fit" T-shirts, or opportunities to lead or select class fitness activities.

Motor skill, fitness, and cognitive standards should guide the development of sequential and progressive instruction. Periodic assessments should be made to ensure the attainment of these standards. Whenever possible, the physical education specialist, who is a certified physical education teacher, should integrate instructional material with other subjects. With these standards in place, middle

Traditional sports such as softball may be offered in middle school physical education. (Photo courtesy Bob Hilliard.)

school students, their parents, and school administrators will value physical education programs of quality. Other important characteristics of middle school physical education include

- Ensuring that the physical education's program goals are consistent with the overall goals of the school
- Collaborating with other educators in interdisciplinary courses or units
- Planning the curriculum to include a scope and sequence of instruction that is appropriate to the needs and diversities of middle school learners
- Adapting instructional approaches to the developmental needs and learning styles of all students
- Providing opportunities for remediation and practice to ensure that all students enjoy success in their movement experiences

SECONDARY SCHOOL PROGRAMS

In the high school grades, students tend to prefer to work at achieving and maintaining a health-enhancing level of physical fitness rather than being placed in classes where they are again taught volleyball, basketball, and softball. Most students want to receive instruction in lifetime sports like bowling, golf, and tennis and in fitness activities such as aerobics or weight training. Facility and equipment limitations can be overcome by using community lanes, courses, and courts and getting students to use personal sports equipment. School

In secondary school physical education, students can be introduced to activities in which they may participate during their leisure hours and later in life. (Photo courtesy Maggie McGlynn.)

gymnasiums can be used for a variety of activities, including aerobics, badminton, rock climbing and rappelling, dance, one-wall racquetball, martial arts, and target archery. Community recreation centers with weight-training equipment and aerobics machines, such as stationary bicycles, stair climbers, and treadmills, may be made available to students during the school day. States and local educational agencies might be more likely to offer a wider range of elective courses to secondary school students if these broadened curricula were available. Learning skills in sports in which students can enjoyably participate throughout their lives should be a primary focus of secondary physical education programs.

Another area of emphasis should be to create opportunities to develop and implement individualized physical fitness programs. While these may be incorporated into aerobic or weight-training classes, students should be encouraged to establish fitness goals using activities they find personally satisfying. Secondary school students are capable of learning how to initiate and sustain fitness programs that they enjoy and are likely to continue throughout their adult lives.

Secondary school physical education classes should meet daily and be equal in length and class size to those for other subjects. Most states, however, have reduced the requirements for physical education for high school graduation. Physical educators face the same issues challenging other secondary school programs: insufficient instructional time, large classes, discipline problems, apathetic students, and meeting the needs of heterogeneous students by gender, race, and ability level. Relevant curricula, committed professionals backed by supportive administrators and parents, and instructional quality can alleviate, or at least reduce, many of these problems.

At all levels of education, it is essential that teachers help their students achieve high standards. If the programmatic characteristics just described are implemented, school-age children will be able to demonstrate proficiency in various movement and motor skills, maintain a physically active lifestyle, and interact positively with others in physical activity settings.

CHANGES IN CERTIFICATION REQUIREMENTS

State control of education has resulted in the establishment of certification standards for public school teachers. Most state departments of education (or the equivalent) specify the standards or competencies that must be completed before a person can teach. This requirement often includes specific courses in instructional methodologies and educational and developmental psychology, as well as a period of supervised student teaching. Physical education programs include disciplinary content, a specialized methodology of teaching, and the application of knowledge to student learning.

More and more states are requiring that students in all disciplines, including physical education, take the *Praxis Series: Professional Assessments for Beginning Teachers* to ensure that they possess both the general and specialized knowledge necessary to teach. Praxis includes assessments of academic skills (general for all teachers), subject matter, and classroom performance. Some states have developed their own competency tests. Many states have reciprocity agreements with other states so that certification in one is equivalent to certification in the other. Certification in a nonreciprocating state requires a teacher to complete one or more courses.

The most common requirement for interscholastic coaches is a teaching certificate (required for all coaches in about half the states). For those states with no established standards (and for those that commonly grant exceptions to the state regulations), liability concerns are paramount. The recent trend of hiring nonteachers to coach has developed because a number of coaching jobs do not have corresponding teaching positions. Those who want to be well-prepared professionals should consult the National Standards for Athletic Coaches (see Chapter 5).

ACCREDITATION

Although not under the jurisdiction of state or federal governments, accreditation helps ensure quality in education. Based on established criteria or standards, accreditation in teacher education, as provided by the National Council for Accreditation of Teacher Education (NCATE), makes institutions accountable for program content. Many schools require that prospective teachers graduate from NCATE-accredited programs. Some institutions, however, choose not to seek NCATE accreditation, believing they can best monitor the quality of their programs.

For physical education, NASPE has been given the responsibility to ensure that physical education undergraduate and graduate programs meet the minimal disciplinary standards. A college or university may submit its curricula (with accompanying explanatory documents) to NASPE on a periodic basis. A national panel of reviewers assesses whether that program is in compliance. If it is not, changes are mandated.

The two phases comprising accreditation are the institutional self-study and the peer evaluation. Nationally established standards and an institution's stated purposes and goals provide the characteristics and criteria for the self-study. The NCATE standards include

- Candidate knowledge, skills, and dispositions
- Assessment system and unit evaluation
- Field experiences and clinical practice
- Diversity
- Faculty qualification, performance, and development
- Unit governance and resources

The institutional report must address each of these standards. Next, a visiting team of evaluators conducts an objective study to determine the accuracy of the report. Its judgments are submitted in writing to the accrediting agency, which decides to grant or to deny accreditation for a five-year period. Thereafter, continuing accreditation is granted every five to seven years if a visiting team positively evaluates the program quality.

Accreditation standards apply in nonschool physical activity settings as well. As described in Chapter 6, certifications are offered by several organizations because employers are requiring that fitness and exercise leaders attain a specified level of competence. Whether leading group exercises, serving as a personal trainer, teaching aquatics activities, providing athletic training, prescribing an exercise program, or coaching youth sports, certifications are increasingly being mandated. People want to participate in programs that are conducted according to standards so they can be confident that the information they receive is accurate and up to date, and the activities they take part in are safe, effective, and appropriate.

Competence as a teacher may include assessing whether students learn proper movement skills such as throwing. (Photo courtesy Lisa Sense.)

Standards are important for instructional programs at all levels. (Photo courtesy Lisa Sense.)

ACCOUNTABILITY

Accountability demands that an individual or institution be held responsible to achieve a specified action. For example, schools are held accountable for increasing students' test scores because these scores are believed to be indicators of student achievement and, hence, inextricably linked with America's economic competitiveness. Accountability matters significantly when incentives and punishments await those who do or do not achieve the performance levels expected by politicians or special-interest groups. While accountability sounds good, this term may gloss over the political agendas of those who believe public schools are failing to meet national academic standards. Some argue that reliance on high-stakes testing fails to address serious fallacies in psychometrics, especially when many of the tests violate construct validity, consequential validity, and fairness. That is, many tests distort or misrepresent what students have actually learned because they do not accurately reflect the content of the curriculum or the typical context in which the curriculum is taught. Huge pressures to raise test scores, however, have led to inordinate amounts of time devoted to test preparation, instruction being geared to the test, and even cheating.

A **standard** is a uniform criterion or foundational guide used to measure quality. Educational standards determine what children at each grade level should know and be able to do. Schools are increasingly being expected to ensure that every child can achieve these standards of performance. Most states have adopted national tests and/or developed their own tests to measure student progress and achievement. State appropriations often depend on the test scores achieved, regardless of the socioeconomic context, the racial and ethnic composition of the student body, or the transient nature of the population. Sometimes the tests used to measure educational achievement bear little relationship to the state or local mandates regarding curriculum. In most cases, these

> **standard:**
> a uniform criterion or foundational guide used to measure quality

achievement tests tend to measure and reward memorization of facts rather than critical-thinking skills.

An **assessment** is a measure of knowledge, skills, and abilities. Assessments are tools used by those considered competent to judge student achievement, such as teachers and specialists. It is incumbent on educators to incorporate a wide range of authentic assessments throughout their programs to deflect an overemphasis on high-stakes test scores. That is, a variety of evaluative measures that reflect the curriculum should be implemented to determine student progress as well as those areas that need more work. Formative assessments are particularly useful for giving students constructive feedback and for determining how to provide individualized remediation. The assessment model in Figure 10-1 illustrates the comprehensiveness of the assessment process in a university setting.

> **assessment:**
> a measure of knowledge, skills, and abilities that leads to the assignment of a value or score

Every physical education class should be designed and taught by a competent and certified physical education teacher (see Box 10-4 for the characteristics

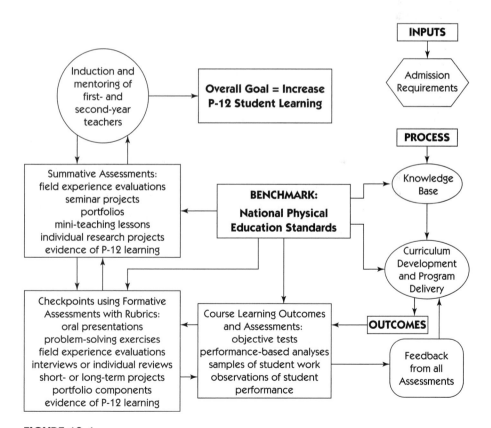

FIGURE 10-1

Assessment model for physical education.

BOX 10-4   COMPETENCIES REQUIRED OF PHYSICAL EDUCATION TEACHERS

General
- Understand the scientific and philosophical bases of physical education and sport
- Develop a comprehensive knowledge for analyzing movement
- Develop a wide range of motor skills, especially those related to the area of teaching
- Study the teaching/learning processes specifically related to the area of physical education and sport
- Become knowledgeable about planning, organizing, administering, supervising, evaluating, and interpreting various aspects of a balanced physical education and sport program

Elementary School Physical Education Teacher
We believe that:
- Professional preparation for the elementary school physical education teacher should focus on the child in preschool through grade 6. The curricula should result in the prospective teacher being competent in:
  - Understanding child growth and development, with an emphasis on motor development
  - A knowledge of and appreciation for the structure function of human movement
  - Observing and assessing children and their movement
  - The knowledge and assessment of health-related and skill-related aspects of physical fitness
  - A knowledge of learning processes, teaching strategies, and factors that affect motor learning
  - Developing curriculum with emphasis on curriculum designs and strategies appropriate for elementary school programs
  - Assessing and working with children who have special needs
  - Personal skills and teaching skills in the content areas of fundamental movement patterns, games/sports, dance, gymnastics, and aquatics to meet the needs and interests of children
- In addition, teacher preparation/staff development will provide:
  - Laboratory and field experiences that are directed and supervised throughout the teacher preparation program
  - Opportunities to become acquainted with a variety of elementary school organizational structures and the administration physical education within those settings.
  - The professional preparation curricula should culminate in certification specific for teaching children in the elementary grades
- Preparation for the classroom teacher should include an understanding of the relationship of physical growth and motor development to the total development and learning experience of the child. Course work in movement skills, methods, and content of elementary school physical education programs should be required. Laboratory assignments that provide for experiences with children in physical education are essential.

(continued)

BOX 10-4 COMPETENCIES REQUIRED OF PHYSICAL EDUCATION TEACHERS (CONTINUED)

- Continuous staff development opportunities should be provided to meet the individual needs of educators concerned with physical education programs for children. Teachers in the field should be involved in the planning of such programs.
- Personnel concerned with teacher preparation and staff development in physical education should have continuous interaction with children. They also need to be aware of current research and legislation, and be able to interpret and apply these to the teaching context.

Middle School Physical Education Teacher

Preparation of teachers should include courses and teaching experiences that pertain to the education of middle school students. The in-service education program for physical education teachers is imperative to assure skilled and knowledgeable teachers to administer the varied programs required for middle schools. Administrators should provide opportunities for teachers to attend workshops, meetings, and conventions to keep physical education personnel current on materials and information.

Educational programs should prepare teachers who:

- Have an understanding of the middle school concept
- Possess teaching certification in physical education
- Avoid gender-role discrimination and gender stereotyping by grouping students according to interest and ability levels
- Understand the physical, social, emotional, and intellectual characteristics that are unique to middle school students
- Possess a positive self-concept and demonstrate respect for the dignity and worth of all individuals
- Have developmentally appropriate knowledge and skills for working with students on a one-to-one basis
- Are familiar with a wide variety of skills and activities in order to implement the exploratory qualities of the program
- Apply various teaching styles and modify rules, equipment, and instructional stations to conform to the needs of the learner
- Continually strive to increase their knowledge and understanding to meet the changing needs of middle school students and their learning environment
- Can interact with students and fellow teachers in a way that supports the special needs of the middle school student
- Will assume leadership in providing for the expanding physical experiences for all students in the school
- Are able to interpret the goals and objectives of the activity programs to students and their parents
- Use instructional strategies based on the developmental and skill level of the student as well as the nature of the activity
- Are able to maintain and manage recordkeeping systems for planning sequential instruction

(continued)

BOX 10-4   COMPETENCIES REQUIRED OF PHYSICAL EDUCATION TEACHERS (CONTINUED)

Secondary School Physical Education Teacher

Educational programs should be conducted by certified physical education teachers who:

- Serve as positive role models of personal health, fitness, skill, and enjoyment of participating in physical activities
- Are knowledgeable in curriculum and instruction, and demonstrate sportsmanship and sensitivity to students' needs
- Know and apply teaching strategies that provide maximum student time on task
- Apply various teaching methods and instructional strategies that personalize physical education classes and allow students to attain optimal personal growth
- Provide for equitable instruction and participation with regard to the individual needs of the student
- Demonstrate professional commitment through involvement in professional organizations and other enrichment experiences
- Plan program activities that promote understanding of cultural diversity
- Accommodate the needs of exceptional students in regular physical education classes
- Understand that the instructional program and athletics are separate and distinct; they strive to keep a balanced perspective between the dual role of teaching and coaching
- Use recognized assessment and evaluation instruments in planning for accountability of the instructional program
- Apply technology in their teaching on a regular and continuing basis

of competent physical educators). Like every other school subject, physical education should include sequential learning activities characterized by objectives, instructional strategies, developmental levels, content standards, and assessments. Objectives should be identified by grade level, and specified outcomes should be assessed at each level by valid and reliable measurements. High-quality physical education programs will help students of all abilities develop physical fitness and motor skills, gain a thorough understanding of fitness, nutritional, and health concepts, enact appropriate social behavior, and value a healthy lifestyle.

Educators cannot achieve these objectives if children and adolescents take part in physical education only one or two days per week. The National Association for Sport and Physical Education recommends that children from kindergarten through grade 5 receive at least 30 minutes of physical education instruction per day; students in grades 6 through 12 should receive at least 50 minutes per day.

Experiences in sport and physical activity programs outside the classroom are also important for children's overall intellectual, social, emotional, and physical development. Whether a recreational youth sport league, individual sports lessons, or a commercial fitness program, appropriate objectives, standards, and

Assessments of program quality may include monitoring heart rates during and following an aerobics session.

assessments will help ensure fun, program adherence, and maintenance of a healthy lifestyle.

LEGAL LIABILITY

One challenge facing professionals working in physical activity–related careers is dealing with the legal issues surrounding injury to participants. The risk of injury mandates that teachers, leaders, supervisors, and administrators understand and comply with their legal obligations to those they serve. Because many people in our society attempt to seek legal redress for any real or perceived mistreatment, physical educators must be especially prudent. **Negligence,** the most frequent claim, occurs when a teacher's or director's failure to act in a reasonable or prudent manner results in injury to another person. Four factors must exist for negligence to be proven:

> **negligence:**
> the legal claim that a person failed to act as a reasonable and prudent person should, thereby resulting in injury to another person

- Presence of a duty (such as providing supervision of a class)
- A breach of that duty (failure to act as a reasonable and prudent person would under similar circumstances)
- Proximate cause of the injury (the action or failure to act caused the subsequent injury)
- The substantial nature of the injuries (the extent of the injuries)

There are two legal defenses against negligence:

- **Assumption of risk** by program participants (however, they must know, understand, and appreciate those risks).
- **Contributory or comparative negligence** by the person injured. Some states have adopted contributory negligence; others use comparative negligence.
  - Contributory negligence refers to behavior by the plaintiff that contributed to the injury. Sometimes contributory negligence can bar recovery for the injury.
  - Comparative negligence apportions damages between a negligent plaintiff and a negligent defendant who each played a part in the injury.

To avoid liability for negligence, you must act reasonably by recognizing potentially hazardous conditions or situations and protecting your students and clients from them. First, **general supervision** is always required when class is in session or activity is occurring. This responsibility includes knowing what to look and listen for, where to stand, how to move around, and what to do when a problem arises. The more dangerous the activity, such as a gymnastics class or a stress test, the closer the **specific supervision** is mandated. Second, you have a responsibility to eliminate not only known hazards (those about which you had **actual notice**) but also those that constitute **constructive notice,** hazards that any reasonable and responsible person should have noticed, such as broken glass on the floor. You bear the responsibility of informing those in charge of necessary repairs or of situations that might lead to injury. Third, you should make regular inspections, involve participants in taking responsibility for their own safety, perform preventive maintenance, and post warnings about using facilities. Fourth, every participant should be warned about potential risks; specifically, each person should understand and appreciate the risks

assumption of risk:
knowing, understanding, and appreciating the risk associated with a chosen activity

contributory negligence:
behavior by the plaintiff that contributed to the injury

comparative negligence:
apportions damages between a negligent plaintiff and a negligent defendant who each played a part in the injury

general supervision:
action required whenever activity is occurring by those for whom the person is responsible

specific supervision:
mandated action required whenever a higher level of risk is associated with the activity of the persons for whom the adult is responsible

actual notice:
refers to the removal of known hazards by a responsible person

constructive notice:
refers to hazards that a responsible person should have noticed and eliminated

One liability issue is what sports activities are appropriate for school and college curricula. (Photo courtesy Lisa Sense.)

and potential for injuries involved in the particular activity. To understand the extent of your obligations to students or clients served, consider these questions:

- Under what circumstances, if any, should you, as a coach, permit your athletes to warm up prior to practice when you cannot be present?
- What are your obligations to a person who will be participating in a research project that involves a submaximal treadmill run?
- What is your obligation to an athlete who has a head or neck injury?
- As a personal trainer, what are your legal responsibilities for the welfare of your client who is participating in a strength training program?
- Under what conditions should the athlete, coach, trainer, or a physician decide when the athlete can return to practice or competition?
- What legal obligations does a sport facility manager have to fans?
- What legal responsibilities does a recreation department have to parents regarding the hiring of personnel to work with children in its programs?
- Under what conditions, if any, does an owner or a manager of a fitness club have legal responsibilities to provide members with equipment that is in safe condition?
- What should an exercise scientist require of a subject in a research study before administering a treadmill test?
- What health and safety responsibilities must the person responsible for a community fun run meet?

Whether dealing with an athlete, a client, or a subject in a research project, an **agreement to participate** helps each participant understand and appreciate the risks involved and any related safety rules. This is not a waiver of responsibility or a guarantee against lawsuits. However, an agreement to participate may help instructors defend themselves against negligence charges because it articulates what

agreement to participate:
a signed acknowledgment of a participant's knowing, understanding, and appreciating the risks associated with an activity

BOX 10-5   TESTING YOUR KNOWLEDGE OF LEGAL LIABILITY

For each situation below, explain why the action was taken by the professional and the term that describes this.

1. During the parent orientation session, the high school coach informs parents and team members that football is a dangerous sport and that serious injuries may occur during practices and games. He provides each parent with a one-page description of the potential risks and requires that the athlete and one parent sign and return this form within one week in order for the athlete to be permitted to continue on the team.

2. During a submaximal treadmill test in an exercise physiology lab, the exercise science researcher monitors all the participant's vital signs to ensure that no overexertion occurs.

3. Following a heavy rain, the physical education teacher uses a mop and towel to ensure that there is no residual water or a slippery spot on the gymnasium floor, since the roof has leaked in the past.

4. A recreation program director requires that each participant in a 5-kilometer road race sign a statement indicating that he or she is participating voluntarily and with an understanding of all risks.

5. As the manager of a public pool, you post signs indicating that no swimming is permitted unless a lifeguard is present.

6. As an athletic trainer attending to a basketball player who has fallen on his neck after being undercut by an opponent, you and a player assist the athlete off the court immediately so you can assess the extent of the injury while the game continues.

7. As the exercise leader in an aerobics class, you observe how vigorously all of your participants are breathing.

assumption of risk means. An agreement to participate, written specifically for each activity, should describe the skills required for safe participation, the possible injuries, and the important rules for safe participation. On this form, the participant should be questioned about any preexisting physical condition and/or limitations. These agreements should include a statement suggesting that at any time a participant experiences discomfort or stress, he or she should discontinue the activity. The final statement signed by the participant should specify that she or he understands and appreciates the risks involved in the activity. In preparing an agreement to participate, the professional should ensure that it is consistent with the legal defense of assumption of risk. (Test your knowledge of legal liability by responding to the questions in Box 10-5.)

Several other steps can also be taken to avoid liability.

• Provide instruction in the proper techniques for skill execution. Meeting this responsibility requires preparation of and adherence to sequential and progressive instructional plans that clearly show individuals are expected to attempt skills beyond their ability to safely execute them.

• Ensure that each participant's fitness, conditioning, and ability levels are appropriate to the expectations. Failure to ascertain limitations or apprehensions may lead to injuries for which you will be liable.

BOX 10-6   MANAGEMENT STRATEGIES TO AVOID THE CHARGE OF NEGLIGENCE

- Follow the guidelines for safe programs established by the school, employers, and state.
- Prepare a statement of safety procedures and distribute it to the program director and to parents, if appropriate.
- Establish an operational system of emergency care in the event of a serious injury.
- Establish a system for identifying, treating, reporting, and recording all injuries.
- Purchase from reputable dealers the best equipment the budget will allow.
- Make sure all facilities are free of hazards.
- Follow sound practices and program-approved activities that specify appropriate skill progressions.
- Learn and teach using the latest and best instructional techniques.
- Closely supervise all activities.
- Carry liability insurance with broad coverage.

- Enforce safety rules and regulations. Strict compliance with school, club, or corporate policies, including those governing the reporting of accidents and injuries, is critical.
- When injuries occur, you must respond appropriately. It is assumed you will hold current cardiopulmonary resuscitation and first aid certifications and thus will know how to respond properly to various injuries. For example, any person suffering from a possible neck, head, or back injury should not be moved without supervision from emergency responders.
- Do not use inadequate, ill-fitting, or defective equipment. You must regularly inspect all equipment, removing any in need of repair or replacement.
- Only qualified individuals should supervise physical activity.

Closely adhering to each of these suggestions and the risk management strategies listed in Box 10-6 not only will help you meet your legal obligation to those you instruct but will also greatly reduce the likelihood that you will become a defendant in a negligence lawsuit. You should also make sure your employer provides adequate insurance protection for you. If such insurance is lacking or inadequate, you should purchase personal liability insurance.

COMMERCIALIZATION OF PHYSICAL FITNESS

When people choose to become physically fit, they face a multitude of choices about how to best achieve that goal. Making a well-informed, wise choice is more difficult in our media-saturated culture. Multimillion-dollar advertisements dominate television, the Web, and print media. Sporting goods manufacturers market their products through highly paid professional athletes. Every imaginable fitness fad is foisted on an often naive public that seeks a quick fix for a lack of physical fitness. The latest fitness gadget guaranteed to "take off pounds quickly" and "with no effort" soon becomes an unused or broken relic in the basement. Commercialization of physical fitness has extended to health and sports clubs that promise fitness results if you join. Sometimes the prospective member is not told about additional charges for aerobics classes, swimming lessons, and personal trainers because these clubs exist more to make a profit than to provide a service.

One additional concern about the commercialization of physical fitness is the subliminal, or sometimes overt, message of sex appeal associated with muscular males and sexy females who look like models. In response, many males have chosen to take drugs such as creatine to build muscle mass and enhance their appearance of masculinity. Many females, in an unending attempt to enhance their appearance of femininity through weight loss, succumb to the dangerous—and at times deadly—triad of anorexia, amenorrhea, and osteoporosis.

Any piece of fitness equipment, program, or drug that is guaranteed to provide immediate and substantial results should automatically be suspect. Research has proven time and again that the only way to safely and effectively reduce body weight is to increase caloric expenditure and decrease caloric intake. Some highly touted devices, such as rubber suits, can be dangerous because they can lead to dehydration. The only safe and effective approach to developing and maintaining physical fitness is regular physical activity combined with a healthy diet.

CAREER BURNOUT

A combination of discipline problems, apathetic students, inadequate facilities, equipment, and other resources, combined with minimal administrative support, often leads to teacher **burnout,** which results in decreased performance. Many physical education teachers feel isolated from other teachers, lack professional mobility, and face the constant threat of spending and program cuts. Thus, many individuals display the signs and symptoms of burnout listed in Box 10-7. People in physical activity–related careers other than teaching may also find their jobs

burnout:
decreased performance quality and quantity resulting from stress, job repetitiveness, lack of support and reward, and overwork

unrewarding or frustrating due to a lack of change or too much change too fast, unchallenging routines, work overload, lack of advancement potential, or threat of elimination.

Often burnout occurs as a result of role conflict. A physical education teacher is often hired to teach a full load of classes and coach one to three sports. Lesson plans, grades, reports, student monitoring responsibilities, and associated

BOX 10-7   SIGNS AND SYMPTOMS OF BURNOUT

- Chronic stress
- Emotional exhaustion
- Depersonalization
- Reduced sense of mastery
- Less enjoyment of work and leisure activities
- Bodily changes such as fatigue, high blood pressure, insomnia, digestive disorders, or increased heart rate
- Overeating or undereating
- Excessive drinking or abuse of drugs
- Frustration with job-related factors such as task repetitiveness, lack of recognition, overwork, or lack of advancement
- Anxiety and depression

teaching duties combine with year-round planning, practices, competitions, and administration of teams to fill most days and nights. One of four patterns then usually develops:

- A tenured teacher/coach decides that the small coaching supplement is not worth the time demands, so she resigns from coaching but continues teaching.

- A teacher/coach concentrates on coaching, putting little effort into teaching because he views it as repetitive and unrewarding.

- A teacher/coach becomes apathetic about both jobs and just goes through the motions instead of being committed.

- A teacher/coach changes careers.

A teacher/coach who resigns may be burned out in part because of the inordinate pressures to win from parents and school administrators. This teacher/coach conflict is aggravated by the higher recognition and rewards for coaching as compared with those for teaching. The chronic, job-related stress resulting from role conflict or role ambiguity can be reduced but probably not eliminated, since the teacher/coach holds two somewhat incompatible positions simultaneously.

Combating burnout has become essential to career survival. Job satisfaction necessitates taking a positive approach toward work responsibilities. Financial rewards, job challenges, recognition, promotion, variety in responsibilities, and professional development all contribute to job satisfaction. Positive feedback is essential. If people are constantly bombarded by negative comments, they cannot continue to function effectively. Recognition and praise for completing responsibilities often lead to positive changes and enhanced self-motivation.

The teacher-coach spends long hours helping students learn and athletes achieve their potential.

When individuals are given the opportunity to take part in the planning process, a greater allegiance to the resultant programs or goals is readily evident. Finally, physical education and exercise science professionals should interact with others on the job by attending seminars, workshops, and conferences. At least once a year, everyone needs to rejuvenate their commitment to and enthusiasm for job responsibilities.

While work-related stress probably cannot be avoided, each of us should understand what causes stress and how to eliminate or cope with it. Physical educators and exercise scientists have a definite advantage in the latter case because they know exercise reduces stress. We need to attain and maintain a personal level of fitness that not only positively affects our productivity and quality of life but also allows us to serve as role models for others.

INSTRUCTIONAL CHALLENGES FACING SCHOOL PHYSICAL EDUCATORS

School teachers, including those in physical education, face many challenges. Among these are insufficient resources for facilities and equipment, apathetic students, drug abuse, lack of family support, heterogeneous students in large classes,

Participation in physical activity, such as volleyball, can help relieve stress and lessen the possibility of career burnout. (Photo courtesy Lisa Sense.)

and discipline and behavioral problems. Despite these factors that negatively affect the instructional environment, teachers are held accountable for student learning.

Limited facilities and equipment need not dissuade physical educators from expanding their programs. The gymnasium can be used for rock climbing, badminton, and aerobics as well as traditional team sports. Community courts, driving ranges, and lanes are often available for tennis, golf, and bowling. Additional equipment can be brought by students, borrowed from recreational departments, leased from companies, and even obtained free from organizations seeking to promote certain sports. Ask students and parents to help construct goals, net supports, weights, and playground apparatus.

Apathetic students who do not want to dress out, participate, or behave present an even greater challenge to teachers. Since each student is unique, teachers need to use whatever resources or referrals they can to determine the causes for this apathy. Only then can they appeal to these students' interests and needs. Replacing dodgeball or unpopular activities with weight training or aerobics may be the only change needed. Rewarding appropriate behavior rather than simply punishing misbehavior encourages positive change. Teaching relevant content, ensuring equal opportunity for all students, and making classes enjoyable may not engage every student, but the number of apathetic ones will certainly diminish. Keeping students busy is not education. Teaching must result in learning.

When students attend school under the influence of alcohol or purchase and use drugs on school grounds, the learning process is severely hampered. Drug education classes and enforcement of school policies for drug-free campuses are

BOX 10-8   ADVOCACY EFFORTS

- Write letters to parents that describe your physical education program and invite them to come to their child's class and observe.
- Develop a physical education program website where you describe the curriculum, announce special events, and share physical activity tips.
- Publish a physical education program newsletter.
- Share position statements developed by professional organizations.
- Distribute press releases about recent research studies that have influenced the welfare of youth and affected your physical education program.
- Invite other teachers, school administrators, board of education members, and politicians to your classes to learn more about your innovative and engaging curriculum.
- Send news stories to the local media about the exciting activities in your program.
- Work with the PTA/PTO or local service organizations to obtain funds to establish a wellness center for students and the general public.
- Distribute public service announcements to the broadcast media.
- Plan special events that publicize the achievements of students in your program.
- Celebrate May as Sport and Physical Education Month.

two ways to help reduce the incidence of these problems. The physical educator should use every opportunity to discourage drug use by showing how it adversely affects physical performance and well-being.

Dramatic demographic and socioeconomic changes are partly to blame for the lack of parental and family support for education in this country. Over half of the children in the United States will spend a portion of their school years in single-parent homes. Most children with two parents will find no one at home after school because both parents work. A quarter of today's children live in households with incomes below the poverty level. Children of minorities already exceed the number of whites in some schools; this population shift will continue. Teachers must overcome a lack of parental support by helping students learn the value of education. Teachers need to help students take greater responsibility for their own education. The physical educator could help by creating an after-school fitness club that could instill self-worth, confidence, discipline, and responsibility in students. Physical education can play a significant role in overcoming some of these problems. Educators need to engage these problems head-on, using their imaginations to create new programs, new teaching methods, and new avenues that serve educational aims. Then educators need to find ways to promote physical education (including these new programs) to parents, students, administrators, and fellow educators. Box 10-8 includes a few suggestions for promoting physical education.

Many states dictate maximum class sizes, but too often these are ignored for physical education. When school administrators believe that physical education is only play, with no instruction where cognitive learning occurs, physical educators may be expected to teach 50 to 60 students in each class. The first objective in this type of situation is to educate your principal about your curriculum and invite decision makers to observe the quality of your program. Working with other professionals, you need to lobby against exceptions to maximum class size. The best rationale you can offer is the increased chance of injury when there is inadequate supervision and crowded instructional and activity conditions. Even with a normal-size class, physical educators face students with heterogeneous abilities. Skill grouping, use of lead-up or progressive games, and curricula that include both cooperative and competitive activities contribute to meeting students' diverse needs.

Discipline and behavioral problems may be the most recurring issue facing teachers. Rather than dissipating in an activity setting, these problems are often exacerbated. Some students with histories of misbehavior may seek to use physical education classes as opportunities to dominate others or show off. Physical educators must establish fair and impartial class policies regarding these behaviors and then enforce them consistently. Using timeouts as punishment, rather than exercises or laps, teaches respect for the rules. Rewarding appropriate behaviors with the opportunity to participate in favorite activities is even more effective than punishments for most students.

In overcoming these challenges, physical educators must be prepared to do a lot more than just teach their favorite sports and games. Each challenge is an opportunity to positively affect the lives of students.

SUMMARY

Physical activity programs are for everyone. They help people learn fitness and sports skills and incorporate them into their daily lives. It is hoped that students and exercise participants of all ages will increasingly enjoy their physical fitness activities, reach their goals, and adhere to their appropriately designed programs. Increasingly, public and private health and sports clubs, work site programs, rehabilitation clinics, and retirement homes will be charged with meeting the fitness and activity needs of adults. There will be a growing need for specialists in these areas. Advances in technology as well as the proliferation of research will continue to have widespread implications for physical education and exercise science in the future. School physical education programs will continue to evolve, with an emphasis on fitness activities and the development of the whole person. Educational reforms of standards, accountability, and assessments will significantly affect funding for school programs and lead to important changes. Although instructional and financial constraints threaten the teaching/learning process, competent teachers must creatively find ways to surmount these barriers while being held accountable for helping each student achieve higher standards. Teachers and exercise and fitness specialists must take their responsibilities seriously to provide safe environments for learning and to act responsibly when injuries occur. Professional involvement and interchange among colleagues are two ways to combat job stress and career burnout.

CAREER PERSPECTIVE

MARTY POMERANTZ
Director of Campus Recreation
University of North Carolina at Chapel Hill
Chapel Hill, North Carolina

EDUCATION
B.S., Pre-Physical Therapy, State University of New York at Binghamton
M.A., Physical Education with a specialization in Intramural Administration, Michigan State University

JOB RESPONSIBILITIES AND HOURS
Marty oversees the operation of a comprehensive university campus recreation program, including intramural sports, sport clubs, fitness and aerobics, and outdoor recreation. This includes managing the program budget, coordinating facilities, supervising seven full-time professional staff, and coordinating long-term strategic planning. He generally works from 8:30 to 5:30 Monday through Friday, fairly typical hours for a director. However, Marty frequently works on weekends, checking on activities, making sure staff members are on duty, and completing work he is unable to finish during the week. Assistant directors and those who oversee programming (i.e., intramurals and sport club activities) work many evening and weekend hours. Depending on school size, type of institution, region of the country, and other variables, salaries for directors range from $35,000 to $100,000, with the average around $50,000. Salaries for other campus recreation personnel start around $20,000 and then advance depending on duties and experiences.

SPECIALIZED COURSE WORK, DEGREES, AND EXPERIENCES NEEDED FOR THIS CAREER
To become a director of a campus recreation program, you need a minimum of a master's degree. The National Intramural-Recreational Sports Association offers a certification for campus recreation specialist, which many professionals hold, but most employers do not require this. Marty states that the following experiences are most helpful in pursuing a career in this field: an internship; a graduate assistantship; a position as an intramural official, supervisor, or sport director; serving as an officer or member of an executive council in club sports; and experience as an instructor, a personal trainer, a monitor in fitness and aerobics, a ropes course facilitator or climbing monitor, or an expedition leader in outdoor recreation. Through these experiences, you develop specialized skills and demonstrate a passion for the field. Marty states that probably the most important course he completed was a basic one in programming and scheduling activities. Other courses, including budgeting, diversity, interpersonal relations, organizational behavior, and facility development, were also helpful in completing his current responsibilities.

SATISFYING ASPECTS
To Marty, the most satisfying aspect of his work is knowing that he makes a tremendous difference in the quality of life on campus. While he may not be responsible for a student learning his or her class material, Marty believes he helps create an environment

that enhances the learning process. By providing opportunities for students to develop lifetime skills, such as leadership, time and money management, problem solving, and interpersonal relationship skills, he and his colleagues help educate the whole person. Also, it is gratifying to help bring good health and smiles to the faces of students, faculty, and staff. While there are occasional conflicts and issues of inadequate facilities, Marty believes he could not have chosen a better career and lifestyle.

JOB POTENTIAL

There are many opportunities for jobs and advancement in campus recreation. If you are willing to relocate, become involved in national and regional committee work, and take time to get to know and network with other professionals, the sky is the limit.

SUGGESTIONS FOR STUDENTS

Marty suggests that you get involved in your campus recreation/intramural program as a paid employee or volunteer. He advises that you see if this field is something you are passionate about; if so, then plunge in. He recommends that you look for a graduate assistantship to complement your graduate work or pursue a full-time internship where you know you will receive a good experience. Most important, he states, you have to really enjoy working with people, including all kinds of people with diverse perspectives and problems.

REVIEW QUESTIONS

1. What are some of the values of physical activity programs?
2. What are several challenges facing professionals in recreation and leisure services?
3. Why do more students choose to specialize in fitness and exercise and sport science than prepare to teach physical education in the schools?
4. How have research and technology changed the quality of scholarship in physical education, exercise science, and sport?
5. How should middle school and secondary school physical education curricula differ?
6. What is accountability, and how does it relate to standards and assessment?
7. What four factors must exist to prove negligence?
8. What are several risk management strategies you should use to ensure that the rights of participants in your program are being protected?
9. What are five factors contributing to career burnout?
10. What are several challenges facing school physical educators?

STUDENT ACTIVITIES

1. Talk with five friends about any individual exercise program in which they are (or were) involved. Summarize the factors that led to their quitting or adhering to their programs.

2. Write a one-page paper about your personal accountability in a job you have held in a field related to your major, such as lifeguard, sport official, camp counselor, or sporting goods salesperson. (If you have not had any of these experiences, talk with people who have and report their experiences.)

3. Ask a faculty member at your institution who led in the development of an undergraduate specialization why this program was established.

4. Secure a copy of the local elementary, middle school, and secondary school standards and curricula for physical education. Analyze them to determine if the standards are being achieved through a progressive and sequential program.

5. Read two articles in any professional journals that describe how an expanded knowledge base and technology in physical education and exercise science have positively affected noneducational programs. Summarize in two or three sentences the impact each has made.

6. Describe two actual examples of people who have suffered from career burnout. What changes would you have recommended that might have prevented these situations?

7. Read two articles about negligent behavior by people in careers associated with physical activity. What action did they take or fail to take? If litigation occurred, what was the outcome?

8. Complete a risk management assessment of a physical activity program, a sporting event, or a sports facility, listing all potentially unsafe actions or situations.

SUGGESTED READINGS

Buckworth J: Exercise adherence in college students: issues and preliminary results, *Quest* 53(3):335, 2001. In this study, the author examines why college students persist in their physical activity programs.

Byra M, Jenkins J: Matching instructional tasks to learner ability: the inclusion style of teaching, *JOPERD* 71(3):26, 2000. The authors stress the importance of adapting instruction to the various learning abilities of all of their students.

Chen W, Rovegno I, Iran-Nejad A: Application of a wholetheme perspective to the movement approach for teaching physical education in elementary schools, *Education* 123(2):401, 2002. After discussing the characteristics of the piecemeal approach to teaching subjects in schools, the authors present the theoretical framework and tenets of the wholetheme approach and apply them to the teaching of movement.

Dyson B: The implementation of cooperative learning in an elementary physical education program, *J of Teach in PE* 22(1):69, 2002. As described in this comprehensive article, cooperative learning is an effective instructional strategy for teaching physical education to children.

Edginton C, Jiang J: Outsourcing: a strategy for improving the quality of leisure services, *JOPERD* 71(4):46, 2000. Outsourcing means acquiring from an outside source a product or service that has traditionally been provided. This article recommends that leisure services agencies explore outsourcing as a way to use their resources more efficiently, increase responsiveness and flexibility, and offer higher-quality services.

Fay T, Doolittle S: Agents for change: from standards to assessment to accountability in physical education, *JOPERD* 73(3):29, 2002. This article describes the importance of using standards as the basis for assessments as physical educators are increasingly being held accountable for student learning.

Gray GR: Safety tips from the expert witness, *JOPERD* 66(1):18, 1995. This paper informs physical educators and coaches about how to avoid negligent actions and decisions through an understanding of how expert witnesses will testify in liability cases.

Greenwood M, Stillwell J, Byars A: Activity preferences of middle school physical education students, *The Phy Educ* 58(1):26, 2001. The authors suggest that to meet the interests and needs of middle school students, physical educators should ask students for their preferences, such as which specific sports should be included in the curriculum and whether or not these should be taught in coeducational classes.

Lee AM: Promotion quality school physical education: exploring the root of the problem, *Res Q for Exer & Sp* 73(2):118, 2002. This researcher states that despite the recognized benefits of regular physical activity, many physical education programs have failed to address weaknesses identified over 50 years ago. A call is made to physical educators to reform their instructional practices based on established standards and assessments of learning.

Malina RM: Adherence to physical activity from childhood to adulthood: a perspective from tracking studies, *Quest* 53(3):346, 2001. The author provides an overview of this topic, as well as an analysis of the factors determining individuals' continued participation in physical activity.

McBride RE, Carrillo D: Incorporating critical thinking into a secondary school wellness unit, *JOPERD* 71(9):20, 2000. The authors share experiences and information specific to a wellness unit to assist physical educators in designing instruction that facilitates the development of critical-thinking skills by high school students.

CHAPTER

11

ISSUES IN SPORTS

KEY CONCEPTS

- Girls and women are increasingly involved in sports and have been aided by Title IX in these advances.
- While minorities, senior citizens, and individuals with disabilities enjoy greater activity, they still struggle for equality in sports.
- Rather than emphasizing winning, the benefits and developmental goals of community youth sports and interscholastic athletics must be reinforced.
- As many intercollegiate athletic programs are besieged with problems associated with commercialized sports, colleges and universities must strive to ensure the attainment of educational outcomes.
- The Olympic Games provide opportunities for friendship among athletes of the world who are seeking to prove their physical superiority; yet they are characterized by politics, nationalism, and excessive commercialization.

Sports participants seek to win. "We're number one" has seemingly become the United States' sports motto from youth leagues to professional teams. To produce the best teams, athletes are often expected to specialize in one sport, to accept coaches' dictates without question, to practice and train with deferred gratification, to excel or face elimination, and to circumvent the rules when necessary. Ethical behavior is often disdained or negatively regarded by coaches, teammates, and spectators, since winning surpasses everything else in importance. (See Box 11-1 for a glimpse at one issue—nutritional supplements—facing sports.)

In contrast, cooperation, discipline, emotional control, fair play, self-esteem, and teamwork are the desired outcomes of sports. Athletes can learn these values as well as respect their opponents both on and off the field. They can also accept officials' decisions without dispute. Even spectators can learn these values. Models of ethical behavior are especially important for young people, who typically imitate the attitudes and behaviors of school, college, professional, and Olympic athletes.

Sports are fun. Sports provide a setting for people to develop their own identities by learning about their capabilities and limitations. Genuine satisfaction comes with making one's best effort regardless of the outcome. A revitalization of body, mind, and spirit through sports can renew one's perspective on life. Overly

---

BOX 11-1 NUTRITIONAL SUPPLEMENTS AND SPORT PERFORMANCE

A major controversy raging through sport at all levels is whether nutritional supplements should be banned. Extensive use of strength-enhancing compounds, readily available at health food stores, via the Web, or just across the Mexican border, has captivated the public as it reads about numerous professional athletes who have stated freely that they have used a variety of nutritional supplements. With no bans on these substances in Major League Baseball, for example, athletes who formerly batted for singles are now swinging for and reaching the fences.

Since athletes of all ages and both genders report using creatine, one of the most widely used supplements, sport organizations are considering whether use of this supplement erodes fair competition. Simultaneously, scientists are conducting research on the long-term physiological effects of high doses of creatine. In addition to seeing significantly increased muscle mass and strength, many athletes have come to believe that creatine enhances multiple bouts of high-intensity efforts and delays the onset of fatigue. The question remains, however, whether users of nutritional supplements are placing winning ahead of other considerations, such as ethical conduct, fair competition, or potential health risks.

---

competitive and commercialized sports undermine this holistic renewal and the character development that is an essential aspect of genuine sport. Administrators, coaches, athletes, and fans must ensure that experiencing the positive side of sports is the right of everyone by working to maintain these values.

Girls and women, minorities, senior citizens, and individuals with disabilities are being treated more equitably in sports today, but they still face discriminatory practices and biases. Public and private youth sports organizations, interscholastic programs, and elite competitions at the collegiate and international levels share some of these common problems and conflicts. This chapter discusses several of these controversial issues (see Box 11-2) and some proposed solutions.

GIRLS AND WOMEN IN SPORTS

Although the Greeks excluded women from the ancient Olympic Games, and the founder of the modern Olympic Games viewed women's role as cheering spectators, there has been a gradual acceptance of girls and women as sports participants. Traditionally both physiological and societal factors contributed to the discriminatory treatment many girls and women experienced when they initially sought to compete in sports. The fact that males beyond puberty have advantages in sports emphasizing speed, strength, and power does not justify the virtual exclusion from sports that females experienced in the past. Research demonstrates that most females are not as strong as men; are shorter and lighter; and, due to total body size, have smaller lungs and lower cardiac output. Yet many female athletes have surpassed the prejudicial limitations placed on them by running and swimming faster and longer than many men. They compete professionally against and with males, achieving high levels of muscular strength and endurance, and

BOX 11-2   THREATS TO THE INTEGRITY OF SPORT

Specialization in one sport, circumvention of rules to gain competitive advantages, pressures to win, and excessive commercialization are the major changes pervading competitive sport from the youth to the collegiate level. Due to these negative factors, many of the lofty values associated with sport, such as fair play, have eroded.

The rationale for early and continued specialization in one sport is that only focused training can lead to victories and attainment of long-term goals such as Olympic medals, professional contracts, or college grants-in-aid. While children aspire for what over 99 percent will never achieve, they miss the enjoyment of playing various sports and risk overuse problems, such as injuries to the epiphysis. Interscholastic athletes are increasingly advised by coaches and parents to focus on only one sport, which again reduces fun and leads to overuse injuries. While some high school students still earn multiple varsity letters, the college dual-sport athlete is almost an anachronism. The time and training required of intercollegiate athletes usually preclude participation in multiple sports.

Coaches often instruct their athletes in how to circumvent game rules without being penalized. At early ages, youth and school sport participants learn that faking an injury to get the clock stopped, calling an opponent's ball out when it helps you win, and lying about one's legal guardian to play on a desired team are acceptable, and even praised, behaviors. Later athletes may take anabolic steroids, accept money from a booster to ensure attendance at a certain university, or cheat on exams to maintain academic eligibility because these actions may later contribute to victories.

Pressures to win are exerted on athletes of all ages by coaches, parents, and fans. Some coaches, overzealous for victories, excessively stress youngsters' arms and bodies, verbally and physically abuse children, and teach and model unethical behaviors. They also emphasize winning so much that by age 12, over 50 percent of all youth sport participants drop out because they are no longer having fun and developing skills. Too many parents try to live through their children by taking fulfillment from their children's sports achievements. Others may even withhold love from children who do not perform to parental expectations. Families have moved, parents have separated or divorced, and other children in the family have been neglected—all in the pursuit of potential lucrative professional sports careers. Fans adore and reward athletes who win and speak disparagingly about and disassociate themselves from the less successful.

Commercialization in sport is both a reality and a necessity in our capitalistic society. Corporate and community funding, fans' financial support, and the media are not inherently bad. Problems occur when these factors outweigh developmental and educational values. Communities may seek recognition and status through winning age-group Pop Warner National Championships or state basketball titles. Corporate sponsorships help youth, school, and college sports teams pay their expenses, but some sponsors have excessive control over the hiring or firing of coaches or the awarding of advertising space in sports arenas. Similarly, fans who donate huge sums of money to athletic programs often want more than preferential seating and parking. Television already dictates, or at least strongly influences, who gets broadcasted and when and where teams compete. Many wonder how long television can charge sponsors increasingly higher prices for advertisements.

While certainly not the only changes, sport specialization, rule violations, pressures to win, and excessive commercialization have made a negative impact on competitive sports at all levels. Combined, they pose threats to the integrity of these programs unless they are moderated or potential abuses are controlled.

are proficient in sports skills once the domain of males only. The physical potential of girls and women is not yet known, since they must first have equal opportunities in sports to achieve their maximum potential. Contrary to the writings of the early 1900s, women do not risk sterility when they train strenuously and compete aggressively. Like males, females benefit in multiple ways when they achieve their physical potential.

Societal attitudes have changed slowly. Sports have traditionally been viewed in the United States as masculine—for males only. Familial and environmental influences have tended to establish fixed gender roles with regard to sports. For example, boys are usually given balls and outdoor toys, while girls usually receive dolls or quiet, passive toys. Early in life, girls learn that if they participate in sports they risk being called a tomboy or being viewed as less feminine or less attractive. Peer group pressure results in a role conflict wherein choosing sports often makes it more difficult to be accepted by one's peers. Therefore, many girls opt out. The more determined ones may compensate by always emphasizing a feminine appearance, deemphasizing their athletic involvement (and their successes), and selecting a sport that is viewed as more acceptable, such as golf, gymnastics, swimming, or tennis. The other alternative is to participate actively in sport, regardless of the consequences. Although few girls chose this route in the past, the situation is changing.

Television commercials that portray women as sports enthusiasts still include sexist overtones and innuendos. Newspapers and periodicals that publish sports stories on women seldom use them as lead stories and never cover them as extensively as they do male sports stories. Since women have lower salaries (today women in the same jobs earn slightly over 70 percent of what men earn), they have less discretionary income to spend for sporting equipment and fitness club memberships. Over 50 percent of American women work outside the home. They usually enjoy less leisure time for recreational activities because of a combination

Joan Benoit won the initial Olympic marathon for women in 1984. (Photo courtesy Kathy Davis.)

TABLE 11-1

IMPACT OF TITLE IX ON SPORTS FOR FEMALES

High Schools*

Number of Participants

	1971	1977–1978	1984–1985	1991–1992	2000–2001
Girls	294,015	2,083,040	1,757,884	1,940,801	2,806,998
Boys	3,666,917	4,367,442	3,354,284	3,429,853	3,960,517

Most popular girls' sports (based on number of schools participating):

Basketball

Track and field

Volleyball

Softball (fast-pitch)

Cross country

Tennis

Soccer

Golf

Swimming and diving

Competitive spirit squads

Intercollegiate Sports (NCAA)†

Average number of sports for women:

1978: 5.61

1982: 6.59

1986: 7.15

1990: 7.24

1992: 7.09

1996: 7.50

2000: 8.14

2004: 8.32

(continued)

of work, family, and household obligations. Tradition and sexism still prevent women from having equal access to public and private recreational facilities.

Today more and more city recreation programs and private clubs are attracting women. The cultural emphasis on fitness has stimulated greater acceptance of women who not only look fit but are fit. Myths die slowly, however, and prejudicial attitudes are even more resistant to change. As girls' and women's sports performances improve, and as each generation of parents lobbies for greater equity, this issue in sports will come closer to resolution.

One leading reason girls and women have enjoyed expanded opportunities to play and compete has been Title IX of the 1972 Education Amendments. (Table 11-1 includes data about changes in competitive and coaching opportunities for girls and women.) Because of this federal legislation, thousands of school

TABLE 11-1 (CONTINUED)

IMPACT OF TITLE IX ON SPORTS FOR FEMALES

Most popular sports:

1. Basketball	6. Tennis
2. Volleyball	7. Track and field
3. Cross country	8. Golf
4. Soccer	9. Swimming
5. Softball	10. Lacrosse

Female coaches of women's teams (since 1998, the number of head coaching jobs of women's NCAA teams has increased by 534; only 10 percent of these positions were filled by women):

1972: over 90%

1978: 58.2%

1982: 52.4%

1986: 50.6%

1990: 47.3%

1992: 48.3%

1996: 47.7%

2000: 45.6%

2004: 44.1%

Female administrators of women's programs (females hold 34% of all administrative jobs in women's programs, yet no females are involved in the administration of 23% of women's programs):

1990: 15.9%

1992: 16.8%

1996: 18.5%

2000: 17.8%

2004: 18.5%

*Data from the National Federation of State High School Associations.
†Data from a study by Vivian Acosta and Linda Carpenter, "Women in Intercollegiate Sport—A Longitudinal Study—Twenty-Seven Year Update 1977–2004" © 2004 Carpenter/Acosta.

In 1960, Wilma Rudolph became the first American woman to win Olympic gold medals in the 100- and 200-meter sprints.

BOX 11-3   *COHEN et al. v. BROWN UNIVERSITY*

In November 1996, the U.S. Court of Appeals for the First Circuit upheld a district court decision finding in *Cohen et al. v. Brown University* that Brown University and its athletic program had violated Title IX. Following the refusal of the U.S. Supreme Court to hear Brown University's appeal, the lower court ruling was upheld, with significant implications for support of equitable intercollegiate athletic programs for females. According to the 1998 settlement agreement, Brown University would be considered in compliance with Title IX as long as it retained its current women's sports programs and maintained a participation rate for female athletes within 3.5 percentage points of the percentage of female undergraduate students at the university. The settlement also stipulated that the university had to upgrade its women's water polo team to varsity status and guarantee funding for four sports—gymnastics, fencing, skiing, and water polo—that had not received adequate support in the past.

---

and college females have achieved greater equity in sport. In 1992, the Supreme Court ruled in *Franklin v. Gwinnett County Public Schools* that monetary damages were available under Title IX. The fact that victims can now be compensated for inequitable treatment for the first time may be just the incentive needed to force schools and colleges to eradicate discrimination. (See Chapter 9, page 287, for a timeline of the most important events related to the impact of Title IX on girls' and women's sports and Box 11-3 for a discussion of a recent landmark Title IX case.)

Title IX's provisions relative to athletics have not been uniformly implemented because of gender biases, limited budgets and facilities, lack of coaches, and resistance to change. Women have benefited, however, by receiving approximately one-third of colleges' athletic budgets for team travel, recruiting, coaches' salaries, medical treatment, publicity, and athletic grants-in-aid. School girls too have gained more teams, better-paid coaches, access to facilities, and other program supports such as new equipment and uniforms.

As these programs have expanded, however, control has shifted to men. Today a much smaller percentage of women coach girls and women than before Title IX, and few women administer athletic programs for females (see Table 11-1). Among the factors contributing to the increasing number of men coaching girls and women are too few women with expertise or interest in coaching, more equitable salaries for coaches of female teams than was the case prior to Title IX, unwillingness of many women to coach highly competitive teams, and hiring practices in which male athletic directors and school principals prefer to hire male coaches. When female and male athletic programs were combined, usually on the premise of equal opportunity, men were inevitably named to the top positions either because of seniority or because of the belief that they "knew" athletics better. Occasionally, though, a female is hired to administer an athletics program that competes at the highest collegiate level. Thus, a major issue confronting athletic programs is the need for more qualified female coaches and sport administrators who are given more opportunities to coach teams as well as direct athletic programs.

Over 30 years after its passage, Title IX remains highly controversial in athletics, even though in other educational settings, equal opportunity for both genders has largely been achieved. At issue, especially at the intercollegiate level, are two major questions. First, many college administrators claim the federal government has failed to provide clear guidance about how to comply with Title IX and its policy interpretations. Second, depending on who is asked, the Office of Civil Rights either has not been effective in enforcing this law or has enforced it in ways that have led to the elimination of men's teams. Each of these points was examined by the 2002–2003 secretary of education's Commission on Opportunity in Athletics, as will be briefly described below.

Title IX provides a three-pronged test for satisfying the requirement of meeting the interests and abilities of male and female students. It states that as long as an institution can meet at least one of these criteria, it is considered in compliance:

- Participation opportunities are substantially proportionate to the undergraduate enrollment of males and females.

- When members of one sex have historically been underrepresented among intercollegiate athletes, there must have been a continuing practice of program expansion in response to developing interests and abilities of the underrepresented sex.

- In the absence of a continuing practice of program expansion, an institution must show that the interests and abilities of the members of the underrepresented sex have been fully and effectively accommodated.

Many athletic directors have chosen the so-called "safe harbor" of proportionality because they believe the other two options are more difficult to measure or prove. In seeking to achieve a substantially proportionate number of female and male athletes, and especially because of the large number of athletes on football teams, many institutions have increased the number of women's teams and even established quotas for the number of walk-on athletes permitted on men's teams. Still, numerous colleges fall significantly below this requirement of meeting the interests and abilities of female athletes.

Regarding whether Title IX has in effect led to the elimination of men's teams, data from the NCAA verify that the average number of men's teams per institution has decreased slightly (read the report online at www.ncaa.org/library/research/gender_equity_study/1999-00/1999-00_gender_equity_report.pdf). However, were these cuts due to the increasing "arms race" associated with trying to keep up commercially in football and men's basketball with conference and national rivals rather than because of the requirements of Title IX to provide women's teams?

The Commission on Opportunity in Athletics, while reaffirming its commitment to equal opportunity for both genders, stated that cutting men's teams was an inappropriate response to Title IX. The commission called on the Office of Civil Rights to provide clear and understandable written guidelines for implementation of Title IX as well as consistent and aggressive enforcement of the law.

EQUALITY FOR MINORITIES

Members of minority groups have found themselves sports outcasts throughout most of this nation's history. Prior to 1950, sports were rarely integrated, with a few exceptions such as Jack Johnson (boxing), Joe Louis (boxing), Paul Robeson (football), Satchel Paige (baseball), Jackie Robinson (baseball), and Jesse Owens (track). Following the Supreme Court's *Brown v. Board of Education* decision in 1954, school desegregation slowly began to open more school and college sports programs to minorities.

Throughout the years, minorities have experienced blatant discrimination in the form of quota systems (only a small number allowed on a team), position stacking (minorities competed for only a limited number of positions because certain others were unavailable to them), social exclusion from clubs and parties, disparity in treatment by coaches, weak academic support, and little tutorial help. Sometimes minority athletes, because of their cultural and educational backgrounds, were ill prepared for the academic demands of college; their athletic prowess had gotten them through a vocational or technical rather than college-preparatory, high school curriculum. Many failed to earn college degrees, thus eliminating themselves from possible coaching positions when their dreams of professional stardom failed to materialize or ended abruptly.

Many minorities oppose the NCAA's rule that to be eligible to compete at the Division I level, prospective student-athletes must graduate from high school having successfully completed the following 14 core courses:

- 4 years of English
- 2 years of mathematics (Algebra I or higher)
- 2 years of natural/physical science (1 year of lab, if offered by high school)
- 1 year of additional English, mathematics, or natural/physical science
- 2 years of social science
- 3 years of additional courses (from any of the above, foreign language, or computer science)

In addition, prospective student-athletes must have a combined score on the Scholastic Assessment Test (SAT) or a sum score on the American College Test (ACT) based on a sliding index that ranges from a core course grade point average (GPA) of at least 3.55 with a 400 SAT or a 37 ACT score to a 2.00 GPA with a 1010 SAT or 86 ACT score. Some argue that the SAT and ACT are culturally biased against minorities, and therefore the test requirements prove that the predominantly white institutions want to limit the domination of minorities on some of their sports teams.

Whether discrimination against minorities in sports is subtle or overt depends on the school or college, the team, and the leadership of both. Many interesting questions persist: Why are the starters on football and basketball teams predominately minorities when the student bodies are predominantly white? Why are

Carl Lewis, shown here receiving the baton (lane 5) in the gold medal—winning 4 × 100 meter relay in the 1984 Los Angeles Olympic Games, has been called by some the greatest athlete ever. (Photo courtesy Paula Welch.)

BOX 11-4   2003 RACIAL REPORT CARD*

This report stated that African Americans continued a decade-long decline in playing college and professional sports, except in basketball. They also lost ground in holding the top management positions in professional and intercollegiate sport. However, there were notable increases in the number of Hispanics in baseball and soccer as well as international athletes in each of the major professional team sports.

The NBA achieved the best record for racial diversity, with 80% of its players, 10 league office vice presidents, 17% of the general managers, and 48% of the head coaching positions. This report provided extensive data to support the grades awarded to each of the sports associations studied in several categories of analysis, such as league officers, head and assistant coaches, front office administrators, and support staff.

*These and other data come from an analysis by the author, Richard E. Lapchick, at the Institute for Diversity and Ethics in Sport of the hiring practices of the National Basketball Association (NBA), National Football Association, Major League Baseball, Major League Soccer, Women's National Basketball Association, and the National Collegiate Athletic Association. This report is available online at www.bus.ucf.edu/sport/public/downloads/media/ides/release_report.pdf.

minorities seldom members of tennis, swimming, golf, and gymnastics teams? Why do fewer minority team members who are marginal athletes receive athletic scholarships than comparably skilled whites? What is the status of the minority female athlete? Why are almost all head coaches and athletic directors white, especially when a high percentage of football and basketball players are African American? (See Box 11-4 for additional information.)

When given the opportunity, formerly underrepresented groups often become dominant forces in sports. (Photo courtesy Maggie McGlynn.)

Some claim that minority athletes are bigger, stronger, and generally more highly skilled than white athletes. Research does not substantiate this. However, it is a fact that minority athletes' opportunities in elite and expensive sports have traditionally been limited, resulting in their devoting greater amounts of time and energy to the school-sponsored sports of football, basketball, and baseball. These three sports also offer the remote possibility for professional careers. Coaches, in seeking to win, must recruit the best athletes. Yet in traditionally white institutions, they may also be encouraged to have as many white players on their teams as possible, which may result in athletic scholarships being given disproportionately to marginal white athletes who play as substitutes, if they play at all.

High cost and lack of opportunities have traditionally prevented many minorities from pursuing tennis, swimming, golf, and gymnastics. Private lessons, expensive equipment, club memberships, and travel requirements for quality competition discourage most minorities from entering these sports; the virtual absence of role models only reinforces the status quo. It should be noted that the minority female athlete must overcome both racial and sexual barriers to equity of sports opportunity. Her greatest opportunities, and hence achievements, have come in basketball and track.

Minority athletes, regardless of gender, sport, or level of competition, deserve to be treated fairly and equitably. All athletes should be expected to complete their academic work in schools and colleges and to earn their degrees in preparation for later life. Because of past discrimination, minorities may deserve to receive counseling to help them derive the most from their education and to learn marketable skills. Since prejudicial attitudes change only gradually, everyone must work together to eliminate discrimination in athletics. Coaches must prohibit mistreatment of minorities on their teams, and administrators must ensure equity for all.

EQUALITY FOR SENIOR CITIZENS

Senior citizens have also had to overcome discriminatory biases to gain sporting opportunities. As the average age of the U.S. population increases, a greater awareness of the needs of seniors to exercise and to compete is emerging. People past 50 years of age are walking, cycling, hiking, swimming, lifting weights, and engaging in a large number of sporting activities with the blessings of their physicians, who view such activities as good preventive medicine. This enthusiasm for exercise and activity has rekindled in many seniors a desire to compete. The National Senior Games and masters events in national, regional, state, and local competitions are providing opportunities for former athletes and newly aspiring older athletes to achieve in sports in unprecedented ways. For example, in the first National Senior Games, which began in 1987, approximately 2,500 men and women competed in sports ranging from archery to volleyball. Held biennially, the National Summer Senior Games now attract over 10,000 competitors in 18 sports. Interest in other sports led to the establishment in 2000 of the Winter National Senior Games, which offer competitions in seven sports. A listing of past competitions, the sports in which competitions are held, and affiliated state organizations can be found at www.nationalseniorgames.org/virtualmall/index.mv?Screen=SFNT&StoreCode=0022. Whether competing for recognition or personal satisfaction, these older Americans are beneficiaries of enhanced strength, flexibility, endurance, and balance, factors that directly improve the quality of their lives. This activity also reduces the stress of lost spouses and friends, and replaces loneliness with new friends and social opportunities.

Public and private recreational programs for older Americans are proliferating. For example, commercial health and fitness clubs offer water aerobics, exercise programs for individuals with arthritis, walking clubs, and other types of programs designed specifically for senior citizens. Many programs for seniors include cardiovascular, muscular strength and endurance, and flexibility components appropriate for individuals with histories of cardiac problems or chronic conditions requiring adaptations. Senior centers, either publicly funded or associated with residential areas, offer stretching sessions, a variety of recreational activities, and aerobic machines. Senior citizens are encouraged to continue their pursuit of lifelong physical activity through age group competitions in tennis, golf, swimming, and many other sports. Through their votes and discretionary incomes, they are demanding and receiving more equitable access to recreational and sporting facilities.

The Paralympic Games showcase the athletic achievements of athletes with spinal cord injuries. (Photo courtesy Paula Welch.)

EQUALITY FOR INDIVIDUALS WITH DISABILITIES

In recent years, individuals with disabilities have increasingly desired equal opportunity to participate and compete in sports. The Amateur Sports Act of 1978 specified that the competitive needs of athletes with disabilities must be accommodated. The Education for All Handicapped Children Act of 1975 mandated that athletics be provided to school students with disabilities, and the 1990 Americans with Disabilities Act called for access to public recreational facilities for those previously denied it. These factors and an eagerness and determination to treat everyone equitably have led to a proliferation of organizations and competitions.

The Paralympic Games, which began in 1952, offer international competitions for individuals with spinal cord injuries. These games, which are now held every four years at the site of the Olympic Games, expanded from 130 athletes from 2 nations to 3,843 athletes from 123 countries at the summer 2000 Paralympic Games in Sydney. (See www.paralympic.org for more information about the history and activities of the International Paralympic Committee.) In 1976 the Paralympic winter games began, and visually impaired athletes were welcomed to its competitions. Since 1980, individuals with amputations and those with cerebral palsy have become competitors; in 1996, mentally handicapped athletes began to compete in these games. The following list of sports attests to the abilities of these remarkable athletes: alpine skiing, archery, boccia, cycling, equestrian events, football (soccer; 5-side and 7-side), goalball, ice sledge hockey, judo, nordic skiing, power lifting, sailing, shooting, swimming, table tennis, track and field, volleyball, wheelchair basketball, wheelchair fencing, wheelchair rugby, and wheelchair tennis.

Since 1968, the Special Olympics has provided competitive opportunities for mentally challenged individuals. Although experts initially questioned this program, the overwhelming success of personal training and state, national, and international competitions has verified the importance of giving individuals with intellectual challenges the chance to achieve and be recognized as winners. The 26 official Special Olympics sports for athletes 8 years and older include alpine skiing, aquatics, athletics (track and field), badminton, basketball, bocce, bowling, cross-country skiing, cycling, equestrian events, figure skating, floor hockey, football (soccer), golf, gymnastics, power lifting, roller skating, sailing, snowboarding, snowshoeing, softball, speed skating, table tennis, team handball, tennis, and volleyball. The 10th Special Olympics World Summer Games for athletes with mental retardation was the largest multisport event in the world held during 1999. Nearly 7,000 athletes from more than 150 countries from around the world showcased their athletic talents.

YOUTH SPORTS

Around 50 million children and adolescents (ages 4 to 18) participate annually in youth sport competitions sponsored by cities, companies, and local and national organizations. These youthful athletes ride derby cars, horses, and dirt bikes; throw baseballs, softballs, footballs, and basketballs; roll bowling balls; hit golf balls, tennis balls, racquetballs, and table tennis balls; kick soccer balls; break boards; turn flips; swim; dive; wrestle; run; and compete in triathlons and many more sporting events. This proliferation of youth sports has been fueled by television, money, civic pride, the desire to produce national champions, parental overzealousness, and professional sports models.

The major issues facing youth sport programs are an overemphasis on winning, poorly trained coaches, parental interference, and eroded ethical values.

Soccer is a popular sport for children. (Photo courtesy Winkie LaForce.)

When winning becomes the primary objective, other potential outcomes are lost. Coaches are usually the ones initially caught up in this win-at-all-costs attitude. To fulfill their own ego needs, coaches too often pressure their young players to play while injured, violate the rules to their advantage, and quit if they are not good enough. Also, coaches' lack of preparation may result in poorly taught skills, improper treatment of injuries, and an inability to understand and deal with children's developmental needs. Some coaches are even guilty of physically, mentally, and sexually abusing their young athletes.

While usually well intentioned, parents often impose their wishes on their children to play a particular sport or several sports. Too often parental aspirations to succeed in sports stem from their own needs rather than the children's needs. Children may experience considerable guilt because their parents invest huge amounts of time and money in lessons and competitions, which only pushes

Youth sports begin to teach a love of competition that for many continues throughout life.

these young athletes to more desperately seek success. Parents too often reward results rather than effort and improvement. And when coaches and parents reinforce cheating to win, abusing officials and opponents, circumventing the rules, and stressing the outcome (winning) over the process (having fun and developing skills), important sporting values as well as essential personal virtues are lost. In addition, adult dominated sports rob children of the opportunity to make decisions, to learn give and take in sports, and to make good judgments.

With such a long list of problems, why do youth sports continue to grow in popularity? First, American children have a genuine interest in and enthusiasm for sports. Second, the positive outcomes in most programs exceed the negative aspects. There are leagues, organizations, coaches, and parents who emphasize fun and participation and ensure positive physiological and psychological outcomes for the children.

Through orientation programs, parents learn about program goals and how to help their children benefit most from their experiences. Program administrators need to emphasize the following:

- Everyone plays in every event and in rotating positions.

- Certificates of participation and team outings are given as rewards instead of huge trophies and championship playoffs.

- Children are asked what they want from their sports experiences to ensure attainment of these aspirations.

- Coaches and parents stress and reinforce cooperation, teamwork, and sportsmanship.

- Outcomes such as individual skill development, participation of everyone, development of intrinsic motivation, learning and playing several sports in varied positions, safe participation, and fun are emphasized. (See Box 11-5 for information about one educational program for volunteers and coaches in youth sport programs.)

BOX 11-5   EDUCATING ADULTS WHO WORK WITH YOUTH SPORT PROGRAMS

The Volunteer Program of the American Sport Education Program seeks to prepare coaches, officials, parents, and youth sport administrators to provide educationally sound and safe environments for players though online learning opportunities (see www.asep.com/learn/VOL_volunteer.cfm). The first level of the coaches' component focuses on coaching essentials, safety, practice and game-day tips, and sport-specific skills; the second level introduces more advanced, sport-specific coaching techniques. In their training, officials learn officiating fundamentals, responsibilities, communication, conflict management, safety, and sport-specific officiating such as proper positioning and mechanics, rules, signals, and the principles of officiating. The parent orientation presents information about why children play sports, the responsibilities of parents to a young athlete, how to communicate with coaches, and how to help children have a fun sport experience. The Directing Youth Sport Program helps administrators improve their management skills, develop staff, build positive parental involvement, evaluate and manage risk, learn financial management and fund-raising tactics, and plan sporting events.

A controversial aspect of youth sports is whether strength training is beneficial or harmful. Assuming qualified adults supervise, instruct, and spot youth at all times, workouts begin with stretching, proper technique is taught and used, realistic goals are set, resistance (weight) is increased gradually, and strength training is a part of a balanced conditioning program, strength training for children and adolescents can be beneficial. For example, strength training benefits coordination and muscle fiber development by improving motor skills and sports performance, increases lean body mass, aids in the development of cardiovascular fitness, enhances self-image and self-esteem, and lowers the incidence of sports-related injuries. There is no scientific evidence that strength training by youth can retard their growth.

Many states also have coaches' associations that either are specific to one sport or have coaches from all sports in their memberships. These groups usually sponsor statewide or regional workshops or clinics on specific coaching techniques or strategies, rule changes, values and ethics in school athletics, and sport psychology. Many volunteer coaches join the National Youth Sports Coaches Association.

Each year, millions of girls and boys ages 8 to 18 years compete in the largest amateur sports program in the United States, the Junior Olympics. The Junior Olympics are organized by the Amateur Athletic Union and recognized by the United States Olympic Committee. These amateur athletes compete in more than 3,000 local meets, state championships, regional events, and national finals. The benefits from being a part of the Junior Olympics include making friends, having opportunities to travel, gaining a sense of achievement, and enjoying the excitement of the competitions. Youth also compete in state games, such as the Empire State Games (New York) and the Keystone State Games (Pennsylvania), which provide a variety of sports opportunities for children of all ages. Most of the athletes in these state games have developed their skills through youth and school athletic programs.

INTERSCHOLASTIC ATHLETICS

The National Federation of State High School Associations promotes interscholastic athletics as an integral part of the educational experiences of high school students (see the "Case for High School Activities" at www.nfshsa.org/case.htm). Most physical educators have traditionally favored and supported interscholastic athletics because they believe adolescents are developmentally and emotionally able to compete. School administrators stress the beneficial outcomes of fitness, sportsmanship, cooperation, self-discipline, and other values for the participants. From a broader perspective, interscholastic athletics enhances school spirit and, in many locales, enlists strong community support for the school.

Today, though, many interscholastic athletics coaches have not been properly prepared to coach. Several factors have contributed to this problem:

- Elimination of some physical education requirements and teaching positions

- The addition of more specialized requirements for prospective physical education teachers and a reduction of coaching-related courses in colleges
- Physical educators choosing not to combine teaching and coaching careers
- Physical educators ceasing to coach
- More school sports teams, especially for girls, requiring coaches
- Teachers of other school subjects seeking coaching positions

The National Federation of State High School Associations (founded in 1920) and the 50 state and associated high school athletic and activities associations work to protect the activity and athletic interests of high schools, promote the growth of educational interscholastic athletics, and protect high school students from exploitation. It publishes *Interscholastic Athletic Administration*. The National High School Athletic Coaches Association (founded in 1965) and the National Federation Interscholastic Coaches Association (founded in 1981) combined have nearly 100,000 members.

The major problem in high school sports in the United States is an overemphasis on winning. Indicative of this compulsion are year-round conditioning programs and practices, students specializing in one sport, students playing while hurt, and coaches' jobs depending on winning records. Advocates of year-round conditioning programs stress that they are needed to develop proper skills, stay competitive with other teams' athletes, and increase chances for college grants-in-aid. Arguments against single-sport specialization include athletic burnout and overuse injuries; denied opportunities to acquire other skills, play with other athletes, and learn from other coaches; and exploitation by coaches concerned only with their teams.

The teacher/coach struggling to meet the demands of two full-time jobs is sometimes overwhelmed when school administrators, parents, and team supporters mandate winning. Coaching supplements are low compared to these pressures, and time expectations are high, although personal satisfaction and community and school recognition may compensate somewhat.

Another controversial issue facing interscholastic athletic programs is the "no pass, no play" policy adopted by some states. Generally, this policy requires that student players obtain passing marks in all (or most) courses taken during the previous grading period. Supporters state that the purpose of schools is education. Thus, participation on a team, or in any other extracurricular activity, is a privilege earned by those who achieve in the classroom. Advocates also claim that this policy will motivate students to achieve academically on a consistent basis. Lawmakers, school administrators, and most parents applaud the effectiveness of this policy because students' performances in their class work have improved overall. Opponents disagree, claiming that extracurricular activities, especially sports, encourage some young people to remain in school. Experience, though, has shown that although a few students may continue their education only because of the appeal of sports participation, many students seem to be taking their schoolwork more seriously because of the "no pass, no play" policy.

The abuse of drugs is all too pervasive in schools. Most adolescents and children, including athletes, have ready access to tobacco, alcohol, marijuana, amphetamines, cocaine, and other legal and illegal drugs. Unless coaches educate their athletes about the harmful effects of these drugs on their bodies, and hence their performances, many interscholastic athletes will succumb to peer pressure and use these drugs. Underage drinking, cigarette smoking, and the use of smokeless tobacco are all too common among interscholastic athletes. Some of these athletes also use anabolic steroids, often resulting in immediate and irreparable physiological damage. Taken to increase muscle bulk and size for appearance and performance purposes, large dosages of anabolic steroids may interfere with normal growth and development, lead to overly aggressive and irrational behaviors, cause sterility, or even kill the user.

School athletic programs also face other problems such as spectator violence, unsportsmanlike conduct by coaches and athletes, cheating to maintain academic eligibility, and program budget cuts. Because of skyrocketing costs, due somewhat to injury and liability insurance and the provision of athletic programs for girls and individuals with disabilities, many schools can no longer afford to provide athletics as a right. Many high schools are adopting a pay-for-play policy, which means educational allocations will no longer finance athletic teams; instead, any student who desires to participate on a team will have to pay for the experience. Although this policy excludes students who are unable to pay, this trend is becoming increasingly popular, especially in private schools.

INTERCOLLEGIATE ATHLETICS

In the realm of college athletics, the regulatory bodies include the National Collegiate Athletic Association (NCAA; founded in 1906), the National Association of Intercollegiate Athletic (NAIA; founded in 1940), and the National Junior College Athletic Association (NJCAA; founded in 1938). The NCAA, with approximately 1,200 members, promotes competition through championships for women and men. The *NCAA News,* published in newspaper format, provides updates on issues and events for its members, along with numerous job announcements. Athletes in small colleges that hold membership in the NAIA compete in 23 women's and men's championships. The NJCAA, representing approximately 500 institutions, conducts championships in the major sports for women and men. Other athletic organizations that encourage the exchange of ideas include the College Sports Information Directors of America, the College Athletic Business Management Association, and the National Association of Collegiate Directors of Athletics.

Ever since the proliferation of college athletic programs for men in the late 1800s, college faculties and administrators have been concerned about the potentially detrimental effects of athletics on academic work. Associated problems then and now include students missing classes because of competing and traveling, receiving unearned grades, and being admitted even though

Track is a popular high school sport for female athletes.

underqualified. The NCAA, NAIA and NJCAA have attempted to administer inter-collegiate athletics on the basis of educational principles, although regulations concerning these issues rest largely with each institution. (Box 11-6 provides one very positive approach to addressing sportsmanship and related values in sport.) The problem that each college faces is how to deal effectively with regulations when winning is almost synonymous with survival, especially at large institutions.

Winning teams appeal to spectators and increase interest. More fans bring in larger gate receipts. More money contributes to hiring coaches with winning reputations and to recruiting and awarding grants-in-aid to better athletes, who combine to win more games. This cycle (winning = fans = money = winning = fans = money) repeats itself with alarming regularity and tends to spiral into an ever-widening circle. The resultant commercialization changes college athletics from an extension of the institution's educational mission to a business venture. When winning becomes the most important objective, rules are frequently violated, both during play and in the recruiting of athletes; sportsmanship, character development, and other values are often lost or at least deemphasized in the process. (See the Research View box for what one study of these issues found.)

Why do intercollegiate athletics continue to thrive? There are three major reasons. First, intercollegiate athletics reflect Americans' attitudes, beliefs, and values. Many people believe that colleges have the responsibility to offer competitive sport opportunities for students, and they defend the concept that sports participation helps prepare the athletes for life by developing physical, intellectual, social, and moral skills. Second, the benefits already mentioned exceed the liabilities. Many people think the problems just listed are sporadic rather than pervasive. They add that participants and spectators enjoy being entertained, while college spirit and allegiance are enhanced. Third, athletic teams are

BOX 11-6   CITIZENSHIP THROUGH SPORTS ALLIANCE

The Citizenship through Sports Alliance (CTSA), composed of amateur and professional sports organizations, was formed in 1997 in response to concerns about the decline in sportsmanship and unethical behaviors within sports in America, a deterioration that permeates all levels of sports competition. This alliance seeks to promote the values realized through sportsmanship and ethical play in sports at all levels. The objective of the CTSA is to help sports participants become better citizens and learn those values necessary to teach and learn respect for self and for others. Among the character-building qualities that CTSA members espouse and seek to engender in their athletes are self-esteem, discipline, courage, responsibility, integrity, honesty, ethics, poise, pride, enthusiasm, respect for others, teamwork, loyalty, compassion, tolerance, courtesy, fairness, and humility.

Leaders in the sports organizations listed below believe that sports have the potential to do great things for youth. Unfortunately, there has been a dramatic rise in poor sporting behaviors displayed by parents and coaches that model the wrong values and threaten the benefits that can come from sports. The CTSA, through its unique relationship with prominent sports organizations, encourages adults to put competition into proper perspective by helping youth use their sport experiences to learn values essential for the development of respect for self and others.

- National Federation of State High School Associations
- National Junior College Athletic Association
- National Association of Intercollegiate Athletics
- National Collegiate Athletic Association
- United States Olympic Committee
- Women's National Basketball Association
- National Basketball Association
- National Hockey League
- Major League Baseball
- National Football League
- National Association of Collegiate Directors of Athletics
- National Association for Sport and Physical Education

valuable public relations tools for institutions. College enrollments often increase as a result of successful athletic programs, especially in football and men's basketball. The provision of entertainment attracts large numbers of spectators to college athletic contests, with an accompanying surge in college loyalty that many claim positively affects legislative appropriations and private donations to academic departments, in addition to generous support for athletics.

Realistically, intercollegiate athletics, regardless of the extent of the challenges, will continue to thrive because of its entertainment value and benefits. To accentuate the positive and reduce the negative, the following actions are possible remedies:

- Sanction intercollegiate coaches and athletes who violate athletic regulations, especially in the areas of recruiting and scholarships, for

🔍 RESEARCH VIEW

The Game of Life*

The authors of this book examined the precollegiate preparation and subsequent academic performance of athletes and other students in the 1951, 1976, and 1989 entering classes at 30 academically selective institutions. Their analysis of the data led to these and other conclusions:

1. Educational opportunities at the institutions studied have increasingly been rationed in favor of athletes; e.g., athletes make up a substantial portion of each entering class.

2. There is a tendency for athletes, regardless of sport, competitive level, and gender, to underperform academically.

3. Sport specialization has resulted in few multisport athletes as well as fewer competitive sport opportunities for nonrecruited athletes.

4. Athletes and athletics are less central to the campus culture.

5. Escalating costs for athletic programs threaten other educational uses of limited financial resources.

6. The commercialization of intercollegiate athletics remains largely unchecked.

As the results of this extensive research study indicated, intercollegiate athletics faces significant ethical, educational, societal, and financial issues. Examining the daily newspaper or listening to the evening news reveals another scandal associated with a fired coach or an athlete arrested for some law-breaking behavior. When the graduation rate of African American players on a team is zero or athletes submit assignments in their classes that are not their own work, education obviously has been devalued. It is hard to defend how coaches can be paid hundreds of thousands of dollars to change teams regardless of existing contracts while athletes lose eligibility for transferring institutions in order to play. When layers of rhetoric are stripped away, the major controversy surrounding Title IX is not about equal opportunity for females versus sports teams for males; the challenge is how an institution can fund a comprehensive athletic program while enmeshed in a spiraling "arms race."

---

*Shulman JL, Bowen WG: *The game of life: college sports and educational values,* Princeton, NJ, 2001, Princeton University Press.

---

the first offense; place violators on a two-year probation from coaching and competing for the second offense; ban violators from college coaching and from intercollegiate competition for life for the third offense.

- Withhold for a period of five years one grant-in-aid for every athlete who does not graduate within six years.

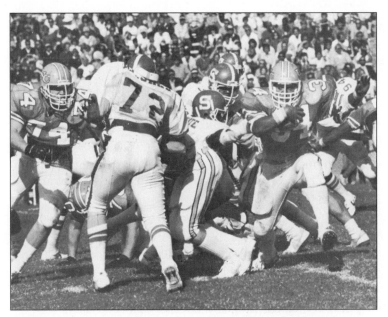

Intercollegiate football teams have become multimillion-dollar businesses in many institutions, challenging the accuracy of the concept of the student athlete. (Photo courtesy UNC Sports Information Office.)

Intercollegiate sports have the potential to help athletes develop their physical, mental, and social skills as long as these positive outcomes are taught and reinforced.

- Base coaches' job security and salaries not on their won–lost records but on the fulfillment of their job responsibilities and the provision of positive experiences for their athletes.

- Restrict schedules of all sports so that no more than one day of class per week is missed.

- Admit only those athletes who meet the academic standards of admission to the colleges they attend.

- Limit grants-in-aid to tuition, fees, and books, and award them only on the basis of need.

If some or all of these suggestions are implemented, intercollegiate athletics may become a more positive, educational experience for athletes.

The abuse of drugs by college athletes and the desire by the NCAA to curtail their use has led to drug testing at football bowl games and NCAA championships (see Box 11-7). Although only a few athletes have been barred from competition because of use of banned drugs, many claim that institutional drug-testing programs have deterred many athletes from the use of performance-enhancing drugs. Still, many college athletes are guilty of perjury when they sign the pledge required by the NCAA stating they do not use these substances. Even the drug education programs offered by colleges and universities have failed to eradicate this blemish on the reputation of intercollegiate athletics.

The use of anabolic steroids is especially dangerous. Besides providing unfair physical advantages, anabolic steroids can severely harm those who abuse them. These drugs may cause users to behave violently on and off the field. Their abuse is often linked with an obsession to earn a starting position, become a star player, or get drafted into a professional league. Amphetamine abuse may also occur under the guise of increasing one's aggressiveness and effort. Cocaine, marijuana, tobacco, and alcohol are more likely to be used socially or for relaxation. As with other college students, most athletes' drug of choice is alcohol, even though most are underage drinkers. Coaches therefore face the challenge of educating their athletes about the negative effects of drug abuse as well as about the rules and values violated through their use.

To preserve the integrity of intercollegiate sports, coaches and athletic administrators must also resolve issues of institutional control. Several institutions have failed to keep overeager supporters from giving money, cars, clothes, and other benefits to athletes. Although not illegal, these actions violate NCAA rules governing payments to athletes. In the intense recruiting battles for blue-chip athletes, coaches may convince admissions committees to lower entrance standards. Many institutions have been criticized for the low graduation rates of athletes, especially African Americans.

Some athletes' conduct also undermines the values thought to be associated with athletics. For example, actions such as taunting opponents and excessive celebrations illustrate that such behavior runs counter to the goals of fair play and respecting one's opponents. Coaches' physical and emotional abuse of players is

BOX 11-7 DRUG TESTING

Sport-governing organizations at the school, college, and professional levels, in an affirmation of their commitment to fair and equitable sports competitions, have specified that certain performance-enhancing drugs are banned. To prevent athletes from gaining artificial advantages through drugs or to deter athletes from the use of drugs that have been proven harmful to health, participants are required to submit to drug testing on a regular and/or random basis. Banned drugs include stimulants such as amphetamines, cocaine, and anabolic steroids. (See www.ncaa.org/sports_sciences/drugtesting/banned_list.html#stimulants for a complete list of drugs banned by the NCAA.)

In NCAA institutions, for example, to be eligible for intercollegiate competitions, student-athletes must sign a consent form indicating their understanding of the drug-testing program and their willingness to participate in it. Member institutions must conduct a drug and alcohol education program once per semester to raise the awareness of student-athletes about the harmful effects of drug use and inform them about institutional and NCAA drug policies. In addition, all student-athletes competing in Division I and II football and Division I men's and women's track and field are subject to random on-campus testing from August through June. During 2001–2002, approximately 9,000 student athletes were tested through this random process for use of anabolic agents, diuretics, and urine manipulators. The National Center for Drug Free Sport randomly selects, based on institutional squad lists, football and track and field programs for short-notice testing (less than 48 hours' notice to the schools).

The World Anti-Doping Code, developed by the World Anti-Doping Agency and adopted internationally in 2003, seeks to level the playing field in Olympic sports. This code, which provides a framework for anti-doping policies as well as rules and regulations, is designed to ensure harmonization of anti-doping efforts across all sports. The code was developed because of increasing abuse of drugs to enhance potential for winning medals in the Olympics despite the fact that doping contravenes the values and fundamental principles of Olympism and medical ethics. Since doping threatens the athlete's health and the integrity of Olympic sport and its ideals, extensive drug testing pervades the Olympic Games and, unfortunately, results in disqualification of gold medalists and public exposure and sanctioning of guilty athletes, as seen repeatedly during the Sydney Games in 2000. Among the prohibited drugs in the Olympics are stimulants, narcotics, anabolic agents, and diuretics. Blood doping and other forms of pharmacological and chemical manipulation are also forbidden.

another example of such destructive behavior. In addition, misdemeanors and felonies, such as driving under the influence of alcohol, using illegal drugs, and sexual assaults and rape, have negatively affected the image of athletes as well as institutions. Booster clubs or athletic foundations have also repeatedly paid off the contracts of coaches with whom they have become disillusioned for not winning enough games or to entice a coach to leave another institution. Such actions always raise the question of who is in control of athletics. These examples describe situations at only a few of the nationally prominent universities that may have failed to maintain institutional control over their big-time athletic programs.

INTERNATIONAL SPORTS

Elite athletes around the world have numerous opportunities to compete in championship events annually, as well as in special events such as the Pan-American Games, the Asian Games, the British Empire and Commonwealth Games, and the World University Games. These events, open to athletes from the countries implicit in the games' titles, are conducted every four years except for

WEB CONNECTIONS

1. http://ed-web3.educ.msu.edu/ysi
   The Institute for the Study of Youth Sports developed the Program for Athletic Coaches' Education and conducts research in many areas relative to youth and school sports.

2. www.paralympic.org
   Learn more about the International Paralympic Games, which are competitions in elite sports for athletes with disabilities.

3. www.specialolympics.org
   The Special Olympics is an international program of year-round sports training and athletic competition for more than 1 million children and adults with mental retardation. Check out this site for a wealth of information about the history, philosophy, and programs of Special Olympics.

4. www.nationalseniorgames.org/virtualmall/index.mv?Screen=
   SFNT&Store_Code=0022
   The National Senior Games Association promotes healthier lifestyles for seniors through education, fitness, and sports competitions and governs the Summer (in 18 sports) and Winter (in 7 sports) Senior Games.

5. www.naia.org/
   Check out this site to find out more about the National Association of Intercollegiate Athletics, which governs intercollegiate competition for over 300 small colleges in 13 sports.

6. www.njcaa.org
   Learn more about the National Junior College Athletic Association, which governs intercollegiate competition in 16 sports for its over 500 member two-year colleges.

Competitive opportunities in international sport include cycling. (Photo courtesy Craig Premo.)

the World University Games, which are held every two years. All of these are important competitions, but the most prestigious internationally are the Olympic Games (patterned after the ancient Greek spectacle). Since 1896 (and 1924 for the Winter Games) athletes from around the world have competed every four years (except during World Wars I and II) under the direction of the International Olympic Committee (IOC). Since 1994, the Winter Games have been held in even-numbered years alternating with the Summer Games.

The Olympic Games have faced numerous threats to their ideals, with politics being the chief detractor. From the inception of the Games through the attempt by the Nazis to prove Aryan supremacy in 1936 to the boycotts of 1976, 1980, and 1984, countries have attempted to use the Olympics to advance their political agendas and influence public opinion. The worst political situation occurred during the 1972 Munich Olympic Games when Arab terrorists massacred 11 Israeli athletes. The banning of some countries and the nonrecognition of others prove that the Olympic Games remain political. Athletes competing as representatives of their nations, the playing of national anthems during the awards ceremonies, national medal counts, team sports, and national uniforms consistently reinforce nationalism. Governments, financially and ideologically, continue to increase their involvement because international prestige and promotion of their political ideologies are at stake. Judging irregularities often result from political alliances, while increased use of drugs verifies the importance placed on winning.

Commercialism has grown exponentially. For example, the 1968 Mexico City Games cost $250 million to stage, while the 1980 Moscow Games reportedly cost over $2 billion. CBS paid $660,000 to broadcast the 1960 events; NBC televised the 1996 Olympic Games at a cost of about $800 million worldwide. One blatant example of the commercialism tainting the Olympics has been the bribes associated with site selection and privileged treatment of IOC members. The athletes are not immune to commercialism either. Although the Olympic Games were begun for amateur athletes competing for the love of sport, today most athletes are professionals, with each sport's governing federation specifying what competitors are allowed to accept monetarily. Many athletes receive money from their countries based specifically on how many medals and what types (gold, silver, or bronze) they win. The list could continue, but the point is that few, if any, Olympic athletes are amateurs in the sense of never having profited from their athletic skill.

In spite of these problems, the Olympic Games thrive and continue to increase in popularity. The development of friendships and the attainment of personal athletic goals are two of the many positive outcomes. Most disdain the boycotts, political maneuvering, unfair judging, and drug abuse, since these incidents only detract from the integrity of the Olympic Games. Commercialization of the overall staging and of the athletes themselves is a nuisance to be tolerated rather than a reason to end the competitions. Many people advocate either reducing the number of events and entries or lengthening the Games and increasing the number of sites and sports. Several support reductions in the symbols of nationalism.

As other nations emphasized Olympic sport success in the decades after World War II, the United States found its traditional dominance lessening, often because of other nations' subsidization of elite athletes. A restructuring of amateur sports in the United States seemed appropriate. Following the passage of the

Jesse Owens, a Big Ten champion from The Ohio State University, won four gold medals in the 1936 Berlin Olympic Games. (Photo courtesy the University of Michigan.)

Amateur Sports Act of 1978, the United States Olympic Committee (USOC) established the United States Olympic Training Center in Colorado Springs, Colorado. It offered to National Governing Bodies for each Olympic sport its resources and facilities as training sites for athletes. The USOC has received some federal funding but relies largely on corporate sponsorships and private donations to support its work. Increasingly, athletes in the lesser-known sports are receiving funding from the USOC to continue training year-round.

SUMMARY

Sports opportunities for girls and women and for minorities of race, age, or ability, often limited in the past, are today more equitable, although some barriers exist that only time and an increased commitment to equity will remove. Youth sports too often overemphasize winning, as do some high school sports. Yet most parents support their children's participation in sports because the positive outcomes outweigh the risks. Balancing educational values with business concerns remains the dilemma facing major college sports today. Abuses abound, yet the public continues to expect colleges to offer athletic programs as entertainment. Similarly, the Olympic ideals, whether real or imagined, seem to ensure people's support of the Olympic Games as politics, nationalism, and commercialization provide insufficient reasons to cancel the spectacle. The pervasiveness of sports (see Box 11-8) in the United States means that people believe sports contribute far more to society than they detract from it. It is the responsibility of those who work in any of these sports arenas to ensure that the potential values to be learned and reinforced through participation in sports are realized by all.

BOX 11-8   SPORTS TIMELINE

Girls and Women in Sports
1972—Congress passed the Education Amendments that included Title IX

Equality for Minorities
1954—U.S. Supreme Court passes *Brown v. Board of Education,* which led to school desegregation with subsequently more equality of opportunity for African American students and loss of positions for African American coaches
1946—Kenny Washington and Woody Strode (Los Angeles Rams) became the first African Americans in the modern era to play in the National Football League
1947—Jackie Robinson (Brooklyn Dodgers) became the first African American in the modern era to play Major League Baseball
1950—Charles Cooper (Boston Celtics) became the first African American in the modern era to play in the National Basketball Association

(continued)

BOX 11-8   SPORTS TIMELINE (CONTINUED)

Equality for Senior Citizens
1987—National Senior Games began

Equality for Individuals with Disabilities
1952—Paralympic Games began to offer competitions for individuals with spinal cord injuries
1968—Special Olympics began to offer competitions for individuals with mental retardation
1978—Amateur Sports Act passed by U.S. Congress mandated meeting the competitive needs of athletes with disabilities
1990—Individuals with Disabilities Education Act passed by U.S. Congress (extended the provisions of Section 504 of the Rehabilitation Act of 1973 and the Education for All Handicapped Children Act of 1975 and subsequent amendments)

Youth Sports
1930—Pop Warner Football began
1939—Little League Baseball established
1950—Biddy Basketball formed
1967—Amateur Athletic Union's Junior Olympics began
1964—American Youth Soccer Organization established

Interscholastic Athletics
1922—National Federation of State High School Associations formed

Intercollegiate Athletics
1852—First intercollegiate sports competition for men held (rowing contest between Harvard and Yale)
1896—First intercollegiate sports competition for women held (basketball game between Stanford and California)
1906—National Collegiate Athletic Association established (began women's competitions in 1981)
1938—National Junior College Athletic Association formed (began women's competitions in 1976)
1952—National Association of Intercollegiate Athletics formed (began women's competitions in 1980)
1971—Association for Intercollegiate Athletics for Women established

International Sports
1896—Modern Olympic Games began
1924—Winter Olympic Games began
1978—Amateur Sports Act passed by U.S. Congress that totally restructured international sport in this country

CAREER PERSPECTIVE

MICHAEL DELONG
Head Football Coach
Springfield University
Springfield, Massachusetts

EDUCATION
B.S., Physical Education, Springfield College
M.A., Physical Education, University of North
Carolina at Chapel Hill

JOB RESPONSIBILITIES AND HOURS

The responsibilities of college and university coaches vary tremendously, depending on the emphasis placed on the institution's program and the sport. Mike organizes and administers an NCAA Division III football program, including directing a staff of two full-time assistant coaches and 12 graduate assistants, recruiting student athletes, planning games and practices, working directly with admissions, raising funds, developing community support, and carrying out on- and off-field coaching duties. He also teaches four semester hours in-season and six to eight semester hours out-of-season, and advises physical education majors—a typical work load at a smaller institution. As with most coaches, Mike's weekly hours, which vary from 85 in-season to 70 off-season to 30 during the summer, are demanding. Salaries are based on each coach's experience and won–lost record, the institution and its reputation, and the sport. At the NCAA Division III level, the salary range is $40,000 to $80,000 for head coaches and $20,000 to $40,000 for assistant coaches.

SPECIALIZED COURSE WORK, DEGREES, AND WORK EXPERIENCES NEEDED FOR THIS CAREER

Although college or university coaching does not require a master's degree, teaching at smaller institutions may require attaining this degree. Physical education is the most common major for coaches at both the undergraduate and graduate levels, although many coaches have degrees in other disciplines. Opportunities to become head coaches usually follow years of coaching high school teams, serving as effective graduate assistants or full-time assistant coaches, or completing successful college or professional playing careers. Volunteering to coach a youth, school, or club team may provide an entry into this career. Mike recommends that prospective coaches emphasize exercise physiology, oral and written communication skills, problem-solving techniques, organizational skills, motivational strategies, and theory and technique courses. He encourages prospective coaches, as well as those already in positions, to visit successful programs and to learn from others.

SATISFYING ASPECTS

People may choose this career because they love a particular sport, want to continue associating with it, enjoy teaching its skills and strategies, like to help athletes develop their talents to their optimal levels, or any combination of these and other reasons.

Mike especially enjoys player/coach relationships, coach-to-coach interactions, and the feeling of accomplishment as the team improves. Coaching can be tremendously satisfying, not only in terms of wins and losses but in watching teams and players grow and mature. For Mike, helping individuals reach their goals is the most rewarding part of coaching.

JOB POTENTIAL

Mike states that to be secure in a college or university coaching position, winning is essential. If you perform within the rules, he says, you will be secure; if you do not perform within the rules, you can expect to be relieved of your duties. Promotion is also based on performance. Coaches who are proven workers have a good chance for advancement in the profession. Politics also plays a role, so it helps to know people. Since getting your foot in the door is difficult and highly competitive, a major part of the initial hiring process is knowing someone who can help you secure a full-time position. Once you have proven your abilities and made connections with people, things generally go a little easier. The job market is extremely competitive, especially for the best jobs. Patience and perseverance are two characteristics essential for success.

SUGGESTIONS FOR STUDENTS

Mike states that coaching is a wonderful career because of the fun and excitement. Coaches are surrounded by great people who like to work and play hard. The rewards of developing players and a team to perform to their fullest potential are tremendous. Mike advises that prior to becoming a coach, make sure you are ready to make a full commitment, because the players you will coach deserve your best effort. Your family also must be aware of the sacrifices they will have to make to the time demands of this career. He adds that you need to be flexible and ready to overcome obstacles and setbacks; there are both extreme highs and extreme lows with which you must cope. The rewards of coaching are directly proportional to the effort you put into the team. If you give your best, coaching is well worth the effort in the long run.

REVIEW QUESTIONS

1. What are three ways in which social factors have inhibited girls' and women's involvement in sports?

2. What have been the positive and negative effects of Title IX on sports opportunities for females?

3. How have minorities faced discrimination in sports?

4. What are three common problems facing youth sports programs, and how would you recommend solving them?

5. What are three issues associated with interscholastic sports, and how would you recommend dealing with each?

6. What do "no pass, no play" and "pay-for-play" policies mean in relation to interscholastic sports?

7. What are three major problems facing intercollegiate athletics today, and how would you recommend solving them?

8. How has the winning = fans = money = winning = fans = money cycle affected the integrity of sports today?

9. How does nationalism pervade the Olympic Games, and what are the positives and negatives of this trend?

10. How can sports contribute to value development?

STUDENT ACTIVITIES

1. Interview students about their attitudes toward girls and women in sport. Ask them what financial support women should receive, which team sports should be available to them, who should coach them, as well as other, related questions. What changes have they observed in society's acceptance of girls and women in sport?

2. Interview two minority athletes on your campus. Ask them whether they have experienced any discrimination during their sports careers and, if so, have them describe it. Have they seen or experienced any changes in how they are treated today as opposed to how they were treated when they first began playing sports at the college level?

3. Based on your attendance at a youth sport event, what were the philosophy and values of that program? What should they have been? Was winning emphasized too much? If so, what indicated that winning was overemphasized?

4. Is the intercollegiate athletic program at your institution a business or a component of education? Can it be both? If so, how?

5. List several possible changes that could improve the Olympic Games. Which of these are realistic alternatives?

6. Interview senior citizens who have participated in Senior Games or masters events or who are active sports participants. What are their reasons for competing and for being active? Has their involvement been lifelong, or is it a recent lifestyle change?

7. Stage a class debate addressing the topic "Athletics do/do not have a place in our educational system."

8. Attend a youth sports practice session and tabulate the number of times the coach(es) provide positive and corrective feedback, the amount of time spent on task such as in drills and observing skill demonstrations, and the methods used for learning motor skills.

9. Locate in a newspaper or magazine an illustration of biased journalism in the coverage of girls and women in sport. Discuss how this article depicts these athletes.

10. Interview a female who participated in sports prior to Title IX. Ask her what has changed in women's sports since that time.

SUGGESTED READINGS

Brown TN, Jackson JS, Brown KT, Sellers RM, Keiper S, Manuel WJ: "There's no race on the playing field": perceptions of racial discrimination among white and black athletes, *J of Sp & Soc Issues* 27(2):162, 2003. The authors provide insights into how differently white and black athletes look at racial issues and discriminatory practices in sport.

Carpenter LJ: Drug testing and the Constitution, *Strategies* 16(6):23, 2003. The author provides an overview of the legal issues associated with the fourth (unreasonable searches and seizures), fifth (self-incrimination), and fourteenth (equal protection under the law) amendments to the U.S. Constitution as they relate to drug testing.

Gilbert WD, Gilbert JN, Trudel P: Coaching strategies for youth sports part 1: athlete behavior and athlete performance, *JOPERD* 72(4):29, 2001 and Coaching strategies for youth sports part 2: personal characteristics, parental influence, and team organization, *JOPERD* 72(5):41, 2001. In these two articles, the authors share insights from 19 volunteer coaches of ice hockey and soccer, who had a combined 166 years of experience, in answering questions about issues that youth sport coaches face and the most effective coaching strategies used to address these issues.

Hartmann D: Notes on midnight basketball and the cultural politics of recreation, race, and at-risk urban youth, *J of Sp & Soc Issues* 25(4):339, 2001. The author examines the late-night recreational basketball leagues that were established mostly in the 1990s for young men in mainly minority, inner-city neighborhoods in the context of contemporary political discourse and public policy. Questions are raised about how effective these leagues are in preventing or reducing crime and delinquency and whether they provide a source of meaning and accomplishment for participants.

Knapp TJ, Rasmussen C, Barnhart RK: What college students say about intercollegiate athletics: a survey of attitudes and beliefs, *Coll Stu J* 35(1):96, 2001. In a survey at the University of Nevada at Las Vegas, college students were found to be supportive of intercollegiate athletics regardless of whether they attended or appreciated these events. Most students did not think student-athletes were serious about their studies and believed that some student athletes received favorable academic treatment from faculty.

McKenzie KB: Grassroots sports for physically disabled becoming a reality, *Parks & Rec* 37(3):60, 2002. Increasingly, recreation programs are providing competitive sports opportunities for individuals with disabilities.

Miller JL, Heinrich MD, Baker R: A look at Title IX and women's participation in sport, *The Phy Educ* 57(1):8, 2000. The results of two surveys reveal that one specific college was in compliance with Title IX though many other institutions are not and that a lower level of interest in sport was expressed by women in comparison with men at that institution. Regarding the latter item, this may be as a result of women having fewer opportunities in sport.

Sullivan KA, Lantz PJ, Zirkel PA: Leveling the playing field or leveling the players? Section 504, the Americans with Disabilities Act, and interscholastic sports, *J Spec Educ* 33(4):258, 2000. This article offers a systematic synthesis of the agency and court rulings that apply Section 504, the Americans with Disabilities Act, and the Individuals with Disabilities Education Act to interscholastic athletics. A framework provides insight into how these federal statutes pertain to the participation of students with disabilities in extracurricular activities.

Watts J: Perspectives on sport specialization, *JOPERD* 73(8):32, 2002. The author presents many of the advantages and disadvantages of high school athletes focusing their training and competition on one sport. An awareness of the issues is suggested if this choice this made.

Wood RH, Reyes R, Welsch MA, Favaloro-Sabatier J, Sabatier M, Matthew LC, Johnson LG, Hooper PF: Concurrent cardiovascular resistance training in healthy older adults, *Med & Sci in Sp & Exer* 33(10):1751, 2001. This study verified the importance of comprehensive training programs that combine resistance and cardiovascular components for the functional fitness of healthy adults.

12

LIVING ACTIVELY IN THE TWENTY-FIRST CENTURY

KEY CONCEPTS

- Life in the twenty-first century will differ dramatically from today's world and significantly affect the role of physical activity programs.
- Leadership is important for physical educators, exercise scientists, and sport professionals.
- A new name for the field of physical education reflects its changing image.
- The promotion of physical activity is essential for increasing participation levels.
- Physical activity is a highly valued part of life.

INTRODUCTORY SCENARIO I—LIVING IN 2050

At 7' 7", 275 pounds, Jimmy broke every national high school scoring and re-bounding record during the 2049–2050 season. A basketball phenomenon, he touched off a recruiting frenzy that quickly exceeded sports fans' wildest imaginations. But to get Jimmy, everyone had to go through James, Sr., who had genetically engineered his son and then relentlessly conditioned, fed, and trained him physically and mentally using the latest technologies and drugs. James, Sr., announced to the world that Jimmy's talents could be obtained, but only for a huge price.

State University offered Jimmy a new car, a condo of his choice, a $100,000-per-year salary, and a bonus to rename the basketball arena in his father's honor if Jimmy helped the semipro Golden Knights win the NCAA Championship.

The New York Kings, the leading professional basketball franchise, tried to entice Jimmy to leap to its league directly out of high school. They implored James, Sr., to allow Jimmy to sign a $30 million-per-year, 20-year, no-cut contract. As an incentive, the Kings added a $50 million bonus for each season Jimmy won the league's Most Valuable Player award.

The NRA conglomerate (formerly Nike, Reebok, and Adidas) promised to introduce the Jamming Jimmy autograph shoe one month later if Jimmy signed its

$1 million-per-week endorsement agreement. If he signed, Jamming Jimmy cloth-
ing and sports equipment would be marketed within six months.

International Sports Marketing (ISM), however, succeeded in getting James,
Sr., to grant it monopolistic control over Jimmy's career. Jimmy would play for
State University for one year before joining the Kings. He would sign with NRA immediately and wear his autograph shoe at the university, but defer the $1 million
per week and other endorsements until he joined the Kings. All of the promised
payouts were guaranteed; plus, ISM would negotiate for Jimmy an additional
$10 million per year in endorsements managed by ISM.

INTRODUCTORY SCENARIO II—LIVING IN 2050

By the midpoint of the twenty-first century most Americans' lives will be completely different from those lived by earlier generations, even as recently as a half-
century earlier. Every school child's education is totally computer based and
individualized according to his or her learning style. Within this somewhat sterile
learning environment, physical education, including dance and sport, has become essential for developing children's social, emotional, and physical skills.
These daily school programs for youth from ages 3 to 20 focus on individualized
fitness programs, environmentally safe outdoor activities, and cooperative sports
in addition to games developed and initiated by the students.

Parents are infused into the school environment—in the classroom and
gymnasium—because the year-round school day starts at 7:00 A.M. and continues
until 7:00 P.M. With more single-parent, non-Caucasian families, schools provide
continuing education for parents, enrichment activities in extended day programs
for children, and leisure-time activities for all ages. Social service and governmental agencies work with and through the schools to provide health care and
counseling, recreational programs, and career education.

Within this technological society, a huge economic gap has developed.
Those without advanced skills and knowledge provide services; those with these
skills work in technology-based careers, expanding the boundaries of knowledge
as they lead the Information Age. Menial tasks, such as manufacturing, are completed by robots or through other nonhuman technologies. Restaurants have
been replaced by food packets and pills to save time and money. Americans' fas-
cination with the automobile has been eradicated and replaced by fast, efficient
mass transit. Work requirements have increased, with most employees choosing
to spend an average of 50 hours per week on the job. Despite these work hours,
with less time needed for transportation and eating, there is greater leisure time,
which is spent mostly in inactive pastimes such as searching the Internet and
watching over 1,000 television channels.

The threat of heart disease, increasingly the number one killer, has finally
begun to catch Americans' attention. Within the past decade, the percentage of
adults engaged in physical activity has risen 50 percent, while 75 percent more
school children are physically active. Extended school programs, private fitness
and health centers, and the use of home exercise equipment have been credited
with these dramatic improvements. The challenge for physical educators, exercise

Children enjoy playing because they have fun.

scientists, recreation directors, health educators, dance specialists, and sport leaders is how to promote the value of physical activity for all.

Are you ready for life in the twenty-first century? Do these scenarios accurately predict reality a half-century from now? This chapter attempts to describe what living in the twenty-first century may be like. It focuses on building on the fields of physical education, exercise science, and sport as described previously to help prepare you for the future.

Physical educators have often followed, rather than led, in Americans' participation in sports and activities. As a result, the importance and prestige of physical education in the schools and sports for all have suffered. Survival of school programs and educationally based sports programs may be in jeopardy. To take a leading role in the sports and fitness movement, physical educators, exercise scientists, and sport professionals in various settings need to improve the quality of their programs and better publicize the potentially valuable outcomes of these programs. Fitness leaders must publicize and document the benefits of active lifestyles for all segments of the population. To add credibility to this advocacy, physical educators, exercise scientists, and sport professionals must become role models of fitness.

Physical educators, exercise scientists, and sport professionals can guarantee accountability in instructional quality by making curricula and programs more humanizing to meet students' and clients' needs, keeping abreast of the knowledge explosion and applying this research-based information, providing equal opportunities for diverse populations, and refocusing athletics to ensure that educational outcomes are imperatives for the future.

LEADERSHIP IN PHYSICAL EDUCATION, EXERCISE SCIENCE, AND SPORT

Leadership is essential for individuals working in physical education, exercise science, and sport careers. Leadership is a behavioral process in which one person attempts to influence other people's behaviors toward the accomplishment of shared goals. Stated another way, leadership is the creation of a vision of potential opportunities along with the empowerment of others who can translate that vision into reality.

Among the descriptors characterizing leaders are the following:

- Visionary
- Creative
- Risk taker
- Global thinker
- Effective communicator
- Committed to excellence and high standards
- Energetic
- Self-confident
- Courageous
- Has integrity

Each of these characteristics will be elaborated on in the context of physical education, exercise science, and sport careers to help you understand the critical role each serves in developing and maintaining quality in our work.

A visionary establishes goals that answer the questions "Where are we going?" "What do we want and why?" and "How will we get there?" In response to the first question, an exercise scientist might investigate several alternative cardiac rehabilitation programs to determine the most effective approach to prescribing exercise programs for patients. Relative to the second question, the goal of the sport manager may be to increase season ticket sales by 50 percent and use the increased revenues to make renovations to the football stadium. In response to the third question, the physical educator may choose to use heart rate monitors, aerobic exercise machines, and the *Physical Best* educational materials to help each student develop and maintain a personal cardiovascular endurance program. A visionary believes passionately in goals or aspirations and diligently works to achieve them. Fitness specialists are willing to spend long hours enhancing their knowledge, learning and using innovative instructional approaches, and expanding their physical activity program offerings to get participants to achieve their fitness goals. The visionary leader possesses charisma that sparks others' interest in and commitment to shared goals; thus, this characteristic is at the heart of leadership.

A leader is creative in determining how to achieve goals through the associated processes or steps. Creativity is evident in the planning of curricula, developing and implementing of a marketing plan for a fitness club or athletic team, and organizing recreational activities for senior citizens.

The leader as a risk taker believes the action or direction to be taken is right even though it may appear difficult or seemingly impossible. The youth sport coach who asks unruly, boisterous, or profane parents to leave rather than allow participants to be yelled at takes a risk of resentment or retaliation. The exercise science researcher explores hypotheses that others have avoided because they take years to explore since the potential benefits outweigh the risks. A leader who is willing to take risks challenges the status quo, continually asking "Why not?" and then proceeding to answer this question.

The leader who is a global thinker refuses to be confined by what has not yet been attempted. The fitness specialist working with senior citizens motivates them to challenge themselves to a higher level of fitness and sports proficiency. The professional sports team manager markets team merchandise internationally through new sales venues and innovative media approaches.

A leader who is an effective communicator shows a respect for others that includes being a good listener and a thoughtful respondent. The physical educator as leader models how each student is equally valued and has the potential to learn. The high school coach ensures that each athlete understands what contributions can and should be made in achieving the team's goals for the season. The athletic administrator convinces donors to finance a new fitness center through a clear articulation of the importance of this facility to athletes' development.

Each leader is committed to excellence and high standards and demonstrates this through daily actions and words. Compromise in expectations and acceptance of inferior performances are not tolerated. The recreational professional insists that safe, organized, equitable, and enjoyable programs be provided for each participant. The exercise physiologist will not permit sloppy research or inaccurate reporting of research findings.

A leader who is energetic appears to work tirelessly. Each class of students, each group of clients, or each team receives the undivided attention and full commitment of the teacher, exercise specialist, or coach. The leader appears to exude energy to others because of a passionate desire to achieve the shared vision. Individuals in physical activity careers are normally role models for fitness, which energizes them to help others achieve a similar high quality of life.

The leader is usually so convinced of the rightness of the vision that self-confidence is readily apparent. No one can deter the self-confident leader from proving that the chosen direction is in the best interests of the group. The personal trainer believes that every client can attain and maintain a physically active lifestyle. The teacher and the coach are knowledgeable in their sports and activities in ways that permeate and positively affect students and athletes.

The leader must be courageous in pursuit of the vision, even when others raise questions or challenges. New teaching approaches or experimental research designs are seldom welcomed and frequently derided. Yet regardless of the disclaimers or adversities faced, the courageous leader advances.

Unless the leader has integrity, the ruse will eventually be discovered. Values such as honesty, fairness, and beneficence are integral to gaining respect from others as well as eliciting their participation in attaining the vision of the physical education, exercise science, and sport professional.

WHAT WILL THE TWENTY-FIRST CENTURY BRING?

The world in the twenty-first century will continue to differ from preceding eras, with numerous changes in the field of physical education, exercise science, fitness, and sport. Several projections based on the continuation of current trends follow. They are divided into the categories of school programs, higher education, athletics, exercise science, and fitness careers. Consider whether these proposed changes and trends will become reality. How will they affect society and you and your career? Are these possibilities desirable? If not, what can be done to avert any undesired outcomes?

School Programs

- Physical education will achieve the established standards for student achievement and, through performance assessment, respond to the call for educational accountability.
- Physical education curricula will emphasize fitness development and maintenance as well as learning psychomotor skills and enhancing social and emotional skills.
- Physical educators will incorporate technology and computer skills into their programs to enhance learning.
- Significantly more minority teachers will be recruited and retained to serve as role models for an increasing number of minority students.
- Coaching certifications will be required of all interscholastic coaches.

The integration of technology into instruction helps students learn.

- Competency entrance and exit tests will be required of prospective teachers.
- Physical educators will continuously upgrade their instructional abilities and content knowledge.
- An appropriate reward system will be implemented to recognize excellence in teaching and coaching.
- Performance, more than longevity, will determine merit pay and career advancement.

Higher Education

- Five-year teacher education programs that include a master's degree will become the standard, while increasingly advanced education and certifications (beyond the bachelor's degree) will be required of sport and exercise practitioners.
- The number of graduates with specializations in fitness, exercise physiology, athletic training, fitness, and sport management will increase.
- Elective physical education activity programs focusing on aerobic activities, weight training, outdoor activities, and lifetime sports will continue to thrive.
- More and more college degrees will be completed online, using a variety of technologies.
- College students will be older, more career oriented, and more diverse in background.

Just as the pole vaulter focuses on the goal ahead, physical educators, exercise scientists, and sport professionals must focus on what contributions they can make in the twenty-first century. (Photo courtesy Maggie McGlynn.)

- College professors will specialize even more in one of the exercise or sport sciences.
- More minority faculty members will be recruited and retained to serve as teachers of and mentors for minority students.
- Increased research productivity will be required for promotion and tenure, although scholarship will be defined more broadly.

Athletics

- Coaching certifications will be required of all youth sport coaches.
- The emphasis on winning in sports at all levels will intensify because of lucrative rewards.
- Value development will still be espoused, although only marginally attained.
- College athletic programs will become more commercialized and more dependent on financial subsidies from educational institutions, sponsors, and donors.
- Drug use and abuse by athletes will increase at all levels.
- The use of technological advances will enhance athletes' skills and performances.
- Competitive opportunities for girls, women, minorities, individuals with disabilities, and senior citizens in sports will continue to increase.

Exercise Science

- Exercise physiologists will collaborate more extensively with physicians and other health care providers in investigating how exercise affects various quality-of-life issues.
- Governmental agencies will increasingly support research that addresses health issues such as obesity and heart disease.

Sports will increasingly attract females who welcome the chance to display their skills. (Photo courtesy Maggie McGlynn.)

WEB CONNECTIONS

1. www.healthy.american.edu/nchfcarln.html
    This site for the National Center for Health Fitness provides information about and posts résumés for full-time and part-time jobs as well as internships.

2. www.ed.gov/free/s-edtech.html
    Check out the free educational technology materials available from this site of the Federal Resources for Educational Excellence.

3. http://sportsvl.com/home.htm
    This site for the Virtual Library of Sport links you to a wealth of Internet resources.

4. www.welcoa.org
    The Wellness Councils of America work with local organizations and individuals to design, deliver, and sustain results-oriented work site wellness programs.

5. www.nal.usda.gov/fnic
    This site of the Food and Nutrition Information Center of the U.S. Department of Agriculture's Research Service provides extensive information about nutrition and related resources.

6. www.americanheart.org
    This site of the American Heart Association offers extensive information about healthy lifestyles and other resources relative to the importance of exercise for all ages.

- Biomechanics and motor learning specialists will use their research and analytical abilities to greatly enhance sport performance into times, distances, and expertise levels thought impossible today.
- Athletic trainers working with physicians and other exercise scientists will expand the scope of their interventions to help athletes prevent and rehabilitate from injuries.
- Exercise physiologists will expand their research through randomized, clinical trials in schools, businesses, recreational programs, and senior citizen residential complexes to answer nutritional and fitness questions.
- Sport psychologists will become increasing important in helping collegiate, professional, and international athletes achieve their potential.
- Exercise scientists will become increasingly specialized in their research focus while working in hospital, clinical, and research laboratories as well as university settings.

- Greater emphasis will be placed on translating research findings in the exercise sciences into practical applications by individuals of all ages as they engage in physical activity.

Fitness

- Fitness instructors and managers will help change participation levels of adults, leading to significant lifestyle changes.
- Physical fitness and sport programs for senior citizens will expand dramatically as individuals live longer and healthier lives.
- Businesses will increasingly provide fitness programs for their employees to help control escalating health care costs.
- Technology will significantly improve fitness equipment, recreational facilities, and physical activity programs.
- Sport and physical activity programs for children, adolescents, and their parents will proliferate through extended day programs in schools.
- Outdoor activities will continue to attract new enthusiasts.
- Consumers will become more discriminating in their purchases of fitness equipment, selection of sports to participate in, and nutritional choices to reduce calories, fat, and cholesterol.
- Baccalaureate and master's degrees, continual upgrading of skills and knowledge, and advanced certifications will be required of instructors and managers in fitness careers.

THE TWENTY-FIRST CENTURY PHYSICAL ACTIVITY SPECIALIST

In education, those who follow you at your college or university will probably have to complete five years of course work if they choose a teaching career in schools. Such a requirement is a likely outgrowth of the emphasis on obtaining a liberal arts education before becoming certified as a teacher. Everyone, in all careers, will be expected—even required—to continually retrain, upgrade, and recertify to keep abreast of the knowledge explosion. If you do not have the sophistication mandated by the Information Age, such as computer literacy for evaluating health risk profiles and prescribing and monitoring exercise programs, you may not be competitive in the job market.

Not only must you be an astute consumer yourself in this era of marketing mania, but you will be called on to help those you teach or direct to discriminate between fact and fallacy. You must teach athletes what food or drugs to consume or training regimens to safely follow in their quest for success. You must be prepared to differentiate between effective and ineffective exercise equipment and diets. You will be questioned concerning whether certain behaviors in sports are ethical, whether the exercises provided by a certain fitness program or instructor are appropriate, and whether the schools, communities, or both should provide fitness programs for school-age children. You may need to become an advocate for "truth in advertising" because quackery in fitness, exercise, health, and nutrition abounds. Because of the increasing popularity of this broad field, many charlatans will eagerly take consumers' money and even allow them to risk their health and well-being unless you help the buyer beware.

Social issues continuing to influence our lives, such as aging and technology, will call for our involvement. Meeting the leisure needs of an older American populace will demand that fitness, recreational, and educational leaders develop and implement programs that are appropriate for these individuals' needs. We will not categorize people of retirement age or older as nonproductive or nonenergetic. This segment of the population will demand to have its fitness needs met through seniors or masters competitions, daily walks in malls, aerobics, bowling leagues, or golf. It will also be important to provide inexpensive physical activity opportunities for those on fixed incomes.

The technology of the twenty-first century will probably astound each of us. Incorporating technology into fitness programs through the use of blood pressure and heart rate monitors on exercise equipment, computers to assess health risks and dietary problems, and videotaping and computer analysis to improve sports performance will allow technology to contribute to exercise safety and skill enhancement. Televised and videotaped exercise classes for home use, for school-age children, at the work site, and in retirement homes may increase due to economic constraints and increased demand for fitness programs.

The environment will also continue to concern many people as they consider what possible irreparable damages our lifestyles may be heaping on future generations. Backpackers, rock climbers, campers, and hikers will be challenged to enjoy nature while leaving it untarnished for those who follow. Ensuring urban green space and protecting state and national parks will be other ways in which recreation specialists will be able to leave a legacy.

CHANGING IDENTITY—FROM PHYSICAL EDUCATION TO EXERCISE SCIENCE AND SPORT STUDIES

When school and college programs involving the development of motor skills were initially developed in the late 1800s and early 1900s, they were called *gymnastics* or *physical training*. Gradually the descriptive term for these programs was changed to *physical education* as an affirmation that this educational field could uniquely contribute to the psychomotor development of students. The term *physical education* continues to appropriately describe school and college programs that focus on participation in fitness, sports, and other physical activities. State requirements determine the number and length of physical education classes attended by school children where they learn fundamental movement skills, develop a variety of sports skills, and learn lifetime fitness practices. College elective and required programs in physical education continue to offer young adults the opportunities to learn new skills, increase abilities in preferred sports skills, and maintain personal fitness.

The term most often used by nonschool agencies, such as public recreational programs or private sports clubs, has never been physical education. Within the past few years, many of these and similar programs have identified themselves using terms such as *fitness, physical activity,* and *wellness.* Since they were not associated with educational institutions, the term *physical education* never appropriately explained their emphases on fun and healthy lifestyles.

Following the emergence of the specialty areas of exercise physiology, sport psychology, motor learning, and others in the 1970s, many in higher education began to question whether the term *physical education* accurately encompassed the tremendous expansion in knowledge in these new fields. These professors did not want to be saddled with what was perceived as an outdated and constricting name, especially one that was alleged to be nonacademic. Years of discussions and national surveys yielded dozens of proposed name changes, but no consensus for a new name for the field emerged. Several advocated for *kinesiology;* others preferred *human movement* or *human performance* as more inclusive of the various specialties. On college and university campuses, departmental names continue to vary widely as each seeks to find an identity that describes the scope of what it does and studies.

Most professionals in the fields associated with physical activity will agree that their professional history is built on physical education. But they prefer to identify themselves as exercise physiologists, motor development specialists, biomechanists, fitness specialists, or athletic trainers. Like many university departments, this book has used the term *exercise science* to encompass these and related fields. Individuals in sport history, sport sociology, sport management, and sport philosophy also believe that *sport studies* more accurately describes what they do. Thus, *sport* has been included throughout this book as a single vital component in the broad definition of this field. Less important than the preferred name is the

Children are our future. They need to enjoy movement and learn to value it during their early years.

commitment to contribute to the knowledge base associated with physical activity and to encourage all people to make physical activity a part of their lives.

PROMOTING PHYSICAL ACTIVITY

Coronary artery disease accounts for over 40 percent of deaths in this country, with physical inactivity being one of the major risk factors. The American Heart Association (AHA) is a leading advocate for each person attaining and maintaining a moderate level of fitness by exercising three to four times a week for 30 to 60 minutes at 50 to 80 percent of maximal capacity. Since physical activity can prevent coronary artery disease and help manage associated risk factors like elevated triglyceride levels, hypertension, and obesity, the promotional activities listed above and others should be supported. For example, health care professionals, exercise scientists, sport managers, and others should model active living, ensure that schools teach psychomotor and sports skills so young people will engage in physically active lifestyles, and encourage communities to develop exercise and sports programs for all ages and ability levels. The AHA is a leader in providing informational and promotional resources, such as the following:

- Just Move with responses to frequently asked questions and links to other fitness resources (www.justmove.org)
- Exercise and Fitness (www.americanheart.org/presenter.jhtml?identifier=1200013)
- Physical Activity in Daily Life (www.americanheart.org/presenter.jhtml?identifier=2155)
- Choose to Move, a self-paced, 12-week program for women (www.choosetomove.org/about.html)

Accountability for program content and results is essential and will continue to grow in importance. Without quality and benefits accruing to those served, no program merits continuation. If children, club members, athletes, senior citizens, or corporate employees are not being taught the skills and knowledge they seek through activity or sports programs, elimination of the activity, or at least replacement of the teacher or leader, is warranted. Individuals hired to teach programs owe it to their participants to ensure learning. Abdication of this responsibility should lead to others being hired to do these jobs. For example, accountability in school physical education necessitates that every student achieve content standards established by the National Association for Sport and Physical Education (see Chapter 1).

Linked closely with accountability is the importance of public relations. Traditionally, the perspective taken by individuals in school programs has been a willingness to serve but not a desire to publicize or market programs. Today this attitude is no longer acceptable. Teachers and program leaders, regardless of setting, must publicize the benefits to those who participate in sport and physical activity. To enlist involvement and financial support, programs must be attractive and successful in meeting perceived needs. An additional outcome of

Karate is an example of a nontraditional activity enjoyed by people of all ages. (Photo courtesy Don Ridgeway.)

this concerted effort to tell others what physical education and sport can do for them is that it brings together, rather than drives apart, all physical activity programs. Here are some examples of ways to promote physical activity and sport:

- Get your governor or mayor to proclaim May as Physical Fitness and Sport Month in your state or city.
- Conduct special events such as a family fitness night, a community fun run, or mall exhibitions of physical education during Physical Fitness and Sport Month.
- Celebrate National Employee Health and Fitness Day in May.
- Initiate daily fitness programs in schools and businesses to encourage everyone to participate in 10 minutes of stretching and 30 minutes of aerobic activities.
- Develop public service announcements for local radio and television stations that promote physical activity and include fitness tips.
- Write and publish a newsletter or local newspaper articles about popular physical activities, sports, and fitness.
- Involve a local service organization and the community in developing a fitness trail.

- Ask the school and city libraries to display books about physical activity, sports, and fitness.

- Involve senior citizens with school-age children in intergenerational walks or other recreational activities.

- Plan special events in schools, businesses, and public agencies to celebrate Heart Month (February), National Nutrition Month (March), and Family Health Month (October).

- Celebrate National Girls and Women in Sports Day (first Thursday in February).

- Initiate a sports attire day each month to encourage everyone to dress for and participate in physical activity.

PHYSICAL ACTIVITY THROUGHOUT LIFE

Many people in the middle and upper classes, some of whom are responding to health concerns or to manage their weight better, are choosing to become more active physically. Because of social needs and feelings of self-worth, people of all ages are motivated to join exercise and sports programs. Jogging, fitness clubs, attending fitness camps, and playing golf are examples of the choices being made.

The sports and fitness movement, recognized now as a part of the American way of life rather than a fad, is initiating dramatic changes in physical activity programs. Consumer demand is readily evident for healthy lifestyles that seek to improve the quality of life through physical activity. Physical educators, exercise scientists, and sport professionals must share their knowledge about physiology, nutrition, psychology, and fitness and skill development. You will conduct your programs at the work site as well as in public facilities and private clubs. While helping the corporate executive, you must not neglect lower-income individuals, whose levels of productivity and lifestyles can also be enhanced.

The group whose needs probably will become paramount in the twenty-first century includes individuals 65 years of age and older. Between 1982 and 2050, the percentage of people in this age category will almost double (to over one-fifth of the population). As Americans live longer, they will need lifetime recreational activities, not only to prevent disease and degeneration but also as a way to enjoy happier, healthier lives.

Advances in medicine and technology not only help us live longer but have greatly changed our lives in other ways. Cures for some diseases, advances in heart surgery to prevent coronaries, and electronically stimulated movement of paralyzed limbs are but a few medical breakthroughs that lengthen and invigorate life. Fewer and fewer household and mundane tasks demand our time and energy as machines free us from routine jobs. Although only some of our free time is currently spent developing fitness and enjoying sports and other leisure-time activities, free time will increase in the future. Technological advances directly influence our leisure-time pursuits as well. Better-designed running shoes, exercise machines equipped to monitor fitness levels, biomechanical analyses of

Physical activity begins early and spans our lifetimes.

tennis strokes or other sport skills, and individualized training paradigms already exist. Undoubtedly advances in sporting equipment, clothing, and facilities will continue to enhance performance as well as pleasure.

The twenty-first century will expand the Information Age. Personal digital assistants (PDAs), cellular phones, instant messenging, and satellite transmissions are only the beginning. With a service economy based on and mandating communications skills and technology as the norm, we will increasingly turn to sport, fitness, and leisure activities during nonwork hours for rest and stress reduction.

Computer technology already permits exercise scientists to assess fitness levels, design and prescribe exercise programs to meet individualized needs, and monitor the attainment of personal fitness goals. Using database management computer software, corporate fitness leaders can determine the impact of each exercise program offered by using attendance numbers and recording fitness parameters. Sport managers can use computers to generate ticket sales solicitations and target marketing campaigns. Computer graphics, desktop publishing, financial forecasts for athletic programs and clubs, students' fitness report cards for parents, biomechanical analyses of athletes' skill performances, and computer-based play calling are a few examples of technological advances affecting programs. (See the Research View box for an exciting development in telemedicine and children's health care.)

Intramural sports give college students opportunities to continue physical activity and competition.

⌕ RESEARCH VIEW

Combining Technology and Health Care

TeleKidcare® is a telemedicine project that helps parents obtain health care for their children in Unified School District (USD) 500 in Kansas City, Kansas, which has a student population of approximately 75 percent ethnic minorities and a similar number on free and reduced lunches. The University of Kansas Medical Center (KUMC) widened the work of its Center for TeleMedicine & TeleHealth (CTT) in 1997 to address the barriers encountered by urban families and school children when attempting to access health care.

School nurses in USD 500 had expressed concern about an emergent alarming trend among school children who were not receiving care for routine acute conditions, such as a suspected strep throat or ear infection, skin irritation, or respiratory ailment. As a result, these children missed several days of school when necessary intervention did not occur in a timely fashion, if at all, due to barriers such as language, inadequate transportation or economic resources, lack of familiarity with the medical community, and citizenship status. When medical treatment was sought, it was often found in the emergency rooms of area hospitals, with their higher costs and adverse impact on scarce medical resources.

TeleKidcare® consists of interactive television (ITV) systems placed in the school health office and in the KUMC Pediatric Clinic that allow the school nurse and the child to see, hear, and interact with the physician. In addition, this state-of-the-art telemedicine technology, equipped with a digital otoscope and an

(continued)

electronic stethoscope, allows physicians to diagnose and treat a wide range of ailments, including acute conditions such as ear and strep infections, as well as chronic conditions, such as attention deficit hyperactivity disorder and asthma.

In addition to the nearly 1,900 health care consultations (consults) in USD 500 via ITV over five years, TeleKidcare® has been instrumental in enhancing the role of the school nurse. No longer simply saddled with various clerical duties, school nurses are enjoying a renewed appreciation from administrators and faculty members alike for their medical assessment skills and ability to inform and educate school children, parents, and school personnel regarding health and wellness concerns.

Parental survey results indicated that 98 percent of parents were "satisfied" or "very satisfied" with services offered through TeleKidcare®, which provides a safe, nonthreatening environment to facilitate the movement of underserved families into an established health care delivery system at school. By utilizing strategies developed by TeleKidcare®, parents can satisfy their children's health care needs without jeopardizing their income, salary, or employment status. By bringing together school nurses, physicians, and parents at the school, this health delivery mechanism provides for a continuum of care unobtainable through traditional school health delivery systems.

One of the most exciting elements of TeleKidcare® is the progress made in its expansion throughout communities in Kansas with funding from the Kansas Children's Initiative Fund. These 15 TeleKidcare® sites in Kansas outside USD 500 are community-focused projects connecting schools with local health care providers. You can learn more about this innovative program at www.osophs.dhhs.gov/ophs/BestPractice/telekidcare_kansas.htm and www2.kumc.edu/telemedicine/programs/telekidcare.htm.

The realm of space travel and the establishment of space colonies broadens our perspective from this country to the importance of viewing how physical education, exercise science, and sport can influence the entire world. Our enthusiasm for sports and fitness is already altering attitudes in other countries. Many professionals share their sports expertise with people in other countries and serve as worldwide models. All of these developments contribute to greater international understanding through the sharing of physical activity.

SUMMARY

Future physical activity leaders hold the keys to the acceptance and promotion of active and healthy lifestyles. Improved curricula based on standards that focus on meeting all students' fitness and lifetime sports and activity skill needs are imperative. The power and potential of physical education, exercise science, and sport is based on a commitment to physical activity, and our nation's health, and maybe even its existence, depends on this commitment. Through technological advances, we must strive to improve the quality of life for ourselves and for others worldwide in the twenty-first century.

CAREER PERSPECTIVE

WINIFRED WARREN LAFORCE
Executive Director
Leadership Triangle
Raleigh, North Carolina

EDUCATION
B.A., University of Florida
M.A., Reading and Language Arts, University of North Carolina at Chapel Hill
M.A., Physical Education with a specialization in Sport Administration, University of North Carolina at Chapel Hill

JOB RESPONSIBILITIES AND HOURS
Through Leadership Triangle, Winkie seeks to build leadership capacity to foster regional awareness, cooperation, and networking across the region's public, private, and civic sectors. She works to recruit and connect emerging and established leaders with people who are committed to understanding the many perspectives of diverse communities. As she crosses boundaries to find common ground on which to address regional issues, Winkie's primary duties are to organize, raise funds, and plan programs and special events. Her key goal is to foster strong local communities working together to preserve and enhance a high quality of life for all residents of the region. She typically works 40 hours a week, except when special events occur that require additional time.

SPECIALIZED COURSE WORK, DEGREES, AND WORK EXPERIENCES NEEDED FOR THIS CAREER
Winkie's varied work experiences have prepared her to advance into this leadership role. Winkie was executive director of the State Games of North Carolina from 1988 to 1990. From 1990 to 1993, she served as president of North Carolina Amateur Sports. She then moved to Atlanta to serve as director of the Sports Department for the 1996 Centennial Olympic Games. She also consulted for the 2000 Olympic Games in Sydney, Australia, and the 1999 Pan American Games in Winnipeg, Canada. Beginning in January 1998, Winkie led North Carolina's effort to bring the 2007 Pan American Games to the Triangle area. During this period, she guided a team of over 600 volunteers and, with the assistance of many corporate citizens, raised over half a million dollars for the bid effort. In 2000, she became executive vice president and general manager of events for Capitol Sports Management, which designed and hosted an Olympic-style, 15-sport event for masters' competitors. Drawing from these extensive management and leadership experiences, as well as her graduate course work, she assumed her current duties in 2002.

SATISFYING ASPECTS
Winkie finds it rewarding to help the region remain one of the best places in the country for all who live and work there. She enjoys the challenges of celebrating the distinctive character and autonomy of local communities while responding to the need to act regionally in dealing with issues such as traffic, water, housing costs, green space, schools, and economic and social equity. She is committed to helping to address these complex issues.

JOB POTENTIAL

Given the increasing popularity of sporting events, opportunities abound for sport managers who are willing to gain skills and knowledge starting in entry-level positions. Salary increases, job security, and career advancement depend on experience, proven performance, and networking. Winkie adds that knowledge and skills learned through sport management can be applied in other settings, such as her current position.

SUGGESTIONS FOR STUDENTS

Winkie states that students must be willing to start at a low salary to "get your foot in the door." She recommends making yourself invaluable to your employers by working hard, including weekends. If you prove your competence and commitment, you can advance in a career that you will find enjoyable and fulfilling.

REVIEW QUESTIONS

1. What factors will influence society and you in your career as the twenty-first century progresses?

2. What changes are projected for school programs in the twenty-first century?

3. What changes are projected for college and university programs in the twenty-first century?

4. What changes are projected for athletic programs in the twenty-first century?

5. What changes are projected for exercise science programs in the twenty-first century?

6. How will technology affect physical activity programs in the future?

7. Should physical education change its name? If so, why?

8. What are several strategies for promoting physical activity for all?

9. Why are even more physical activity programs for senior citizens essential in the future?

10. What is the greatest challenge you will face in your career within the next few years?

STUDENT ACTIVITIES

1. Find five magazine advertisements that validly use physical activity or fitness in marketing their products. Find five magazine advertisements that make outlandish claims about their fitness-related products.

2. Interview three people who teach physical activities in any type of program. Ask them what they think the problems and challenges are for people in their careers or similar careers. What suggestions for improvement do they have?

3. Describe the program offerings of an elementary school, secondary school, college activity program, health club, or recreation department that you think meets the needs of the individuals currently being served. Will these needs differ by 2010? If so, how will these needs be met?

4. Write a two- or three-page paper describing "Living in the Year 2020," when you will be around the midpoint of your career.

SUGGESTED READINGS

Baker JAW, Pan DW, Wade MG: Multidimensional scaling: the name revisited, *Int J Phys Educ* 33(2):76, 1996. In this study, 85 chairpersons of physical education departments were asked to rate attributes associated with 13 potential departmental titles. All except the physical education/teacher education group preferred the name *sport and exercise science*.

Edginton CR, Davis TM, Hensley LD: Trends in higher education: implications for health, physical education, and leisure studies, *JOPERD* 65(7):51, 1994. Access, delivery systems, privatization, curricular innovation, accountability, strategic thinking, and entrepreneurship are among the trends that will influence the future of health, physical education, and leisure studies programs.

Harrington WM: Our collective future: a triumph of imagination, *Quest* 51(3):272, 1999. This Thirty-Third Amy Morris Homans Commemorative Lecture deals with the collective future of physical education. Harrington presents a scenario for 2015 that optimistically predicts the physical education profession will continue to thrive if professionals collectively plan for the future.

Haskell WL: Physical activity, sport, and health: toward the next century, *Res Q Exer & Sp* 67:37, September, 1996 supplement. In this section of a special issue on physical activity, sport, and health, the writer discusses the key issues for taking advantage of the growing scientific evidence that regular physical activity is beneficial. He states that the two major changes that will increase the need to promote physically active lifestyles are the impact of new technology on work and leisure time and the general aging of the population.

Hill J, McLean DD: Technology and leisure, introduction: defining our perspective of the future, *JOPERD* 70(8):21, 1999, and Introduction: possible, probable, or preferable future? *JOPERD* 70(9):15, 1999. In these two articles, the authors discuss the relationship between, and integration of, technology and leisure as well as possible implications of how technology will affect leisure in the future.

Kennedy E, Offutt SE: Healthy lifestyles for healthy Americans: report on USDA's year 2000 behavioral nutrition roundtable—an update on USDA's latest forum on what we know about changing nutrition-related behavior, *Nutr Today* 35(3):84, 2000. Because Americans eat too much and exercise too little, they suffer from excessive rates of heart disease, some cancers, and diabetes. Even though healthy people are more productive at work and play, more satisfied with their personal lives, and more capable of achieving their aspirations, too many smoke, consume alcohol excessively, and remain inactive.

Kretchmar RS: The challenge of telling our story effectively, *Quest* 51(2):87, 1999. The author states that the future of physical education, exercise science, and sport in higher education requires professionals to communicate powerfully and effectively in describing what they do.

Saunders RP, Fee RM, Gottlieb NH: Higher education and the health of America's children: collaborating for coordinated school health, *Phi Delta Kappan* 80(5):377, 1999. Good health behaviors, say researchers, are linked with academic results and the reduction of specific dangerous behaviors of students. Coordinated school health programs can increase these positive outcomes.

Zeigler EF: From one image to a sharper one! *Phys Educ* 54:72, Spring 1997. This article advocates that the traditional field of physical education must select and support an appropriate name (with attendant knowledge, skills, and scholarship), and coalesce around the professional competencies associated with working with physical activity programs.

Zeigler EF: The profession must work "harder and smarter" to inform those officials who make decisions that affect the field, *Phys Educ* 56(3):114, 1999. Professionals must promote activity throughout a person's life. The author suggests 13 principles that should guide programs in the twenty-first century.

Appendix A

SELECTED PHYSICAL EDUCATION, EXERCISE SCIENCE, AND SPORT JOURNALS

Journal	Publisher/Contact Information	Article Type
ACE FitnessMatters	American Council on Exercise 4851 Paramount Drive San Diego, CA 92123 1-800-825-3636 www.acefitness.org	Information about a variety of fitness issues
ACSM's Health and Fitness Journal	American College of Sports Medicine 401 West Michigan Street P.O. Box 1440 Indianapolis, IN 46202-3233 317-637-9200 www.acsm-healthfitness.org	Practical information for fitness instructors, personal trainers, exercise leaders, program directors, and other health and fitness professionals
Adapted Physical Activity Quarterly	Human Kinetics Box 5076 Champaign, IL 61825-5076 1-800-747-4457 www.humankinetics.com/products/ journals.journal.cfm?id=APAQ	Scholarly papers related to physical activity for special populations
American Fitness Magazine	Aerobics and Fitness Associations of America 15250 Ventura Boulevard, Suite 200 Sherman Oaks, CA 91403-3297 1-877-968-7263 www.americanfitness.com/100.amf	Popular articles about fitness, nutrition, and health
American Journal of Clinical Nutrition	American Society for Clinical Nutrition, Inc. 9650 Rockville Pike Bethesda, MD 20814-3998 301-530-7038 www.ajcn.org	Practical articles dealing with nutritional issues
American Journal of Health Education	American Association for Health Education 1900 Association Drive Reston, VA 20191-1598 1-800-213-7193 www.aahperd.org/aahperd/template. cfm?template=ajhe_main.html	Scholarly and applied research in topics in health education
American Journal of Sports Medicine	American Orthopaedic Society for Sports Medicine 6300 North River Road, Suite 500 Rosemont, IL 60018 1-877-321-3500 www.ajsm.org	Scholarly articles in sports medicine
Clinics in Sports Medicine	W.B. Saunders Curtis Center Independence Square West Philadelphia, PA 19106-3399 1-800-654-2452 www.harcourthealth.com/fcgi-bin/ displaypage.pl?isbn=02785919	Academic and scholarly articles in sports medicine

Journal	Publisher/Contact Information	Article Type
Exercise and Sport Sciences Reviews	American College of Sports Medicine 401 W. Michigan Street P.O. Box 1440 Indianapolis, IN 46206-1440 317-637-9200 www.acsm-essr.org	Reviews of scientific, medical, and research-based topics in sports medicine and exercise science
Fitness Management Magazine	Fitness Management 4160 Wilshire Blvd. Los Angeles, CA 90010 323-964-4800 www.fitnessworld.com/home/fr/home.html	Popular articles about fitness and fitness products
Health and Fitness Journal	American College of Sports Medicine 401 W. Michigan Street P.O. Box 1440 Indianapolis, IN 46206-1440 317-637-9200 www.acsm-healthfitness.org	Scientific research, education, and practical applications of sports medicine and exercise science
Journal of Aging and Physical Activity	Human Kinetics Box 5076 Champaign, IL 61825-5076 1-800-747-4457 www.humankinetics.com/products/journals/journal.cfm?id=JAPA	Research associated with physical activity and aging
Journal of Biomechanics	Elsevier Health Sciences Division The Curtis Center 625 Walnut Street Philadelphia, PA 19106-3399 215-238-7800 www.jbiomech.com/	Scholarly articles dealing with sport biomechanics
Journal of Applied Biomechanics	Human Kinetics Box 5076 Champaign, IL 61825-5076 1-800-747-4457 www.humankinetics.com/products/journals/journal.cfm?id=JAB	Research associated with biomechanics in sport, exercise, and rehabilitation
Journal of Applied Physiology	American Physiological Society 9650 Rockville Pike Bethesda, MD 20814-3991 301-634-7164 http://jap.physiology.org/	Scholarly and applied articles in physiology
Journal of Applied Sport Psychology	Association for the Advancement of Applied Sport Psychology Robert S. Weinberg, Editor Department of Physical Education, Health and Sport Studies Miami University, OH 45056 513-529-2728 www.aaasponline.org/journal.html	Scholarly articles related to sport psychology
Journal of Athletic Training	National Athletic Trainers' Association 2952 Stemmons Fwy. Dallas, TX 75247-6196 214-637-6282 www.journalofathletictraining.org	Education and research about the prevention, evaluation, management, and rehabilitation of injuries

Journal	Publisher/Contact Information	Article Type
Journal of Cardiopulmonary Rehabilitation	Lippincott-Williams & Wilkins 530 Walnut Street Philadelphia, PA 19106-3621 215-521-8300 www.lww.com/product/ 0,,0083-9212,00.html	Scholarly works dealing with cardiac rehabilitation
Journal of Exercise Physiology	American Society of Exercise Physiologists Department of Exercise Physiology The College of St. Scholastica 1200 Kenwood Avenue Duluth, MN 55811 218-723-6297 www.css.edu/users/tboone2/asep/fldr/ fldr.htm	Online research-based journal for scholars and practitioners in related fields
Journal of Leisure Research	National Recreation and Park Association 22377 Belmont Ridge Road Ashburn, VA 20148-4501 703-858-0784 http://rptsweb.tamu.edu/Journals/JLR/	Dedicated to the creation of new knowledge and understanding in the leisure services field
Journal of Motor Behavior	Heldref Publications 1319 Eighteenth St., N.W. Washington, DC 20036-1802 1-800-365-9753 www.heldref.org/html/jmb.html	Scholarly articles dealing with motor control, learning, and development
Journal of Orthopedic and Sports Physical Therapy	1111 North Fairfax Street, Suite 100 Alexandria, VA 22314-1436 877-766-3450 www.jospt.org	Scientific articles about clinical procedures in orthopedics and sports medicine
Journal of the Philosophy of Sport	Human Kinetics Box 5076 Champaign, IL 61825-5076 1-800-747-4457 www.humankinetics.com/products/ journals/journal.cfm?id=JPS	Research and theory about the philosophic thought in sport
Journal of Physical Education, Recreation and Dance	American Alliance for Health, Physical Education, Recreation and Dance 1900 Association Drive Reston, VA 20191-1598 1-800-213-7193 www.aahperd.org/aahperd/template.cfm? template=johperd_main.html	Research and applied articles associated with physical education, recreation, and dance programs
Journal of Sport and Exercise Psychology	Human Kinetics Box 5076 Champaign, IL 61825-5076 1-800-747-4457 www.humankinetics.com/products/ journals/journal.cfm?id=JSEP	Research about the interactions of psychology with exercise and sport performance
Journal of Sport History	North American Society for Sport History Available online (since 2000) at www.aafla.com5va/history_frmst.htm www.nassh.org/index1.html	Scholarly research about sport history
Journal of Sport Management	Human Kinetics Box 5076 Champaign, IL 61825-5076 1-800-747-4457 www.humankinetics.com/products/ journals/journal.cfm?id=JSM	Research about the theory and application of sport management

Journal	Publisher/Contact Information	Article Type
Journal of Sport Rehabilitation	Human Kinetics Box 5076 Champaign, IL 61825-5076 1-800-747-4457 www.humankinetics.com/products/ journals/journal.cfm?id=JSR	Scholarly information about rehabilitation from sport injuries
Journal of Sport and Social Issues	Sage Publications, Inc. 2455 Teller Road Thousand Oaks, CA 91320 1-800-818-7243 www.sagepub.com/journal. aspx?pid=149	Research-based articles about sport within the social context
Journal of Strength and Conditioning Research	National Strength and Conditioning Association P.O. Box 9908 Colorado Springs, CO 80932 719-632-6722 www.nsca-lift.org/Publications/ default.shtml	Research information for strength and conditioning practitioners
Journal of Teaching in Physical Education	Human Kinetics Box 5076 Champaign, IL 61825-5076 1-800-747-4457 www.humankinetics.com/products/ journals/journal.cfm?id=JTPE	Descriptive, theoretical, and research articles about the teaching of physical education at all levels
Measurement in Physical Education and Exercise Science	Measurement and Evaluation Council of the AAALF 1900 Association Drive Reston, VA 20191-1599 1-800-213-7193 www.erlbaum.com/shop/tek9. asp?pg=product&specific=1091-367x	Research articles associated with measurement and assessment in physical activity programs and settings
Medicine and Science in Sports and Exercise	American College of Sports Medicine 401 W. Michigan Street P.O. Box 1440 Indianapolis, IN 46206-1440 317-637-9200 www.acsm.org/publications/MSSE.htm	Articles from basic and applied science, medicine, education, and allied health fields
Motor Control	Human Kinetics Box 5076 Champaign, IL 61825-5076 1-800-747-4457 www.human.kinetics.com/products/ journals/journal.cfm?id=MC	Articles about the multidisciplinary examination of the movement of humans
Palaestra	Challenge Publications, Ltd. P.O. Box 508 Macomb, IL 61455 309-833-1902 www.palaestra.com	Articles about sport, physical education, and recreation for individuals with disabilities
Parks and Recreation	National Recreation and Park Association 22377 Belmont Ridge Road Ashburn, VA 20148-4501 703-858-0784 www.nrpa.org/department.cfm? department ID=188publicationID=11	Articles of general and applied interest

Journal	Publisher/Contact Information	Article Type
Pediatric Exercise Science	Human Kinetics Box 5076 Champaign, IL 61825-5076 1-800-747-4457 www.humankinetics.com/products/ journals/journal.cfm?id=PES	Reporting about scientific knowledge of exercise during childhood
Performance Training	National Strength and Conditioning Association P.O. Box 9908 Colorado Springs, CO 80932 719-632-6722 www.nsca_lift.org/publications/ default.shtml	Online journal www.nsca-lift.org/perform with practical and research-based articles
Quest	Human Kinetics Box 5076 Champaign, IL 61825-5076 1-800-747-4457 www.humankinetics.com/products/ journals/journal.cfm?id=QUEST	Research about contemporary issues in physical education in higher education
Research Quarterly for Exercise and Sport	American Alliance for Health, Physical Education, Recreation and Dance 1900 Association Drive Reston, VA 20191-1598 1-800-213-7193 www.aahperd.org/aahperd/template. cfm?template=rqes_main.html	Scholarly research in the exercise sciences
SCHOLE: A Journal of Leisure Studies and Recreation Education	National Recreation and Park Association 22377 Belmont Ridge Road Ashburn, VA 20148-4501 703-858-0784 www.uncwil.edu/spre/SCHOLE/ schole.html	Scholarly inquiry into all aspects of parks, recreation, and leisure education
Sociology of Sport Journal	Human Kinetics Box 5076 Champaign, IL 61825-5076 1-800-747-4457 www.humankinetics.com/products/ journals/journal.cfm?id=SSJ	Research, critical thought, and theory in the sociology of sport
Strategies: A Journal for Sport and Physical Education	National Association for Sport and Physical Education 1900 Association Drive Reston, VA 20191-1598 1-800-213-7193 www.aahperd.org/aahperd/template. cfm?template=strategies_main.html	Applied sport and physical education articles
Strength and Conditioning Journal	National Strength and Conditioning Association P.O. Box 9908 Colorado Springs, CO 80932 719-632-6722 www.nsca-lift.org/publications/ default.shtml	Articles about resistance training, sports medicine and science, and other issues of interest to strength and conditioning professionals
The Physical Educator	Phi Epsilon Kappa Fraternity 901 W. New York Street Indianapolis, IN 46202 317-637-8431 http://www2.trumann.edu/pek/public.html	Scholarly articles about physical education

Journal	Publisher/Contact Information	Article Type
The Physician and Sportsmedicine	McGraw-Hill Companies 4530 W. 77th Street Minneapolis, MN 55435 952-835-3222 www.physsportsmed.com	Scholarly articles about medical aspects of sports
The Sport Psychologist	Human Kinetics Box 5076 Champaign, IL 61825-5076 1-800-747-4457 www.humankinetics.com/products/ journals/journal.cfm?id=TSP	Applied research in sport psychology

Appendix B

CERTIFYING ORGANIZATIONS

Aerobics and Fitness Association of America
15250 Ventura Boulevard, Suite 200
Sherman Oaks, CA 91403-3297
1-877-968-7263
www.afaa.com/10000.asp

American Sport Education Program
1607 N. Market Street
Box 5076
Champaign, IL 61825-5076
1-800-747-5698
www.asep.com

American College of Sports Medicine
401 W. Michigan Street
P.O. Box 1440
Indianapolis, IN 46206-1440
317-637-9200
www.acsm.org

American Council on Exercise
4851 Paramount Drive
San Diego, CA 92123
1-800-825-3636
www.acefitness.org

American Red Cross (national headquarters)
2025 E. Street, NW
Washington, DC 20006
202-303-4498
www.redcross.org

The Cooper Institute
12330 Preston Road
Dallas, TX 75230
972-341-3200
www.cooperinst.org

National Athletic Trainers' Association
2952 Stemmons Fwy.
Dallas, TX 75247-6196
214-637-6282
www.nata.org

National Strength and Conditioning Association
P.O. Box 9908
Colorado Springs, CO 80932
719-632-6722
www.nsca-lift.org

Young Men's Christian Association of the USA
101 North Wacker Drive
Chicago, IL 60606
312-977-0031
www.ymca.net

Glossary

Academic discipline a formal body of knowledge discovered, developed, and disseminated through scholarly research and inquiry

Actual notice refers to the removal of known hazards by a responsible person

Adapted physical education a program for exceptional students who are so different in mental, physical, emotional, or behavioral characteristics that, in the interest of quality of educational opportunity for all students, special provisions must be made for their proper education

Aesthetics the philosophical area that focuses on the artistic, sensual, or beautiful aspects of anything, including movement

Affective development an educational outcome that focuses on the development of attitudes, appreciations, and values, including both social and emotional dimensions

Agoge an educational system for Spartan boys that ensured the singular goal of serving the city-state

Agreement to participate a signed acknowledgment of a participant's knowing, understanding, and appreciating the risks associated with an activity

Anthropometrics bodily measurements used to evaluate physical size and capacity

Arete all-around mental, moral, and physical excellence valued by the Greeks

Asceticism a doctrine that renounces the comforts of society and espouses austere self-discipline, especially as an act of religious devotion

Assessment a measure of knowledge, skills, and abilities that leads to the assignment of a value or score

Assumption of risk knowing, understanding, and appreciating the risk associated with a chosen activity

Athletic training the study and application of the prevention, treatment, and rehabilitation of sports injuries

Athletics organized, highly structured, competitive activities in which skilled individuals participate

Axiology a philosophy that deals with the value of things and discovering whether actions, things, or circumstances are good or virtuous

Battle of the Systems a controversy raging in the 1800s over which system of gymnastics was most appropriate for Americans

British Amateur Sport Ideal concept espoused by upper-class males in Great Britain that values playing sports for fun and competition and not for remuneration

Burnout decreased performance quality and quantity resulting from stress, job repetitiveness, lack of support and reward, and overwork

Calisthenics the term used in the 1800s to describe Catharine Beecher's program of exercises designed to promote health, beauty, and strength

Categorical imperative the belief that moral duties are prescriptive and independent of consequences

Cognitive development an educational outcome that emphasizes the acquisition, comprehension, analysis, synthesis, application, and evaluation of knowledge

Comparative negligence apportions damages between a negligent plaintiff and a negligent defendant who each played a part in the injury

Constructive notice refers to hazards that a responsible person should have noticed and eliminated

Contributory negligence behavior by the plaintiff that contributed to the injury

Dance bodily movements of a rhythmic and patterned succession usually executed to the accompaniment of music

Day's Order Swedish systemized, daily exercises that progressed through the whole body from head to toe

Deontology an ethical theory advocating that actions must conform to absolute rules of moral behavior, which are characterized by universality, respect for the individual, and acceptability to rational beings

Eclecticism a combination of theories and doctrines from several philosophies into a consistent and compatible set of beliefs

Education of the physical a belief that physical education's unique contribution within education should be to develop individuals' physical fitness and sport skills

Education through the physical a belief that physical education should uniquely contribute to the education of the whole person through physical activities; promoted educating children to live in a democratic society through social and intellectual interactions within physical education

Epistemology the branch of philosophy that examines what people know and how and why they hold certain beliefs

Ethics the study of moral values or the doing of good toward others or oneself

Exercise physical movement that increases the rate of energy use of the body

Exercise physiology the study of bodily functions under the stress of muscular activity

Exercise science the scientific analysis of the human body in motion; broadly encompasses exercise physiology, biomechanics, kinesiology, anatomy, physiology, motor behavior, and some aspects of sports medicine

Existentialism a twentieth-century philosophy that centers on individual existence and advocates that truth and values are arrived at by each person's experiences

Games activities ranging from simple diversions to cooperative activities to competitions with significant outcomes governed by rules

General supervision action required whenever activity is occurring by those for whom the person is responsible

Grand tourney or melee combats fought under conditions similar to war between two teams of knights

Greek Ideal unity of the "man of action" and the "man of wisdom"

Gymnasium a site for intellectual and physical activities for Greek citizens

Gymnastics term used to describe Greek athletics, European systems of exercises with or without apparatus, and a modern international sport

Halteres handheld weights used by jumpers to enhance their performances

Health wellness of body and mind; absence of disease or illness

Health-related fitness attaining the level of well-being associated with heart function (cardiovascular endurance), muscular function (strength and endurance), and flexibility as a deterrent to debilitating conditions

Hygiene the science of preserving one's health

Idealism a philosophical theory advocating that reality depends on the mind for existence and that truth is universal and absolute

Inclusion the placement of students with physical, mental, behavioral, or emotional disabilities or limitations into regular classes with their peers

Jousting   an event at medieval tournaments in which two mounted knights armed with lances attempted in a head-on charge to unseat each other

Knight   warrier during the medieval period

Leisure   freedom from work or responsibilities so that time may be used for physical activity

Light gymnastics   Dioclesian Lewis's program based on executing Beecher's calisthenics along with handheld apparatus

Metaphysics   a philosophy that refers to the nature of things, or how actions or events are related to one another

Motor behavior   broad term encompassing motor control, motor learning, and motor development

Motor control   an area of study that deals with the neurophysiological factors that affect human movement

Motor development   the maturation and changes in motor behavior throughout life

Motor learning   the study of cognitive processes underlying motor acts associated with skill acquisition through practice and experience

Movement education   a child-centered curriculum that emphasized presenting movement challenges to students and encouraging them to use problem solving and guided discovery to learn fundamental skills

Muscular Christianity   the philosophy that moral values can be taught through sport

Nationalism   a pervasive theme stressing promotion and defense of one's country that was the desired outcome of several European systems of gymnastics in the 1800s

Naturalism   a belief that the scientific laws of nature govern life and that individual goals are more important than societal goals; everything according to nature

Negligence   describes the legal claim that a person fails to act as a reasonable and prudent person should, thereby resulting in injury to another person

New physical education   a curriculum focused on developing the whole individual through participation in play, sports, games, and natural, outdoor activities

Normal school   a specialized institution for preparing students to become teachers in one or more subjects

Page   term used for the boy during the first seven-year training period (ages 7–14), under the guidance of the lady of the castle, to become a knight

Paidotribes   the first physical education teacher, who taught Greek boys wrestling, boxing, jumping, dancing, and gymnastics at a palaestra

Palaestra   a Greek school where boys learned wrestling, boxing, jumping, dancing, and gymnastics

Pancratium   an event in Panhellenic festivals that combined wrestling and boxing skills into an "almost-anything-goes" combat

Panhellenic festivals   festivals open to all Greeks in which athletic contests were a focal point

Pedagogy   the art and science of teaching

Pentathlon   a five-event competition that included the discus throw, javelin throw, long jump, stade race, and wrestling

Philosophy   a love of wisdom; the pursuit of truth

Physical activity   all movements that can contribute to improved health

Physical education   a process through which an individual obtains optimal physical, mental, and social skills and fitness through physical activity

Physical fitness   developed through endurance and resistive exercises of sufficient frequency, duration, and intensity to enhance heart and other bodily functions

Play   amusements engaged in freely, for fun, and devoid of constraints

Pragmatism an American movement in philosophy emphasizing reality as the sum total of each individual's experiences through practical experimentation

Profession a learned occupation that requires training in a specialized field of study

Psychomotor development an educational outcome that emphasizes the learning of fundamental movements, motor skills, and sports skills

Purpose a stated intention, aim, or goal

Realism a philosophical system stressing that the laws and order of the world as revealed by science are independent from human experience

Recreation refreshing or renewing one's strength and spirit after work; a diversion that occurs during leisure hours

Renaissance a period from the fifteenth to seventeenth centuries marked by a renewed appreciation for classical culture

Scientific method the process of making observations, developing hypotheses, conducting experiments, analyzing data and information, reporting findings, and establishing theories or drawing conclusions

Skill-related fitness refers to achieving levels of ability to perform physical movements specific to a sport, such as serving a tennis ball effectively, or a physical activity, such as executing safe and proper technique in an aerobics class

Specific supervision mandated action required whenever a higher level of risk is associated with the activity of the persons for whom the adult is responsible

Sports physical activities governed by formal and informal rules that involve competition against an opponent or oneself and are engaged in for fun, recreation, or reward

Sport and exercise psychology the study of human behavior in sports, including an understanding of the mental processes that interact with motor skill performance

Sport biomechanics the study of the effects of natural laws and forces on the body through the science and mechanics of movement

Sport history the descriptive and analytical examination of significant people, events, organizations, and trends that shaped the past

Sport management the study of the management of personnel, programs, budgets, and facilities in various sports settings

Sport philosophy analyzes sport from aesthetic, epistemological, metaphysical, and ethical perspectives

Sport sociology the study of the social units and processes within the sporting context

Squire term used for the boy during the second seven-year training period (ages 14–21), under the direction of a knight

Stade race a footrace in Panhellenic games run the length of the stadium

Standard a uniform criterion or foundational guide used to measure quality

Teleological refers to theories that focus on the end results or consequences of processes or occurrences

Thermae facilities in Rome for contrast baths of varying water temperatures and other leisure activities

Turners individuals who exercised at a turnplatz

Turnfests festivals for the exhibiting of German (turner) gymnastics

Turnplatz an outdoor exercise area established by Friedrich Jahn

Utilitarianism a theory that refers to the goal of creating the greatest good for the largest number of people

Wellness mental, emotional, spiritual, nutritional, and physical factors that lead to healthy behaviors

Credits

Chapter 1

Unit one photo courtesy Corbis.
P. 5, Reprinted from *Moving into the Future—National Standards for Physical Education* with permission from the National Association for Sport and Physical Education, 1900 Association Drive, Reston, VA 20191-1598.
P. 8, Photo, Reprinted with permission of the University of Tennessee Press. From Kozar AJ: *R. Tait McKenzie, the sculptor of athletes,* 1975, The University of Tennessee Press.
P. 19, Reprinted with permission of the American Alliance for Health, Physical Education, Recreation and Dance, 1900 Association Drive, Reston, VA 20191-1598.

Chapter 3

PP. 76–77, Reprinted with permission of the American Alliance for Health, Physical Education, Recreation and Dance, 1900 Association Drive, Reston, VA 20191-1598.
P. 94, Reprinted with permission of the Interstate New Teacher Assessment and Support Consortium, a program of the Council of Chief State School Officers.

Chapter 4

Figure 4.6, Reprinted with permission of the National Athletic Trainers' Association, 2952 Stemmons Frwy, Dallas, TX 75247-6196.

Chapter 5

PP. 151–154, Reprinted from *Quality Coaches, Quality Sports: National Standards for Athletic Coaches* with permission from the National Association for Sport and Physical Education, 1900 Association Drive, Reston, VA 20191-1598.

Chapter 7

P. 233, Puzzle, Reprinted with permission of Jane Jenkins.

Chapter 8

P. 236, Reprinted with permission of Human Kinetics, Champaign, IL 61825-5076.
P. 252, This article is reprinted with permission from the *Journal of Physical Education, Recreation and Dance,* April 1960, p. 27. The journal is a publication of the American Alliance for Health, Physical Education, Recreation and Dance, 1900 Association Drive, Reston, VA 20191-1598.

Chapter 9

P. 265, *NEA Proceedings,* 32:621, copyright 1893, National Education Association. Reprinted with permission.

Chapter 10

Table 10.1, Reprinted from "Developmentally Appropriate Physical Education Practices for Children" with permission of the National Association for Sport and Physical Education, 1900 Association Drive, Reston, VA 20191-1598.

Chapter 11

Figure 11.3 (high schools), National Federation of State High School Associations. (2000). (available from P.O. Box 690, Indianapolis, IN 46206).
Figure 11.3 (intercollegiate sports), Acosta R.V. and Carpenter L.J. (2004). Women in intercollegiate sport—a longitudinal study twenty-seven-year update 1977–2004 (available from the authors, P.O. Box 42, West Brookfield, MA 01585-0042).

Index